American Politics: Playing the Game

Houghton Mifflin Company   Boston

Atlanta   Dallas   Hopewell, New Jersey
Geneva, Illinois   Palo Alto   London

American Politics: Playing the Game

Susan Rouder

City College of San Francisco

To Anna, my sister

Printed in the U.S.A.
Library of Congress Catalog Card Number: 76–13962
ISBN: 0–395–24971–6

Contents

Preface

This is a *practical* introduction to American government and politics. It is written for you, the frustrated citizen. It communicates *how to get the system to budge*—whatever the goal.

Because of the book's focus, information about American political culture and institutions is consistently pragmatic. For example, the discussion of political culture conveys information to help you identify the problems associated with mobilizing support for a cause or candidate. It also paves the way for an introduction to political socialization and persuasion techniques.

The institutional chapters emphasize effective political action through the application of a game framework, introduced in Chapter 2. Discussed are the unique characteristics of legislative, executive, and judicial games; the arenas of action; and key institutional players and how they can be influenced. The rules of each institutional game are also described. Included are those that distribute advantages to various players, those that give citizens access to each institution, and those that apply to persuasion tactics. Finally, each institutional section contains case studies of citizens who use a variety of techniques to get through to decision-makers to win political games.

So, little about this book is an abstract account of American government. Even key concepts such as "federalism," "democracy," and "pluralism" unfold in the context of political action. The hope is that after reading this book, you will have *confidence* in your ability to participate politically, will be *more inclined* to participate, and will *know how* to win political games, should you choose to play.

The assumptions are clear. One is that the game of American politics is indeed worth playing. The second is that *this* system of government is capable of responding to diverse needs and interests—those that go beyond the economic. And third, that knowing how to play the game of American politics increases the probability of winning.

An American government text that really prepares people to be effective citizens—that's what this book is about.

Susan Rouder

Acknowledgments

More than any other factor, my association with Ralph Goldman, Professor of Political Science at San Francisco State University, inspired this book. I thank him warmly. Professors Delmer D. Dunn, University of Georgia; Judith A. Gillespie, Indiana University; Kenneth Meriam, Los Angeles Valley College; Allan Wolk, Bronx Community College; and Peter DeGroot, City College of San Francisco were consultants on the book. Their reviews and critiques were extremely valuable. They are, however, in no way responsible for any of the book's deficiencies.

I would like to thank those who initially commented on the introductory chapters, Professors Jim Downton, University of Colorado; Kay Lawson, San Francisco State University; Sam Schwartz, College of Marin; and Ted Taylor, City College of San Francisco. And most important, I would like to thank my dear friend, Professor Sandra Powell, San Francisco State University. Her intellectual and moral support allowed this book to be completed.

Text Credits

Gabriel A. Almond and Sidney Verba, *The Civic Culture: Political Attitudes and Democracy in Five Nations* (copyright © 1963 by Princeton University Press; © 1965 Little, Brown and Company) pp. 82, 108, 109. Reprinted by permission of Princeton University Press.

American Institute of Public Opinion Survey, reported in 1965 Gallup Opinion Index: "Proportion of Americans Knowing Their Congressman and Various Things about Him." Reprinted by permission.

Sherry R. Arnstein, "Maximum Feasible Manipulation," *Public Administration Review*, Special Issue, September, 1972, p. 378. Reprinted by permission.

From Howard Bloomenthal, *Promoting Your Cause*. Copyright © 1971 by Howard Bloomenthal. Used by permission of Funk & Wagnalls Publishing Company, Inc.

Book of the States, "Provisions for Recall of State Officials," "Provisions for Referendum of State Legislation," and "Initiative Provisions for State Legislation," Council of State Government, pp. 48–49, 50, 170. Reprinted by permission.

William W. Boyer, "Policy Making by Government Agencies," *Midwest Journal of Political Science*, August 1960, Wayne State University Press. This article subsequently appeared as Chapter 1 in William W. Boyer, *Bureaucracy on Trial: Policy Making by Government Agencies* (Bobbs-Merrill, Indianapolis, 1964).

Claude Brown, *Manchild in the Promised Land* (copyright © Claude Brown, 1965). Reprinted by Permission of Macmillan Publishing Co. Inc., and Jonathan Cape Ltd., London.

Carol W. Cagle, "Privacy Campaign: Eye on the Spys," *ACLU News*. Copyright © 1974 by the American Civil Liberties Union, Inc. Reprinted by permission.

Jonathan D. Casper, *The Politics of Civil Liberties* (Harper & Row, Publishers, Inc., New York, 1972), p. 262. Reprinted by permission.

Stephen Chaberski, "Inside the New York Panther Trial," *ACLU News*. Copyright © 1973 by the American Civil Liberties Union, Inc. Reprinted by permission.

Thomas Cottle, *Black Children, White Dreams* (Houghton Mifflin Company, Boston, 1974). Copyright © 1974 by Thomas Cottle. Reprinted by permission of The Sterling Lord Agency, Inc.

Congressional Quarterly, "25 Top Spenders," August 6, 1971, p. 1681, and June 9, 1973, p. 1425. Reprinted by permission.

Congressional Quarterly, "Writing Tips," November 14, 1969, p. 2282. Reprinted by permission.

Congressional Quarterly, "Intensive Lobbying Marked Civil Rights Debate," February 21, 1964, pp. 364–366. Reprinted by permission.

Congressional Quarterly, "Congressional Votes on Roll Calls that Produced Party Division," January 15, 1972, pp. 86–87. Reprinted by permission.

Scott M. Cutlip and Allen H. Center, Effective Public Relations, p. 302. Copyright © 1952. Reprinted by permission of Prentice-Hall, Inc., Englewood Cliffs, New Jersey.

Matthew P. Dumont, "Down the Bureaucracies." Published by permission of Transaction, Inc., from *Transaction*, vol. 7, no. 12. Copyright © 1970 by Transaction, Inc.

Samuel J. Eldersveld and Richard W. Dodge, "Personal Contact or Mail

Propaganda" in *Public Opinion and Propaganda,* ed. Daniel Katz et al. (Holt, Rinehart and Winston, Inc.), 1954, pp. 532–542. Reprinted by permission.

Lewis A. Froman, Jr., *People and Politics: An Analysis of the American Political System,* copyright © 1962, p. 22. Reprinted by permission of Prentice-Hall, Inc., Englewood Cliffs, New Jersey.

William A. Gamson, *Power and Discontent,* Homewood, Ill., The Dorsey Press, 1968, pp. 94–98. Reprinted by permission.

Ira Glasser, "Grass Roots Campaigning: The Key to Success," *ACLU News* (March/April 1974), p. 4. Reprinted by permission. Copyright © 1974 by the American Civil Liberties Union, Inc.

Mark J. Green, James M. Fallows, and David R. Zwick, *Who Runs Congress?* Copyright © 1972 by Ralph Nader. Reprinted by permission of Grossman Publishers, a division of Viking Penguin, Inc.

Charles Hamilton and Stokely Carmichael, *Black Power,* Random House, Inc./Alfred A. Knopf, Inc., New York, 1967, pp. 58–84. Reprinted by permission.

Louis Harris, *Confidence and Concern:* "Inclination of Americans to Join Groups," p. 21; "Political Activities Citizens Say They would Engage In," pp. 21–22; and "Citizens Opinions on Interest Group Activity," p. 23. (King's Court Communications, Inc.) Reprinted by permission.

Louis Harris, *The Anguish of Change,* W. W. Norton & Company, Inc., New York, 1973, pp. 173–174. Reprinted by permission.

Chester Hartman, *Yerba Buena,* Glide Urban Center Publications, San Francisco, 1974. Reprinted by permission.

Martin Luther King, Jr., *Why We Can't Wait,* pp. 81, 84–86. Copyright © 1963 by Martin Luther King, Jr. Reprinted by permission of Harper & Row, Publishers, Inc., and Joan Daves.

Martin Luther King, Jr., *Stride Toward Freedom,* Copyright © 1958 by Martin Luther King, Jr. Reprinted by permission of Harper & Row, Publishers, Inc. and Joan Daves.

Samuel Krislov, "The Amicus Curiae Brief," *Yale Law Review,* April 1963. Reprinted by permission.

League of Women Voters of the San Francisco Bay Area and Los Angeles County, "Local Government in California and Citizen Participation," 1974, table V. Reprinted by permission.

Anthony Lewis, *Gideon's Trumpet,* Random House, Inc./Alfred A. Knopf, Inc., New York, 1964, pp. 5–6. Reprinted by permission.

Seymour Martin Lipset, *Political Man: The Social Bases of Politics,* copyright © 1959, 1960 by Seymour Martin Lipset. Reprinted by permission of Doubleday & Company, Inc.

Gerald C. Lubenow, "The Action Lawyers," *Saturday Review,* August 26, 1972, pp. 36–42. Reprinted by permission.

Margaret I. Miller and Helene Linker, "Equal Rights Amendment Campaigns in California and Utah." Published by permission of Transaction, Inc., from *Society,* Vol. 11, No. 4. Copyright © 1974, by Transaction, Inc.

Gary Orfield, *Congressional Power*, Harcourt Brace Jovanovich, Inc., New York, 1975, pp. 99–103, 270–271, 103–116. Reprinted by permission.

John De J. Pemberton, Jr., "The Rights of Access to Mass Media" in *The Rights of Americans*, ed. Norman Dorsen, Random House, Inc./ Alfred A. Knopf, Inc., New York, 1970, p. 290.

Public Opinion Quarterly, 1972, pp. 62, 75. (R. R. Bowker, New York, 1972. Copyright © 1972 by Columbia Broadcasting System, Inc.) per permission of CBS Inc.

Charles A. Reich, "Bureaucracy and the Forests," 1962. Reprinted by permission of The Center for the Study of Democratic Institutions/ Fund for the Republic, Inc., Santa Barbara, California.

John S. Saloma III and Fredrick H. Sontag, *Parties: The Real Opportunity for Citizen Access*, Random House, Inc./Alfred A. Knopf, Inc. New York, 1972, pp. 122, 155, 159. Reprinted by permission.

Kenneth E. Scott, "Standing in the Supreme Court," *Harvard Law Review*, February 1973.

Jay A. Sigler, *An Introduction to the Legal System*, The Dorsey Press, Homewood, Ill., 1968, p. 122. Reprinted by permission.

John C. Wahlke, Heinz Eulan, William Buchanan, Leroy C. Ferguson, *The Legislative System*, New York: John Wiley & Sons, Inc., 1962. Reprinted by permission of the authors.

J. Allen Whitt, "Californians, Cars, and the Technical Death." Published by permission of Transaction, Inc., from *Society*, Vol. 10, No. 5. Copyright © 1973 by Transaction, Inc.

Deil S. Wright, "Executive Leadership in State Administration," *Midwest Journal of Political Science*, February 1967, table, p. 4. Reprinted by permission of Wayne State University Press.

I
Political Games:
Who Plays,
How to Play

1
About Political Games

It was a Friday night. Cyril Cuevas and his neighbors had just begun their meeting—a meeting to demand that the city put stop signs at a nearby intersection. The meeting hadn't been going long when someone ran in the room shouting. Six-year-old Jennifer Cuevas had just been hit by a car. She was dead. The accident had occurred at *that* intersection, the one under discussion. For four years Mr. Cuevas and his neighbors had been trying to get someone to pay attention. But with slide-rule estimates and traffic flowcharts establishing traffic safety priorities, and with everyone else also competing for the attention of the Board of Supervisors, nothing had been done.[1]

Stories of the frustration of dealing with "city hall" abound. Not all are as tragic as the one just described; some are much more tragic. Most contain a very clear message: It's impossible for the "little guy," the average person, to get the system to budge. Only those people who have "contacts," or "are on the inside," or "have money" can get anywhere with politicians.

Wrong. Sure it helps to have contacts and money, and it's great

---

[1] Larry Liebert, "And Now She's Dead," *San Francisco Chronicle*, August 8, 1973.

if you're on the inside, but it is possible to get the system to budge without these particular assets. There is a second clear message in the story of Jennifer Cuevas. Most people do not know how to get through to government officials. Mr. Cuevas and his neighbors didn't. The result is that most people don't even try, or if they do, they give up in frustration.

To be active is to be aware, committed, and potent.[2]

The political system is open to citizen influence, but getting through means knowing *how* to play the game of American politics. It means knowing how to analyze a problem and establish goals; how to develop a strategy and select appropriate tactics; how to identify the players, both allies and opponents, and their resources; and how to use information to assess the likely moves of the other players. Finally, playing the game successfully means knowing the rules of the game—particularly the ones that are likely to help.

Sounds complicated, doesn't it? But it doesn't have to be. The point is, if you *care* about something that requires political action, you can't use a haphazard, play-it-by-ear approach and expect to be successful.

The game begins with caring, but additional ingredients are essential for its successful completion. There must be a recognition of an ability to act, resources that make effective action possible, and access to power—to decision-makers.[3]

Frequently in this country people care, but they feel powerless. There is little recognition of an ability to act effectively. People don't know how. In addition, people often feel that "politics" is unrelated to their lives. The immediate problems being faced seem to have no political answers. When a family is unable to find adequate housing at a price they can afford, when a woman returning to college is unable to find an inexpensive day-care center for her children, when a

---

[2] Amitai Etzioni, *The Active Society* (New York: The Free Press/Macmillan Publishing Co., 1968), p. 4. Copyright © 1968 Amitai Etzioni. Reprinted by permission.
[3] *Ibid.*, pp. 4–5.

family's life savings are exhausted by one member's illness, people *still* do not see the relevance of politics.

Although access to decision-makers is usually possible, individual and group resources can be mobilized, and people do care about the quality of their lives, these two ingredients are still missing. Their absence, in part, explains inaction. Without this recognition of an ability to act and sense of the relevance of the political process, the number of players is seriously reduced. The chances that the problems about which people care will be resolved are also reduced.

The Greek term for citizen, *politēs*, comes from the same root as politics and means, he who collaborates openly or publicly in making a common union. The citizen, then, is essential to politics, not merely an appendage.[4]

What is the meaning of a *political* game? How does it differ from games like chess, tennis, or football? The word "political" has to do with the process through which *authoritative* decisions are made. Authoritative decisions are those that are *binding* on society. They are binding because they are perceived as legitimate and because there is a capacity for enforcing them. The result is, usually, obedience. But citizens don't call just *any* decision authoritative. In this country the authoritative decisions are those made by government, by duly elected or appointed public officials. Citizens consider these decisions binding for a variety of reasons, among them habit, tradition, respect for certain procedures, a loyalty to particular persons or institutions, and fear. Activities are political when they are directed toward defining these decisions, determining who the decision-makers shall be, implementing the decisions, and resolving any conflicts over their meaning or application.

If a group of friends get together and formally agree to recycle all their newspapers, is that a political decision? No, for there is nothing except perhaps friendship and respect for the decision to make it binding. There is nothing *compelling* obedience. If one person breaks the agreement, chances are he or she won't even be ostracized

---

[4] Robert J. Pranger, *The Eclipse of Citizenship* (New York: Holt, Rinehart and Winston, 1968), p. 89.

by the group. However, if this same group of friends decide to try to get their city council to appropriate funds so that all newspapers in their community can be collected for recycling, is that a political decision? Yes, it is. Whether successful or not, the act of trying to influence public officials is part of the authoritative decision-making process. If the decision to allocate the necessary amount was made, it would be accepted as binding on the community.

The result of the political process is that things which at least some citizens value get distributed. They include such things as money for schools, roads, and weapons; rights to equal education, to privacy, and to impartial justice; and obligations to pay taxes, join the military, and respect other people's property. Frequently what gets distributed is determined by who is playing the game and how well they play it.

Who Usually Plays

Americans are a strange breed. We say we believe in something called democracy, yet few of us are willing to participate in it. Saul Alinsky[5] called this accepting democracy intellectually but rejecting it emotionally. But who *does* participate; who *is* willing to play the political game?

Who usually plays the game depends in part on where it is played and in part on the issues involved. Is the location the voting booth, a party caucus meeting, the convention floor, a courtroom, legislative houses, or administrative offices? In addition, is the game being played at the local level, state level, or national level? Is the issue urban redevelopment, public education, an excess profits tax, or impeachment? [6]

My mother gets $7.10 a month for gas and electricity. She pays about $30 (every two months). You want to know why? I'll tell you why.

We use the stove to heat the rooms. We burn the lights at night so the rats won't go near the baby. Also, it's dark where we live, even during the day. So if I am reading or sewing or studying from a book, I've got to burn the lights. The Welfare knows all this, and they are supposed to do something about it, but they never do. Every month we get this bill, and my mother pays it

[5] Saul Alinsky was one of this country's most famous community organizers. Born in Chicago in 1901, he spent most of his life organizing the poor—showing them how to use power.

[6] For a study of how group influence changes with the issue, see Robert Dahl, *Who Governs?* (New Haven, Conn.: Yale University Press, 1961).

with the food money. Then she has to prove to the Welfare that she has used the food money to pay for the lights. . . .
I can remember the last time they turned off the lights. It was winter. My mother was so cold she started to cry. Then we all started to cry because it was so dark. We had to eat cold food out of tin cans until the Welfare called Con Edison and they turned the lights back on again. When he comes, my mother is angry with the man. "Pray to God you have not hurt these children. Believe me." Afterwards my little sister was sick for a week.

The Poor House State[7]

The problems of this desperate family are partially political, yet the mother of this family is statistically unlikely to play the political game. Unlikely to play also are the other approximately 15 million adults in this country who are classified as "poor."

Individual Players
But you don't have to be poor to be unwilling or unable to participate politically. Wherever the game takes place and whatever the issue, most people are only marginally involved. Even the most traditional form of democratic participation, voting, illustrates the unwillingness of thousands of American citizens to play. Presidential elections produce the highest turnout, and yet not since 1916 has more than two-thirds of the potential electorate been willing to vote. On two occasions, 1920 and 1924, less than half actually turned out. The 1972 election was a more recent participation fiasco. Only 55 percent of all eligible voters actually voted.

Not only do great numbers of people fail to vote, for a variety of reasons, but those people who do vote hardly represent a cross section of the country. Voting tends to be higher among men than among women, and higher among the better educated, higher-income groups, those between the ages of 35 and 65, metropolitan residents (particularly suburbanites), whites, and homeowners.[8]

Voting, of course, isn't the only form of participation to consider. Other traditional forms include running for political office, becoming active in party and campaign work, making financial contributions to political candidates or causes, belonging to organizations that support

[7] Richard M. Elman, "If You Were on Welfare," *Saturday Review*, May 23, 1970, p. 27.
[8] See the Michigan Survey Research Center Study in Fred I. Greenstein, *The American Party System and the American People* (Englewood Cliffs, N.J.: Prentice-Hall, 1963).

or oppose candidates or take stands on political issues, and attempting to influence friends politically.[9]

While opportunities for all forms of political participation abound, most people simply don't respond. About one-third of American adults are politically apathetic or passive; in most cases they are unaware of the political world around them. Another 60 percent are just spectators. Only 1 or 2 percent could be called really active.[10]

Those involved in these other forms of participation are also not proportionately a cross section of the community. As with voting, higher-class persons are more likely to participate than lower-class persons.[11] Take the simple act of writing letters. Business executives are four or five times as likely to write to their representatives as manual laborers are. In addition, college graduates are far more apt to write to their representatives than people in the lowest educational category.[12]

What are the implications of this low-level, unrepresentative participation? Those who do play the game have an obvious advantage. Their resources and tactical opportunities are magnified. They play the game knowing that except for particularly controversial rewards, their influence will be exaggerated. Those in the lowest income and educational groups have an obvious disadvantage.

Interest Group Players

Thus far the focus has been on individuals as players. But a great many people have discovered the necessity of playing the game in groups. Government, particularly on the state and national levels, is just too big and too complex for most citizens to confront individually. An organized group provides a way of bringing individual resources (money, effort, skills) together to focus more efficiently on some concern that is shared by others.

Some political scientists say this country functions relatively smoothly because it is pluralistic. *Pluralism* means that political power is shared by a number of different groups—groups that have different religious, economic, ethnic, and cultural interests. According to the

[9] Lester Milbrath, *Political Participation* (Chicago: Rand McNally and Company, 1965), p. 18.
[10] *Ibid.*, p. 21.
[11] *Ibid.*, p. 116.
[12] E. E. Schattschneider, "The Scope and Bias of the Pressure System," in *The Semisovereign People* (New York: Holt, Rinehart and Winston, 1960).

pluralistic view, these groups compete actively and relatively equally in the political decision-making process. As groups direct their attention to particular issues, they check one another's power. Through competition, they keep one another from exceeding or abusing their power.[13]

One of the many criticisms of the pluralist view is that it fails to recognize the class bias of groups—the fact that many people and many interests are not represented by competing groups.

As with individual forms of participation, the higher a person's income, the more education he or she has, and the higher the occupational status, the more likely that person is to belong to a group.[14] Specifically, V. O. Key notes, in professional households, over one-half of those responding to a 1952 questionnaire on group membership claimed to belong to three or more groups. Only 5 percent of those in unskilled workers' households maintained this frequency of involvement. Over 40 percent of those in the latter occupational group reported no membership in any formal or informal group, as against only 19 percent for professionals' and 25 percent for business executives' households.

The inclination to join groups—whether political, semipolitical, or nonpolitical—is not shared equally by all classes. As with voting, great numbers of people will not or cannot play.

On the basis of this information, can we then conclude that basically this country is ruled by a wealthy elite? Some people do. Their view is that the members of groups with power (corporate, military, and governmental) are drawn largely from upper-income groups. Further, they believe that the policies made and implemented by these groups protect and promote the interests of the wealthy and big business.[15]

The weakness of this point of view is not in its observation that most political elites are relatively wealthy or, to put it another way, that the wealthy have more than their proportionate share of the

[13] Works by leading pluralists include Robert Dahl, *Who Governs?*; Edward Banfield, *Political Influence* (New York: The Free Press, 1961); Nelson Polsby, *Community Power and Political Theory* (New Haven, Conn.: Yale University Press, 1963).

[14] V. O. Key, Jr., *Public Opinion and American Democracy* (New York: Alfred A. Knopf, 1961), pp. 502–503.

[15] See C. Wright Mills, *The Power Elite* (New York: Oxford University Press, 1956), and William Domhoff, *Who Rules America?* (Englewood Cliffs, N.J.: Prentice-Hall, 1967).

many resources on which political power is based. Instead, this view falls short in failing to recognize that political power often depends on other than economic resources. In addition, and Domhoff recognizes this, the wealthy are not always in agreement on policy matters.

So while the pluralists have failed to recognize the class bias of the groups playing the political game, the *elitists* have failed to recognize that the results of class bias are not always predictable or that groups with other than economic resources can and do win.

But the elitists do have a point. Neither the economic bias nor the economic motives of most political groups can be ignored. It is quite clear that those who join together in groups to play the political game *usually* do so to protect or promote an economic interest.[16] This has also been true historically, particularly since the late nineteenth century. The major interest groups have had economic goals.[17]

Business groups are out to promote the economic interests of business; labor groups promote the economic interests of labor; professional groups do the same. A look at the top lobbying spending illustrates the degree to which this is true (Table 1-1).

Campaign contributions also indicate who plays the game. Some of the largest come from groups that may, directly or indirectly, want to influence policy that affects them economically.

In the 1972 campaign big corporations were particularly active, secretly contributing amounts of $100,000 and more to the Committee for the Re-election of the President.[18] By the fall of 1973 several companies had pleaded guilty to violating the Corrupt Practices Act of 1925, which, among other things, barred corporations and labor unions from contributing to campaigns and limited individual contributions to a campaign committee to $5,000.[19]

Big business has not been quite so willing to contribute to the Democrats. This is labor's territory, although their usual generosity was not apparent in 1972. Herbert Alexander estimates that while labor organizations spent almost $6 million on the 1968 presidential campaign, they probably gave less than $750,000 in 1972 to help the

---

[16] Some important exceptions to this, which will be discussed throughout the book, are emerging.

[17] See Thomas H. Greer, *American Social Reform Movements* (Port Washington, N.Y.: Kennikat Press, 1949 and 1965), pp. 274–275.

[18] For a detailed account of the Senate Watergate Committee disclosures on secret $100,000 contributions, see Richard L. Strout, "Pattern of Firms' Gifts to Nixon Campaign Seen," *The Christian Science Monitor*, November 19, 1973.

[19] The Federal Election Act of 1972, which emphasized disclosure of contributions rather than limits on the size of contributions, had not yet taken effect.

The Now Society

12-5

I heard a funny one from a guy in big oil
yesterday — or was it big labor? Anyway . . .

William Hamilton

Table 1-1

25 top spenders

The 25 top spenders of the organizations that filed lobby spending reports for 1970 are listed below, with the amounts they reported spending in 1970 and 1969.

Organization	1970	1969
Veterans of World War I, U.S.A. Inc.	$341,244[1]	$ 9,955
National Association of Letter Carriers (AFL-CIO)	277,125	295,970
United Federation of Postal Clerks (AFL-CIO)	228,325	250,827
Council for a Livable World	214,626	112,603
AFL-CIO (National headquarters)	197,493	184,938
American Farm Bureau Federation	163,553	146,337
American Hospital Association	153,241	69,925
National Association of Home Builders of the United States	151,605	138,472
United States Savings & Loan League	149,794	126,421
Citizens Committee for Postal Reform Inc.	138,545	83,951
Record Industry Association of America	123,286	115,334
Disabled American Veterans	117,134	15,368
National Committee for the Recording Arts	99,886	139,726[2]
Livestock Producers Committee	96,945	7,255
American Medical Association	96,064	91,355
National Association of Postal Supervisors	94,661	68,365
National Council of Farmer Cooperatives	94,307	82,486
National Housing Conference Inc.	92,549	95,562
The Farmers' Educational and Cooperative Union of America	80,738	73,264
Common Cause (and Urban Coalition Action Council)	79,347	3,754
National Cotton Council of America	79,036	34,084
American Legion	78,939	114,609
Brotherhood of Railway, Airline & Steamship Clerks, Freight Handlers, Express and Station Employees (AFL-CIO)	75,056	80,985
American Trucking Associations Inc.	74,484	80,896
International Brotherhood of Teamsters, Chauffeurs, Warehousemen & Helpers of America	72,626	56,053

[1] Increase results from change in reporting, with entire budget listed in 1970.
[2] Reflects group's final reported figures.

Source: *Congressional Quarterly*, August 6, 1971, p. 1681.

Table 1-1 (cont'd.)

The top 25 spenders of the organizations that filed lobby spending reports for 1972 are listed below with the amounts they reported spending in 1972 and 1971.

Organization	1972	1971
Common Cause	$558,839	$847,856
American Federation of Labor–Congress of Industrial Organizations (AFL-CIO)	216,294	205,101
Veterans of World War I of the U.S.A. Inc.	213,743	308,946
American Postal Workers Union	208,767	257,093
United States Savings and Loan League	191,726	158,727
National Council of Farmer Cooperatives	184,347	60,000
Disabled American Veterans	159,431	129,881
National Association of Letter Carriers (AFL-CIO)	154,188	135,334
American Trucking Associations Inc.	137,804	115,287
The Farmers' Educational and Cooperative Union of America	113,156	97,438
United Mine Workers of America	110,045	93,352
American Nurses' Association Inc.	109,643	no spending record
National Association of Home Builders of the United States	99,031	125,779
American Medical Association	96,146	114,800
Brotherhood of Railway, Airline & Steamship Clerks	88,540	91,642
Recording Industry Association of America Inc.	88,396	41,875
American Insurance Association	82,259	65,812
National Federation of Federal Employees	82,080	67,856
National Housing Conference Inc.	77,906	99,924
International Brotherhood of Teamsters	76,897	63,716
National Limestone Institute Inc.	75,777	3,278
American Civil Liberties Union	73,131	23,853
National Association of Real Estate Boards	70,941	74,952
Liberty Lobby Inc.	70,019	56,125
New York Committee of International Committee of Passenger Lines	66,636	100,342

Source: *Congressional Quarterly*, June 9, 1973, p. 1425.

Democratic presidential candidate. They did contribute a great deal more to Democratic candidates for the House and Senate.[20]

If campaign contributions and lobbying spending are partial measures of which groups play the game, the message is clear: Those playing most frequently at the national level are indeed protecting and promoting economic interests.[21] This doesn't mean, however, that, once elected, candidates will *consistently* respond to the economic interests that put them in office and may now be nourishing them in office. What it probably means is that their general line of policy will be favorable to that economic interest. And it may mean that, where possible, specific decisions favorable to that interest will be made.[22]

In either case, the economic interests primarily responsible for the election have an advantage. A different kind of advantage is apparent when a group has money to spend on lobbying. At a minimum, these groups can expect their point of view to be effectively communicated.

What about those people not playing the game? Does their failure to play mean that their point of view won't be heard? Not necessarily. Many public officials believe they have an obligation to promote and defend the interests of all their constituents, regardless of how active they are. And to the extent this occurs, there is some compensation for the class bias of participation, individual and group. But is that good enough? Abraham Holtzman, speaking about those unwilling or unable to play the game in groups, answers in this way:

> The unorganized are dependent upon others who have primary concerns of their own. Therefore, intervention by such groups on behalf of the unorganized is unpredictable, haphazard, and uncertain. At any point, the organized group may be forced to compromise in time, effort, and substance. The aspirations of the unorganized are easily sacrificed if the espousal of their interests raises a threat to the internal units or the advantage of the orga-

---

[20] Labor has consistently violated the spirit of the Corrupt Practices Act by funneling campaign contributions through a Committee on Political Education (COPE). This has been legally acceptable.

[21] Thomas R. Dye suggests this is also true on the state level. At least, state legislators agree that business interests are the most powerful groups. See Thomas R. Dye, "State Legislative Politics," in *Politics in the American States: A Comparative Analysis*, eds. Herbert Jacob and Kenneth N. Vines, 2d ed. (Boston: Little, Brown and Company, 1971), pp. 201–202.

[22] For example, dairy farmers pledged at least $2 million to President Nixon's re-election campaign. Immediately following the contribution, President Nixon ordered an increase in milk price supports paid to dairy farmers. Denying any wrongdoing, the President said "normal political considerations" played a part in the decision.

nized group. And the politician is not only aware that the unorganized tend to participate less frequently in voting and party activity relevant to his own future but also he recognizes their ineptness in exerting pressure upon government.[23]

Holtzman's point is clear. It's dangerous to rely on others to play the game for you, yet that's what most Americans are doing. Beyond the activity of voting, citizens are allowing groups concerned with economic interests to define the game. What is needed is greater participation and more individuals and groups pursuing interests that go beyond the economic—groups such as Common Cause, The National Committee for an Effective Congress, The People's Lobby, Public Citizen, Inc., and the many public-interest law firms. While the pursuit of private economic goals may ultimately benefit great numbers of citizens, it is just as likely to conflict with broader social interests such as clean air and water, tax reform, adequate health care and housing, and the conservation of energy.

The flaw in the pluralist heaven is that the heavenly chorus sings with a strong upper-class accent. Probably about 90 percent of the people cannot get into the pressure system.[24]

Why Play

It would be nice to believe that the reason some people play the game of American politics has to do with their commitment to *democracy*. Democracy is all about people and how they should relate to one another in a society. It's both a political system and a moral system.[25] Politically, it means that ultimate political authority is vested in the people. Morally, it promotes certain values: (1) *individualism:* the government must enable each individual to achieve the highest potential of development; (2) *liberty:* each individual must be allowed the greatest amount of freedom consistent with order; (3) *equality:* people should have equal rights and equal opportunities; and (4)

---

[23] Abraham Holtzman, *Interest Groups and Lobbying* (Toronto: The Macmillan Co. of Canada, 1966), p. 7. Copyright © 1966 Abraham Holtzman. Reprinted by permission.
[24] Schattschneider, *The Semisovereign People*, p. 35.
[25] E. E. Schattschneider examines democracy from both perspectives in *In Search of Government* (New York: Holt, Rinehart and Winston, 1969).

fraternity: people should cooperate and work together to create a wholesome society.

Americans say they value democracy, at least in the abstract.[26] But values are meaningless unless people are willing to act on them, unless they are willing to promote and preserve them. To say you are appalled by the existence of poverty in this country because you value human life and health as well as human dignity, and then to do nothing about these values, is a mockery. These values become meaningless.

To be active is to be in charge; to be passive is to be under control, be it of natural processes, of social waves and streams, or—of active others.[27]

The values of democracy basically reflect an affection and concern for humankind, for people. Unless people are willing to *act* in their private lives and public lives to preserve and nourish these values, any verbal commitment to democracy becomes absurd. Action for humankind means opposing any denial of rights to racial and other minorities; opposing the prevalence of poverty in a rich society; and helping to promote the interests of the least free members of the society, those whose most basic needs for life, security, and personal freedom are unmet and whose basic political and social affiliations are denied.[28] It's this kind of action that makes any commitment to democracy more than mere rhetoric.

The Antiaction Point of View

Not everyone would agree on the necessity for sustained political action in a democracy. Some people feel that it is not necessary, or particularly desirable, for most citizens to play the game actively. This antiaction point of view has several parts, each of which should be considered.

The size and complexity of society make sustained political action unrealistic. This antiaction argument usually begins by criticizing Jean

---

[26] For a study of citizen attitudes toward democracy, see James W. Prothro and Charles M. Griff, "Fundamental Principles of Democracy: Basis of Agreement and Disagreement," *Journal of Politics*, May 1960, pp. 276–294.

[27] Etzioni, *The Active Society*, p. 4. Reprinted by permission.

[28] Edgar Litt, *Democracy's Ordeal in America: A Guide to Political Theory and Action* (Hinsdale, Ill.: The Dryden Press, 1973), p. 20.

Jacques Rousseau, an eighteenth-century French philosopher. Rousseau had the odd notion that democracy, as government, required action by the people. Envisioning a city-state rather than a nation, he wrote, "the sovereign can act only when the people are assembled." The fact that, even at that time in history, it would have been difficult to have the French people "constantly assembled in a public place" didn't faze him. After all, citizens ought to be willing to make any sacrifice necessary to attend their public duties.[29]

Rousseau might have been a little impractical, and E. E. Schattschneider is probably correct in saying that "an all-American town meeting in Rousseau's style would be the largest, longest, and most boring and frustrating meeting imaginable," and that it would produce total paralysis. But does this mean we should just forget the idea of "government by the people" to which Abraham Lincoln referred in his Gettysburg Address?

Schattschneider and others say yes. People have misinterpreted Lincoln; 200 million people do not and cannot govern in Rousseau's sense. Jefferson's idea of democracy seems more realistic to these critics. It is "government by consent of the governed." Representatives are elected and must return to the people to be re-elected. Consent is given or denied. "The American people are in the situation of a very rich man who owns so many businesses that he cannot personally run all of them. He controls them by selecting agents to act for him, giving them a great deal of latitude in their operations, but holding them responsible for the results they get." [30] Let the government take the initiative to do what is necessary. It sometimes has to deal with problems before the people understand them. As long as the people have the last word and demand that leaders do the best job they know how to do, the system will work well.

Lester Milbrath seems to share this antiaction point of view. Citizens need only confine their participation to voting responsibly, and the political system will function smoothly. Channels of communication will stay open between the public and their leaders.

> As we think about the role of the average citizen then, we should not expect him to give a lot of attention to, and be active in resolving, issues of public policy. Nor should we expect him to stand up and be counted on every issue that comes along. The

[29] This discussion draws heavily on Schattschneider, *In Search of Government*, pp. 59–76.
[30] *Ibid.*, p. 72.

most we can expect is that he will participate in the choice of decision-makers and that he will ask to be heard if an issue comes along that greatly concerns him or on which he can make some special contribution. Many citizens do not even vote or speak up on issues, yet their passive role has the consequence of accepting things as they are. Indeed it is impossible to escape at least a passive role in the choice of decision-makers. The choice process can proceed and government can continue to function even if many citizens choose to be so inactive as to fail to vote.[31]

This part of the antiaction point of view seems incompatible with the idea of democracy as a moral system. How prepared will citizens be to make that ultimate election decision when so little is being asked of them in other civic arenas? How can citizens possibly implement their values if they're told they can't be expected to be informed and can't be expected to communicate actively and consistently with their representatives? How will citizens be able to hold public officials accountable; and how will they be able to judge performance?

Somewhere between the rainbows of Rousseau and the pragmatism of Jefferson, there is a more effective approach to political action. Such an approach should encourage citizens to act on those values that are consistent with democracy as a moral system. It should oblige citizens to work to understand and communicate consistently and persistently with elected officials. It should emphasize citizen awareness so that public officials can indeed be held responsible at election time, as well as in between.

Subjection in minor affairs breaks out every day, and is felt by the whole community indiscriminately. It does not drive men to resistance, but it crosses them at every turn, till they are led to surrender the exercise of their will. Thus their spirit is gradually broken and their character enervated; whereas that obedience, which is exacted on a few important but rare occasions, only exhibits servitude at certain intervals, and throws the burden of it upon a small number of men. It is vain to summon a people, which has been rendered so dependent on the central power, to choose from time to time the

[31] Milbrath, *Political Participation*, p. 145.

representatives of that power; this rare and brief exercise of their free choice, however important it may be, will not prevent them from gradually losing the faculties of thinking, feeling, and acting for themselves, and thus gradually falling below the level of humanity.[32]

But there is more to the antiaction approach to democracy. It can be summarized in this way. In addition to being impractical and unnecessary, sustained political involvement is also disruptive. It may promote unnecessary conflict and cleavages—cleavages that are difficult to bridge. To understand this point of view, one need only think of the civil rights issue, particularly as it manifested itself in the sixties. The intense feelings on both sides of that issue stimulated active participation in politics by many who were formerly apathetic, but their political activities also deepened the cleavages between people, making consensus increasingly remote.[33] The war in Southeast Asia provoked the same kind of domestic conflict and promoted serious cleavages. The level of intense participation seemed to make consensus impossible.

This argument fails to recognize the possibility that intense political participation and the resulting conflict may be functional to society. Lewis Coser argues this position. Far from being a negative factor that tears apart, Coser says, conflict may fulfill a number of important functions—it may be an essential element in group formation and group life.[34]

Speaking about small groups, for example, Coser explains that conflict is often necessary to maintain relationships. Without ways to vent hostility toward each other and to express dissent, group members may feel completely crushed and may react by withdrawing. Relationships are maintained by freeing pent-up feelings of hostility.[35]

What does this have to do with this second antiaction argument? In essence, this: Minimal participation contributes to order, with the potential for serious outbursts; active involvement forces readjustment of the system. This is how it works. If only minimal participation is encouraged, this participation acts like a safety valve. The potential

---

[32] Alexis de Tocqueville, *Democracy in America* (New York: Alfred A. Knopf, 1945), Vol. II, p. 320.
[33] Milbrath, *Political Participation*, p. 147.
[34] Lewis A. Coser, *The Functions of Social Conflict* (London: Routledge & Kegan Paul, 1956), p. 8.
[35] *Ibid.*, p. 47.

for real involvement and real conflict is drained away. While safety-valve processes and institutions may produce order, the social system and the individual lose something. The system is not forced to modify itself to meet changing conditions; the dammed-up tension in the individual creates the potential for a more serious disruptive explosion.[36]

The increased participation and accompanying conflict during the civil rights struggle and the more intense involvement of some segments of society during the period of United States involvement in Southeast Asia might well be viewed as constructive. However inadequately and slowly, the government was ultimately forced to reassess its positions, in part because of internal conflict.

The conflict of the Gilded Age (1880s), the ensuing depression years (1893–1897), and the Progressive era (1901–1920) further brings into question the argument that intense citizen participation is likely to produce cleavages that are dysfunctional to society. During the 1880s, dozens of groups emerged with visions of an improved society. There were demands for civil service reform, the eight-hour day, scientific agriculture, women's suffrage, enforcement of vice laws, factory inspection, nonpartisan local elections, trust-busting, wildlife conservation, tax reform, abolition of child labor, businesslike local government, regulation of railway rates, and hundreds of other ideas that would later be identified as progressivism. Even with all this activity, change didn't come quickly. All the pressure for reform during the Gilded Age couldn't conceal the fact that individuals and groups remained fragmented.[37]

The depression following this period seemed to dramatize the need for reform. The failures of industrialism and national partisan politics became increasingly apparent. Hundreds of discussion groups emerged where people, regardless of background, gathered to find remedies.[38]

The payoff from heightened participation and its accompanying conflict didn't come in any significant way until the Progressive era. The groups of this period, different in style and composition, began to cooperate and to win. The middle classes of the cities joined with earlier Populists in a common demand for social, economic, and political reform. Still, conflict was far from absent. Neither big business

---

[36] *Ibid.*, p. 48.
[37] David P. Thelan, "Social Tensions and the Origins of Progressivism," *The Journal of American History*, September 1969, p. 335.
[38] *Ibid.*, p. 337.

nor the urban political machines appreciated being the target of reformist zeal. But out of that conflict, out of that heightened citizen participation, came legislation that transcended private interests, legislation that responded to the broader needs of the community as they were perceived at that time. It included opportunities for citizens to be more directly involved in state politics through the initiative process and popular referendum, the establishment of the direct primary in many states, and the widespread adoption of the recall.[39] The participation and accompanying conflict of these three periods seemed to produce beneficial results, not cleavages difficult to bridge.

A final argument against intense citizen involvement has to do with the general incompetence of people. It goes this way: Except in abstract form, citizens are not very committed to the democratic rules of the game, nor are they very informed politically. Leaders, on the other hand, are much more committed to democratic values and believe in the rules of the game. For example, they will compete in elections and will abide by the decisions of the electorate.[40]

At least two objections to this argument can be voiced. First, if participation in politics builds a commitment to democratic values, why not encourage greater citizen participation? Second, what about those elites that do not follow the democratic rules of the game? The 1972 election illustrated their presence dramatically. Illegal campaign contributions were accepted eagerly; "dirty tricks" were conducted openly. Because there *are* exceptions, because not *all* elites are committed to democratic principles, citizens must become responsible. Citizens must be more than minimally involved.

So much for the antiaction argument. A final answer to "Why play?" is, "You can win." A citizen doesn't have to be rich, to be famous, to have abundant "inside contacts." All that is needed are commitment, skill, and opportunity.

A new and very exciting political phenomenon is occurring among students in this country. At least 400,000 college students in over nineteen different states are now, through their schools, dues-paying

[39] For a thorough discussion of the nature of citizen participation during the Progressive era and the resulting legislation, see Richard Hofstadter, *The Age of Reform* (New York: Vintage Books, 1966).

[40] Several studies suggest that participation in politics builds a commitment to democratic values and that elites are much more likely to understand and adhere to specific applications of general democratic principles than are average citizens. Milbrath, *Political Participation*, p. 150.

members of public interest research groups (PIRGs, as they are commonly called). These are social action groups made up of students who are developing skills and resources and taking advantage of the opportunities for change. Acting out democratic values is what they are all about. And they are winning. Take a look at some of their accomplishments.

- The appointment of an ombudsman for prisoners in the St. Louis jails.
- A new state law that regulates ambulance services in Massachusetts.
- New regulations that forbid lumber companies to clear-cut swaths of forests without federal approval.
- State regulation of private employment agencies in Oregon.
- Increased accessibility to state and local records in Massachusetts through a new state law.
- The wearing of nameplates by the police in Minneapolis so officers who misbehave can be more easily identified.
- A new plan in Detroit that forces landlords to repair dilapidated housing.
- A cleanliness grading system for restaurants in St. Louis.[41]

These are only a few examples of what can be done if citizens are willing to play. Students involved in PIRGs are winning because they know how and are willing.

So what can be said about political games thus far? Most people do not play actively. Those who do, either individually or in groups, tend to be among the more advantaged segments of society. And the payoff they seek is frequently economic. Those unconcerned with the small number of players seem to like the relative stability that comes from limited and narrowly defined participation. No one ever seems to win too much or lose too much. If new players joined actively, the existing ones might have to watch their moves more carefully, or even move in different ways. In addition, the rewards of the game might ultimately get dispersed differently. And finally, the rules defining the game might be changed in order to accommodate the interests of additional, increasingly competent players.

Political games, then, are relatively stable in this country. Who

---

[41] Richard Lyons, "College Crusaders for Consumerism," *San Francisco Examiner and Chronicle, This World,* October 21, 1973; originally reported in the *New York Times.*

wins is fairly predictable. Only greater and more diverse participation would alter the nature and rewards of the game.

Key Words

Political
Pluralism
Elitists
Democracy

Suggested Activities

1. Conduct a political participation survey of the class. What percentage of the class regularly does the following:
   a. Votes
   b. Works for a candidate or election issue
   c. Works for a political party or group with a political interest
   d. Communicates with public officials (through letters, telegrams, visits, etc.)
2. Conduct a political participation survey of the parents of class members. Gather the same information. Compare the results.

2
How to Play the Game of American Politics

If people care about winning, playing the game of American politics involves careful analysis and planning. Both of these activities are costly. They consume time and energy. For people without a basic commitment to the importance of political action and without a basic commitment to a goal, the cost will seem to be too great. You may as well forget it. But assuming the commitment and opportunity are there, there are nine steps to effective political action.

1. Identify the problem
2. Formulate the goal
3. Determine strategic options
4. Collect strategic information and make a strategic choice
5. Identify players—potential allies and opponents
6. Calculate player resources
7. Determine tactical options
8. Collect tactical information and make tactical choices
9. Identify rules

Following these steps requires knowing a few things about political games in general and a few things about the *key concepts* involved.

What all games have in common is that they involve decision makers with intertwined goals and objectives. Each player is dependent on other players.[1] For both parlor games and political games, winning involves anticipating the moves of your opponent. The best move in a chess game or the best way to bid or the best card to lay down in a bridge game depends on what one's opponents are likely to do.[2]

In parlor games, however, each player's options are more limited. These games are usually well defined, they have an explicit and efficient set of rules, the information available to players is specified at every point, and the scoring procedure is complete. Political games are far less well defined. Some rules are indeed explicit, but other implicit, informal rules may be more crucial to success; and, probably most important, information is imperfect. The number of players is usually very large and changing, their objectives are not always known, their tactical understanding and inclinations may be only vaguely apparent, and some of them may not act in a rational way—a way that maximizes gains and minimizes losses.[3] Quite obviously, political games are more difficult to play than parlor games.

Both political games and parlor games involve a certain degree of conflict and a certain degree of cooperation. The fact that all players value the same prize draws them together. However, not everyone can always win. Not everyone can become mayor; no more than one tennis player can win the set in singles. When there is scarcity, there is conflict.[4]

Even with conflict, many political games allow competing players to win something. Winning may not necessarily involve destroying all of what your opponent values. Think about the political game of war. Modern war is limited war. Although warring nations may have conflicting values, they have a powerful common interest in reaching an outcome that is not enormously destructive to both sides. The same is true in a labor strike. A successful strike is not one that destroys the employer financially.[5] Legislative games are of this type. Through

[1] Martin Shubik, "The Uses of Game Theory," in Contemporary Political Analysis, ed. James C. Charlesworth (New York: The Free Press, 1967), p. 240.
[2] T. C. Schelling, "What Is Game Theory?" in Contemporary Political Analysis, ed. James C. Charlesworth (New York: The Free Press, 1967), p. 277.
[3] Ibid., p. 277.
[4] See Ralph Goldman, Contemporary Perspectives on Politics (New York: Van Nostrand Reinhold Company, 1972), pp. 331–340.

bargaining and compromise all players usually win something. Not all of what the "losing" players value is destroyed.

So two kinds of political games are possible—games that allow only one winner, such as elections, and games that allow everyone, even the losers, to win something.

The *type* of political game being played will influence *how* the game is played. Games where only one winner is possible, where the other player(s) must lose, are not conducive to interaction and cooperation among the players. Because the players are in a very real sense opponents, there is no need for communication or bargaining. In contrast, if the game is played in court, in party caucus meetings, or on the legislative floor, communication among opposing players is crucial as each tries to get the best deal. Bargaining opportunities are built into the strategy.

Enough about the general dynamics of games. The specifics of *political* game-playing are more important. Let's examine the nine steps to political action.

Identify the Problem

Except for voting, most people will not act politically unless they see a problem. They only see a problem when they see a discrepancy between what they value and what they see as reality. Black citizens living in the South would never have identified their inability to vote as a problem unless (1) they valued the right to vote, and (2) they perceived that they really were not able to vote. People living in urban centers would never have identified air pollution as a problem unless (1) they valued clean air and the good health that accompanies it, and (2) they perceived the deteriorating quality of the air and believed that poor health might result.

One difficulty people committed to political action have is communicating to others the fact that a value-reality gap exists. Unless people know the facts of a situation, and are convinced that what they know is an accurate reflection of reality, they are unlikely to act politically. In addition, unless activists have *correctly* identified the dominant values among the people they are trying to arouse, a following is not likely to develop. Political failure frequently occurs be-

[5] Thomas C. Schelling, *The Strategy of Conflict* (Oxford: Oxford University Press, 1960). Reprint issued in 1970 by special arrangement with Harvard University Press, pp. 5 and 6.

cause activists *assume* that because *they* are strongly committed to a certain value, everyone else must be. For example, perhaps the activist believes a particular legislator should be removed from public office because of a conflict of interest. The legislator is helping to make policy decisions in areas where he has a substantial financial interest. However, the activist may discover that while constituents can be convinced that a conflict of interest exists, people will not assist in removing the legislator from office because they don't share the belief that a conflict of interest per se is bad. To reach constituents, the activist may have to go one step farther and demonstrate clearly how this conflict of interest is shortchanging *them*.

Political problems are those that can be dealt with through the authoritative decision-making process. They are problems that can be eliminated or eased through decisions by public officials. It is also important to realize that the problems themselves may have been created by the political process; for example, a particular decision may not have been fairly or efficiently implemented.

Ultimately, the dimensions of a particular political problem will have to be communicated if people are to be convinced. The action-oriented citizen will have to be able to explain the origin and persistence of the problem. Answering these questions will help:

- What policies have been developed regarding the problem?
- How have these policies been implemented nationally, statewide, or locally?
- Where are the policy gaps and policy failures?
- What and who are responsible? [6]

Of course, answering these questions requires information, and that means research. Good intentions are not enough.

Formulate Goals

A *goal* is what one specifically wants to accomplish through political action. It is what one wants to win—the pay-off. Unless it is perceived as *important*, it won't sustain the necessary interest or commitment. It won't be worth the cost either to the activist or to essential followers.

[6] For further discussions, see Dieter T. Hessel, *A Social Action Primer* (Philadelphia: The Westminster Press, 1972), pp. 75–80.

In addition to being perceived as important, the goal should be *specific*. Unless a new party is being launched or the existing party structure is being used, stick to a single issue. A citizen who is counting on the assistance of others must realize that more often than not, increasing the range of issues tends to splinter allies.[7]

The goal should be *realizable*. It should be consistent with capabilities and with resources. The quickest way for an action effort to disintegrate is through failure to achieve results.

But unless the political game allows only one winner, be prepared to *compromise*. Compromise doesn't mean failure, it means getting part of what one asks for; maybe another time it will be possible to get the rest. What people get relative to what they give up will depend on how skillfully they play the game.

Some people see compromise as an essential part of the political process in a free and open society. For Saul Alinsky, a society devoid of compromise is totalitarian. Specifically, he believes "a free and open society is an on-going conflict, interrupted periodically by compromises—which then become the start for the continuation of conflict, compromise, and on ad infinitum."[8]

Don't be discouraged by initial disinterest in your goal. Although this may be difficult to understand, disinterest may actually produce an advantage. Burkhart calls this "issue slack." He believes it is far easier to arouse people and mobilize their support if they do not know about a problem—a plan to put another shopping center on marshland or a plan to expand the airport. It is more difficult where no slack, no citizen disinterest, is evident, since people then have some information about a problem and have already made up their minds about where they stand.[9]

Think through the possible *side effects*. Doing so may alter a goal or may produce a way of eliminating the negative effects. In either case, in order to mobilize support and deal with the reservations of potential allies, these side effects must be identified. Failing to do so can be a major miscalculation.

Martha is a college sophomore. She is also a prostitute. Asked to join a citywide effort to improve the working conditions of those in her profession, she refused. Specifically, Martha was asked to help

[7] See Michael Walzer, *Political Action* (Chicago: Quadrangle Books, 1971), p. 28.
[8] Saul Alinsky, *Rules for Radicals* (New York: Random House, 1971), p. 59.
[9] James Burkhart et al., *Strategies for Political Participation* (Cambridge, Mass.: Winthrop Publishers, 1972), pp. 82–83.

unionize prostitutes throughout the city and to work to convince state legislators that prostitution and other "victimless crimes" should no longer be classified as crimes. Although she was logically a potential ally, Martha believed that the implementation of these goals might make her life even more difficult. With improved working conditions and the elimination of police harassment, more women would be attracted to the profession. These were the negative side effects she and other potential allies perceived, but the organizers didn't.

Determine Strategic Options

Once a goal has been established and the action-oriented group or individual is convinced that it won't be weakened by adverse side effects, the next step is considering strategic options. A *strategy* is an overall plan that the players adopt in order to achieve a specific goal. The tactics, which are the hows, come later.

The strategic options available include (1) levels of government, (2) institutional arrangements, and (3) electoral or pressure politics. Can the goal be achieved at the local, state, or national level? Can it be achieved through the legislative, executive, or judicial branch of government? Can it be accomplished by influencing those who already hold political power, or does it require electing someone new? These are the available strategic choices. The first two are determined by *who has the authority to act*. Depending on the goal, some choices will be automatically eliminated. The others will have to be considered and weighed carefully.

How does one decide at what level of government the political game should be played? Determining where the game should be played requires understanding the geographic distribution of power in this country; it requires understanding the concept of *federalism*.

Federalism is the division of power between national and state governments. It was a bait used in 1787 to entice some of the participants in the Constitutional Convention to accept the idea of a new government. Unless states could be assured that they were not relinquishing all their independent power by getting together to form a United States, they would have no part of the deal. Through federalism the union could be established.[10] Federalism offers the citizen a

---

[10] The basic principle of American federalism is found in the Tenth Amendment to the Constitution, which provides that the national government is to have only those powers delegated in the Constitution, with all other powers reserved to the states.

number of different points of access—local government, state government, or national government. The question becomes, of those levels of government with the relevant authority, where would the goal be easiest to implement and yet still have an impact?

If citizens are inexperienced or if resources are limited, the local level of government might seem the logical place to start. However, before coming to this conclusion, it is important to think about how power is distributed within each level. Who holds power in the community? Who holds power statewide? [11] Sometimes communities and states are dominated by particular interests—a dairy interest, a mining interest, union interests. In fact, the smaller the geographic area, the less diverse interests are likely to be. James Madison had this problem on his mind when he argued for a large republic:

> The smaller the society, the fewer probably will be the distinct parties and interests composing it; the fewer the distinct parties and interests, the more frequently will a majority be found of the same party, and the smaller the compass within which they are placed, the more easily will they concert and execute their plans of oppression. Extend the sphere and you take on a greater variety of parties and interests; you make it less probable that a majority of the whole will have a common motive to invade the rights of other citizens. Or if such a common motive exists, it will be more difficult for all who feel it to discover their own strength, and to act in unison with each other.[12]

As James Madison explained it, competing interests appear as the geographic area becomes larger. The power of any one group diminishes as others, with resources of their own, appear on the scene. Dairy farmers, for example, are likely to have more power in a rural county of New York than in the state of New York as a whole.

The strategic question to be asked is, then, will the goal be blocked by a dominant local interest? Could action at the state level make it possible to gain support and substantially reduce the influence of that one opposing interest?

The importance of this strategic question can be seen in the civil rights battle. Not until it was fought and won on the national level did black citizens begin to make significant gains. Local and state governments, with the power given them through federalism, were

---

[11] See Grant McConnell, *Private Power and American Democracy* (New York: Alfred A. Knopf, 1966), p. 104.
[12] James Madison, *The Federalist*, Number 10 (New York: Modern Library), pp. 60–61.

easily influenced by segregationist interests. William H. Riker, in his analysis of federalism, argued this point:

> The main beneficiaries (of federalism) throughout American history have been the southern whites, who have been given the freedom to oppress negroes, first as slaves and later as a depressed caste. Other minorities have from time to time also managed to obtain some of the benefits: e.g., special business interests have been allowed to regulate themselves, especially from about 1890–1936. . . . But the significance of federal benefits to economic inests pales beside the significance of benefits to the southern segregationist whites. The judgment to be passed on federalism in the United States is therefore a judgement on the values of segregation and racial oppression.[13]

This division of power, then, provides opportunity of access but also strategic pitfalls. The easiest level to penetrate may bring forth the strongest opposition. If the community has diverse interests, or if the goal poses no threat to a single dominant interest, the local level may well be the place to start. This assumes, of course, that the goal can be satisfactorily fulfilled at the local level.

The U.S. Constitution and public law define authority—where certain games *can* be played. If the goal has to do with international affairs, the game generally has to be played at the national level; if the goal has to do with interstate commerce, the game must again be played at that level. However, if the goal involves public education or public safety, there is a choice. Ordinarily these games are played at the state and local levels. An examination of the U.S. Constitution and the *Congressional Record* gives some indication of federal concerns. Another partial indication of who does what is spending. When interpreting the statistics in Table 2–1, remember that the data can be somewhat misleading because state governments supervise most local government spending and make important decisions about how and to whom the money should be distributed.[14]

Finally, when determining strategic options associated with levels of government, don't disregard the possibility of action at more than one level. If there is a national organization that has explained the problem in a similar way and is pursuing similar goals, it seems logical

---

[13] William H. Riker, *Federalism: Origin, Operation, Significance* (Boston: Little, Brown and Company, 1964), pp. 152–153.
[14] See Herbert Jacob and Kenneth N. Vines, eds., *Politics in the American States*, 2d ed. (Boston: Little, Brown and Company, 1971), p. 6.

that the citizen would work through that organization. Many national organizations are organized federally for that very reason. They often have the resources to conduct political action at more than one level simultaneously. An example is Common Cause's nationwide campaign to end the influence of money and secrecy in government. So the first question is, what levels of government, given the goal, *could* be involved?

The next strategic question is, *what institutional choice is available?* At each level of government, there are three kinds of decision-making institutions—executive, legislative, and judicial. This *separation of power* was a convenient device used by the framers of the Constitution to keep all government power from falling into the hands of any one individual or group. One institution, Congress, was to be primarily responsible for *making* laws; the second institution, the presidency and its accompanying executive departments, was to be primarily responsible for *implementing and enforcing* the law; the Supreme Court and subsidiary courts would have the job of *interpreting and applying* the law.

While this separation is not complete (there is some functional overlap), it does contribute to a system of *checking and balancing power*. No institution can do its job without cooperation from at least one other institution. But more about that later.

The distribution of power among institutions is particularly important to activists. It provides alternative avenues of access to government. If it seems impossible to get the executive branch of government to enforce a law passed by Congress, the citizen can go to court to compel enforcement. If the court sees no negligence on the part of the executive branch, the citizen might work with others to strengthen the law itself.

Usually individuals and groups seeking change do not have the resources to play the game in each institution. In addition, the goal might only be reachable through one. That is, only one institution might have the authority to act. The answers to these questions might help determine the right institution for action.

1. Are there already laws or constitutional provisions that complement the goal? For example, if the goal is safer public housing, are there already laws that purport to guarantee safe public housing? If the answer is yes, the executive branch needs to be pushed to enforce them. If the answer is no, the legislative branch would seem to be the appropriate focus.

Table 2-1
State and local finances and employment

No. 419. Governmental general expenditure (direct and intergovernmental): 1972 and 1973

| | Expenditure (mil. dol.) | | | | | | Percent | | | |
| | 1972 | | | 1973 | | | 1972 | | 1973 | |
Function	All governments	Federal	State and local	All governments	Federal	State and local	Federal	State and local	Federal	State and local
Total	321,389	188,100	204,203	344,233	204,813	222,710	100.0	100.0	100.0	100.0
National defense and international relations	79,258	79,258	(X)	79,624	79,624	(X)	42.1	(X)	38.9	(X)
Space research and tech	3,369	3,369	(X)	3,270	3,270	(X)	1.8	(X)	1.6	(X)
Postal service	9,366	9,366	(X)	9,572	9,572	(X)	5.0	(X)	4.7	(X)
Education	69,990	13,045	86,134	75,690	14,783	92,963	6.9	42.2	7.2	41.7
Highways	19,442	5,540	21,683	19,173	5,834	21,624	2.9	10.6	2.8	9.7
Natural resources	14,215	11,729	3,244	16,372	13,764	3,393	6.2	1.2	6.7	1.5
Health and hospitals	17,033	5,478	13,946	18,669	6,591	14,864	2.9	6.8	3.2	6.7
Public welfare	23,558	15,739	28,203	26,967	15,482	31,380	8.4	13.8	7.6	14.1
Housing and urban renewal	5,411	4,611	2,897	7,345	6,301	3,333	2.5	1.4	3.1	1.5
Air transportation	3,575	2,538	1,191	3,147	1,960	1,475	1.3	0.6	1.0	0.7
Social insurance admin.	2,291	1,911	1,136	2,525	2,047	1,281	1.0	0.6	1.0	0.6
Interest on general debt	23,077	17,114	5,962	25,117	18,332	6,785	9.1	2.9	9.0	3.0
Other and combined	50,805	18,402	39,806	56,762	27,253	45,612	9.8	19.5	13.3	20.5

X Not applicable.

[Local government amounts are estimates subject to sampling variation; see source. Aggregates exclude duplicative transactions between levels of government. See also *Historical Statistics, Colonial Times to 1970*, series Y 534–566, Y 744, Y 750–782, and Y 820–848]

Table 2-1 (cont'd.)

No. 420. Governmental expenditure for capital outlay: 1967 to 1973

Year and function	Total capital outlay		State and local			Construction expenditure only		State and local		
	All governments	Federal	Total	State	Local	All governments	Federal	Total	State	Local
1967	42,101	17,868	24,233	11,544	12,689	23,832	4,470	19,362	9,550	9,811
1968	47,057	21,326	25,731	12,210	13,521	24,772	3,972	20,800	10,053	10,747
1969	47,246	19,006	28,240	12,701	15,539	26,836	3,932	22,904	10,610	12,294
1970	47,519	17,869	29,650	13,295	16,355	28,402	4,150	24,252	11,185	13,067
1971	48,823	15,686	33,137	14,736	18,402	31,051	4,081	26,970	12,446	14,524
1972	55,053	20,816	34,237	15,283	18,953	32,908	4,801	28,107	13,022	15,085
1973, total	55,348	20,091	35,257	14,677	20,580	32,875	4,632	28,243	12,327	15,916
National defense and international relations	14,133	14,133	(X)	(X)	(X)	1,283	1,283	(X)	(X)	(X)
Space research*	108	108	(X)	(X)	(X)	45	45	(X)	(X)	(X)
Education	7,932	1	7,931	2,807	5,124	6,251	(X)	6,251	2,168	4,083
Higher education	2,731	(X)	2,731	2,288	443	2,036	(X)	2,036	1,702	334
Local schools	4,856	(X)	4,856	175	4,681	3,913	(X)	3,193	164	3,749
Other	345	1	344	344	(X)	302	(X)	302	302	(X)

Highways	11,524	65	11,459	9,120	2,339	9,974	56	9,918	8,005	1,913
Natural resources	3,278	2,504	774	526	248	2,670	2,109	561	342	219
Health and hospitals	1,263	198	1,065	582	483	1,025	154	871	504	367
Sewerage	2,428	(X)	2,428	(X)	2,428	2,346	(X)	2,346	(X)	2,346
Local parks, recreation	863	(X)	863	(X)	863	595	(X)	595	(X)	595
Housing, urban renewal	3,024	1,113	1,911	216	1,695	1,216	(X)	1,216	215	1,001
Air transportation	1,442	431	1,011	194	817	1,195	315	880	152	727
Water transport†	490	143	347	79	267	301	66	235	64	171
Local utilities	3,656	(X)	3,656	(X)	3,656	2,790	(X)	2,790	(X)	2,790
All other	5,207	1,395	3,812	1,153	2,660	3,185	604	2,581	875	1,705

X Not applicable.

* Includes technology.

† Includes terminals.

[In millions of dollars. Local government amounts are estimates subject to sampling variation; see source. See also *Historical Statistics, Colonial Times to 1970*, series Y 523–524, Y 593–594, Y 673–674, Y 740–741, and Y 787–788]

Source: United States Bureau of the Census, *Statistical Abstract of the United States, 1975*, 96th ed., Washington, D.C., United States Government Printing Office, 1975, p. 254.

2. Is the executive branch unwilling or unable to enforce the law? If the answer is yes, the relevant department seems unwilling to enforce the law, then legislative or court action compelling enforcement might be required. If the answer is yes, but it seems *unable* to enforce the law because of inadequate financial resources or an inadequate staff, two institutional answers are possible. A legislative effort could produce an increased budgetary appropriation. An executive effort at a higher level might produce a different distribution of money—a shift in where money is spent.

The answers to these questions will probably become apparent during the problem analysis stage. In substance, they should indicate what the institutional possibilities are, given the goal.

The final strategic question involves a choice between *pressure politics* and *electoral politics*. Since *power* is the ability to get what one wants, particularly the ability to persuade others to do what they might not ordinarily do, the question becomes, can existing decision makers be persuaded?

While a variety of tactical possibilities are available to individuals and groups interested in persuading public officials, it is possible that none of the usual approaches will work. If a legislator or governor, for example, is philosophically opposed to the sought-after goal, if it is inconsistent with his or her party's position, or if support of the goal would mean antagonizing major campaign contributors, it may be necessary to work for that legislator's or governor's political defeat. This step, however, would only be undertaken if his or her opposition were considered serious. Sometimes the mere mention of this intention by a group with political clout will neutralize the public official's position: both active support and active opposition could be perceived as too costly.

To summarize, the strategic options are these: level of access—local, state, or national; institutional access—legislative, executive, or judicial; and method of access—pressure politics or electoral politics.

Strategic Information

The ultimate strategic combination might reflect not the only choice, but rather the best choice given the individual's or group's resources, experience, and goal. If one strategic combination doesn't work, another will have to be tried. Whatever the choice, it should be arrived at on the basis of carefully assembled information.

This information is of a special kind. It is called *probability information* and is frequently used in games to avoid haphazard moves. It includes whatever information will help in predicting the probability of success. At this stage, the information should help the activist make a sound *strategic choice*. For example, if the goal is improving the conditions at the county jail, and one strategic option involves getting the county board of supervisors to increase their jail appropriation, what information is available that would indicate the likelihood of a positive response? Does checking the minutes of full board and committee meetings reveal that only 25 percent of the members would support this? Do public statements and votes by board members reveal little likelihood of support? If so, would there be a greater probability of success from using the judicial process? Careful research might reveal a judicial trend in the state toward making conditions in jails consistent with state law. It is this kind of information that would lead to a sound strategic choice. The chess player, the tennis player, and the football player need the same kind of information to develop a winning strategy. How do the other players usually play the game?

The Strategic Choice

Using the information collected, an evaluation should be made of the combination most likely to succeed. For example, to achieve the goal of a guaranteed national income for all Americans, the initial choice would probably be the national level, the legislative branch, and pressure politics. Some of the information directing the activist to this combination might include the following:

1. Only national decision makers have the financial resources and constitutional authority to enact policy affecting citizens of more than one state.
2. The current federal welfare legislation doesn't, even implicitly, guarantee anyone income. So the executive branch cannot be pressured to do something it hasn't the statutory authority to do.
3. Because there is no apparent violation of either statutory or constitutional obligations, the federal court system could not help implement the goal at this stage.
4. The only institution capable of providing the statutory authority for a guaranteed income at the national level is Congress.
5. Because of the changes in the composition of Congress since President Nixon first sent them a similar piece of legislation,

pressure politics might now work. Generally, more liberal legislative players could provide the extra leverage needed to overcome the resistance of any one unsympathetic committee chairperson. Electoral politics shouldn't be necessary.

Once the strategic choice has been made and the general plan developed, it is time to carefully identify all the essential players, including the potential players.

Players

The players in the political game may be individuals or groups, operating in either a private or a public capacity, who are likely to interact in relation to the established goal. Some will work together in pursuit of the goal (allies); others will work together in opposition to the goal (opponents). Individual players include citizens who write letters to public officials, vote, bring court actions, etc. Their activities are not defined by any organized group. Also included in this category are individuals with a particular status, skill, or position who can help other individuals or groups gain access to institutions. A lawyer helping a client, a legislator helping a constituent, and a folksinger assisting an organization in fund-raising are examples.

Interest Groups and Political Parties

Group players include organized *interest groups* whose members share common views and objectives. In addition to their nonpolitical activities, interest groups attempt to influence public officials in those specific policy areas relevant to the group's objectives. *Political parties* are also group players. They consist of individuals who, very broadly, share certain beliefs and who organize to win elections, operate government, and influence public policy.

The differences between interest groups and political parties define their limitations. Knowing these help the action-oriented citizen decide on which kind of group is more likely to help implement the goal. First, parties are entirely political. Their primary interest is placing people in public office and influencing policy in that way. Interest groups, on the other hand, may be political only part of the time. When they are acting politically, they are pursuing rather specific, usually private, goals. They become political when they must—when getting what they want or keeping what they have involves influencing government. For example, the American Medical Association normally concerns itself with such things as medical standards and the professional development of doctors, but for years the AMA acted politically to prevent the establishment of Medicare.

The methods used by interest groups, unlike those used by parties, are varied. They include both pressure politics and electoral politics—primarily the former, for the emphasis is on policy, not personnel.

Still another difference between the two relates to membership. Party members don't formally pay dues, although they may make campaign contributions, and they don't formally enroll as party members, except through voter registration procedures. Membership in a party is usually informal. At a particular time a citizen simply identifies with a certain party and the candidates it promotes. While this identification, for most people, is fairly constant, an individual who can't support the party's candidate in a given election doesn't "lose" membership. Interest-group members do pay dues and do formally join. They indicate through money and effort whether or not the group is effectively promoting their individual interests. This evaluation occurs yearly as they decide whether or not to renew their membership.

The different focus of each of these institutions determines the kinds of people who will identify with each. The party, to survive, has to continue to attract enough supporters to get its candidates elected. The result is a group whose membership is very diverse and that espouses, through its candidates, a broad range of policies. The members of interest groups are more homogeneous. They have a more limited number of objectives and a greater number of shared attitudes. If interest-group leaders were to promote issues inconsistent with or outside the range of the group's defined objectives, members might withdraw support.[15]

Governmental groups must also be considered players. Various departments and agencies may help citizens gain access to other institutions and may even join the citizens' group in an intensive lobbying effort. Since this action is formally against the law, government groups lobbying at the national level call their activities "supplying information." One reason why these groups may be particularly valuable allies and particularly difficult opponents is that they represent an area of expertise. They have at their disposal abundant information in a fairly well-defined policy area. This information becomes a particularly important resource in interaction with others (that is, members of the

[15] See Abraham Holtzman, *Interest Groups and Lobbying* (Toronto: The Macmillan Company, 1966), p. 7. The above discussion relies strongly on this source. Copyright © 1966 Abraham Holtzman. Reprinted by permission.

legislative branch) who may have relatively little information. Ordinarily this important resource is apparent at all levels of government.

All these groups are possible players in any political game, yet, for the average citizen seeking to influence government, interest groups may be the most valuable means of access; this may be the place to start.[16]

If a group approach seems realistic, the goal will often require additional player support. The question is, *how does one get people to join a cause?* How is it possible, once they are attracted, to direct their energies toward a specific goal?

Mobilizing Player Support

The answer has to do with mobilization.[17] *Mobilization* means bringing together resources. In addition, the answer has to do with controlling the resources that are gathered. One important resource, of course, is people.

Two points about mobilization should be kept in mind. First, effectiveness is not necessarily related to the *absolute* amount of resources that are brought together. Rather, it is related to the amount that can be *controlled* relative to that of the opposition. What resources can the activist really count on using?

The second point about mobilization is more obvious. That is, mobilization is easier during periods of crisis. People seeking change will frequently time their efforts at mobilization to take advantage of an existing crisis (e.g., the energy crisis, a prison riot). Or, through an intensive educational effort, they may communicate the existence of a crisis about which people have been unaware (e.g., the environmental crisis). If the effort is successful, mobilization of people and other resources becomes easier.

One form of mobilization is *coalition formation*. Bringing together groups with a common interest increases the total resources available. These groups become essential players. But if mobilization also involves controlling the resources (i.e., personnel), there are certain informal rules to follow.

---

[16] The names of many interest groups are listed in the *Encyclopedia of Associations*. Others can be contacted through local volunteer bureaus, local switchboards, and chambers of commerce.

[17] See Amitai Etzioni, *The Active Society* (New York: The Free Press/Macmillan Publishing Co., 1968), pp. 388–398.

1. *The groups should not be so diverse that control is impossible.*
2. All parties to the coalition must perceive a *mutually* beneficial goal based on *each* party's conception of its own self-interest.
3. Each party to the coalition must have a genuine *power base* and must not depend for ultimate decision-making on a force outside itself.
4. The coalition must deal with *specific* and *identifiable*—as opposed to general and vague—goals.
5. The coalition must not be so difficult to coordinate and manage that it becomes too costly and time-consuming. Mobilize only the number and quality of resources that are really necessary. Remember, it is not how many groups are in the coalition that counts, but whether or not their resources and activities can be efficiently controlled. If one or more groups take independent action or make statements inconsistent with the overall strategy, the coalition will become a *liability.*[18]

Issue Salience

There is one other crucial factor related to players that activists must keep in mind. In addition to knowing who the allies are likely to be in the game being considered and how to mobilize their support, *issue salience* is important. Salience refers to how strongly players feel about the issue. The side with far fewer allies and resources may end up winning because of their intensity of commitment.

The significance of high issue salience is that it magnifies the resources of the players. Those who feel strongly about an issue will give more time and/or money to the cause. For example, large numbers of people who are against gun control, against abortion, or against school busing feel so strongly that their efforts appear to have far greater impact than their numbers would suggest. On the other hand, those players with low issue salience but who are still in favor of the goal may be of little value to your side. They will either not get involved or become involved in causes they perceive to be far more crucial. For example, a majority of citizens in this country favor eliminating the electoral college system, but few feel strongly enough to fight for the required constitutional amendment. So the job for the activist

---

[18] For a discussion of rules 2 through 5, see Charles Hamilton and Stokely Carmichael, *Black Power* (New York: Random House, 1967), pp. 58–84.

involves not just identifying issue positions of players but identifying how strongly key players are committed to that position.

To summarize the points to keep in mind about players, it is important to remember the various types, both individual and group, and their different levels of commitment and skill; the necessity of not just bringing people and groups together in support of a goal, but exerting some control over their resources and activities; and the rules of coalition formation, if implementing the goal requires a coalition.

Allies and Opponents

Before we leave the subject of players, a rather obvious distinction should be made between allies and opponents. If one or more groups are needed to implement the goal, identify both actual allies and potential allies. Based on the earlier problem analysis, who, inside or outside of government, has supported a similar goal? For example, what legislators have proposed or voted for similar bills? What interest groups and government officials have testified on behalf of a similar goal in committee hearings? What courts and judges have ruled favorably in related areas? The same questions asked a different way can help in the identification of opponents.

Opponents are those likely to work against the goal, and certainly those who were responsible for the conditions leading to the goal. Those opponents particularly should be carefully identified. One of Saul Alinsky's rules is, "Pick the target, freeze it, personalize it." The people responsible must be singled out as the target, not an easy thing when "individuals and bureaus one after another disclaim responsibility for particular conditions." [19]

John Gardner, chairman of Common Cause, seems to agree with the Alinsky approach. The 1974 struggle to get campaign reform legislation through Congress, particularly legislation requiring the public financing of campaigns, was a difficult one. While a number of legislators were far from enthusiastic about this effort, one man, Rep. Wayne L. Hays of Ohio, was in a particularly good position to do something about his opposition. As chairman of the House Administration Committee, which considered campaign reform, he could stall the bill and in fact see to it that the public financing provisions were eliminated. His reasons for doing this might have had something to do with a conflict of interest. In 1974, he was responsible for the

[19] Alinsky, *Rules for Radicals*, pp. 130–131.

Democratic campaign fund raising and money dispensing. Public financing of campaigns would eliminate this job, with all its advantages.

The problem was, how to get Wayne Hays to budge. Traditional
methods didn't seem to be working. While they were not abandoned
entirely, a new, particularly dramatic approach was taken. In a full-
page advertisement in the *Washington Post*, Common Cause asked,
after identifying Hays as the enemy and pointing out the apparent
conflict of interest, "Is it any surprise that his appetite for meaningful
reform is near zero? How can the House Democratic leadership
sanction such a scandal?"

"Pick the target, freeze it, personalize it"—that's what Common
Cause was doing.

Using this tactical advice isn't always easy. At all levels of government, within various institutions, there may be several people responsible. Not everyone can be the target. One criterion in picking the target is the target's vulnerability relative to the individual's or group's
resources.

Once an opponent is singled out, others are likely to come out of
the woods. This is particularly true if the opponent is personalized.
Instead of identifying "City Hall" as the enemy, pick a target with an
identity.[20] Common Cause picked Wayne Hays, not Congress. Those
rushing to the person's defense can then be placed in the opposition
category. The next step involves assessing their strength.

Calculate Player Resources

Resources are assets; they are what the players have going for them or
what they seek to mobilize to win. Ultimately they help to define
power.

Once a strategy has been selected and players identified, resources
must be carefully assessed. Who is likely to have the greatest influence
on those decision makers in a position to fulfill the goal? To answer,
it is necessary to understand specifically the relationship between resources and influence.

A group has *influence* if its point of view and methods of persuasion were among the factors affecting the outcome of a decision or
action. Players are more likely to have influence if they have *actual*
resources rather than merely *potential* resources. Potential resources

[20] *Ibid.*, p. 133.

are those that are not being controlled; they have not been mobilized. Actual resources are already highly liquid and can be activated immediately.[21]

Players are likely to have influence only if they are willing and able to use the resources they have. A group might have resources, but its leadership might be unwilling to use them without the consent of the membership. Or, a citizen might have resources but be unwilling to use them because the costs in time and energy are perceived as too great. In addition, groups or citizens might be unwilling to use the resources they have if they feel their resources are inadequate relative to those of the opposition. Finally, they may be unwilling to use them for fear of a backlash. Additional opponents might join the game.[22] Influence is also related to how resources are used. A group may lose the game if it spends its resources inefficiently, wasting them and producing less effect on a decision than it might have had.[23] "Skill in Politics," according to Robert Dahl, "is the ability to gain more influence than others, using the same resources." [24]

Resources may lead to additional resources. They may lead to future influence. Political actions, even those that appear to fail, should be judged not simply in terms of their immediate success, but according to whether or not new resources have been created from the action. In one sense the civil rights march on Washington in 1963 failed, because it did not change any votes in Congress. However, it may have prompted thousands who had previously never taken part in the civil rights movement to participate.[25] Potentially, the new resources created could lead to a more important future success.

People are resources strictly in terms of their numbers, but also in terms of their individual assets. They may bring money, skill, an official position, popularity, status, knowledge, information, and an organization to a political effort. Successful strategists try to calculate the actual and potential resources of all players—both allies and opponents. They also try to determine the players' ability to mobilize resources. Finally, they attempt to assess how the resources are likely to be used.

All these calculations require more information. How does each

[21] William A. Gamson, *Power and Discontent* (Homewood, Ill.: The Dorsey Press, 1968), pp. 94–95.

[22] *Ibid.*, p. 96.

[23] *Ibid.*, p. 97.

[24] Robert Dahl, *Who Governs?* (New Haven, Conn.: Yale University Press, 1961), p. 307.

[25] Gamson, *Power and Discontent*, p. 98.

player usually play the game; how do players usually employ their resources; what proportion of resources is each player likely to use; how willing is each player likely to be to commit resources? With this information tactical considerations begin. What tactics are consistent with the overall strategy and realistic relative to actual and potential resources?

Tactical Options

Tactics are the specific moves—the hows consistent with the overall plan. While the choice of tactics will ultimately depend on one's resources and goal, it also depends on the nature of the game to be played. For example, how many players will the political game have? Do the rules allow anyone to join the game at any point? Do the rules allow only one winner, as in an election and many court cases, or is it possible for everyone to win something?

To illustrate, if the rules allow more than one winner, then each player will try to maximize the gain by using tactics designed to (1) promote negotiation, (2) convince the opposition that substantial resources are available as well as the skill to use and increase them, and (3) demonstrate that players are available with whom a "better deal" could be made. If the appropriate tactics are selected and used with skill, winning will mean getting most of what was sought. At a minimum, it should mean getting more than was given up.

Tactical options can be categorized in terms of how they are perceived. Are they "acceptable"? Acceptable political tactics usually means those that are not disruptive, that involve only those people who want to be involved, and that are part of the traditional and legal way of communicating politically in this country.[26]

This group of tactical options includes such activities as campaigning, letter-writing, lobbying, circulating petitions, registering potential voters, submitting *amicus curiae* briefs, and holding public meetings. Some of these activities are designed to influence public officials directly, while others are methods of indirect influence. Some are appropriate to pressure politics, others to electoral politics. What they have in common is that they are viewed as *normal*—as consistent with the norms or rules of the political community involved.

[26] Disruptive tactics have little citizen support. See Hazel Ersking, "Polls: Demonstrations and Race Riots," *Public Opinion Quarterly*, Winter 1967–1968, pp. 655–677.

A second category of tactical options includes those that are disruptive, and usually confrontational, but still legal. Most citizens consider them less acceptable than those in the first category, although they have been used frequently throughout U.S. history. They include demonstrating, marching, boycotting, picketing, holding teach-ins, and fasting. These could be classified as *extraordinary legal tactics*. In terms of the community's perceptions, they violate the *informal* rules of political behavior.

The third category of tactical options includes those that are both *extraordinary* and *illegal*. Among the possibilities are violent demonstrations, kidnapings, sit-ins, refusals to pay taxes, courtroom disruptions, and, if there is a draft, refusals to be drafted. These violate both the informal and *formal* rules of political behavior.

If objectives can be achieved through the use of "normal" tactics, these should be selected. The advantages of built-in citizen and decision-making support for the methods, if not yet the goal, are numerous. Perhaps the most important advantage is that time, energy, and other resources will not have to be spent convincing the public and decision makers that the goal warranted extraordinary methods of communicating. For indeed, indirectly and subtly, tactics as well as goals may have to be justified to be accepted.[27]

Extraordinary tactics are verbal, physical, or economic forms of protest.[28] They are used by individuals and groups (usually the latter) to promote political response directly or indirectly. Protest tactics, even when legal, should not be used indiscriminately. Ordinarily they are used under the following conditions:

1. When normal channels of political communications seem to be blocked and/or decision-makers seem unwilling to budge
2. When resources seem inadequate for normal tactics
3. When additional resources such as public interest and new supporters need to be mobilized through protest
4. When a group requires action to bolster morale and confidence among its members

[27] Louis Harris provides evidence of the relationship between the perceived legitimacy of the issue and opinions of the tactics used. See *The Anguish of Change* (New York: W. W. Norton & Company, 1973), pp. 173–174.
[28] Michael Lipsky defines protest as "a mode of political action oriented toward objection to one or more policies or conditions, characterized by showmanship or display of an unconventional nature, and undertaken to obtain rewards from political or economic systems while working within the systems." See "Protest as a Political Resource," *American Political Science Review*, December 1968, p. 1145.

PUNCH

1975 Los Angeles Times

''The anti-dog lobby seems to be growing.''

Copyright, Punch Magazine. Reprinted by permission of Los Angeles Times Syndicate.

Protest activity can most easily be understood as an aspect of *bargaining*. To bargain, you have to have something to exchange, find someone who wants what you have and who, in return, has something you want, and have the opportunity to make the exchange. The problem is that some groups are left out of the bargaining process because they don't have anything to exchange.[29] Protest activities are a way of increasing resources so that participation in political bargaining is possible.

This is how the process works. Groups with inadequate resources who are trying to bargain with public officials attempt to get other people, or "third parties," on their side. Specifically, the idea is to gain the support of people to whom public officials are usually sensitive (certain constituents, campaign contributors, etc.). These third parties are the people who usually bargain with specific public officials because they have something to offer (votes, status, money, etc.). If a variety of protest activities gains their support, an opportunity for negotiation will probably arise. Understandably, the mass media are crucial to success in attracting third parties.[30]

Protest tactics are not unique to the modern civil rights or antiwar movements. Historically they have been used by unions, farmers, and women—by any group not able to achieve its goals through normal political methods.

Although they are frequently associated with causes on the political left, protest tactics have not been used only by those holding this particular point of view. For example, in the 1960s, the proponents of racial equality and integration used almost every form of nonviolent protest to achieve their goals. Learning from these efforts, white parents in some northern cities picketed school boards that tried to end de facto segregation in the schools and boycotted their school systems. As black citizens had done in the south, white parents in some communities further demonstrated their discontent by establishing short-term private schools.[31] Both protesting groups found it difficult to remain within the confines of extraordinary legal activity.

Some groups find it politically advantageous to combine normal

---

[29] James Q. Wilson views protest activity as a part of bargaining. See "The Strategy of Protest: Problems of Negro Civic Action," *Journal of Conflict Resolution*, September 1961, pp. 291–303.

[30] Michael Lipsky explains this process and its accompanying problems. "Protest as a Political Resource," pp. 1144–1158.

[31] See Arthur Waskow, "The Meaning of Creative Disorder," in *From Race Riot to Sit-in* (New York: Doubleday & Company, 1966), pp. 276–290.

tactics with extraordinary legal tactics. The efforts of the Student Nonviolent Coordinating Committee (SNCC) to get black voters registered in Albany, Georgia, in the 1960s were closely connected with street marches for equal access to public accommodations and economic boycotts against discriminatory employers. Each tactic strengthened and complemented the other.[32] The Right-to-Lifers in the 1970s are picketing the hospitals that perform the greatest number of abortions while simultaneously lobbying for a U.S. constitutional amendment and the election of antiabortion candidates.

Do protest tactics work? That is a difficult question to answer because other social and political processes are operating simultaneously. The Gallup Poll showed that American public opinion reversed itself on the subject of the war in Vietnam in a period of three or four years. This reversal coincided with a great many antiwar protests. Still, a cause-and-effect relationship cannot be demonstrated. A closer relationship was established in a study of 23 cities in which riots occurred and 20 nonriot cities of similar size. While the objective of the riots was not necessarily an increase in governmental expenditures, a year after the riots there was a marked increase in city and state expenditures on welfare in riot cities. Nonriot cities did not have the same pattern of welfare expansion.[33]

Whether or not there is a relationship between protest tactics and positive policy may ultimately have to do with the issue and the decision makers. If the issue has the *potential* for attracting widespread attention and sympathy, protest tactics are worth considering, particularly if normal tactics have failed. If decision makers are *capable* of responding but haven't been moved by normal tactics, again extraordinary legal methods may be suitable. However, public officials might perceive response as too costly. They might feel it would mean losing the next election or failing to get reappointed to a particular position. Response from decision makers with these perceptions of political reality would be unlikely, unless they had no choice.

Let's take a closer look at protest tactics that are extraordinary and illegal. They are of two types—nonviolent and violent. They are used when normal and/or extraordinary legal moves do not produce the desired result or when the proponents perceive those moves as being futile.

---

[32] *Ibid.*
[33] Michael Betz, "Rioting and Welfare: Are They Related?," *Social Problems,* December 1974, pp. 345–355.

The effectiveness of nonviolent illegal tactics is also related to how they are perceived by observers. If they, like extraordinary legal tactics, are viewed as legitimate forms of social protest, they are more likely to produce positive policy results. But what influences this view? If they are perceived as *credible* activities, if they are perceived as an *appeal* rather than a threat, and if they are *sanctioned* as legitimate protest by public officials, the opportunity for successful bargaining is more likely.[34]

The Reverend Martin Luther King, Jr., understood the relationship between public perceptions of the goal and acceptance of the tactics. Writing to fellow clerics from a Birmingham, Alabama, jail in 1963, he explained that illegal tactics are only justifiable when they are used in relation to unjust laws.

You express a great deal of anxiety over our willingness to break laws. This is certainly a legitimate concern. Since we so diligently urge people to obey the Supreme Court's decision of 1954 outlawing segregation in the public schools, at first glance it may seem rather paradoxical for us consciously to break laws. One may well ask: "How can you advocate breaking some laws and obeying others?" The answer lies in the fact that there are two types of laws: just and unjust. I would be the first to advocate obeying just laws. One has not only a legal but a moral responsibility to obey just laws. Conversely, one has a moral responsibility to disobey unjust laws. I would agree with St. Augustine that "an unjust law is no law at all."

Now, what is the difference between the two? How does one determine whether a law is just or unjust? A just law is a man-made code that squares with the moral law or the law of God. An unjust law is a code that is out of harmony with the moral law. To put it in the terms of St. Thomas Aquinas: An unjust law is a human law that is not rooted in eternal law and natural law. Any law that uplifts human personality is just. Any law that degrades human personality is unjust. All segregation statutes are unjust because segregation distorts the soul and damages the personality. It gives the segregator a false sense of superiority and the segregated a false sense of inferiority. Segregation, to use the terminology of the Jewish philosopher Martin Buber, substitutes an "I—it" relationship for an "I—thou" relationship and ends up relegating persons to the status of things. Hence segregation is not only politically, economically and sociologically unsound, it is morally wrong and sinful. Paul Tillich has said that sin is separation. Is not segregation an existential expression of man's tragic separation, his

[34] This is the view of Ralph H. Turner, "The Public Perception of Protest," *American Sociological Review*, December 1969, pp. 815–833.

awful estrangement, his terrible sinfulness? Thus it is that I can urge men to obey the 1954 decision of the Supreme Court, for it is morally right; and I can urge them to disobey segregation ordinances, for they are morally wrong.

Let us consider a more concrete example of just and unjust laws. An unjust law is a code that a numerical or power majority group compels a minority group to obey but does not make binding on itself. This is difference made legal. By the same token, a just law is a code that a majority compels a minority to follow and that it is willing to follow itself. This is sameness made legal.

Let me give another explanation. A law is unjust if it is inflicted on a minority that, as a result of being denied the right to vote, had no part in enacting or devising the law. Who can say that the legislature of Alabama which set up that state's segregation laws was democratically elected? Throughout Alabama all sorts of devious methods are used to prevent Negroes from becoming registered voters, and there are some counties in which, even though Negroes constitute a majority of the population, not a single Negro is registered. Can any law enacted under such circumstances be considered democratically structured?

Sometimes a law is just on its face and unjust in its application. For instance, I have been arrested on a charge of parading without a permit. Now, there is nothing wrong in having an ordinance which requires a permit for a parade. But such an ordinance becomes unjust when it is used to maintain segregation and to deny citizens the First Amendment privilege of peaceful assembly and protest.

I hope you are able to see the distinction I am trying to point out. In no sense do I advocate evading or defying the law, as would the rabid segregationist. That would lead to anarchy. One who breaks an unjust law must do so openly, lovingly, and with a willingness to accept the penalty. I submit that an individual who breaks a law that conscience tells him is unjust, and who willingly accepts the penalty of imprisonment in order to arouse the conscience of the community over its injustice, is in reality expressing the highest respect for law.[35]

Even with "justice" on his side, King did not use nonviolent illegal tactics impulsively. He used them to produce good-faith negotiations with leaders of the community, negotiations that would result in more than the previous broken promises.

"Why direct action? Why sit-ins, marches and so forth? Isn't negotiation a better path?" You are quite right in calling for negotiation. Indeed this is the very purpose of direct action. Non-

[35] Martin Luther King, Jr., *Why We Can't Wait* (New York: Harper & Row, Publishers, 1963), pp. 84–85. Copyright © 1963 by Martin Luther King, Jr. Reprinted by permission of the publisher.

violent action seeks to create such a crisis and foster such a tension that a community which has constantly refused to negotiate is forced to confront the issue. It seeks so to dramatize the issue that it can no longer be ignored.[36]

Extralegal nonviolent action more recently worked for American independent truckers. After attempting normal methods of influence, truckers took advantage of the issue. Most drivers could sympathize with the truckers' dilemma—contracts to fulfill but gas shortages and high prices. There are between 100,000 and 200,000 independent truck drivers in this country. The rigs they own and operate cost between $25,000 and $45,000. In 1972 and early 1973 they were paying 25 to 30 cents a gallon for unlimited supplies of diesel fuel. By early 1974 prices ranged as high as 60 cents a gallon, and rigs with a fuel capacity of 200 to 300 gallons had to settle for 25 gallons or less at crowded truck stops. Truckers simply had to absorb the additional cost of fuel and the money they lost because runs took longer.[37] Even the inconvenience trucker blockades and strikes caused to citizens was not enough to detract from the "justness" of the issue.

However, the truckers weren't dealing with one community, they were dealing with the federal government—ultimately with the President of the United States. Were sympathetic public opinion and increasingly threatening tactics enough to force negotiation? In this case, they were. A mutually acceptable compromise was worked out.

The second type of extraordinary illegal tactic was also employed by some truckers. Violence was so widespread in a few areas that the governors of eight states called out the National Guard to protect highway overpasses and patrol truck stops. Violence against both persons (assault) and objects was involved.

What is violence and are all violent activities to be viewed in the same way? Ultimately the definition of violence is political. The kinds of specific acts that are classified as violent or that are not classified in that way depend on who is doing the defining and who has the resources to disseminate and enforce the definition. In a war, for example, each side typically labels the other side the aggressor and calls many of its violent acts atrocities. The winner's definition usually prevails.[38] Also, the tendency of political regimes to exaggerate the

---

[36] *Ibid.*, p. 81.
[37] "The Times They Are A-Changin,'" *Newsweek*, February 18, 1974, pp. 19–20.
[38] Jerome H. Skolnick makes this point in *The Politics of Protest*, one of several staff reports presented to the National Commission on the Causes and Prevention of Violence (Washington, D.C.: U.S. Government Printing Office, 1970).

tactics of those who challenge established institutions, in order to discredit the behavior of the challenging groups and mask their own violence, should not be overlooked.

For example, the burning of draft cards and records was officially viewed as a violent form of unlawful protest, while the subject of the activity, i.e., the war in Indochina, was officially seen as simply a policy with unfortunate consequences, such as civilian massacres, random dispersal of unarmed people, and acts that some would call genocide.[39] Still, whether it is engaged in by those with power, protecting "order," or by those with fewer resources, seeking change, violence is behavior designed to inflict injury to people or damage to property.

What are the costs of violence used tactically compared with those of extraordinary illegal tactics that are nonviolent? A rational tactic is one that produces for players more than is given up—the perceived benefit is greater than the perceived cost. Violent tactics used by individuals and groups attempting to maximize the impact of relatively insubstantial resources have the potential for being irrational. If death, serious physical injury, and loss of freedom and legitimacy are considered maximum costs, this is what players using violent tactics are exposing themselves to.[40]

When some left-wing organizations went "underground" in the late 1960s and early 1970s and began engaging in "guerrilla" tactics, they were attempting to minimize potential costs. When they bombed Selective Service headquarters in various cities, post office buildings, police stations, and corporate headquarters, they had no intention of "dying for the cause," or even of getting caught. Nor was there any *expectation* that civilians would be harmed. After interviewing several members of guerrilla organizations in this country, *Scanlans'* editor, Warren Hinkle, made this observation:

> There is a delicate balancing act, and guerrillas occasionally blow it. But an integral part of guerrilla strategy is that civilians aren't suppose to get hurt, just scared. This doesn't necessarily make a Mr. Nice Guy out of a bomber; but true is true, and it simply is contrary to all guerrilla theory to go around blowing up people whom they expect, inevitably, some year, to side with the movement against the government.
>
> The political safety-first among American guerrilla terrorists is why so few casualties have been sustained—despite the horrendous

[39] Edgar Litt, *Democracy's Ordeal in America* (Hinsdale, Ill.: The Dryden Press, 1973), p. 142.
[40] Peter K. Eisinger, "The Conditions of Protest Behavior in American Cities," *American Political Science Review*, March 1973, p. 13.

noise of all those bombings going off in the United States the last few years. Most bombing attacks are on buildings or other inanimate objects and usually take place at night when the premises are safer on both sides to blast. A warning is routinely delivered before the blast in case of a night watchman or unknown laggards.[41]

However, as Hinkle points out, sometimes guerrillas do "blow it." The result is often severe injury to themselves and others. Nonviolent protestors, by relying for their impact on the *implicit threat* of violence, may win without facing these potential costs.

A second cost can be the issue itself. The media may pay so much attention to the violence that the issue is obfuscated—except to the few already committed. Not many people understood the reason for the 1973 killing of Oakland, California, school superintendent Marcus Foster by Symbionese Liberation Army (SLA) members. Most people forgot about the goal of feeding hungry people as the media focused on the 1974 kidnaping of Patricia Hearst. Even some hungry people forgot.

Still another cost of using violent tactics is that violence may also be used in reaction. To deal with those who engage in this form of activity, officials may feel compelled to use measures that ordinarily would be unacceptable. In the process, those not directly involved may also have their rights abridged. Some revolutionary organizations expect this response and perceive it as a gain rather than a cost. They believe that when the political system overreacts, when it uses measures that are perceived as illegitimate, society will be polarized. With polarization, the "enemy" will be more easily identified, as will their potential supporters. This approach assumes, of course, that there will be potential supporters willing to join "the cause" and fight against the reaction of the political system. It further assumes that the cost will not be so great as to preclude further activity.

A final cost is the tactic itself. Ultimately, to win, it must be discarded. Even if it did succeed in calling attention to an issue and the seriousness of an organization, even if it did succeed in mobilizing new members and heightening morale within the group, any gains, to be consolidated, will require other tactics. The violence of early labor organizing, whether generated by workers, employers, or police, was accompanied by nonviolent tactics and followed by normal political activity. Labor was able to move away from violence once it was ac-

[41] "Suppressed Issue: Guerrilla War in the U.S.A.," *Scanlans*, January 1971, pp. 7–8.

cepted as a serious player—one that had resources and a willingness and ability to use them.

The ethical reasons for accepting or rejecting violent tactics will have to be assessed by each individual. Still, if people value an egalitarian society and individual dignity, are violent tactics, particularly those directed toward people, compatible? Pacifist Mulford Sibley has this to say on the subject:

> All violence tends to be reactionary, whatever may be the avowed objectives of those who employ it. While in the long run, the effects of violence can no doubt be counteracted in some measure, it always leaves scars and such progress as is made in the direction of an egalitarian society is always achieved primarily *despite* violence and not because of it.
>
> Violence tends to force us to forget the notion of limits to human action: all methods become permissible in a situation where the opponent is destined for obliteration. But if the "logic" of violence is physical destruction of the opponent, what becomes of such demands as equality, respect for personality, and other revolutionary claims? Dead men cannot be equal, nor can their personalities be respected.[42]

So those are the options to consider—normal, extraordinary legal, or extraordinary illegal tactics. The tactical choices, to repeat, will depend on the resources of the players, the type of game being played, and the goal sought. Making those choices, however, requires still more information.

Tactical Information

Generally, the information that needs to be gathered relates to the conditions under which specific tactics have previously worked or failed. Certainly the fact that a tactic has worked in the past under similar conditions is no guarantee of success, but an analysis of other political games and the moves of other players may increase the possibility of winning.

The following questions will guide this stage of the information-gathering process. Considering a previous case of political action,

1. How similar was the goal to the one presently being sought? (For predictive purposes, they should be as similar as possible.)
2. What was the institutional setting? (What specific policy-making

---

[42] Mulford Q. Sibley is professor of political science at the University of Minnesota. These comments are from "Revolution and Violence," *Peace News*, 1964.

institution was involved and how open was it to communication? Was there an institutional choice?)

3. What level of government was involved? Did the players have a choice, or were they limited by formal rules and their own resources to a particular level of government?

4. What was the attitudinal climate? Did attitude surveys, public-opinion polls, or recent votes indicate that players were operating in a favorable or unfavorable attitudinal climate?

5. What tactics were employed by the proponents and the opponents?

6. What were the resources of each side, and how did they define the tactical opportunities?

7. What costs were apparent (financial, political, psychological, etc.)?

Players should not be dissuaded from action by dissimilarities. The above questions are merely designed to assist tactical planning. For example, if the attitudinal climate does not seem ripe for action at present, then educational tactics could first be employed. If the present resources of the proponents are not sufficient, given even minimal tactical requirements, then effort and existing resources must be spent to mobilize additional resources.

While the preceding questions ask players to analyze past attempts to achieve similar goals, another approach may also be used. The analysis may focus *initially* on the tactics. Apart from the goal being sought, under what conditions are specific tactics likely to work? An advantage to beginning with a tactical survey and analysis is that this reduces the possibility of eliminating tactical possibilities simply because they haven't been used to win similar goals. A disadvantage is that frequently the goal defines both the strategic choice and the tactical options. Perhaps the goal can *only* be achieved through the federal court system, where the tactical possibilities are severely limited. Still, players need to think about both approaches. Whichever is used, the above questions will be helpful during this information-gathering stage.

Timing considerations are also part of tactical information. When should the game begin? Ultimate success might mean a delay. Common timing miscalculations involve proposals that will be enormously costly during a period of extreme inflation or proposals that are likely to be vetoed by an unsympathetic executive. If information indicates that the timing is bad, postpone any tactical moves or be prepared for only limited success.

The tactical choices can now be made. They may include only normal tactics or a combination of normal and extraordinary, depending on the stage of the strategy. However, the choices are always the result of acquired tactical information.

Rules

Just as formal and informal rules operate in a community, they operate in games. Political games are no exception. They define how one *ought* to play, how one *gets* to play, and how one is *rewarded* during the course of the game. For example, in a card game informal rules may establish the amount of money that will admit players and how they ought to play the game (i.e., no talking across the table). Formal rules define how many cards each player may receive, how much each card is worth, when players draw additional cards, what is winning, etc. If one wants to play a political game in the congressional arena, rules establish how to become a direct player (gets elected to Congress), how to behave as a congressional player, how advantages get distributed (i.e., leadership positions or important committee assignments), and how bills become law (a win). There are also rules for indirect congressional players (i.e., lobbyists and citizens).

Something to think about
Which of these congressional rules are formal and which are informal?

In both parlor games and political games, which rules players choose to follow will depend on the players, their goals, their relative resources, the kind of game being played, and the sanctions applied when rules are broken.

Let's get more specific. If one wants to know the rules relevant to political games, these questions must be answered:

1. What formal rules provide access to the particular arena (to legislatures, courts, executive hearings)?
2. What rules guide the moves, or tactics of the players in that arena?

3. What informal rules suggest how one ought to behave in the particular game?
4. What formal and informal rules distribute advantages to players, and under what conditions are those advantages distributed?
5. How do the rules define a win?

The rules are a crucial part of any political action. Community organizer Saul Alinsky felt so strongly about their importance that he devoted an entire book to them. In general, his point of view was this:

> There are certain central concepts of action in human politics that operate regardless of the scene or the time. To know these is basic to a pragmatic attack on the system. These rules make the difference between being a realistic radical and being a rhetorical one who uses the tired old words and slogans, calls the police "pig" or "white fascist racist" or "mother fucker" and has so stereotyped himself that others react by saying, "Oh, he's one of those," and then promptly turn off.[43]

From this discussion it should be clear that each political action step is dependent on the others. Rules are related to strategic and tactical choices, to one's resources as well as the resources of one's opponent, and to the goal sought. As a package these interdependent steps suggest a way to win. The remaining chapters explain and illustrate how action-oriented citizens may apply this model. They also provide information relevant to strategic and tactical choices.

Key Words

Strategy
Information
Federalism
Power
Interest group
Political party
Mobilization
Coalition
Salience
Resources
Influence
Tactics
Rules

[43] Saul Alinsky, *Rules for Radicals*, p. xviii.

Suggested Activities

From the local newspaper select a political conflict. Gather information about it. Determine the following:

1. The problem involved
2. The conflicting goals
3. The general strategies used by each side
4. The specific players involved and their resources
5. The tactics being used by each side
6. The rules each side appears to be following

II
Political Culture
and Socialization

3
What Americans Think and Feel about Politics—
Its Relation to How They Act

Nobody seemed to care much about Harlem, not the people who could do something about it, like the mayor or the police.

Some of the cats I knew had gone into the police department. They seemed to be exploiting Harlem too, once they got there. These were the same cats who had come up in Harlem. They didn't care any more either. They just wanted to go out there and get some of that money too.

Harlem was getting fucked over by everybody, the politicians, the police, the businessmen, everybody. There were a lot of things that we knew about but didn't think about when we were high: how nobody cared too much about cleaning up the junkies or making drugs legal so that they'd stop robbing people, since it was just Harlem and East Harlem; how nobody gave a fuck about some niggers and some Puerto Ricans, so that's why nothing was going to be done about it. It seemed that when we got high off pot and stuff and started philosophizing, we really knew things. . . .

We'd laugh about how when the big snow storms came, they'd have the snowplows out downtown as soon as it stopped, but they'd let it pile up for weeks in Harlem. If the sun didn't come out, it might have been there when April came around. Damn sending snowplows up there just for some niggers and people like that.[1]

[1] Claude Brown, *Manchild in the Promised Land* (New York: The Macmillan Company, Signet Books, 1965; London, Jonathan Cape Ltd.), p. 198. Copyright © Claude Brown, 1965. Reprinted by permission.

As Claud Brown writes about growing up in Harlem, he is describing what many ghetto dwellers think about politics. Apparent in this excerpt is the belief that if you are poor and nonwhite, politicians aren't going to look after your interests. If people think public officials don't care about their problems, why should they bother to participate or be generally supportive?

The Importance of Political Culture

Political culture refers to the way citizens are oriented to their political system. It includes political attitudes, feelings, and beliefs. What people think and feel about politics is important to know for a variety of reasons. First, this information can be used as a way of thinking about the functioning of the total political system. For example, the government of the United States calls itself, among other things, a democracy. That requires some citizen participation. It also requires public officials to be responsive to the public, for ultimate political authority in a democracy is vested in the people. Now, if large numbers of citizens do not use the authority they have, because they feel politically powerless and/or because they feel public officials are not responsive, this may affect the government's ultimate ability to solve the nation's problems. Without continuing communication from all segments of society, how are public officials to know accurately what those problems are? James David Barber describes the relationship between political culture and systemic functioning in this way: When citizen consensus breaks down, and democratic political institutions and processes are no longer perceived as legitimate, it is very probable that the government will break down "either by becoming a stable but unresponsive structure of repression or by becoming a disordered flux of accidental alternations between complete ineffectiveness and personalized tyrannies." [2]

Defining political thinking and feeling is also important to action-oriented citizens for a second reason. The political culture of a nation helps to shape political behavior. Of course this is not the only factor influencing how people behave, but it is an important one.[3] Knowing the way people think and feel about politics, then, becomes a guide to

[2] James David Barber, *Citizen Politics* (Chicago: Markham Publishing Company, 1969), p. 94.
[3] For a more precise discussion of the relationship between political culture and political behavior, see Donald J. Devine, *The Political Culture of the United States* (Boston: Little, Brown and Company, 1972), pp. 6–14.

mobilizing support. How willing will people be to join a cause if they are disillusioned about government? How ready will they be to join with other citizens if there is little trust? It is important strategic and tactical information.

A third reason for the activist to understand the political culture is that this information also becomes a guide to *predicting how public office holders might respond* to a particular goal. For the politician is guided not only by personal political orientations, but also by how constituents think and feel. The politician wants to know how constituents feel about particular issues, about the job the politician is doing, etc. This information, then, becomes an important item in politicians' political calculations as well as in the calculations of those seeking to influence them.

Defining the American Political Culture

In order to begin defining the American political culture, it might help to think more precisely about the relationship between the political culture and the *political system*. A system generally consists of units so interrelated that a change in the functioning of one will produce changes in the others. The units of a political system include all those institutions and roles that are part of the authoritative decision-making process. Those political units don't exist in a vacuum; they have an environment, and that environment includes the political culture.

This is how it works. Environmentally, people are part of an ecological system and other social systems. They also have certain biological and personality characteristics. Out of this environmental mix certain wants evolve. These wants get screened by certain cultural values as well as shaped by them. Only those wants that survive the screening process can become, ultimately, political demands and political supports. The influence of political culture doesn't stop there. It also affects the way public officials and particular structures respond. In a sense, the political culture of a nation pervades the entire political system as well as the environment in which it rests.[4]

If political culture is so pervasive, how can the specific political orientations that define that culture be identified? The logical place to start is with those that shape *inputs* and the input process. Figure 1 shows that this is the process through which citizen demands

[4] The above discussion is essentially the point of view of Donald J. Devine. See *Political Culture*.

Figure 1
Relationship between the political culture and the political system.

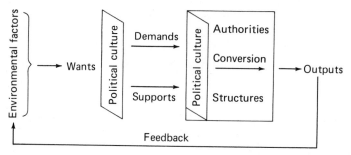

Adapted from Donald J. Devine, *The Political Culture of the United States.* Boston: Little, Brown, 1972, p. 25.

and supports are communicated to political authorities. (Supports include citizens' paying taxes, obeying laws, voting, etc.) In a sense, inputs are the resources that ultimately allow demand to be implemented. After this it seems appropriate to deal with those orientations that influence the *conversion* process—the process through which demands and supports get converted into something that some citizens and public officials want. And finally, orientations related to the *delivery* (or output) process will be examined. What do citizens think and feel about how policy is being implemented? The quality and quantity of output, of course, will in turn influence the environment and affect new demands. This is called *feedback.*

Thinking and Feeling about the Input Process
Political culture, we've said, is *one* of the factors influencing political behavior—the behavior of citizens as well as that of public officials.[5] Of particular concern to the activist seeking allies is how citizens *feel* about the input process. Do citizens feel they can effectively get through to public officials to register their support or rejection? Do they have confidence in their own citizen role? Are they willing to join with others to effect change? In addition to understanding how citizens feel, political activists need to understand something about the level and substance of their political awareness. How much do citizens

---

[5] Other factors include such things as socioeconomic status, the degree to which structures and rules promote or allow participation, the degree of economic and political heterogeneity in a community or state, and individual personality.

know about political issues and candidates, the focus of political action?

These are only some of the questions related to the input process that you, the action-oriented citizen, must answer. The answers begin to define the American political culture.

One place to begin this definition is with *perceived* citizen roles. About half the citizens in this country do not share the perceptions of the Harlem residents about whom Claud Brown spoke. They feel they *can* do something about unjust or harmful laws, at both the local level and the national level. They feel citizens *should* participate.

Even among those who feel powerless, voting is the most common form of political participation. Between 70 and 80 percent of the people in this country *report* voting regularly, at least in presidential elections.[6] Of course, not everyone believes this is an effective way of communicating politically. Most just get some form of gratification from the process.[7]

> To me, voting is the thing, the right to put in the guy you want— that's the big thing. I mean, I know that over there they don't have that and they have a lot of trouble. That kid that was born to Princess Elizabeth—he is going to be the king someday. Nobody else is going to run it, know what I mean. . . . Here, there is a contest against each other trying to serve the people the best way they could to stay in power. And that's a good thing.[8]

This is DeAngelo, a factory worker, talking. He is like most people. Voting is his only *regular* political activity. He doesn't belong to a political club or organization, he never contributes money to a campaign, he doesn't join community organizations or contact public officials, but he *does* vote.[9]

However, what about those citizens who are more active than DeAngelo, who perceive the citizen's role as a more involving one? Meet Fred Plowkowski.

[6] Sidney Verba and Norman H. Nie, *Participation in America* (New York: Harper & Row, Publishers, 1972), p. 31.

[7] In 1952, according to a Survey Research Center study, 80 percent of the population perceived voting to be effective; by 1968 that figure had dropped to 57 percent. Devine, *Political Culture*, p. 42.

[8] Robert E. Lane, *Political Ideology* (New York: The Free Press, 1962), p. 166.

[9] Verba and Nie report the percentage of people who *say* they engage in certain political acts. In addition to voting, they found that 69 percent of those they interviewed engaged in one other political act, but not necessarily regularly. One-third of their respondents reported engaging in no other political act. *Participation in America*, p. 33.

He couldn't believe it. Ten years with the same firm, in the city where he had grown up, and now "let go." His engineering degree wasn't the ticket he once thought it would be. Still, he was one of the lucky ones. He would be moving to a new city soon. A job with another company would be waiting. It wasn't quite as good as the one he was leaving, but he could make it. After all, he was still young, 40 years old. His wife and kids would adjust. Sure it would be hard leaving his old neighborhood, where his family had lived—aunts, uncles, cousins—in fact almost all the Poles in the city. Well, this was a new start; they would manage.

Fred's life is changing, yet politically it probably won't. He is one of those people with a strong "sense of citizen duty." His political orientations and behavior are fairly well established and predictable. Because he is male, white, and over 35 years old, has a formal education, derives a good income from his profession, and has grown up in one city, he is likely to feel confidence in his citizenship role and is likely to participate—he will certainly vote (Table 3–1).

Still, what about the approximately 50 percent of the population who are not like Fred Plowkowski—who feel politically powerless, who feel they can't even be successful periodic players? [10] On the basis of the evidence presented in Chapter 1, we know who they are likely to be. The lower a citizen's level of income, education, and occupational status, the more likely that citizen is to feel politically ineffective and the less likely he or she is to participate politically.[11]

Something to think about
Can the politically alienated ever be mobilized for political action? Under what conditions would they be likely to participate? What forms might that participation take?

The most important predictor of political action appears to be level of education. The alienated tend to have less education. Does

[10] A 1973 Louis Harris survey, commissioned by the U.S. Senate Subcommittee on Intergovernmental Relations, reported that an average of 55 percent of all Americans feel alienated and powerless. This represents an increase of 26 percent since 1963. See *Confidence and Concern* (Cleveland, Ohio: Regal Books/Kings Court Communications, 1974).

[11] Studies have consistently established these relationships. See Ada W. Finifter, "Dimensions of Political Alienation," *American Political Science Review*, June 1970, p. 399.

Table 3–1
Social correlates of political involvement

High Involvement	Low Involvement
Males	Females
Whites	Negroes
35 years of age and over	Under 35 years of age
High formal education	Low formal education
High income	Low income
Urban residence	Rural residence
Membership in several organizations	No organizational membership
Occupations:	Occupations:
Professions	Farm workers
Business executives	Unskilled labor
White-collar workers	
Skilled labor	

Source: Adapted from Seymour Martin Lipset, *Political Man* (Garden City, N.Y.: Doubleday & Company, 1960), p. 184. See also Lester W. Milbrath, *Political Participation* (Chicago: Rand McNally & Company, 1965), chap. 5.

that mean that political activists are likely to be informed just because they generally have more education than the inactive and alienated? Let's take a look.

Political knowledge and the input process.   Since voting is the most common form of political action, *how informed are voters?* Do they know who their representatives are and something about their record in office? As the survey in Table 3–2 reveals, the answer clearly is *no.*

Nor do voters know the issue positions of the candidates who receive the greatest publicity—presidential. They frequently don't even know the positions of the candidates whom they are supporting. Take a look at the results of the poll conducted for the Associated Press by the Roper Organization of New York. By May 15, 1976, after most of the presidential primaries had occurred, an average of more than half the potential voters didn't know where their favorite candidate stood on five major issues (government guaranteed jobs, breaking up the major oil companies, abortion, military spending, welfare reform). For example, on only *one* of five issues could the supporters of Jimmy Carter, the leading Democrat, identify his position correctly. President

Table 3–2

Proportion of Americans knowing their representatives and various things about them

	Percentage Correct
1. Do you happen to know the name of the present representative in Congress from your district?	43
2. Do you happen to know when he or she comes up for election next?	30
3. Do you know how he or she voted on any major bill this year?	19
4. Has he or she done anything for the district that you definitely know about?	14

Source: 1965 AIPO Survey, reported in 1965 Gallup Opinion Index. Also in Robert T. Golembiewski, J. Malcome Moore, and Jack Rabin, eds., *Dilemmas of Political Participation* (Englewood Cliffs, N.J.: Prentice-Hall, 1973), p. 298.

Ford's supporters did somewhat better. They correctly identified his position on three issues, missed on one, and split evenly on the other. Only the supporters of Morris Udall could correctly identify Udall's position on all five issues.

Well, citizens don't know much about office holders—who they are and what they are doing—or much about those running for office, but perhaps they have some understanding of ballot issues. After all, several state and local governments have initiative and referendum processes where citizens can vote directly on issues that concern them.

One way of determining how aware of issues citizens are is to ask them how they would rate themselves on their knowledge of what is going on in government. The Louis Harris organization did this in 1972 and submitted its report to a Senate subcommittee.

Without dealing with knowledge of specific issues, the researchers found that 60 percent of the people gave themselves negative marks on their general understanding of developments in the federal government. Professed knowledge of governmental activities at the state level is even worse. Only 27 percent felt they were fundamentally conversant with the issues. Issue understanding seems strongest at the local level, where 43 percent seem to know what is happening. This figure, however, drops to 33 percent in big cities.[12]

[12] See Harris, *Confidence and Concern*, p. 17.

Public-opinion polls are a way of determining what, if anything, citizens know about specific issues and their general predispositions. They are a *guide* to how citizens are likely to act politically. Bernard C. Hennessy defines public opinion as "the complex of beliefs expressed by a significant number of persons on an issue of public importance." The crucial elements in this definition are *issue, public, complex of beliefs, expression,* and *number of persons.* For public opinion to exist, according to Hennessy, there must be an issue, a contemporary situation on which there is likely to be disagreement; there must be a recognizable group concerned with the issue, a public; and there must be the possibility of some distribution of opinion on the issue—there must be two or more possible points of view. It is this *total* constellation of views on an issue that Hennessy calls a complex of beliefs. Public opinion also requires expression. While people may have unexpressed opinions (predispositions that may later crystallize into opinions), they are only public when they are expressed. Finally, for public opinion to exist, a significant number of persons must be involved. A few friends expressing their private opinions does not count.[13]

Now that we know what is meant by public opinion, the next step should be simple. To identify what and how much citizens know about issues, check the public-opinion polls. Not quite. There are a few problems that should first be recognized. While people say their opinions reflect some awareness,[14] frequently they do not; people give opinions to pollsters when they do not have an opinion. In fact, they may not have even the barest minimum of factual information on which to base an opinion. Well then, won't the respondents just tell the pollster they "don't know" or have "no opinion?" According to Michael Rappeport, no. He says that citizens don't want to admit their ignorance, and answering a pollster's questions doesn't force them to reveal that they really don't know anything about the issue or people reflected in the question. Whether or not someone has knowledge about an issue clearly influences that person's expressed opinion.[15]

So failure to consider the "ignorance factor" when examining

13 Bernard C. Hennessy, *Public Opinion* (Belmont, Calif.: Wadsworth Publishing Company, 1965), pp. 97–103.
14 The figure is 70 to 80 percent, according to Hazel G. Erskine, "The Polls: The Informed Public," *Public Opinion Quarterly,* Winter, 1962, pp. 669–677.
15 Michael Rappeport, "The Distinction the Pollsters Don't Make," *The Washington Monthly,* March 1974, p. 13.

"That's the worst set of opinions I've heard in my entire life."

Drawing by Weber; © 1975, The New Yorker Magazine, Inc.

public-opinion polls can lead to an incorrect assessment of citizen opinions and, for the activist, a major strategic miscalculation. For as discussion about an issue or candidate intensifies and citizens become more knowledgeable, opinions are likely to shift. This must be considered in planning any political action.

Well, when they are interviewed by pollsters, why aren't people honest about their lack of knowledge? It would certainly make life easier for action-oriented citizens who require that information. The answer, in part, is that people *believe* citizens should be informed about issues and what the government is doing, but they feel overwhelmed. A 1968 election study revealed that 45 percent of the citizens interviewed agreed with the statement, "Sometimes politics and government seem so complicated that a person like me can't really understand what's going on." [16] To be consistent with their own norm, then, many citizens may try to hide their ignorance.

Other problems with using public-opinion polls as precise measures of orientations toward issues and predictors of political behavior are very important for the activist to consider. They include distortion of opinion because of the way questions are worded, the changing of opinions over time, the discrepancy between opinions and action, and the tendency to generalize about opinions on the basis of a single opinion.

Let's take a closer look at one of these additional problems—the connection between citizen opinions on issues and their expressed or actual willingness to *act* on those opinions. The difficulty is that people's opinions and actions, for a variety of reasons, are not always consistent. When people interact with their friends, their citizenship orientations may be quite different from those operating in the presence of a pollster. Social and economic pressures may prevent people from acting in a way that is consistent with their expressed opinions. Then, too, attitudes and opinions are not always clear and uncontradictory—conflicting attitudes may produce conflicting opinions and behavior.[17]

For example, among the American public at large, 92 percent agree that cities "must be better places to work and live in," and 60 percent report a sense of urgency about the urban problem. But are

[16] University of Michigan, Survey Research Center, 1968 Election Study, Variable 167. Reported in John P. Robinson, Jerrald G. Rusk, and Kendra B. Head, *Measures of Political Attitudes* (Ann Arbor, Mich.: Institute for Social Research, 1968), pp. 635 and 637.
[17] Hennessy, *Public Opinion*, pp. 187–188.

people willing to act on that opinion? Of those polled, 69 percent were against paying higher taxes for urban improvement.[18]

An even greater problem and more difficult relationship to assess is the connection between what people say they are for and how that will *actually* influence their behavior.

Public opinion on the health hazards of cigarette smoking illustrates the point. As a result of a massive educational campaign about the relation of cigarette smoking and lung cancer, something happened. After the Surgeon General's report appeared and the information campaign was under way, not only did per capita consumption of cigarettes begin to drop, but opinion surveys revealed that many smokers were *trying* to reduce their smoking. Three out of five smokers accepted the idea that smoking was a cause of lung cancer. However, although the opinion persisted, for many the behavior change did not.[19]

Although most people are concerned about the relationship just discussed—how major information affects opinions and ultimately action—there is another interesting relationship to be considered, also of practical value to the activist. Sometimes action influences information and opinions. For example, the haphazard purchase of a product may lead a person to formulate opinions that justify the choice. Once the product has been tried, the probability of a repeat purchase increases because the user has tried it and found it acceptable. A person who accidentally attends a political demonstration may act with the crowd first and only later declare himself or herself an adherent on principle.[20]

Something to think about
What are some of the ways this information may be used by the political activist?

Well, with all the problems associated with public-opinion polls, why even bother to use them? They are useful because they convey *some* information relevant to the input process. As long as those using the polls are aware of the interpretation pitfalls, they can serve as a *guide* to how citizens feel at a particular time about a particular issue.

[18] Leo Bogart, *Silent Politics* (New York: John Wiley & Sons, 1972), p. 57.
[19] *Ibid.*, p. 84.
[20] *Ibid.*, p. 103.

We know they rarely indicate the level of knowledge associated with the opinion, the intensity of the opinion held, or the likelihood that citizens will act on the opinion. Still, why spoil all the fun? Not being able to perfectly predict the moves of players helps to make the game interesting.

From examining the political participation orientations of Americans as well as their political understanding, a picture begins to emerge. Citizens believe participation is important but fail to participate regularly in more than one activity. An increasing number of people feel politically powerless. Citizens believe they should be politically informed, but most say they are not—and evidence reveals that indeed they are not. Still, people will express opinions about specific issues without any real understanding of those issues. The fact that people are inclined to *say* they know something about an issue may indicate how strong the knowledge norm is in this country. What is beginning to emerge is a picture of a political culture full of conflicts between what citizens feel and believe to be politically important, on the one hand, and what they actually know and do politically, on the other.

The picture is not complete, however. There are other input orientations that need to be identified. For example, what do people think about their fellow citizens as political actors? What are their views of the input institutions—political parties, interest groups, the mass media? And finally, what do Americans think about various types of political activity, normal and extraordinary? These too are important pieces of *strategic and tactical information.*

Political trust and the input process.   Effective political action usually requires getting together with other people who have common concerns. Cyril Cuevas was doing that the night his daughter was killed. For people to be willing to join with others in a common political endeavor, there must be at least some degree of mutual trust. Determining the way citizens feel about each other, then, is crucial to predicting whether or not they are likely to work together for political goals.

David Schuman says America is a country of individuals mistrustful of others. This state of mind has evolved, according to Schuman, because governmental leaders and even our founders have led us to believe that people are essentially evil, self-serving, and self-centered.[21]

---

21 Schuman develops this point of view by examining the assumptions of James

Why would governmental leaders have us believe this? Schuman's view is that it is in the interest of those who have held and presently hold power to make us distrustful, for that divides us and makes us politically impotent.

Whether or not Schuman has correctly identified the message and motive of governmental leaders in this country, has he correctly described the way citizens feel toward one another? Are we mistrustful and suspicious? What are the implications for political action?

If the inclinations of Americans to join organizations can be considered partial evidence, the answer is clear. More than three out of every four Americans engage in some kind of organizational activity. These include religious organizations (55 percent), social groups (26 percent), school organizations (23 percent), charitable groups (21 percent), labor unions (16 percent), professional organizations (14 percent), civic groups (14 percent), fraternal orders (14 percent), veterans' organizations (12 percent), political clubs (12 percent), sports organizations (12 percent), business organizations (10 percent), cultural or art groups (7 percent), and fan or booster clubs (3 percent). The list seems endless. While only religious organizations involve more than one in four people, there does seem to be a willingness to join with others in some common endeavor.[22]

There is an upper-class bias to membership in voluntary associations. It is more common among the professional and managerial classes, among college-trained people, and among people with high incomes. However, there are particular associations that attract large numbers of middle-class and lower-middle-class people (unions, churches, sports clubs, etc.). Of course, some people are group members in name only. A considerable number have only a paper connection with the organization.[23]

It would seem, however, that if membership in voluntary association, however superficial, is one measure of citizen trust, that trust is present. If low-income citizens do not join, it seems reasonable to

---

Madison in *Federalist* No. 10. For Madison, a republican form of government would reduce the possibility of particular factions having unchecked power. Schuman claims that Madison's prescription was based on a particularly negative view of humanity. See *Preface to Politics* (Lexington, Mass.: D. C. Heath and Company, 1973), pp. 7–27.

[22] Harris, *Confidence and Concern*, p. 21.

[23] The Verba and Nie study of political participation reported that one-third of those who are members of voluntary associations say they are inactive. *Participation in America*, p. 41.

assume that it is because they don't have the time, financial resources, or perceived skills that membership frequently requires. They do not necessarily fail to join because of mistrust.

Another measure of citizen trust is what people say. An attitude survey of youth also indicates that mistrust is not very pervasive (Table 3–3).[24]

If citizens do not mistrust one another, how willing are they to join together politically? While very few people actually come together in political organizations, they still have positive orientations toward interest-group activity. A great many people feel interest-group activity is bringing results. The Louis Harris surveyors found, for example, that 49 percent of the people interviewed expressed the view that "groups of citizens and organizations are having more effect in getting government to get things done, compared with five years ago." The main reasons they cite are that "people are more involved today," "groups of people can get more done than one person," "government is listening to people more today," "people are more organized and persist more," "people are more knowledgeable," and "the media has given groups such as that good coverage." [25]

For group players seeking to mobilize support, the signs are encouraging. Citizens are not mistrustful; they feel hopeful about effecting change by joining with others. And, more precisely, they say they would be willing to do many of the things political groups ask their members to do. Look at this list of what people say they would do:

- 94 percent would "vote against a public official"
- 91 percent would "talk to friends and neighbors"
- 84 percent would "write their Congressman"
- 81 percent would "write their U.S. Senator"
- 79 percent would "work through a group they belong to"
- 76 percent would "contact local law enforcement officials"
- 75 percent would "contact someone in local politics"
- 72 percent would "join a local citizens group"
- 66 percent would "join a political party and work to make changes"
- 65 percent would "write a letter to the newspaper"
- 62 percent would "send money to support a local citizens group to demand action"

[24] Robert Chandler, *Public Opinion* (New York: R. R. Bowker Company, 1972), p. 62.
[25] Harris, *Confidence and Concern*, p. 23.

Table 3–3
Political trust

Which of the following statements do you *strongly agree* with, which do you *partially agree* with, and which do you *strongly disagree* with?

	Percent Total Youth	Percent College	Percent Noncollege	
1. Most people will go out of their way to help someone else				
Strongly agree	14%	6%	16%	Not asked of
Partially agree	57	60	56	parents
Strongly disagree	29	34	28	
2. No sane, normal, decent person could even think of hurting a close friend or relative				
Strongly agree	38	18	43	
Partially agree	39	45	38	
Strongly disagree	23	37	19	
3. Anyone who completely trusts anyone else is asking for trouble				
Strongly agree	17	15	18	
Partially agree	37	43	36	
Strongly disagree	46	42	47	
4. Most people can be depended on to come through in a pinch				
Strongly agree	21	17	22	
Partially agree	57	61	55	
Strongly disagree	22	22	22	
5. People are basically good, but our society brings out the worst in them				
Strongly agree	31	24	33	
Partially agree	41	45	40	
Strongly disagree	27	30	26	

Source: Robert Chandler, *Public Opinion* (New York: R. R. Bowker Company, 1972), p. 62. Copyright © 1972 by Columbia Broadcasting System, Inc. per permission of CBS Inc.

- 61 percent would "talk to a newspaper reporter or editor"
- 55 percent would "vote against the public official's party at the next election" [26]

It's an impressive list. Even though we know citizens don't actually engage in these activities, the fact that they say they would be willing

[26] *Ibid.*, pp. 21–22.

to shows an enormous *potential* for group activity. If only some of these citizens could be mobilized, the gap between norms and behavior would decrease.

Just as orientations toward interest groups are positive, so are orientations toward political parties. The previous list gives some indication of that. In addition, in a 1964 survey in Wisconsin, about two out of three citizens agreed that "people who work for parties during political campaigns do our nation a great service" and that "democracy works best where competition between parties is strong." They disagreed with the statement that "it would be better if, in all elections, we put no party labels on the ballot." [27]

This Wisconsin study agrees with other evidence that indicates that party identification is one of the most stable forces in American politics. As of 1968 approximately 88 percent of the American public expressed some degree of party preference, and almost a third of these were *strongly* attached to a party.[28]

This positive way of thinking about this important input institution, however, may be changing. A more recent study concluded that, increasingly, Americans are satisfied with neither party. The findings demonstrated emphatically that distrust of the government was related to dissatisfaction with both parties.[29] Consistent with this 1972 study is the definite indication that more and more Americans are identifying themselves not as Democrats or Republicans, but as Independents.[30]

This shift may not be an indictment of the party system per se, but rather an expression of disenchantment with the dominant parties. This distinction is crucial to the organizer who is relying on electoral rather than pressure tactics.

To summarize orientations toward these two traditional input institutions (political parties and interest groups), they are generally positive. Citizens believe interest-group activity and party activity are important. They *say* they would be willing to engage in activities associated with these institutions. They are, however, a little dis-

[27] J. Dennis, "Support for the Party System by the Mass Public," *American Political Science Review*, Summer 1966, pp. 600–615.
[28] Hugh A. Bone and Austin Ranney, *Politics and Voters* (New York: McGraw-Hill Book Company, 1963), pp. 7–9.
[29] "Report that Government Is Losing Public Trust," *San Francisco Chronicle*, September 12, 1972.
[30] A Harris poll in late 1973 showed 28 percent identifying themselves as "Independent," up from 17 percent who so classified themselves in 1968. In 1975, George Gallup reported the figure to be 32 percent.

enchanted with the major parties at present, and are increasingly registering as independents. This may, however, be only a temporary phenomenon associated with Watergate. More important is the continuing gap between norms and behavior. Citizens say these institutions are important, but they fail to participate actively in them.

To complete the picture of orientations toward input institutions, let's take a look at the media. The mass media, in the traditional sense, are not viewed as political input institutions, but in fact they are. (They may also be viewed as output institutions.) Used by public officials to communicate with other public officials, by journalists to communicate directly with office holders as well as with the general public, and by individuals to communicate with other members of the public and with officials, they are an integral part of the political process. They assist in getting citizens' demands heard and perhaps met. They also assist in conveying signs of public support to public officials. The media can also help to build support for an issue among third parties —groups to whom public officials may be sympathetic—which is particularly important to groups with inadequate resources.[31]

Because of the increasingly important role of the media in the political process, we need to know what citizens think about them. Can they be used effectively to build public opinion?

Orientations toward the media are not constant. They seem to change dramatically depending on what is happening in the country. For example, in 1965, 29 percent of the citizenry had confidence in the press, in 1972 this had dropped to 18 percent, and in 1973 it was back up to 30 percent. Confidence in television news in 1965 was at 25 percent, in 1972 it dropped to 17 percent, and in 1973, as with confidence in the press, it rose significantly to 41 percent. Interestingly, only 17 percent of the public officials sampled had confidence in television reporting in 1973.[32]

Press coverage of Watergate and related affairs seemed to be responsible for the 1973–1974 upturn in citizen confidence in the media.

[31] See Chapter 2, page 48.
[32] Louis Harris and Associates poll, New York Times, December 3, 1973, p. 34. A Gallup poll in 1973 indicated greater confidence in the media. A "great deal" of confidence was registered by 15 percent toward newspapers and 16 percent toward television; "quite a lot" of confidence was indicated by 24 percent toward newspapers, 22 percent toward television; "some" confidence was expressed toward both newspapers and television. See Gallup Opinion Index, July 1973, pp. 10–17.

By a 5 to 1 majority, the public felt that "in exposing the facts about Watergate, the Washington *Post* and other newspapers were an example of a free press at its best." A 3 to 1 majority also agreed that "if it had not been for the press exposés, the whole Watergate mess never would have been found out." [33]

Does confidence in the media mean, in part, that its messages are believable? According to a 1963 study by a Roper research team, 44 percent considered television to be the most believable medium, 21 percent mentioned newspapers, and 11 percent said magazines. This believability seems to be related to the fact that citizens interviewed felt by more than 2 to 1 that television rather than newspapers helped people understand candidates and issues.[34]

The relative advantage enjoyed by television is less at the state level, but it is still significant. Here, many people continue to gain their clearest understanding from television (42 percent), but a rather large number (37 percent) say this understanding comes from newspapers. (Also, 6 percent identify the radio, 1 percent magazines, and 9 percent "other people.")

Television really loses its paramount importance in local elections (26 percent). Here, newspapers predominate (40 percent). In addition, 6 percent continue to identify radio and 1 percent magazines. A larger number than at other levels (23 percent) identify "other people." [35]

Taken together, the evidence suggests that, depending on the poll examined, between 40 and 70 percent of the population have some degree of confidence in the media and most agree on the importance of a free press. Orientations, however, change rather quickly, depending on what is occurring—race riots, antiwar demonstrations, or Watergate. What is happening in the country influences levels of confidence.

For the activist, it is important to know not only these general media orientations, but relative orientations. How the public feels about television as opposed to radio and newspapers, and how these

[33] Louis Harris, *The Anguish of Change* (New York: W. W. Norton & Company, 1973), p. 284.
[34] Herbert E. Alexander, "Communications and Politics: The Media and the Message," *Law and Contemporary Problems*, Spring 1969, p. 258.
[35] These data are from B. Roper, *A Ten-Year View of Public Attitudes toward Television and Other Mass Media, 1959–1968,* also reported in Alexander, "Communications and Politics," p. 258.

feelings change from the national level to state and local levels, become guides to action. They help to answer the question, Should the media be used?

Political tactics and the input process.   A final set of input orientations that need to be identified are those dealing with types of political participation. While we already know that citizens don't participate politically to any great degree, although they believe participation is important, feelings and ways of thinking about particular political behavior have not been identified precisely. In Chapter 2, tactics were classified as normal, extraordinary legal, and extraordinary illegal. In addition, it was suggested that whether or not a goal is ultimately accepted as legitimate by the public will be determined by a variety of factors, one of which is feelings about the tactics used. So, what are legitimate tactics, according to public perceptions?

There are two different approaches to estimating citizen orientations toward forms of participation—focusing on known participation practices to arrive at citizen feelings and thinking about participation, or focusing on surveys that define citizen opinions toward various forms of participation.

Their actions tell us that citizens generally accept *normal* forms of political participation, although participation decreases in direct proportion to the amount of energy required (Table 3–4).

In addition to the large percentage who regularly vote, at least in presidential elections, we know that 69 percent engage in at least one other normal political act and almost half engage in two or more acts.[36]

Failure to participate in a particular political act, however, doesn't necessarily imply disapproval. On the contrary, in normal political activity, citizens are far more likely to express approval of forms of participation than to actually participate. For example, in one study conducted several years ago in Albany, New York, 32 percent of those interviewed believed that writing to a representative was one way in which an ordinary citizen could influence the government. Yet only 11 percent reported that they had written such a letter.[37] Even this figure of 11 percent may be inflated, for in voting studies, where it is possible to compare the number of people who actually vote with

[36] Verba and Nie, *Participation in America*, p. 33.
[37] V. O. Key, Jr., *Public Opinion and American Democracy* (New York: Alfred A. Knopf, 1961), pp. 418–419.

Table 3–4
Citizen participation: how much? how widespread?

Percentage Engaging in Twelve Different Acts of Political Participation

Type of Political Participation	Percentage
1. Report regularly voting in presidential elections*	72
2. Report always voting in local elections	47
3. Active in at least one organization involved in community problems†	32
4. Have worked with others in trying to solve some community problems	30
5. Have attempted to persuade others to vote as they were	28
6. Have ever actively worked for a party or candidates during an election	26
7. Have ever contacted a local government official about some issue or problem	20
8. Have attended at least one political meeting or rally in the last three years	19
9. Have ever contacted a state or national government official about some issue or problem	18
10. Have ever formed a group or organization to attempt to solve some local community problem	14
11. Have ever given money to a party or candidate during an election campaign	13
12. Presently a member of a political club or organization	8

Number of cases: weighted, 3095; unweighted, 2549

* Composite variable created from reports of voting in 1960 and 1964 presidential elections. Percentage is equal to those who report they have voted in both elections.

† This variable is a composite index where the proportion presented above is equal to the proportion of those in the sample who are active in at least one voluntary association that, they report, takes an active role in attempting to solve community problems. The procedure utilized was as follows: Each respondent was asked whether he or she was a member of 15 types of voluntary associations. For each affirmative answer the respondent was then asked whether he or she regularly attended meetings or otherwise took a leadership role in the organization. If yes, the respondent was considered an active member. If the respondent was an active member and reported that the organization regularly attempted to solve community problems, that respondent was considered to have performed this type of political act. Membership in expressly *political* clubs or organizations was excluded from this index.

Source: Sidney Verba and Norman H. Nie, *Participation in America* (New York: Harper & Row, Publishers, 1972), p. 31. © 1972 by Sidney Verba and Norman H. Nie.

the ones who say they did, the discrepancy is obvious. For example, in one survey of voting in the 1964 election, approximately 80 percent of the respondents in most regions of the United States said they had voted. The actual figure was 62.8 percent.[38]

So while most people don't engage in any form of normal political activity other than voting, they still approve of other forms of involvement. How far does this approval extend? Does it extend to extraordinary legal forms of political participation? *Ordinarily* it doesn't, although acceptance does depend on the protestors, certain characteristics of the audience, and the nature of the goal.

Legal forms of protest are usually dramatic and somewhat disruptive ways of exercising the constitutional right of free speech. In its abstract form, most citizens accept the importance of this right. In surveys conducted in the 1950s and 1960s, only a few respondents failed to agree with such statements as, "the minority should be free to criticize majority decisions," and "I believe in free speech for all no matter what their views might be." [39]

So there is no problem, apparently. Wrong. The problem is that when this abstraction is turned into a specific, acceptance disintegrates. For example, in the 1950s, if anyone's speech were "tinged with socialism," only a slight majority would allow it. Only 27 percent would allow an admitted Communist to make a speech in the community. If religion or the church were attacked in any way, only 37 percent would declare this a legal form of speech.[40]

Still, these are the 1970s. We are no longer living in the Cold War atmosphere of the 1950s. Surely the intolerance of controversial speech that existed then does not exist now. In fact, it does. A nationwide telephone poll conducted by CBS News in 1970 revealed that over half of the 1136 people interviewed said that they would not give everyone the right to criticize the government if the criticism were thought to be damaging to the national interest. An even greater percentage of those interviewed indicated disapproval of free speech

[38] See Lester W. Milbrath, "Individuals and Government," in *Politics in the American States*, 2d ed., eds. Herbert Jacob & Kenneth N. Vines (Boston: Little, Brown and Company, 1971), p. 34.

[39] See James W. Prothro and C. W. Grigg, "Fundamental Principles of Democracy: Bases of Agreement and Disagreement," *Journal of Politics*, May 1960, pp. 276–294; and Herbert McClosky, "Consensus and Ideology in American Politics," *American Political Science Review*, June 1964, pp. 361–382.

[40] See S. A. Stouffer, *Communism, Conformity and Civil Liberties* (New York: Doubleday & Company, 1955), pp. 29, 33, 36, 41.

expressed in an extraordinary way. Specifically, three-quarters of those questioned said extremist groups should not be permitted to organize demonstrations against the government, even if there appeared to be no clear danger of violence. Freedom of speech is fine as long as no one hears it.[41]

Even when the goals of protestors generate sympathy and tolerance, their tactics are often not condoned. After 1970, for example, the rising antiwar sentiment came from two different categories of people: a highly educated, articulate minority who opposed the war for moral reasons, and a larger number from lower socioeconomic groups who opposed the war as a nuisance and, pragmatically, as a losing cause. However, this support for the goals of the antiwar movement did not include support of the tactics. Of those who felt the war was a mistake, 63 percent were definitely hostile to the protests. This reaction was even shared by a majority of those favoring immediate withdrawal.[42]

Although even sympathizers could not condone protests, large numbers of citizens accepted as important the right of free speech—in this case, the right to discuss this controversial question. A Louis Harris poll in the late 1960s reported that by 81 percent to 11 percent, a majority of citizens agreed with the statement that "the antiwar demonstrators may not be entirely right, but they are raising real questions which ought to be discussed and answered." [43] Were Americans becoming more tolerant of controversial free speech, or had this particular speech become more and more acceptable? While that question is difficult to answer, what can be concluded is that extraordinary legal tactics are *generally* not accepted.

Predictably, extraordinary illegal tactics are even less acceptable to most citizens, even when the goals of the protesting group are perceived as legitimate. After the race riots of the 1960s, when ghettos were burned and looted, large majorities could sympathize with the desperate plight of the blacks, and over 80 percent favored a "domes-

---

[41] A study by M. E. Olsen confirms the fact that people accept as legitimate more normal forms of free speech—public meetings and even peaceful protests—but when it comes to more direct tactics—strikes, sit-ins, demonstrations—majority support withers. "Perceived Legitimacy of Social Protest Actions," *Social Problems*, Winter 1968, pp. 297–309.

[42] See Philip Converse and Howard Schuman, "Silent Majorities and the Vietnam War," *Scientific American*, June 1970, pp. 17–25. Also reported in Bogart, *Silent Politics*, p. 95.

[43] Harris, *The Anguish of Change*, p. 173.

tic Marshall Plan to rebuild the ghettos of the big cities." Yet by 73 percent to 18 percent, a large majority condemned the tactics of the riots—if they were indeed tactics.[44]

Interestingly, black citizens themselves also rejected violent tactics, but not overwhelmingly. A 1970 Louis Harris poll revealed that 58 percent of black citizens agreed that they could win their rights without violence. Seven years earlier 63 percent had agreed with that statement.

Still, even black citizens—who, along with other minorities, have suffered the greatest inequities—prefer normal tactics. In 1970, in answer to the question, "how will blacks make real progress?" 92 percent said, "electing more blacks to public office," 83 percent said, "working more closely with whites who want to help blacks," and 68 percent said, "organizing boycotts where whites discriminate against blacks." Only 42 percent said, "taking to the streets in protest." [45]

Approval for extraordinary tactics is higher among youth, particularly college students. But even most college students believe extraordinary violent activity is never justified. Table 3–5 describes the attitudes of youths toward various forms of political participation.[46]

So citizens generally support only normal political activity, although support for extraordinary activity increases among black and young people.

At this point, how can citizen thinking and feeling about the input process be summarized? This list should help:

Citizen Orientations Toward Themselves as Players

1. Most citizens feel they can be politically effective, although the percentage is decreasing.
2. Most citizens feel people should be active politically.
3. Most citizens are not politically active—many don't even vote.
4. Most citizens think they should be informed about issues, their representatives, and community problems.
5. Most citizens are not informed. Almost half feel government and politics seem too complicated.

---

[44] *Ibid.*, p. 174.
[45] "The Black Mood: More Militant, More Hopeful, More Determined," *Time*, April 6, 1970, pp. 27–29.
[46] Chandler, *Public Opinion*, p. 45.

Table 3–5
Attitudes of youth toward political tactics

	Percent Total Youth	Percent College	Percent Noncollege
For those activities you have not been involved in, which of these would you like to be involved in?			
Sit-ins	11	20	9
Strikes	9	14	8
Riots	3	4	3
Marches	11	20	8
Political campaigns	25	35	22
Organization meetings	12	15	12
Civil rights protests	12	24	9
Join organizations like SDS and YAF	6	8	5
Be arrested	3	3	3
None	59	36	65

Which of the tactics listed on this card do you feel are *always* justified, which are *sometimes* justified, and which do you feel are *never* justified?

Sit-ins				
Always justified	5	12	3	Not
Sometimes justified	66	78	63	asked of
Never justified	28	10	33	parents
Ultimatums to those in authority				
Always justified	7	6	8	
Sometimes justified	65	75	63	
Never justified	26	19	28	
Blockades of buildings				
Always justified	3	2	3	
Sometimes justified	36	46	34	
Never justified	59	52	61	
Destruction or mutilation of property				
Always justified	1	—	1	
Sometimes justified	12	16	12	
Never justified	86	84	87	

Source: Robert Chandler, *Public Opinion* (New York: R. R. Bowker Company, 1972), p. 45.

Table 3–5 (cont'd.)

	Percent Total Youth	Percent College	Percent Noncollege
Resisting or disobeying police			
Always justified	3	1	4
Sometimes justified	34	62	27
Never justified	62	37	69

Orientations Toward Other Citizens

6. Citizens generally have positive feelings about other people, if membership in voluntary organizations is one indication.

Orientations Toward Input Institutions

7. Although most citizens are not active in political parties or interest groups, they feel these groups, plus the mass media, are politically important. People even say they would be willing to engage in some interest-group activities that are not presently part of their routine.

Orientations Toward Input Methods

8. The tactics used by groups are accepted as legitimate when they are normal. Extraordinary legal and illegal tactics are generally not accepted, even when the goals of the protesting groups are perceived positively.

Something to think about
Why is each of these input orientations relevant to political action?

Thinking and Feeling about the Conversion Process

When people talk about "government" and what the government is doing or not doing, they are usually talking about *conversion* institutions and processes. Without really knowing how they all come together, citizens are referring to the legislative, executive, and judicial branches of government. These are the institutions constitutionally responsible at each level of government for converting citizen demands and supports (i.e., votes and tax dollars) into outputs. The degree to which they are *perceived* to be succeeding will influence

Table 3–6
Attitudes toward national government

	Percentage
Yes, tend to improve	76
Sometimes improve, sometimes not	19
Better off without them	3
Other, don't know, etc.	2
Total	100

Source: Gabriel Almond and Sidney Verba, *The Civic Culture* (Boston: Little, Brown and Company, 1963), p. 48.

other input orientations as well as citizen participation. How likely will citizens be to cheat on their income tax if they think public officials usually cheat? And this information is crucial to the activist.

An extraordinary thing is happening to the way citizens think and feel about government. It is changing in an alarming direction. The five-nation study done by Almond and Verba in the 1960s indicated very positive feelings about government. Table 3–6 gives the responses of American citizens to the question, "On the whole, do the activities of the national government tend to improve conditions in this country or would we be better off without them?" [47]

So how are things changing? While the figures vary somewhat, polls indicate that the national government is losing public trust. For example, Arthur Miller, a political scientist from Ohio State University, found that while 20 percent distrusted the government in 1964 this had risen to 39 percent by 1970. Among black citizens, distrust was at 56 percent in 1970. Breaking the figures down by age groups, he found distrust to be far more profound among people over 60 than among those under 30. [48]

As if this decline in government trust were not enough, the 1973 findings of Louis Harris are even more disturbing. He found that a *majority* of Americans—53 percent—agreed there is something deeply wrong in America (37 percent disagreed, and the remainder were not sure). The Harris organization said that this was the first time since

[47] Gabriel Almond and Sidney Verba, *The Civic Culture* (Boston: Little, Brown and Company, 1965), p. 48.
[48] "Report that Government Is Losing Public Trust," *San Francisco Chronicle*, September 12, 1972, p. 7. Also reported in *Society*, July-August 1974, p. 13.

the assassinations of Martin Luther King and Sen. Robert F. Kennedy in 1968 that a majority had answered the question affirmatively. Asked to explain their concern, one-quarter of those sampled said that "government leaders are corrupt and immoral." More people gave that answer than any others.[49]

How does this growing distrust of national government manifest itself in political behavior? In a variety of ways. Sometimes people fail to vote—they withdraw; sometimes people vote negatively—vote against everything in local elections; sometimes people become more active. Just how they behave will depend on both their socioeconomic characteristics and their *precise* political feelings.[50]

Another way to think about citizen orientations toward the conversion process is to look at how people feel about specific conversion institutions and their key players. Again, evidence reveals that feelings toward most institutions are becoming more negative. The same 1973 Louis Harris survey revealed that feelings about the national *executive branch* of government were particularly bad. In 1965, 41 percent of Americans had confidence in that institution, in 1972 it had dropped to 27 percent, and by 1973 it was at 19 percent. The legislative branch wasn't doing much better. In 1965 confidence in the Senate was at 42 percent, in 1972, at 21 percent, and in 1973 it had rallied to 30 percent. Confidence in the House of Representatives was about the same.[51]

Feelings about the U.S. Supreme Court were also not that positive, certainly not at the 1965 level. While in 1965 the confidence level was 51 percent, in 1972 it plunged to 28 percent, and by 1973 it had improved only slightly, to 33 percent.[52]

How do these figures compare with feelings about other governmental and nongovernmental institutions? Look at Figure 2.

Oh to be a doctor instead of a politician!

Perhaps local conversion institutions and players fare better? Not at all. A 1975 Louis Harris poll revealed that among people who live in the central cities, only 7 percent have confidence in local government leaders. Residents of cities have seven times more confidence in their garbage collectors than in their mayors.

---

[49] See *New York Times*, December 3, 1973, p. 34.
[50] For an explanation of how different forms of political alienation can influence different types of political behavior, see Ada W. Finifter, "Dimensions of Political Alienation," pp. 389–410.
[51] *New York Times*, December 3, 1973, p. 34.
[52] *Ibid*.

Figure 2
Degree of confidence in various institutions.

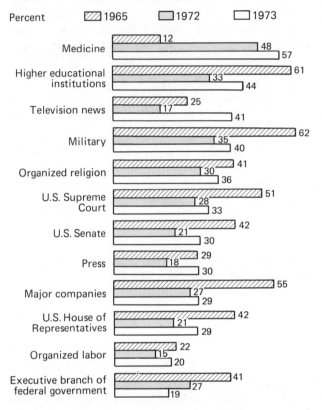

Percent   ▨ 1965   ▧ 1972   ☐ 1973

Medicine — 12, 48, 57

Higher educational institutions — 61, 33, 44

Television news — 25, 17, 41

Military — 62, 35, 40

Organized religion — 41, 30, 36

U.S. Supreme Court — 51, 28, 33

U.S. Senate — 42, 21, 30

Press — 29, 18, 30

Major companies — 55, 27, 29

U.S. House of Representatives — 42, 21, 29

Organized labor — 22, 15, 20

Executive branch of federal government — 41, 27, 19

While feelings do fluctuate, at this point orientations toward neither government generally nor specific institutions are very positive. What the precise effect will be on political behavior is difficult to predict. Activists need to know that this is the kind of political climate with which they are dealing. They need to look for clues to the ways in which it is going to affect their job of mobilizing support among the general population or specific groups.

Thinking and Feeling about Outputs and the Output Process

Outputs are the things that get distributed as a result of the conversion process. They include such things as *money* for schools, rapid transit, and veterans' affairs; *rights* to equal employment opportunities, equal education, and due process of law; *obligations* to pay taxes and serve on juries; etc.

The way people feel about outputs and the output process, like the other parts and processes of the political system, affects the way the system works. And the range of citizen feelings is wide. James David Barber puts it this way:

> The apathetic citizen who has given up on government, thoroughly disillusioned, expects little and hopes for even less. His view of the future is pessimistic; things are likely to get worse and there is not much he can do about it. At the other end of the scale is the political fanatic who wants and expects utopia tomorrow. Living on logic, he can see no reason why the political system should not be transformed immediately into perfection, into a political heaven on earth. If the apathetic lacks hope, the fanatic lacks a sense of history, of the ways the human organism grows stage by stage.[53]

Most Americans fall between these two extremes, according to Barber. Not all the hopes of citizens are wrapped up in what the government may or may not do, and skepticism about politics and politicians helps to protect Americans against massive disillusionment.[54]

Let's look at the evidence. Both the political system and the economic system in this country help to define the quality of life. To the extent that government is partially responsible for distributing things that define that quality, Americans nationally are quite satisfied. A 1972 Gallup poll indicated that 74 percent were satisfied with their housing, 84 percent with the work they do, 60 percent with their children's education, and 78 percent with their standard of living. In all, a majority (58 percent) said they were satisfied with the future facing them and their family. Does this optimism pervade orientations toward the outputs of state governments?

The citizens and public officials interviewed in a California study in 1973 also expressed general satisfaction. However, respondents were discriminating. As can be seen from Table 3–7, those living in different types of communities had different points of view.

Interestingly, even though Americans are satisfied, they don't seem to attribute their satisfaction to what the government does. At least

---

[53] Barber, *Citizen Politics*, p. 97.
[54] *Ibid.*

Table 3-7
Evaluation of services provided by local government

Service	Percent Rating Service			Most Favorable Comments Came From	Most Negative Comments Came From
	Good	Fair	Poor		
Air quality	26	39	35	rural areas	unincorporated areas
Water quality	70	24	6	special districts	unincorporated areas
Sewage disposal	54	31	15	elected officials, staff	unincorporated areas
Garbage disposal	55	32	13	elected officials	cities over 500,000
Streets and roads	54	38	8	elected officials	cities over 500,000
Fire protection	84	13	3	cities over 500,000	counties
Law enforcement	64	31	5	elected officials	cities under 25,000
Health care	57	31	11	cities between 25,000 and 50,000	unincorporated areas
Land use planning	26	42	32	elected officials	unincorporated areas
Libraries	71	23	6	cities between 25,000 and 50,000	unincorporated areas
Parks, recreation	52	38	10	special districts	unincorporated areas
Transportation	11	23	66	cities under 25,000	appointed officials
Housing	20	46	34	elected officials	unincorporated areas
Cultural affairs	36	39	25	elected officials	unincorporated areas
Assessment practices	40	38	22	special districts cities between 150,000 and 500,000	unincorporated areas

Source: The League of Women Voters, Local Government in California and Citizen Participation (League of Women Voters of the San Francisco Bay Area and Los Angeles County, 1974).

one survey indicates that less than a majority of white citizens expect very much at all from the government. For example, only 30 percent of white citizens interviewed (but 81 percent of blacks) agreed with the statement, "the federal government should make sure everyone has a job and a good standard of living." [55]

So Americans are satisfied with their situation in life but don't attribute what they have, necessarily, to government outputs. In fact, most don't expect very much in the way of government outputs, although this expectation differs dramatically among white and black citizens.

Well, what about feelings toward the people who deliver these outputs? The contact most citizens have with government is usually with these players—bureaucrats. The police officer, the clerk at the department of motor vehicles or unemployment office, the mail carrier —these are the people who help to staff output institutions. What do citizens think about the job they are doing? After all, these are the people responsible for seeing that governmental outputs get distributed efficiently.

The most pervasive feeling, at least in the early 1960 Almond and Verba study, is that citizens will be treated *equally* by governmental bureaucrats (Table 3-8). These were the questions asked:

> Suppose there were some questions that you had to take to a government office—for example a tax question or housing regulation. Do you think you would be given equal treatment—I mean, would you be treated as well as anyone else? If you had some trouble with the police—a traffic violation maybe, or being accused of a minor offense, do you think you would be given equal treatment? That is, would you be treated as well as anyone else?

Less overwhelmingly positive are the feelings about governmental officials being *responsive* (Table 3-9). These were the questions asked:

> If you explained your point of view to the officials, what effect do you think it would have? Would they give your point of view serious consideration, would they pay only a little attention, or would they ignore what you had to say? If you explained your point of view to the police, what effect do you think it would have? Would they give your point of view serious consideration, would they pay only a little attention, or would they ignore what you had to say?

[55] Survey Research Center, University of Michigan, 1968 election survey.

Table 3–8
Expectations of treatment by governmental bureaucracy and police

Percent Who Say	From Bureaucracy	From Police
They expect equal treatment	83	85
They don't expect equal treatment	9	8
Depends	4	5
Other	—	—
Don't know	4	2
Total	100	100

Source: Gabriel Almond and Sidney Verba, The Civic Culture (Boston: Little, Brown and Company, 1965), p. 70.

Table 3–9
Amount of consideration expected for point of view
from bureaucracy and police

Percent Who Expect	From Bureaucracy	From Police
Serious consideration for point of view	48	56
A little attention	31	22
To be ignored	6	11
Depends	11	9
Other	—	—
Don't know	4	2
Total	100	100

Source: Gabriel Almond and Sidney Verba, The Civic Culture (Boston: Little, Brown and Company, 1965), p. 72.

Taken together, these somewhat dated answers show that most citizens in this country feel that they will be treated equally by police and bureaucrats and that their point of view will be considered seriously, or at least moderately seriously. So not only are they satisfied with what they are getting out of life, but, to the extent that government is perceived as playing a role, they are satisfied with the way in which things are being distributed.

What does all this add up to? Can the way citizens think and feel about governmental institutions, players, and processes as well as their

Figure 3
Citizen input.

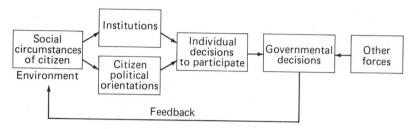

Adaptation of tables on pp. 8 and 19 from *Participation in America: Political Democracy and Social Equality* by Sidney Verba and Norman H. Nie. Copyright © 1972 by Sidney Verba and Norman H. Nie. Reprinted by permission of Harper & Row, Publishers, Inc.

own political role be summarized? More important, how do these orientations influence behavior?

This variation of a diagram (Figure 3) developed by Verba and Nie summarizes the relation between political culture (citizen political orientations) and participation. It also reminds us that more than just citizen participation influences governmental decisions. Let's briefly put the pieces together.

Both the social circumstances of the individual and broader environmental factors influence citizen political orientations. In this country, as we've seen, political orientations tend to be positive. The only exceptions are an increasing sense of powerlessness and distrust of conversion institutions. Precisely who is most likely to have positive orientations, however, is influenced by socioeconomic factors. Income, level of education achieved, occupational status, age, race, and sex are all relevant. Generally, positive political orientations are more likely to be associated with high socioeconomic status. These are the citizens who have more interest in and information about politics and who feel more politically effective.

However, these orientations alone do not determine whether or not an individual will participate politically. Institutional factors are also relevant. Participation in organizations and identification with a political party increase the tendency toward other participation, regardless of socioeconomic status. Somehow, this institutional involvement socializes citizens politically.[56] Understanding that process re-

[56] See Chapters 11 and 12 of Verba and Nie, *Participation in America*, for a precise discussion of the influence of institutional factors on participation.

quires knowing something about how citizens generally acquire their political orientations. On to that discussion.

Key Words

Political culture
Political system
Public opinion

Suggested Activities

1. Determine the political orientations of class members, focusing on input, conversion, and output orientations.
2. Determine the political orientations of the parents of class members.
3. Compare the results.
4. Re-examine the results of the class and parent political participation surveys. Can any tentative generalizations be made on the basis of the two surveys?

4
Influencing Political Thinking and Feeling

"Knowing where people's political heads are," as the expression goes —how they generally think and feel about political institutions, processes, products, and themselves as players—is only the first step. The second step for the person or group interested in building support for an issue, candidate, or cause is knowing how political orientations develop and change. Only then is it possible to begin thinking about influencing the behavior of potential players.

Adrien Keller lives in a black ghetto of Boston. Although she is only 12 years old, she has some definite feelings and beliefs about the government and the laws it makes and enforces. The skepticism and disappointment that one more frequently finds among adults are already apparent. These are some of her political views, expressed in an interview with Thomas J. Cottle.

> "Here's the way I feel about it," Adrien resumed. "Sure, a person's religion plays an important part, and so does what their family thinks. But there are just some things that people need the government for, even when the government isn't that fair, which is a lot of the time. See, if they don't make any laws, then we're going to be in lots of trouble. Rich families don't need to have a lot of laws. They'll do what they have to do anyway. But poor people...."
> She looked embarrassed suddenly, fearing that I should see her family as being poor.

"... If we don't have laws to protect us," she was saying, "then we don't really have very much. Like at school. If there's a law that says we have to be given hot food with our lunches, then they have to give it to us whether they like to or not, cause the law says they have to."

"But aren't there times, Adrien, when the law says they have to but they still don't give what they promised?"

"I guess so," she answered quietly. "I guess that's right."

Adrien continued to look puzzled. She stared at me before speaking again.

"I guess I want laws to make a difference but I know that they don't. Or else, it takes so long for them to ... to. ..."

"Institute them?" I offered.

"Yeah. Make them come true. I think kids want to believe in the law, and the government too. We keep going back to it. I mean, nobody I know really questions it that seriously. Nobody's really even going to be able to change it. Lots of kids will say we have to be represented in it. Even if we don't have the vote, we have to have our say. But I worry whether we would help in the right away. Do you know what I mean?" [1]

So at the age of 12, this is where Adrien is politically. How did she develop these political feelings and beliefs? Is she likely to retain them as an adult, or will they change? How will they influence her political behavior? To answer these questions requires some understanding of political socialization.

Political Socialization

Political socialization is the process through which people acquire their political orientations and patterns of behavior. It is the way a political culture gets shaped and transmitted from generation to generation.

Some definitions might help in describing the process. Political thinking and feeling involve what people *believe* to be true, what they *value*, and their general *attitudes*.

Values

Values are the most basic ingredient. Our feelings about what is right and wrong, what is unjust or just, are reflections of what we value.

[1] This interview is one of many with black children conducted by the sociologist-psychotherapist Thomas J. Cottle. The occasion around which this book revolves is a political one: the U.S. election of 1972. See *Black Children, White Dreams* (Boston: Houghton Mifflin Company, 1974).

They become aspects of our personality. From her comments it is easy to see that Adrien values the rule of law and equal application of the law. This is only one kind of value, an expression of what is *desirable*, what *ought* to be.

There are two additional kinds of values. One is an expression of a person's *wants and needs*. For example, "I want to go to Europe" and "I want a new car" are statements that indicate that the individual places a value on the *object* to which the statement refers. The final kind of value is an expression of a *relationship* of means to an end. For example, "I value clean air because it contributes to my good health," or "I value dieting because it allows me to wear a size 10." Dieting certainly doesn't have any intrinsic value; it is the relationship that creates the value.[2]

People don't value all things equally. They *order their preferences*. For example, when people say all they want out of life is good health for themselves and their families, economic security, and enough leisure time to enjoy what they earn, they are expressing values. Yet they don't value each of these ingredients of a happy life to the same degree. Someone who gives up a secure job because it offers little leisure time probably prefers leisure time to economic security.

Sometimes values pose problems for people. They may conflict. For example, people are likely to value both public safety and various civil rights guaranteed by the U.S. Constitution. If those people think crime is getting out of hand, if they think citizens are no longer safe walking city streets, they may be willing to accept a denial of certain aspects of due process of law in favor of protecting the public and ensuring safety. In a value conflict one sees particularly clearly how preferences are ordered.

The reason values are an important part and product of the socialization process is that they help to influence the way we experience the world. Along with knowledge, they help to define one's personality, which in time influences perceptions and ultimately political behavior. Heinz Eulau emphasizes the importance of identifying values if one wants to understand political behavior:

> Values can serve as central organizing principles in studying the personal basis of political behavior. Presumably a person's values

[2] For additional clarification of these three types of values, see Ralph M. Goldman, *Contemporary Perspectives on Politics* (New York: Van Nostrand Reinhold Company, 1972), p. 110; and Lewis A. Froman, Jr., *People and Politics* (Englewood Cliffs, N.J.: Prentice-Hall, 1962), p. 19.

are sufficiently structured to constitute a value system; and if they do, the value system may well be the most stable component of political behavior. Therefore it is a critical task of research to discover the content of a person's value system, its arrangement and degree of internal consistency, and its relation to the culture that patterns the politics of the group to which the individual belongs. More than any other aspect of personality, personality-rooted values express the personal basis of political behavior.[3]

On a still more practical level, personal values are closely tied to persuasion. Persuasion is more possible when the communicator and the receiver have common values.[4] So those values need to be identified.

Beliefs

A second important concept associated with political socialization is *belief*. Beliefs are ideas we assume to be true. Sometimes they are based on carefully accumulated evidence. Frequently they are based on personal experience. Always they are influenced by what we value and our personalities in general. A mother in Lansing, Michigan, may believe school busing to promote integration is going to be harmful to her child's education. She probably hasn't read or heard any available evidence on the subject, but her belief may be based on any one or more of the following factors: conversations with another family whose child had to attend an integrated school and who "suffered" as a result; a sense that black people are not as smart or well mannered as white people, so integration couldn't offer any learning advantages; a feeling that the neighborhood school offers parents a chance to influence their children's education more directly and positively; a knowledge that riding on a bus takes time that could be used more advantageously at home or in the classroom. Whatever the ingredients and regardless of their validity, they help to define a particular belief, one that might be related to an entire belief system.

Attitudes

Attitudes are influenced by both values and beliefs. Generally, they are predispositions to respond in a certain way to certain events, people, and processes. As long ago as 1935, Gordon Allport surveyed

[3] Heinz Eulau, *The Behavioral Persuasion in Politics* (New York: Random House, 1963), pp. 95–96.
[4] See Otto Lerbinger, *Designs for Persuasive Communication* (Englewood Cliffs, N.J.: Prentice-Hall, 1972), p. 127.

the way the concept of "attitude" was being used. After reviewing 16 different definitions, he decided that an attitude has at least five aspects:

1. It is a mental and neural state
2. Of readiness to respond
3. Organized
4. Through experience
5. Exerting a directive or dynamic influence on behavior[5]

To illustrate the relation between attitudes, values, and beliefs, Arthur Froman discusses what can happen when one of the ingredients changes. He says, let us assume we *value* equal representation of all interests in the United States. Further, let us assume that we *believe* that Congress allows for equal representation of all interests within the United States. On the basis of this value-and-belief connection, if everything else is equal, we would predict a favorable *attitude* toward Congress. If it could be demonstrated that Congress does not *in fact* allow for equal representation of all interests within the United States, the attitude toward Congress might change. However, under certain conditions a change of belief may not produce a change in attitude. Even with this change in belief, we may like Congress for other reasons. Our attitudes are based on many values and beliefs. If one belief is shown to be false, that doesn't necessarily mean that people will change their attitude. It may be necessary to challenge a number of beliefs before they will change their minds.[6]

Something to think about
How could the activist use this information?

Those of us involved in a cause that requires building popular support need to know how people acquire their values, beliefs, and attitudes, particularly during adulthood. Still, let's not get ahead of ourselves. How does the process of political socialization generally work? How are political orientations and patterns of behavior acquired? The process takes place throughout a person's lifetime. It involves *directly* picking up messages from individuals and groups who are trying to

[5] G. W. Allport, "Attitudes," in *Handbook of Social Psychology*, ed. C. Murchison (Worcester, Mass.: Clark University Press, 1937), pp. 798–884.
[6] Froman, *People and Politics*, p. 22.

teach political principles (i.e., from family, schools, and political leaders), but it also involves the *indirect* acquisition of political orientations. Quite accidentally, a child might acquire a political party identification through overhearing father and mother discuss politics.[7] ("Damn those Democrats, they never do anything right," or "those Republicans always get us into economic chaos.")

The Process of Political Socialization

When does it all begin? It is difficult to say exactly, but every piece of evidence indicates that a child's political world begins to take shape well before the child even enters elementary school. At this point, the child obviously is not politically informed, but he or she *emotionally identifies* with the political community, its political leaders, and even a political party. What parents say prompts that identification.

Between the ages of 7 and 13, children, like Adrien, become more politically sophisticated. They acquire some political information and knowledge. They begin to be able to differentiate between different political leaders and institutions. Particularly interesting is the fact that by this age the child has sorted out the relative weights of various political figures. The President consistently emerges as a person of special distinction. One 8-year old interviewed put it this way:

Question
"What does the President do?"
Answer
"He runs the country, he decides the decisions that we should try to get out of and he goes to meetings and tries to make peace and things like that. . . ."
Question
"When you say he runs the country, what do you mean?"
Answer
"Well, he's just about the boss of everything. . . ." [8]

Regardless of the power children of this age attach to the President, they still think he is within easy reach. He can be written to, telephoned, and even visited in Washington. A 9-year-old interviewed had this to say on the subject: [9]

[7] Richard E. Dawson and Kenneth Prewitt, *Political Socialization* (Boston: Little, Brown and Company, 1969), p. 39.
[8] David Easton and Jack Dennis, *Children in the Political System: Origins of Political Legitimacy* (New York: McGraw-Hill Book Company, 1969), p. 145.
[9] *Ibid.*, p. 173.

Question
"Can you ever tell the President of the United States what kinds of things you think he should do?"
Answer
"Yeah, you can talk with him. . . ."
Question
"How—just call him up on the telephone and tell him or what?"
Answer
"Yeah, you go to the White House, most people do. . . ."
Question
"Some people do go and tell him what they want?"
Answer
"Yeah. . . ."

By the early teens, the child, to a great extent, has become the political person he or she will be as an adult. Basic political attachments and identifications are now established. They are no longer strictly emotional. In addition, political interest is likely to increase. Teenagers may follow political events and even participate in political groups.[10]

While childhood is the most important period for the acquisition of political orientations and parents are the most important agents of socialization, political learning continues throughout adulthood—fortunately for the activist. If a person's political outlook changes as an adult, it is because that person is involved in new social groups and roles. "Moving from one part of the country to another, shifting up (or down) the social and economic ladder, becoming a parent, finding or losing a job, getting old, are common experiences that can result in modified political perspectives."[11]

Peer groups are the most important agents of socialization for adults. The reason has to do with the high degree of interaction involved in peer groups and the emotionally laden personal relationships that exist within them. Friends and coworkers are both available and needed.[12]

Of course, not all peer groups influence members to the same extent. The degree to which an individual is influenced by peers depends on the degree to which that individual values the peer group. This, in

[10] Dawson and Prewitt, *Political Socialization*, pp. 44–52.
[11] *Ibid.*
[12] *Ibid.*, p. 132.

turn, seems to depend on the number and type of needs satisfied by the group, the existence of alternative ways of satisfying these same needs, the degree of power or even force that the group can potentially exercise over its members, and the particular status of the individual within the total group.[13] However, even taking variations in the degree of influence into consideration, for most adults, orientations are stabilized or altered through peer interaction.

Something to think about
In putting together a political strategy, how can this information be used?

Peers are even more important in the political socialization process than the *media*, not only because the media attract less attention than peers and certainly evoke less emotional involvement, but for other related reasons as well. First, when peers interact, politics comes up unexpectedly—as a sideline or marginal topic in a casual conversation. Thus, a political message is more likely to get through. On television, when an explicit political message comes on the air, perhaps in the form of a documentary, people are likely to change the channel. It is harder to "switch off" a friend. Second, when peers interact, they are flexible whenever their ideas are resisted. Unlike the media, an individual trying to influence another can choose the right occasion. An individual can adapt the message to the other person's interest and ability to understand. Third, when there is agreement, there is immediate reward. When someone yields to personal influence as opposed to media messages, the reward for the influencer is both quick and personal. Fourth, peer interaction is more effective in political socialization because the individual is able to trust a known and intimate source, and because peer groups share many of the same predispositions. An unknown media editorial writer just hasn't the same influence. Finally, peer interaction allows for persuasion without conviction. Because of the personal affection and loyalty that operate in close associations, an individual may be influenced simply to sustain or strengthen the relationship.[14]

[13] Lerbinger, *Designs for Persuasive Communication*, p. 96.
[14] See Paul F. Lazarsfeld et al., *The People's Choice*, 2d ed. (New York: Columbia University Press, 1948), pp. 150–151.

Does that mean that the media are not at all effective as agents of adult political socialization? Not quite, but their role is difficult to assess.

Whether or not someone actually receives a message through the mass media seems to depend on a number of factors. The very basic ones include:

1. The kind of *exposure* a message gets
2. The particular *medium* used to communicate the message
3. The *content* of the message itself
4. The attitudes and psychological *predispositions* of the audience
5. *Interpersonal relations*—an individual's social attachments to other people, and the character of the opinions and activities shared with them[15]

How does it all work? Let's examine *message exposure* first. Is it true that the more a person is exposed to a media message, the more likely it is that it will be accepted? Advertisers must believe this, for they constantly bombard the public with the same commercials. However, various studies seem to indicate that although repetition of a message is of value, sheer parrotlike reiteration may begin to irritate the audience. Repetition with variation, on the other hand, seems to be more persuasive. During World War II, a popular singer named Kate Smith was very successful in selling war bonds over the radio. Each appeal she made was somewhat different from the others, but they all had the same goal—to create and reinforce the desire to buy a war bond, and then to intensify that desire to the point of actual purchase. According to researchers, "each new entreaty sought out a new vulnerability to some listeners," and repeated exposure to these varying appeals reinforced the growing response tendency in individual listeners.[16]

The second factor affecting whether or not a media message is likely to get through is the *medium* itself. According to Katz and Lazarsfeld, the message will be more widely accepted when it appears in a source thought to be trustworthy.[17]

[15] Elihu Katz and Paul Lazarsfeld, *Personal Influence* (Glencoe, Ill.: The Free Press, 1955), pp. 21–25.

[16] Joseph T. Klapper, *The Effects of Mass Communication* (Glencoe, Ill.: The Free Press, 1960), p. 120. Apparently, each variation in the message identified a different reason to buy the bonds, and persons given more than one reason were more likely to do so.

[17] See experimental findings in Carl I. Hovland and Walter Weiss, "The Influence of Source Credibility on Communication Effectiveness," *Public Opinion Quarterly*, Winter 1952, pp. 635–650.

Sounds logical, doesn't it, and we know from Chapter 3 the degree to which the public has confidence in each medium at each level of government. Television is not only the major source of news for most people,[18] it also, among the mass media, receives the highest confidence rating (although this is not overwhelming).

The *content* of the message is the next factor to consider. The ideas that usually get through to people are those that are consistent with what they already believe. So the dominant effect of mass communication is *reinforcement* of opinion. However, content may also intensify a belief or attitude. This, in turn, may propel a person to act politically. The media can cause minor changes in opinion, but this is more difficult, and opinion conversion is very rare.[19]

A study by the Bureau of Applied Social Research illustrates the reinforcing tendency of the media. They interviewed 560 adult residents of Springfield, Missouri, before and after a week-long media and public relations campaign designed to improve public attitudes toward the oil industry. Of those interviewed, 78 percent retained their original views of the oil industry (whether "pro" or "anti"). In addition, 13 percent switched from "anti" to "pro," and 9 percent actually switched in the opposite direction.[20]

One additional point should be made about the relation of content to messages received. Consistently, studies in the past have indicated that very little substantial political content gets communicated to people. What does get communicated is images—impressions of people.[21]

A more recent study by the Citizens Research Foundation, however, concluded that more than images may be getting through. They conducted a survey of 600 voters who were monitored while viewing commercials sponsored by Democrats for Nixon in the 1972 presidential campaign. The three commercials used in the study were selected because they seemed "the most controversial, best publicized and, by some accounts, the most effective TV spots in the presidential race." Specifically, these 60-second commercials accused Sen. George McGovern of South Dakota, the Democratic presidential nominee, of

---

[18] See B. Roper, "Emerging Profiles of Television and Other Mass Media," in *Public Attitudes* (New York: Television Information Office, April 5, 1967).
[19] Klapper, *The Effects of Mass Communication*, p. 15.
[20] *Ibid.*, p. 17.
[21] See "Television and the Emerging Cults of Political Personalities," in Harold Mendelsohn and Irving Crespi, *Polls, Television, and the New Politics* (Scranton, Pa.: Chandler Publishing Company, 1970), pp. 264–280.

planning to cut military spending to a point jeopardizing national security, favoring making half the people in the country eligible for welfare, and continually changing his stand on public issues. Voter reaction, according to the study, indicated that these political spots were an important source of information for certain voters, those with *only low or moderate interest*. This is not an insignificant number, depending on the campaign. The spots appeared to be more effective, surprisingly, when they communicated information about issues rather than an image. Voters with high political interest seem to be less susceptible to the influence of commercials, probably because they rely on other sources of political information.[22]

Something to think about
How can political activists use this information?

Katz and Lazarsfeld have identified still another important factor in media influence: the attitudes and psychological *predispositions of the audience*. The Citizens Research Foundation study made a similar point. They found that after seeing the three pro-Nixon commercials in the study, the undecided voters and those who switched support were usually moved in the direction of their basic predispositions. This may or may not have benefited the candidate sponsoring the commercials. Consistent with the idea of the media as basically a reinforcing and intensifying agent, the opposition viewers (pro-McGovern) became even stronger opponents after viewing the 60-second spots.

The final ingredient to consider in evaluating the role of the media in the political socialization process is the effect of *interpersonal relations*. How do other people and the character of the opinions and activities a person shares with them influence that person's response to media messages? Messages from the mass media are seldom received and interpreted by isolated individuals. Reactions are influenced by the *social location* of the individual—the immediate social setting.[23]

---

[22] For a summary of the study, entitled, "Political Advertising: Voter Reaction to Televised Political Commercials," see John T. McQuiston, "T.V. Spots' Impact on Voter Studied," *New York Times*, February 17, 1974, p. 17. The above is a digest of the original article.
[23] See Eliot Freidson, "The Relation of the Social Situations of Contact to the

This view is consistent with studies that have demonstrated that media messages are usually not communicated to people in a direct way, but through various stages. Each stage involves personal influence. This is how it works. Within peer groups there are *opinion leaders*—people who exert a disproportionately greater influence on others. These opinion leaders exist in all occupational, social, and economic groups. They have subject matter interest and expertise. Some are likely to acquire political messages directly from the media and communicate them to their peers, who then, in turn, communicate them to others. Obviously, a little personal interpretation and filtering occur in the process.[24]

Something to think about
Who are the opinion leaders you know? What is their area of expertise?

Because of the various stages involved, messages usually take some time to get transmitted. For example, in January 1971, high Texas officials were identified as being part of what came to be known as the Sharpstown Bank scandal. It took nearly a year and a half before public awareness and revulsion built up to the point where Texas voters threw out of public office the governor, the lieutenant governor, the speaker of the house, and more than half the legislature.[25] The public reaction to Watergate and related incidents was similarly slow to take hold.

It is only when a particularly sensational news bulletin appears that this several-step flow of communication significantly disappears. One study of citizen reaction to President Lyndon Johnson's decision not to seek another term indicated that 75 percent of the respondents aware of LBJ's announcement learned of it instantly via the electronic media, principally television. An additional 17 percent learned of it later, but again from the media. Only 5 percent of those who knew about it heard it by word of mouth.[26]

Media in Mass Communication," *Public Opinion Quarterly*, Summer 1953, pp. 230–238.
[24] Katz and Lazarsfeld, *Personal Influence*, p. 32.
[25] Reported by Roscoe Drummond, "Will Congress Vote Real Reform?," *Christian Science Monitor*, December 12, 1973.
[26] See I. L. Allen and J. David Colfax, "The Diffusion of News on LBJ's March 31 Decision," *Journalism Quarterly*, Summer 1968, pp. 321–323.

Except for these major events, opinion leaders are a crucial part of each social setting. They communicate media messages by talking about them.[27] As they do this, their own perceptions, influenced by their experience, personalities, and values, surround and shape the message.

It would be particularly nice for activists to know who these opinion leaders are, or at least how to locate them. For without a doubt, they are crucial not only to the political socialization process, but to the communication process generally. However, locating them is difficult, for who they are depends on *situational, structural,* and *cultural* factors. Certain people may be more influential in some situations than in others. A nurse might be influential when dispensing medical advice to friends in *situations* requiring that kind of communication. Specific people may be particularly well situated to relay information because of the *structure* of the situation. The boss's private secretary may be the one who influences office workers. One study concluded that the group member who has the highest "centrality"— access to all others in the group—is most likely to be in control and to be more influential.[28] Others are particularly influential in transmitting *subcultural* information. Teenagers tell their parents about the latest music, the latest fads, etc.[29]

Regardless of their particular sphere of influence, opinion leaders read more magazines and books than non-opinion leaders, focusing, of course, on the subject associated with their leadership.[30] Interestingly, even with greater media exposure, public affairs opinion leaders do not acknowledge the effect of the media on *their* personal decisions. They attribute their own opinions to the influence of other people.[31]

A summary might be helpful at this point. Political socialization, we've said, is life-long, but particularly important in childhood. Basic orientations are acquired during this period. Of all the agents of polit-

---

[27] This process is ordinarily referred to as the two-step flow of communication. For summaries of related studies, see Elihu Katz, "The Two-Step Flow of Communications: An Up-to-Date Report on an Hypothesis," *Public Opinion Quarterly,* Spring 1957, pp. 61–78.

[28] Harold J. Leavitt, "Some Effects of Certain Communications Patterns on Group Performance," in *Readings on Social Psychology,* eds. Guy E. Swanson, Theodore M. Newcomb, and Eugene L. Hartley (New York: Henry Holt and Company, 1952).

[29] Katz and Lazarsfeld, *Personal Influence,* p. 118.

[30] *Ibid.,* p. 310.

[31] *Ibid.,* p. 318.

ical socialization with whom children come in contact, *parents* are most important. For adults, *peers* are the most important influence. They transmit political messages in subtle ways, often without meaning to do so. Among peers, influence in certain subject areas will vary. Different opinion leaders within each group will transmit messages that they find important and interesting, which they receive directly from the media, to their acquaintances (friends, coworkers, and relatives). Thus, the media usually play an important but indirect role in the political socialization of adults.

With this introduction to political socialization as background, action-oriented citizens must consider several crucial questions: To what extent can peer influence be used in any political campaign? Given the time it takes for media messages to be communicated, should the media be used? If peer and media influence are used in a campaign, can political orientations be influenced? In addition and more important, can political behavior be affected? The answers to the first two questions will depend on the resources of players involved, the environment in which the campaign is occurring, and the scope and length of the campaign. The answers to the final two questions should evolve out of the discussion that follows.

Influencing others.   We know a person has influence if conveying his or her point of view was one of the factors affecting the outcome of a decision or action. Leo Bogart introduces us to what this process of influence is all about and the conditions under which it occurs:

> An attempt to influence is less likely to be successful the more structured and familiar the subject of discussion, the greater the individual's emotional involvement with it, the less prestigious the source, and the more disparate the message from the individual's attitude source, and the more disparate the message from the individual's attitude at the start.[32]

This overview includes the basic ingredients of influence: the communicator, the message, the setting, and the audience.

Let's talk first about the *communicator*—the one trying to influence another person. How does the communicator affect whether or not someone is likely to be persuaded? It has to do with the communicator's *credibility*. Highly credible sources of information seem to have a substantially greater *immediate* effect on the audience's reac-

[32] Leo Bogart, *Silent Politics* (New York: John Wiley & Sons, 1972), p. 105.

tion.[33] Interestingly, the effect is not the result of the amount of attention paid to the message or the comprehension of the message. Rather, variations in the credibility of the source seem to influence the audience's motivation to accept the conclusions advocated.[34]

Credibility can have at least two bases. One is related to the communicator's *expertness* on a subject. If the communicator is perceived as expert, the message is perceived as true. The second has a social context. It is perceived *trustworthiness*. The same speaker may not appear trustworthy to two different groups.[35]

One experiment exploring the effect of a trustworthy communicator involved introducing the same communicator in different ways to two different audiences. With one group an introduction was used that was designed to arouse suspicion. The group was expected to infer that the communicator had something to gain from pushing the point. With the second group the introduction was designed to inspire belief in the speaker's impartiality. The speaker was introduced as an economist from a leading American university. With both groups the content of the speech and the conclusions were identical. Yet the speaker introduced as "motivated" was rated as less fair and honest and as having given a poorer presentation than the supposedly impartial speaker.

Something to think about

What does this suggest about what speakers to send to groups and about how a speaker should be introduced?

In this particular experiment, the amounts of attitude change did not vary.[36] Attitudes were probably reinforced and intensified. If attitudes were nonexistent, they may have been developed.

[33] S. W. Alper and T. R. Leidy find that unless other influences are introduced to support the original information, the long-range impact of a credible source is less certain. See "The Impact of Information Transmission through Television," *Public Opinion Quarterly*, Winter 1969–1970, pp. 556–562.

[34] See Carl I. Hovland, Irving L. Janis, and Harold H. Kelly, "Communication and Persuasion," in Michael A. Malec, ed., *Attitude Change* (Chicago: Markham Publishing Company, 1971), pp. 66–67. Originally published in Carl I. Hovland, et al., *Communication and Persuasion* (New Haven, Conn.: Yale University Press, 1953), pp. 269–281.

[35] Lerbinger, *Designs for Persuasive Communication*, p. 93.

[36] C. I. Hovland and Wallace Mandell, "An Experimental Comparison of Conclusion-Drawing by the Communicator and by the Audience," *Journal of Abnormal and Social Psychology*, July 1952, pp. 581–588. Also reported in Arthur K.

More than this may occur, however. Those theorists who focus on beliefs to explain attitude development and change argue that a credible communicator can more easily create an internal conflict that encourages attitude change. If a source credible to an audience denounces the ideas the audience is for and supports the ideas it is against, the audience should become disoriented and confused. This is an environment conducive to attitude change.[37]

In addition, and related to credibility, an important characteristic of the communicator is *prestige*. When prestige is attached to suggestions, they are more likely to influence. Attitudes may even be altered. Quite understandably, people are more likely to believe statements from those who are respected because of their position or expertise. Is this Walter Cronkite's advantage?

The relationship between prestige and attitudes was tested in an American college. A group of students was given a set of statements concerning conservative or liberal opinions. The students were asked to identify those with which they were in agreement. A month later the same test was again given. This time, however, the students were told that a number of eminent educators had accepted certain of the liberal views on the paper. The result was a shift toward the liberal end of the scale, obviously brought about by this prestige suggestion.[38] The permanence of this shift, if it is not reinforced, is doubtful, however.

If we compare the various characteristics of a communicator that are important in any attempt at influence, one is dominant—the degree to which the communicator is perceived as *trustworthy*. If the communicator can convey a sense of fairness and impartiality, aspects of trust, this should be even more effective than any prestige or expertness.[39]

Something to think about
How does a communicator convey trustworthiness?

Cohen, *Attitude Change and Social Influence* (New York: Basic Books, 1964), p. 25.

[37] Lerbinger, *Designs for Persuasive Communication*, p. 75.

[38] J. A. C. Brown, *Techniques of Persuasion* (Baltimore, Md.: Penguin Books, 1963), pp. 75–76.

[39] Cohen reviews the relevant studies, *Attitude Change and Social Influence*, pp. 26–27.

What about the *message?* It certainly must have something to do with whether or not particular attitudes get developed or altered.

Apparently, the way in which an argument is *organized* makes a difference. Hovland and his associates talk about using message *incentives.* These may include substantiating arguments so that the other person will judge the communicator's message as "true" or "correct." Or they may include both positive and negative appeals. *Positive* appeals are those that call attention to what can be gained by accepting the message. *Negative* appeals usually include words that arouse fear and depict the unpleasant consequences of a failure to accept the message.[40] The most effective appeals are likely to be those that serve as reassurances, that allow the audience to anticipate escaping from or averting the threat.[41]

Another kind of appeal that is sometimes used as a message incentive is one that is directed at group norms. When a message calls attention to the listener's *group membership,* if that membership is important, the message should be more believable. Arguments compatible with the group's norms are likely to be accepted; those that are in conflict are likely to be rejected.[42] So if a speaker were interested in convincing a taxpayer association that crimes without victims should no longer be classified as crimes, what appeal should be used?

In addition to the message, another aspect of the process of influence is the *setting* itself.

The most important way in which a setting can help to influence attitudes is through *social interaction.* J. A. C. Brown says that if a group can be created whose members feel a sense of belonging, an individual may begin to accept a new system of beliefs through this sense of belonging to the group.[43]

An experiment conducted several years ago clarifies this point. In this situation, group discussion encouraged a sense of belonging that in turn influenced attitudes and even behavior. The particular experiment involved six small groups of housewives living in the same neighborhood. They were divided into lecture and discussion situations. The aim was to determine whether a lecture or group discussion

---

[40] Hovland, Janis, Kelly, "Communication and Persuasion," p. 67.
[41] I. L. Janis and S. Feshbach, "Effects of Fear-Arousing Communication," *Journal of Abnormal and Social Psychology,* January 1953, pp. 78–92. Also described in Hovland, Janis, and Kelly, "Communication and Persuasion," p. 68.
[42] H. H. Kelly, "Salience of Membership and Resistance to Change of Group-Anchored Attitudes," *Human Relations,* August 1955, pp. 275–290.
[43] Brown, *Techniques of Persuasion,* p. 67.

could increase the home consumption of milk. The same person appeared at all group meetings, in some as a discussion leader, in others as a lecturer. The content was always the same. A checkup after two weeks and again after four weeks revealed that the *discussion*, and the group decision that followed it, was considerably more effective in increasing milk consumption and in changing family food habits than the lecture.[44]

Not to be overlooked, however, is the fact that the new attitude probably didn't conflict in any substantial way with other beliefs. If discussion groups had been established with the aim of convincing the members to believe something that was at odds with a previously held belief that had substantial social support outside the discussion group, behavior change would have been unlikely.[45]

When peer socialization was discussed, the importance of social interaction was explained. Indeed, it was emphasized that for adults, peers play the most crucial role in sustaining and developing political orientations. Depending on the degree of attachment to a peer group, the social situation can have two interesting effects, one predictable and one not so predictable. First, there will be greater *resistance* to altering those attitudes that have peer support. Second, however, there is a greater *willingness* to expose oneself to discussions with people holding opposing viewpoints. The strong group identification and sense of belonging seem to give people confidence in the attitudes they hold. This, in turn, allows them to venture into dangerous attitude territory.[46]

So a sense of group belonging can both encourage and restrict attitude development. It all depends on how important the individual perceives the group to be and how strongly initial attitudes are held.

---

[44] Kurt Lewin, "Group Discussion and Social Change," in *Readings in Social Psychology*, eds. Guy E. Swanson, Theodore M. Newcomb, and Eugene L. Hartley (New York: Henry Holt and Company, 1952), p. 466. Another study that demonstrates the impact of discussion as opposed to lecture groups is Jacob Levine and John Butler, "Lecture vs. Group Decision in Changing Behavior," *Journal of Applied Psychology*, February 1952, pp. 29–33. While these studies are not flawless, they offer some clues to the process through which groups can influence attitude development and change. Both are described in Katz and Lazarsfeld, *Personal Influence*, p. 75.

[45] An experiment substantiating this position is in E. B. Bennett, "Discussion, Decision, Commitment, and Consensus in Group Decision," *Human Relations*, August 1955, pp. 251–274.

[46] See Gary I. Schulman, "Who Will Listen to the Other Side? Primary and Secondary Group Support and Selective Exposure," *Social Problems*, Winter 1971, pp. 404–415.

Where new attitudes emerging in secondary groups (more impersonal social contexts) do not conflict with those reinforced by the primary group, and where discussion is used to encourage at least a minimum sense of belonging, new attitude development can occur.

The situation or setting, to summarize, influences attitude development and change by *socially* influencing the degree to which attitudes will be held or altered. Wherever a group sense of belonging exists or develops, attitudes consistent with the norms of that group will predominate. Secondary groups can produce new attitude development through the use of discussion techniques, as long as the new attitudes don't conflict with those held by primary groups. The stronger a person's feeling of belonging to a group, the more willing that person will be to be exposed to discordant attitudes, and the less likely the person will be to alter original attitudes.

A picture of the *audience* in the influence process has emerged from the discussion of these other ingredients. The fundamental point is that if the audience—the people whose attitudes others are trying to influence—is strongly committed to a group, it will resist messages that it perceives to be inconsistent with group norms.[47] As we know, the more intensely an attitude is held, the more resistant the person will be to change. Weakly held attitudes are the ones susceptible to change.[48] It would seem that these are the attitudes not consistently reinforced by peers or strengthened by any of the personal need-satisfying properties identified earlier.[49]

One other point about the behavior of audiences in attitude development and change situations is worth mentioning. Assume for the moment that a person's opinion is an honest reflection of an attitude. Studies seem to indicate that people will behave differently when they have been *forewarned* that someone wants to change their opinion.

Around 1770, Benjamin Franklin observed this same tendency. He put it this way:

The way to convince another is to state your case moderately and accurately. Then scratch your head, or shake it a little and say that

[47] H. H. Kelly and E. H. Volkart, "The Resistance to Change of Group-Anchored Attitudes," *American Sociological Review*, August 1952, pp. 453–465.
[48] P. H. Tannenbaum, "Initial Attitude Source and Concepts as Factors in Attitude Change through Communication," *Public Opinion Quarterly*, Summer 1956, pp. 413–425.
[49] Paul H. Wright discusses the conditions that could affect the fate of persuasive communication. "Attitude Change under Direct and Indirect Interpersonal Influence," *Human Relations*, May 1960, pp. 199–211.

is the way it seems to you, but of course you may be mistaken about it; which causes your listener to receive what you have to say and like as not, turn about and try to convince you of it, since you are in doubt. But if you go to him in a tone of positiveness and arrogance, you only make an opponent of him.[50]

Current research seems to support Benjamin Franklin. Indirect influence in the form of casual or nonpurposive conversation is more effective than direct influence. Without a forewarning the recipient of the remark does not have the critical and defensive frame of mind that is typical when people know that others are out to influence them.[51]

The response to the forewarning also depends on whether the audience has *expressed* an opinion or not. When they know in advance that someone is going to challenge an *unexpressed* opinion, people (the audience) will tend to tone down their own opinions in the subsequent discussion; there is nothing to lose by being accommodating. If the opinion has already been *expressed*, however, and then the audience is forewarned that it is going to be opposed, there is a strong likelihood that the opinion will be defended vigorously. Discussion resembling debate, it seems, polarizes the views of the committed and brings the uncommitted closer to the center.[52] Verbalizing a commitment to an attitude or opinion serves to strengthen it, as we saw earlier.

The previous discussion should suggest that influencing others is neither simple nor easy to accomplish. It should also suggest the particular difficulties involved in *changing* attitudes. Possessing an attitude implies commitment; individuals are to some degree involved in their positions. A more highly involved individual is more likely to reject alternative views. So it is the less committed person who might respond to persuasive communication.

Most political campaigns and general advertising campaigns pay particular attention to these people.[53] Those involved in campaigns believe that while attitudes are fixed tendencies to respond in certain

[50] From Readers Digest Association, *Getting the Most Out of Life* (Pleasantville, N.Y.: Readers Digest Association, 1946), p. 54. Also reported in Paul H. Wright, "Attitude Change under Direct and Indirect Interpersonal Influence," p. 199.
[51] See P. F. Lazarsfeld, B. Berelson, and H. Gandit, *The People's Choice: How the Voter Makes Up His Mind in a Presidential Campaign* (New York: Duell, Sloan & Pearce, 1944), pp. 152–153.
[52] Bogart, *Silent Politics*, p. 106.
[53] See Dan Nimmo, *The Political Persuaders* (Englewood Cliffs, N.J.: Prentice-Hall, 1970), p. 180. Also Carolyn W. Sherif, et al., *Attitude and Attitude Change* (Philadelphia: W. B. Saunders Company, 1965), pp. 11–17.

ways, these tendencies are often so vague in content that they may give rise to conflicting responses, depending on the stimuli. So, given the stable quality of attitudes, it makes more sense for the mass persuaders to contrive stimuli and settings that trigger a favorable response than to attempt to change attitudes.[54]

What guarantee is there that if a favorable response has been triggered, it will result in consistent behavior? What is the likelihood that a person who is convinced of the merit of an idea will act accordingly? Because most activists are interested in more than persuasion, the answer to this question is fundamental.

Attitudes and Action

The most obvious thing that can be said about the relationship between attitudes and action is that it is highly tenuous. People do not necessarily act in a way that is consistent with their expressed attitudes. Early studies of racial prejudice indicated, for example, that a person's verbal acceptance or rejection of minority groups might be quite unrelated to what that person would actually do in an open social situation.[55]

This doesn't mean that there is *no* relationship. However, predictions of likely behavior are more reliable if the person making the prediction understands to whom the individual or group looks for approval, acceptance, etc. It's the same old important element reappearing—personal influence. People's norms and guides to action are likely to be derived from family, friends, or other persons used as *reference groups*. In one study seeking to explain the relationship between attitudes and action, two-thirds of the people interviewed *acted* in a way that was consistent with their expressed attitudes and one-third in an inconsistent manner. For both groups, however, the possible approval or disapproval of reference groups was the crucial guide to behavior.[56]

---

[54] This approach is based on a theory of mass persuasion. See John C. Maloney, "Advertising Research and an Emerging Science of Mass Persuasion," *Journalism Quarterly*, Autumn 1964, pp. 157–528. Summarized in Nimmo, *The Political Persuaders*, pp. 31–33.

[55] See Richard T. La Piere, "Attitudes vs. Actions," *Social Forces*, December 1934, pp. 230–237; and Joseph D. Lohman and Dietrich C. Reitzes, "Deliberately Organized Groups and Racial Behavior," *American Sociological Review*, June 1954, pp. 342–348.

[56] Melvin L. De Fleur and Frank R. Westie, "Verbal Attitudes and Overt Acts: An Experiment on the Salience of Attitudes," *American Sociological Review*, December 1958, pp. 667–673.

"Understand what's going on in China? . . . I don't even understand Washington."

Mr. Graysmith/San Francisco Chronicle

Be careful. Don't equate expressed attitude change with probable behavior. The few studies that have been done on this subject indicate that expressed attitude changes are very poor predictors of subsequent behavior.[57]

One explanation of this discrepancy is that in order to produce a *stable* behavior change, a supporting environmental change must occur. For example, the person holding a new attitude must have it reinforced in some kind of consistent social setting. Otherwise, the same factors that produced the initial attitude (the one held prior to the change) and initial behavior will continue to operate to nullify the effect of the change.[58] Given what we know about adult socialization, particularly the influence of peers, this explanation seems plausible. It is one explanation criminologists use to explain the difficulty a drug addict who tries to "kick the habit" has. If the social environment isn't reinforcing, the addict rarely succeeds.

To introduce a different way of looking at the nebulous relation between attitudes and action, it is important to note that a change in behavior may not be related to a change in attitude. This could certainly be the case, for example, when people are expected to publicly conform, particularly when they are under surveillance (i.e., by a boss). Still, behavior changes without consistent attitude changes can gradually produce those attitude changes. Integration legislation, although initially resisted by many, has come to be accepted positively by a majority of the population.

Some observers think attitude change is following behavior change in the South. Although traditionally oriented toward the Democratic party, southerners have been voting for Republican presidential candidates—Eisenhower, Goldwater, and Nixon. These were the candidates whose political attitudes were perceived to be consistent with those of the voters. This continuing perceptual shift and habit of

---

[57] See N. Maccoby, A. K. Romney, J. S. Adams, and Eleanor E. Maccoby, *Critical Periods in Seeking and Accepting Information*, Paris-Stanford Studies in Communication (Stanford, Calif.: Institute for Communication Research, 1962); see also the article on the toilet training of children, E. Fleishmann, E. Harris, and H. Burtt, *Leadership and Supervision in Industry: An Evaluation of a Supervisory Training Program* (Columbus, Ohio: Ohio State University Bureau of Education Research, 1955); I. Janis and S. Feshbach, "Effects of Fear-Arousing Communication." All three studies are discussed in Leon Festinger, "Behavioral Support for Opinion Change," *Public Opinion Quarterly*, Fall, 1964, pp. 404–417.

[58] Leon Festinger, "Behavioral Support for Opinion Change."

voting for Republican presidential candidates seems to be producing a gradual movement to the Republican party among large numbers of Southern voters. Over time, the rewards of voting for a Republican presidential candidate seem to have reinforced or rationalized that action.[59]

Well, lets see where we are. To summarize the relation between attitudes and action, several points are clear. First, attitude change is very difficult because attitudes develop and are socially reinforced over time. So most persuaders concentrate on developing new attitudes consistent with those that already exist, or simply triggering a favorable response without tampering with attitudes at all. Second, *expressed* attitude change is a poor predictor of behavior. Attitude change and subsequent consistent behavior normally only occur when these changes are not in conflict with reference groups. In addition, unless they are socially reinforced, neither the attitude change nor the new behavior is likely to persist. The activist would do well to think through how peer groups, particularly reference groups, could be used to aid attitude development and change or perceptual shifts, and ultimately to influence desired political behavior. The research discussed in this chapter suggests *rules* to follow as one tries to persuade an audience. If observed, they should help distribute advantages to your side. While they offer no guarantee of success, they could significantly reduce the possibility of failure.

Key Words

Political socialization
Values
Beliefs
Attitudes
Opinion leaders
Message incentives
Reference groups

Suggested Activities

1. Attempt to reconstruct how you were politically socialized.
    a. Was a particular parent, friend, or acquaintance unusually influential?

[59] Nimmo, *The Political Persuaders,* p. 182.

    b. Did events influence your political socialization?

    c. In recent years have you experienced any *change* in your political attitudes or beliefs? Can you explain those changes?

2. Attempt to influence three or four people outside the class politically.

    a. What reaction did you get?

    b. How was their reaction related to your relationship and to their predispositions?

III
Techniques of
Persuasion

5
Direct Techniques of Persuasion

As activists try to mobilize support from potential players, they are usually involved in a two-step tactical process. The first step is *educational*. It involves using various techniques of communication to get people to increase the *attention* they pay to a situation and their *comprehension* of the situation. The second step is *persuasion*. It involves getting people to *yield* to what they now comprehend.

The last chapter introduced some of the research relevant to persuasion. By focusing on how political orientations develop and change, the conditions under which attempts at persuasion might be successful were identified. What hasn't been considered thus far are particular techniques that can be used in both stages. This is the concern of this section. What tactics work?

First things first. Before we look at techniques, direct and indirect, we need to know something about educational campaigns generally and communication specifically.

About Educational Campaigns

Educational campaigns, which culminate, hopefully, in persuasion, may be *long-term* or *short-term*. Long-term campaigns are frequently those requiring an actual attitude shift or change. On the other hand, short-term campaigns may only require the acquisition of an opinion and a consistent form of political behavior (i.e., a consistent vote).

For example, various groups in this country are trying to change the public attitude toward marijuana. Specifically, they are trying to change public attitudes toward its being dangerous and ultimately toward its being illegal. This long-term campaign has involved the widespread publication of any medical reports favorable to this point of view and the promotion of arguments dealing with the high cost to taxpayers of classifying marijuana use as criminal. Initiative campaigns in several cities and states have been one vehicle used to increase discussion of the issue. The proponents of decriminalizing marijuana use expect no immediate policy results, only an eventual change in attitude that will be conducive to those results. Their entire strategy and tactics are based on this long-range approach.

Short-term campaigns are more obvious. They usually are directed toward a specific legislative or executive proposal, but election of a candidate also involves a short-term persuasive campaign. The scope of these efforts varies. They range in magnitude from a few newspaper advertisements to campaigns involving outlays of millions of dollars. V. O. Key, Jr. described the large-scale, but short-term, program of the American Medical Association in 1950. The AMA was opposing any form of national health insurance. Prior to the campaign, congressional mail was running 2½ to 1 in favor of health insurance; nine months later it ran 4 to 1 against it.[1]

In addition to being long- or short-term, educational campaigns may be *direct, indirect,* or both. Direct campaigns involve person-to-person attempts at education and persuasion. Indirect ones involve a mass medium that separates the proponent of a cause from his or her audience. Whatever the approach and duration, and these will be discussed shortly, the campaign must involve effective communication. In this chapter we deal with direct techniques of persuasion. However, many of the principles of communication are applicable to both types.

Communication

Saul Alinsky said that a person could lack any of the qualities of an organizer save one and still be effective and successful. The exception

[1] Valdimer O. Key, Jr., *Politics, Parties, and Pressure Groups,* 5th ed. (New York: Thomas Y. Crowell Company, 1964), p. 132.

is the art of communication. It doesn't matter what you know about anything if you cannot communicate. Without that ability, you're just not in the game. In *Rules for Radicals* he described how communication occurs:

> Communication with others takes place when they understand what you're trying to get across to them. If they don't understand, then you are not communicating regardless of words, pictures, or anything else. People only understand things in terms of their experience, which means you must get within their experience. Further, communication is a two-way process. If you try to get your ideas across to others without paying attention to what they have to say to you, you can forget about the whole thing.[2]

Something to think about
What communication techniques would allow an activist to "get within the experience" of your student body?

The process of communicating a new idea, then persuading people of the idea and seeing it acted on positively, first requires that audience attention and interest be developed. To do this the communicator needs to know several things. The communicator must know the *audience*, the *objective*, how to *motivate* an audience, and how to *research* the subject. In addition, the communicator must know how to make the presentation, whether written or verbal, *understandable*, and how to select the appropriate *medium* for communicating it.[3]

Establishing the *objective* is the place to start. After determining whether it is to be a long-term or short-term objective, the problem is to make it *realistic*. The objective of persuading the residents of a lumber town to support a building moratorium would hardly seem realistic. However, the same residents might ultimately be convinced, through education, that building and conservation are not necessarily incompatible. What follows is a description of a public information campaign designed to reduce the number of highway traffic accidents. Planned by the Communication Arts Center of the University of Denver, the campaign involved establishing what are called "middle-range objectives." While this particular effort relied on indirect forms

2 Saul Alinsky, *Rules for Radicals* (New York: Random House, 1971), p. 81.
3 Howard Bloomenthal discusses each of these components of effective communication in *Promoting Your Cause* (New York: Funk and Wagnalls, 1971), pp. 4–26. © 1971 by Howard Bloomenthal. Used by permission of Funk and Wagnalls Publishing Co., Inc.

of communication, the message about objectives is applicable to either type.

An Informational Campaign Designed to Generate
Public Self-awareness

If an information campaign starts with the assumption that large segments of its potential audience will be indifferent, it becomes essential to identify targets well before the campaign is actually implemented. However, before targets can be delineated, the objectives of the campaign must be spelled out explicitly, specifically, and realistically. For example, suppose a mass communications information campaign is to be launched for the purpose of effecting control over highway traffic accidents in which bad drivers are involved. The first targeting task is to pinpoint "bad drivers." Research accumulated over time has indicated that in at least eight out of ten cases operators of motor vehicles consider themselves to be either good or excellent drivers. Additionally, studies conducted by the Center showed that for the most part drivers tended to ignore the more than 300,000 persuasive traffic safety messages that appear annually in our print media alone.* How then should a mass media information campaign be directed to "bad drivers"— given the conditions that the great majority of vehicle operators consider themselves to be "good drivers," and that most people tend to ignore most traffic safety messages most of the time? Further, what can such an information campaign really expect to accomplish—the elimination of *all* highway accidents; the abolition of a small proportion of accidents? Indeed, is it feasible to believe that mass communications by themselves can do anything at all either to eliminate or to reduce such complex phenomena as highway traffic accidents?

Questions such as these immediately came to the fore when the Center was asked to participate in developing a television traffic safety program together with the Columbia Broadcasting System and the National Safety Council. It was clear from the beginning that if public indifference to traffic safety information was to be overcome, a completely innovative format designed to attract a high level of public attention must be developed. Second, it became obvious that the stereotyped didactic approach, which simply tries to inform people that they may be bad drivers, would be met with audience resistance. Consequently, it was considered vital to develop techniques whereby potential viewers of the proposed programming would be given some insights into their driving defi-

---

* See H. Mendelsohn, *Mass Communication for Safety: A Critical Review and a Proposed Theory* (Chicago: National Safety Council, 1963). Also, H. Mendelsohn, *The Dogmas of Safety* (Denver: Communication Arts Center, University of Denver, 1967) (offset).

ciencies without offending them. Finally, it was thought necessary to afford potential viewer-drivers the opportunity of actually doing something about correcting whatever deficiencies they were able to uncover. In short, it was decided that a television program directed to the driving public would be developed in pursuit of three middle-range objectives and no more: (1) to overcome public indifference to traffic hazards which may be caused by bad driving; (2) to make bad drivers cognizant of their deficiencies; (3) to direct viewers who become aware of their driving deficiencies into social mechanisms which had already been set up in the community to correct such deficiencies.

Note the specificity of these objectives. They are succinct, reasonable, and amenable to objective post hoc evaluation. Realizing that propaganda alone cannot alter the incidence of traffic accidents per se, it was decided to opt for a lower-level effect manifestation.

Communications researchers, traffic safety experts, and television production personnel combined their expertise in implementing the objectives they themselves had promulgated. What resulted from this mix was "The CBS National Drivers Test."

Aired originally just prior to the 1965 Memorial Day holiday weekend, "The National Drivers Test" attempted to attract maximum public attention by publicizing the program in a massive promotional campaign. All in all, some 50 million official test answer forms were distributed via newspapers, magazines, and petroleum products dealers throughout the nation prior to air-time.

"The National Drivers Test" sought to overcome both prior public apathy and overconfidence in its ability to operate motor vehicles correctly by allowing drivers to measure their own abilities and then to decide for themselves whether or not they were sufficiently proficient. If drivers discovered themselves to be less accomplished than they had expected, they were directed to enroll in driver improvement programs which were already available in their communities.

During the airing of the program and afterward, evaluation research was carried out in order to determine the program's success in meeting the specific objectives it had set up for itself. In introducing his book, *The National Drivers Test* (Random House, New York, 1965), Warren V. Bush, the producer of the program, summed up the immediate effects of the presentation:

> The response was enormous, beyond all expectations. One of the highest public-affairs broadcast of all time, "The National Drivers Test" was viewed by approximately 30 million Americans. Within days following the broadcast, CBS News had received mail responses from nearly a million and a half viewers.
>
> Most importantly, preliminary research indicated that nearly 40 percent of the cross-section of *licensed* drivers who had par-

ticipated in the broadcast had failed to pass The National Drivers Test. Perhaps it is this kind of individual self-discovery that is the necessary first step to genuine self-improvement. (pp. x–xi)

It should also be pointed out that according to the National Safety Council, some 35,000 drivers actually enrolled in driver improvement programs throughout the nation following the initial telecast of the "Test."

In terms of the specific goals set, the first airing of the program was judged to have been effective. In addition to the 30 million viewers who were made aware of certain high-risk traffic hazards, at least 600,000 individuals were made to realize their own driving deficiencies and presumably the need to correct them in some way. The 35,000 who actually enrolled in driver training and improvement courses immediately following the first airing of the program represented an estimated threefold increase in previous *total annual* voluntary enrollments in such courses. One need not go much beyond these gross figure to realize that the one-hour program was effective well beyond any prior expectations on the part of the planners.

The lessons learned from this exercise suggest that innovative information-giving formats, abetted by strong prior promotion, can overcome preexisting so-called public apathy to a great degree. Second, it is clear that reasonable middle-range goals, narrowly defined and explicitly stated, can be successfully accomplished.[4]

The highway traffic campaign just described illustrates the relation between establishing objectives and knowing the audience. That understanding can come only from a systematic analysis of the audience.

What, precisely, should one know about the *audience* in order to effectively communicate? What tendencies are apparent? The questions below can be a guide:

1. What *general group* does the audience represent? Does it consist largely of homemakers, students, laborers, proprietors of small businesses, etc.?
2. What *specific group* or organization does it represent? Is it a political party, a church group, or a service club? Does the group have a particular point of view? What is its status in the community?
3. What are the *general characteristics* of the audience? Is the audience homogeneous or heterogeneous in terms of cultural or envi-

---

[4] Harold Mendelsohn, "Some Reasons Why Information Campaigns Can Succeed," *Public Opinion Quarterly*, Spring 1973. This case study is reprinted from pp. 50–61. Reprinted by permission.

ronmental background? What is the general educational level? Do the members of the audience have common interests?

4. What are the *specific characteristics* of the audience? Are any specific characteristics, such as sex, age, religion, or political affiliation, identifiable?
5. What are the probable *motivations* of the audience? Does it represent the satisfied or dissatisfied elements of the community— the haves or the have-nots? Can its probable aspirations, expectations, and goals be identified?
6. What is the likely *attitude* of the audience toward the communicator? [5]

Something to think about
What did the Communication Arts Center know about its audience?

Particularly relevant to direct communication, the answers to these questions will provide an audience profile. That profile, then, can help define the communication objective or, if the objective has been predetermined, help the communicator predict the likely effect. For example, the profile could suggest how interested the audience might be. If the audience consists of 18- to 25-year-old men and the objective is to persuade them that the military draft should be restored, the audience will probably be very interested and perhaps hostile.

The next step in the communication planning process, *motivational analysis,* is a difficult one for political activists, for motivation involves many factors that incite and direct an individual's actions.

One approach to understanding motivation is the classic drive model. According to this approach, a person who experiences a deficiency or disruption in himself or herself or the surroundings seeks to correct the situation in order to restore some internal balance. So a *motive* is the internal stimulus that impels a person to act in a way that reduces the tension that originally created the motive.[6]

Some assumptions are basic to this approach. One is that people are goal-seeking; they are constantly striving to reduce the tensions within them. As they do, they successfully adjust to the environment.

[5] These audience analysis questions are from Jan Eisenson, J. Jeffrey Auer, and John V. Irwin, *The Psychology of Communications* © 1963, pp. 279–280. Reprinted by permission of Prentice-Hall, Inc.
[6] For further information, see Neal E. Miller and John Dollard, *Social Learning and Imitation* (New Haven, Conn.: Yale University Press, 1941), pp. 18–21.

A second is that they can be influenced from the outside. A communicator does not have to view motives as innate. Relying on these two assumptions, W. Phillips Davison makes this point about communication:

> The communicator can influence attitudes or behavior only when he is able to convey information that may be utilized by members of his audience to satisfy their wants or needs. If he has control of some significant aspect of his audience's environment, his task may be an easy one. All he must do is tell people about some environmental change or expected change that is important to them.[7]

Something to think about

What did the Communication Arts Center conclude was necessary to motivate its audience?

Probably the best known application of this approach to motivation is in the field of marketing. Ernest Dichter, a psychologist specializing in motivational research, applies his results to designing soap, automobiles, or just about anything else that can be sold. He illustrates the same tension-reducing approach to motivation by discussing his longing for a car:

> I am unhappy with my car for a number of reasons. My children have complained about the fact that it looks shabby and all their friends have much better-looking and new cars. Furthermore, I read in the papers about new cars. I see advertisements extolling the improvements of the new cars. Finally, something minor happens to my car, which could easily be repaired, but it provides the final stimulus to visit a showroom and to shop for a new car. What happened as far as my motivations were concerned? Why indeed did I buy this new car? . . .
>
> The tension differential, borrowing this term from the physical sciences, has become so great that the action is finally triggered off.[8]

It is apparent from Dichter's account that motivation research applied to marketing involves *discovering* consumer motives related to

---

[7] W. Phillips Davison, "On the Effects of Communication," *Public Opinion Quarterly*, Fall 1959, p. 359. These assumptions and Davison's application are also in Otto Lerbinger, *Designs for Persuasive Communication* (Englewood Cliffs, N.J.: Prentice-Hall, 1972), pp. 80–81.

[8] Ernest Dichter, *The Strategy of Desire* (Garden City, N.Y.: Doubleday & Company, 1958), p. 38.

a product and *reshaping* the product—actually or psychologically—so that its ability to satisfy the discovered needs is more obvious. The product is assigned a suitable personality and status, so to speak.[9]

Not without controversy, motivational research has also been applied to marketing political candidates and issues. In both direct and indirect campaigns, audience analysis allows motives to be discovered.[10] Then appeals that will link up with people's motives are built into messages. Attitude change is not necessary.

Something to think about

How would a campaign manager discover the motives of the electorate? How would the manager then shape the candidate to appeal to these motives? Do you have any feelings about the ethics of this process?

After motivation analysis, the next thing to think about is carefully researching the subject matter.[11] Get facts, opinions, reasons, and examples. Then, remembering the principles of message design and organization discussed in the last chapter, plan the approach.

Even with all this preparation, effective communication ultimately requires the obvious—being understandable. Try to be *concise* and *clear*. Say what you mean and only what you mean. Specify precisely what action is being called for, if the campaign is action-oriented. Use language that is familiar to the specific audience. Interject only one idea at a time, then develop it and present it in the most human way possible.[12]

Communication that does not employ the appropriate *medium* can be wasted. If it doesn't serve as a transmission line between you and your audience, it has failed. Even with direct forms of communication, the basic criterion for choosing the medium is: Will it transmit what you want to say to the people you want to say it to? Will it reach the right audience? For example, will a telephone enable you

---

[9] Lerbinger, *Designs for Persuasive Communication*, p. 83.

[10] Ordinarily this is done through depth interviews that allow selected respondents to answer open-ended questions and to associate freely. Various projective tests usually supplement this technique. For technique illustrations, see Dichter, *The Strategy of Desire*, pp. 283–288.

[11] One particularly good source on how to research is Donald K. Ross, A *Public Citizens' Action Manual* (New York: Grossman Publishers, 1973).

[12] Bloomenthal, *Promoting Your Cause*, pp. 19–24.

to get the message through, or is it too impersonal? Other criteria are the degree of confidence your audience has in each medium and the degree to which they use it. Of course, using more than one medium will reinforce and intensify a message.[13]

Choosing Direct Techniques

Assuming media and audience analysis have been completed, the research has been carefully completed, and the objective realistically set, what would make the activist use direct techniques of communication?

Of all the ways of communicating, those involving direct personal contact are the most effective. This is fortunate for the average citizen who at some time gets concerned about a problem and needs to do something that requires political action. The citizen should know that if the rules are followed, contacting public officials personally and/or talking directly to citizens' groups are potentially very effective tactics. Even the most professional, large-scale campaigns will supplement elaborate media communication with direct contact if they have "people" resources available.

Direct forms of communication vary. The choice will depend on whether the activist is interested in contacting an individual, a small group, or a large audience. Lobbying a public official, having a personal discussion with a potential financial contributor, canvassing a neighborhood, and writing letters to or telephoning would-be supporters are examples of one-to-one communication. Small-group discussions or more formal public-speaking activity are the two main ways of communicating directly to groups.

Now, how do these approaches work, and more important, do they?

Prestige Conversations

Let's say that a person has just become aware of a problem and wants to convince someone with some prestige that the problem exists and needs resolution. Obviously the prestige factor is perceived as important, because the person thinks, "who would take *me* seriously?" It can be important because getting the support of someone who has special status can give the activist leverage. It can help the activist

[13] *Ibid.*, pp. 28–30.

gain access to community organizations, the media, or other prestige people. Public officials, a college professor or president, a professional person with publicly recognized expertise, and a well-known cleric are examples of prestige contacts.

But how can Joe or Sarah Nobody get these people to listen? Identifying a prestige person who has had a similar interest in the past would help. Daily papers covering related problems contain names. An activist who is informed, sounds serious, and is patient should be able to make an appointment with someone in this category—particularly a public official who has a vested interest in being perceived as responsive. If that initial appointment should prove difficult to obtain, forming a small organization and/or obtaining signatures from other citizens who have a similar concern will help. This provides the added leverage that may be needed for even the first contact.

Once the appointment has been made, the citizen should follow the communication rules and think about the principles of persuasion. Every face-to-face contact takes preparation, and unless a prestige person is convinced the first time around, the opportunity may well be lost.

While conversing with one other person is a particularly effective means of communicating because ambiguous information can be immediately cleared up and otherwise undetected nuances can be noted, it does pose some unique problems. First, the communicator has less control over the content because it can be influenced by both parties to the conversation. This doesn't happen as easily when the communicator is formally addressing an audience. So, in a one-to-one conversation the person attempting to influence has to be prepared for changes in direction. Second, even conversations that are face-to-face can lead to verbal confusion, in part because the communicator can't stick to a prepared script. Knowing thoroughly the problem to be discussed and the action being recommended helps, but there are some rules for conversations that should be followed.[14]

1. *Talk about reality*   Resist the other person's attempts to discuss the words used rather than the reality they represent. This may require saying every now and then, "I don't believe I said

[14] These rules are elaborated on in Bloomenthal, *Promoting Your Cause*, pp. 47–59.

that. What I thought I said was. . . ." To know whether or not the listener has indeed understood the message, get some feedback —conversational clues to whether or not you've gotten through.

2. *Avoid judgments*   Perhaps the other person in the conversation will not be entirely cooperative. Maybe the person disagrees with either the way the problem is being explained or the approach being recommended. Ask the other person for his or her point of view. Try to remain open and nonjudgmental. Failing to do so will inhibit the development of the conversation and may keep you from accepting the other person's perfectly good suggestion. If you know in advance that the other person will disagree with some points, start with points of agreement, then proceed to the more sensitive areas.

3. *Use silence*   People are ordinarily afraid of gaps in a conversation. Silence can allow your idea to take hold, can provide evidence that you are thoughtfully considering the other person's point of view, and can serve to emphasize particular points.

4. *Organize yourself and your thoughts*   Relying on the information about message design previously discussed, organize your thoughts in some logical order. Do not overdo it; limit the number of ideas you are trying to communicate. Prepare yourself by remembering to be yourself. Regardless of the prestige of the other person, if you are sincere, informed, and have an important concern, being yourself in the conversation will be effective.

5. *Maintain eye contact*   Eye contact does a variety of things in a conversation: It sustains the other person's involvement in what you have to say; it demonstrates your interest while listening; and if a third person is present who should be involved in the conversation, eye contact with that person can draw him or her into the conversation.

6. *End the conversation on time*   Unless a designated amount of time has been set aside for the conversation, it is sometimes difficult to know when to end it. Look for clues. People show when they begin to mentally "tune out." Their eyes start to wander, their voices lose some intensity, they interrupt at illogical moments or make comments that are not responsive to what has just been said. Ideally, the conversation should be ended before these signs are evident, and it should be ended with a reminder of what you are requesting, what the next step will be, and, obviously, a word of thanks—even if the conversation is unsuccessful.

Letter-writing

Using the same rules of communication and principles of persuasion, letter-writing campaigns can be another important direct technique.[15] A particularly important rule, in this case, is personal influence. If people write to people they know, to their friends, they are more likely to be effective. Or if a prestigious person in the community, state, or nation lends his or her name to a campaign, and the letter appears to be from that person, it can also be effective.

Both these approaches are frequently used in fund-raising campaigns. For example, individuals are asked to write to 10 friends each, soliciting contributions to a cause. Personal influence makes it far more difficult to refuse a request from a friend than from a stranger. In addition, friends are more likely to persuade one another that an issue is worth supporting. Or a prestige person will sometimes allow a fund-raising letter to be sent to others in his or her name. Knowing the leverage a credible communicator and/or reference individual has, the activist should not hesitate to use this technique. A letter sent by a prestigious organization can have the same effect if the recipient respects the organization and the causes it normally promotes.

Telephone Contact

Because of the strength of personal influence, telephone communication should also be considered in any persuasive campaign. If such communication is properly organized, a particular message can reach more people quickly in that way than in any other direct way.

A telephone network is an important organizational asset for established groups or groups trying to get established. Large numbers of members can be notified and activated immediately. This is how Common Cause, the interest group, structures its telephone network. At the top of the pyramid is the *network coordinator*, next come *activators*, and below them *telephoners*. When members need to be contacted, the coordinator phones the activators. Each activator is responsible for maintaining a year-round team of six to eight telephoners. Under the coordinator's direction, the activators alert telephoners to make their calls and pass on necessary information. Also, these activators will relay the telephoners' results to the coordinator. The telephoners themselves are responsible for actually conveying the

---

[15] The effectiveness and rules of writing letters to public officials will be discussed in subsequent chapters.

essential message to between five and ten members. Ordinarily they alert them to crucial lobbying situations requiring action (i.e., letters and telephone calls to key legislators). When they have made their calls, they report to the activator how many members were reached and the names of anyone who may have dropped out or moved.

According to organization leaders, this highly structured telephone network has been a primary reason for the group's success. Through it, Common Cause is able to *control* an important resource—its members.

Canvassing

Canvassing involves talking to people in or around their homes. It is the most *certain* way of getting information out to a large number of individuals, but it is by no means the easiest or quickest. This is certainly true in get-out-the-vote campaigns, one of the most common reasons for canvassing. A get-out-the-vote experiment conducted by a graduate seminar at the University of Michigan required an investment of 400 hours to induce 39 persons out of 203 probable nonvoters to vote, a cost of 10 person-hours per vote.[16]

As costly in time as this technique is, if people are available, it should be used. Compared with contacting people in other ways (i.e., distributing literature by mail and telephone canvassing), it seems to be *the most* effective method of affecting voter behavior.[17] More precisely, face-to-face canvassing makes people more likely to vote, it increases interest in a particular campaign, and it even makes people feel more politically effective.[18] In elections that are rather dull and uninteresting, canvassing becomes particularly important for the group with a stake in the outcome. It can actually result in *persuasion*, as opposed to merely getting favorably inclined people to the polls.[19]

Persuasion is not, however, the *usual* effect of canvassing. At best it normally influences voter preferences not by producing conversions, but by reinforcing voting habits and reducing the likelihood of defections from a candidate or cause.[20]

[16] Samuel J. Eldersveld, "Experimental Propaganda Techniques and Voting Behavior," *American Political Science Review*, March 1956, pp. 154–165.
[17] Michael Lupfer and David E. Price, "On the Merit of Face-to-Face Campaigning," *Social Science Quarterly*, December 1972, pp. 534–543.
[18] Lester W. Milbrath, *The Washington Lobbyist* (Chicago: Rand McNally & Company, 1963), pp. 41 and 58. Reprinted by permission.
[19] Raymond E. Wolfinger, "The Influence of Precinct Work on Voting Behavior," *Public Opinion Quarterly*, Fall 1963, pp. 387–398.
[20] Lupfer and Price observed, however, actual persuasion effects from door-to-

Given what has been said about the role of personal influence in the political socialization process, the superiority of face-to-face canvassing is understandable. This direct personal contact, like conversations, draws attention to the message for a longer period of time than other forms of communication. In addition, it gives the communicator instant feedback from the listener so that the message can be modified if it hasn't been understood or well received.[21]

If canvassing does become part of an educational persuasive campaign, some rules might help.

1. Canvass, if possible, in *groups of two*, preferably with one man and one woman. Since homes are frequently visited when one person in a couple is away, access will be easier.
2. An inexperienced canvasser should join an *experienced* one.
3. *Carry something* with you—a leaflet, a petition, or an information packet. Canvassers need a reason for coming to people's doors beyond the issue itself.[22]
4. Know *what you are talking about*, not just how you feel about the issue. Be prepared to answer questions, but don't overwhelm anyone with information.
5. *Avoid anger*, recriminations, and long arguments. They won't help, and this will save the canvasser's energy.
6. *Ask for action*—a signature on a petition, turnout at the polls, support in the coming election for a particular issue or candidate, attendance at a forthcoming neighborhood meeting, etc.
7. Note who would benefit from a *return visit*, either on the day of an election or in general.

Most of these rules were followed by Republicans working on the 1964 presidential election. Canvassing was a major tactic employed in the Goldwater campaign. Canvassers were urged to work in pairs, and couples were recruited from activists in local civic organizations. Generally, they were people familiar with suburban neighborhoods. Detailed instructions from the national headquarters advised canvassers to carry flashlights and never enter the house. That precaution was not

door canvassing in their study of the 1970 U.S. Senate race in Tennessee between incumbent Albert Gore and Republican Congressman William Brock. "On the Merit of Face-to-Face Campaigning."

21 *Ibid.*, p. 542.
22 Michael Walzer discusses these and other things to remember about canvassing. *Political Action* (Chicago: Quadrangle Books, 1971), pp. 97–98.

for reasons of safety, but for reasons of expediency. It uses up too much time.

This was the suggested conversation:

> "Good evening, Mr. or Mrs. _____. I'm _____, and this is _____. We are volunteers calling tonight to ask you to vote for Barry Goldwater for president. May we count on your vote?"
>
> "We also want you to vote for the other Republican candidates. May we count on your vote for them?"
>
> "We want you to know that we think enough of your vote and our candidate to come by and ask you to vote for them."

The canvassing effort was enormous. Almost 3,400,000 voters in 912 counties in 46 states were contacted. When canvassing was completed, what residents told canvassers proved to be an excellent predictor of the percentage of popular votes Goldwater later received.[23]

So canvassing, prestige conversations, telephone contact, and writing letters are four frequently used direct-communication techniques. Which to use depends on the reason for the contact as well as the resources of the individual or group involved. Each is effective because it allows for flexible communication and personal influence. The face-to-face approaches, however, have additional attention-drawing advantages.

Next to be considered are *direct contacts with groups*. Not nearly as costly in time or people, communicating in small discussion groups as well as large groups through public-speaking engagements can educate as well as persuade. Before getting into actual techniques, a few things should be noted about groups in general.

While people communicating indirectly through the mass media direct their messages to *secondary groups* (members of the community, state, or nation; workers; young people; etc.), those involved in discussions or public-speaking engagements are frequently directing their messages to *primary groups*. The unique characteristic of this type of group, as we know from the last chapter, is that these are face-to-face associations. The people in them know or at least recognize one another; they communicate with one another over a span of time.

---

[23] From John H. Kessel, *The Goldwater Coalition* (Indianapolis and New York: The Bobbs-Merrill Company, 1968). Also reported in Dan Nimmo, *The Political Persuaders* (Englewood Cliffs, N.J.: Prentice-Hall, 1970), p. 21.

Not all primary groups are alike, and anyone from outside a group who plans to persuade the individuals in it should know its characteristics. There are seven specific characteristics that seem to differentiate groups. Thinking about them should make *group analysis* easier.[24]

1. *Group conformity*   In discussing the political socialization process, the conformity-producing effect of groups—particularly peer groups—was noted. Individuals tend to act in ways that will gain recognition, admiration, respect, or approval from significant groups. The degree to which group members conform should influence both the content of the message and the way it is delivered.

2. *Group prejudices*   Among strongly cohesive groups, prejudice of one sort or another is not rare. Environmentalists may be prejudiced against builders, trade unionists against management, faculty against school administrators. While these may also be prejudices of individual members, the group, if it is cohesive, will intensify them.

3. *Group resistance to change*   Individuals, we know, have difficulty accepting new ideas. Group resistance is usually even greater. It is important to think about the *degree* to which a particular group is likely to resist change and *how* it might resist.

4. *Group structure*   Large groups often have subgroups or particular ways of structuring themselves to make their interaction easier. Knowing the structure will help one understand both the internal process of communication and the process of control.

5. *Group values*   Each group has a set of values or goals. Analyzing them will help an outsider understand how the group is likely to behave (i.e., react toward a particular idea).

6. *Group patterns of decision*   How are decisions in the group made—by one person, by a small executive committee, or by the group as a whole? What group decision rules prevail—are decisions made by majority vote or by consensus? If a speaker is calling for group support and action, knowing who the decision makers are and how decisions are made is crucial.

7. *Group patterns of discussion*   Some groups encourage free, open discussion; others restrict informal communication. Whether a formal presentation should be made to the group or a discussion approach used will be influenced by this characteristic.

---

[24] Eisenson et al., *The Psychology of Communication*, pp. 256–258.

Discussion Groups

Gilman Elementary School encourages parent participation in the total operation of the school. For this approach to be successful, parents must attend regular meetings. There is no group leader per se. Instead, parents, teachers, and administrators establish objectives through open, and often intense, discussion. Planning for the implementation of objectives is also the focus of the discussion. Because participants *care* about making this approach to public education succeed, they realize the importance of participation. They attend regularly.

Discussion groups, such as the one at the Gilman School, are particularly conducive to attitude development. They are a setting that can easily trigger a favorable response. Moreover, as noted in the last chapter, discussion groups are even conducive to attitude change. The reason has something to do with the special forces operating in a discussion situation as opposed to a passive group setting. For example, a greater *cohesiveness* is likely to develop—an attraction to the group. A higher level of *motivation* and greater *coordination* are also likely to develop. Individual members are more likely to discover *common goals*. This, in turn, promotes a common definition of and attempt to realize *group goals*. Finally, because there is great *internal interaction* —every member is both a speaker and a listener—common values, beliefs, and attitudes are more frequently and intensely communicated.[25]

All these special forces were operating in the Gilman discussion group. As a result, participants were willing to try new approaches to education. They were *persuaded* that particular educational alternatives were worth a try. But these results are not unusual, according to the research available.[26] A number of important things can and do happen as a result of the discussion setting, for example:

1. Both attitudes and overt behavior can be significantly altered.
2. Participants are more likely to feel personal involvement in a problem and greater responsibility for any decisions made to deal with it. This is particularly true if the decision was arrived at on the basis of consensus.
3. Those who reach conclusions through discussion tend to hold on to them more tenaciously, if they are reinforced.

Still, if an activist tries to use an existing discussion group as the

[25] *Ibid.*, pp. 264–265.
[26] *Ibid.*, pp. 267–268.

target of a persuasive effort, there are several problems. First, the activist must gain the trust of the group. The activist must demonstrate a willingness to be a participant. If an activist has an interest consistent with the group's goals, and can articulate the common ground, trust should evolve. If the activist is known by other participants or represents an organization that is respected by the group, the development of trust will be facilitated.

However, a second problem must be considered. As with prestige conversations, in a discussion group it is difficult to control the direction of the communication. The activist-participant must use any opportunity that presents itself to contribute relevant information and to move the group toward the consideration of the objective. Most groups will provide the available "space," since the members were interested enough initially to invite the activist to participate. If the goal is to trigger a favorable response rather than to alter attitudes, the special factors operating in the group should make up for any loss of control.

Let's take a look at another discussion situation where the activist is keeping group characteristics in mind. Penny was invited to talk about "what she is into" with a small, very cohesive group of women. In this case the women were feminists who had been meeting for a prolonged period to discuss in personal ways the problems women face. While the group ordinarily did not ask "outsiders" to come to meetings, an exception was made. Penny was a friend of a regular participant and was a feminist. Besides allowing her access, these two factors also tended to promote trust.

One problem Penny knew she would face was skepticism about any significant change occurring politically. She knew that most of the people who would be present believed that social change begins at the personal level. It would be difficult to get the group to support her cause, the election of feminist political candidates, or even to recognize elections as a viable means of change. Still, because she and the women's organization she represented were so committed to the importance of dealing with social problems at the political level, she would persist.

At the meeting, after establishing her own feminist orientation, she confronted the problems directly. Not wanting to negate the norms of the group, she explained why she believed working for change at the political level was not inconsistent with approaching it at the personal level. Indeed, she argued, they were complementary.

She hoped to establish the relationship between her cause and the group's activity and norms.

Penny's particular manner of communicating in the discussion group also tended to complement the nature of the group. She knew that the group communicated very personally, and that it was informal and open. She obviously couldn't try to persuade the group by using a lengthy, highly statistical presentation. If she did, not only would it be difficult to start a discussion, but attitudes about the impersonality and callousness of the political process might be provoked.[27] So her comments were brief, informal, and personal. The group was encouraged to express feelings openly, to interact as usual, and to come to its own conclusions about the issue.

The result? No campaign workers were forthcoming, but Penny was smart enough not to ask for or expect that. Instead, she saw signs of reduced hostility toward the political process and received a request for information about the next public meeting involving feminist candidates.

Something to think about
What rules of audience analysis did Penny follow?

Before we conclude this section on the group-discussion approach to persuasion, ask yourself this question: Have you ever been to a small group meeting where you were simply talked to, where you felt the agenda and decisions had previously been established, or where you felt "used" or, at a minimum, "left out"? This shouldn't happen if activists are aware of the conditions under which people are more likely to participate. Here are a few:

1. When people believe that what they are talking about or working for is of some *consequence*—that the results of their thinking will be used

2. When the situation is really *open-ended* and members feel the conclusions were not decided in advance

3. When the *purpose* of the decision is clearly *stated* and the group can direct itself to that purpose[28]

---

[27] Lerbinger says "the communicator must be highly sensitive to any cues he inserts into his message that might bring unwanted group norms into the audience's psychological field." *Designs for Persuasive Communication*, p. 96.

[28] These and other conditions are identified by Harleigh B. Trecker in *Group*

So if a discussion technique is used, the activist has three particular things to think about in addition to the general rules for persuasive communication. The activist should think about the special group characteristics, the unique advantages of a discussion situation, and the conditions that are likely to promote participation. These considerations should influence both the message design and the manner of presentation. Now let's turn to a second way of approaching groups directly.

Public Speaking

As intimidating as public speaking is to many people, just think about what it really is—a planned conversation with a group of listeners.[29] It's different from discussion situations. Where direct contact through discussion groups is characterized by informality, flexibility, and little control over content, direct contact through public speaking has just the opposite characteristics. Prepared notes, an outline, or a completely written speech contribute to the formality, inflexibility, and control of the situation. In addition, the audience is usually larger in size and seated in a way that would make interaction difficult, if not impossible.

The groups activists are likely to visit are those generally referred to as *voluntary associations*. They can be categorized in terms of interests.[30]

- Veterans, military, or patriotic
- Civic, service, or both
- Lodges, fraternal, or professional
- Cultural, educational, or alumni
- Social, sports, hobby, or recreational
- Church or religious
- Political or pressure

Whether or not the message gets through to any of these groups and results in the sought-after response depends in part on the skills of the speaker. If the group has offered a choice, the activist should carefully assess these skills in order to decide whether or not to even try public speaking. An informal discussion might be more appropri-

---

Process in Administration (New York: Woman's Press, 1946, 1960), pp. 164–165.

[29] James N. Holm, *Productive Speaking for Business and the Professions* (Boston, Allyn and Bacon, 1967), p. 311.

[30] From Lerbinger, *Designs for Persuasive Communication*, p. 170.

ate to the talents of the person involved. However, if a group requests a speaker, then it should be someone with particular skills. These usually relate to knowing how to gain attention, maintain interest, and, ultimately, persuade.[31] It all begins with establishing credibility. A credible speaker tends to be more persuasive.

Something to think about

How would a speaker establish credibility?

Even a credible speaker must be able to draw attention and maintain interest. The distinction between attention and interest is a thin one. In a sense, attention "turns us on" and interest "keeps us there." Very generally, a speaker can gain attention by communicating with intensity and enthusiasm, varying what the audience has previously been exposed to, and offering novel or dramatic images, where possible. The purpose of interest devices is to minimize the attention disruptions. Research on the subject suggests that *experience with a subject* is most effective in creating interest. When speakers are talking about familiar things, the audience is least likely to lose interest.

Something to think about

How could an activist use the experience of clerical workers to develop interest in a campaign?

In addition to this general guide to maintaining interest, here are some other clues.

1. *Animation*   Just as change and intensity attract attention, animation maintains interest. Shifts in vocal quality, gestures, and varying expressions provide a visible index of how the speaker feels about the subject. They reinforce what is being said.
2. *Novelty*   Like familiarity with a subject, novelty can maintain audience interest. Unusual illustrations of familiar problems and/or principles are an effective combination.

When Roy Wilkins, executive secretary of the NAACP, was testifying before the Senate Commerce Committee on July 22, 1963, he seemed to be using a novel approach. He asked the U.S. senators

---

[31] See Eisenson et al., *The Psychology of Communication*, pp. 239–240.

*"A word to the wise, Benton. Don't
squander your credibility."*

Drawing by Lorenz; © 1974 The New Yorker Magazine, Inc.

he was addressing to imagine a familiar situation with a different twist:

> For millions of Americans this is vacation time. Swarms of families load their automobiles and trek across the country. I invite the members of this committee to imagine themselves darker in color and to plan an auto trip from Norfolk, Va., to the Gulf Coast of Mississippi, say, to Biloxi. Or one from Terra Haute, Ind., to Charleston, S. C., or from Jacksonville, Fla., to Tyler, Texas.
>
> How far do you drive each day? Where, and under what conditions can you and your family eat? Where can they use a restroom? Can you stop driving after a reasonable day behind the wheel, or must you drive until you reach a city where relatives or friends will accommodate you and yours for the night? Will your children be denied a soft drink or an ice cream cone because they are not white? [32]

Not many Americans, including senators, have not experienced the fatigue that comes from a long day of travel, particularly with small children. Including this situation in a speech designed to persuade could not help but maintain interest. The audience must have empathized with a father not often able to stop to rest and eat because he and his family were black. It was an unusual illustration of a familiar problem. Other interest-maintaining devices include the following:

3. *Conflict*   Developing a speech by portraying conflicting forces is another approach to maintaining interest. Real estate developers versus environmentalists, pacifists versus militarists, rentors versus landlords—the conflict situation sustains interest. In a way it is another method of achieving definiteness of form. It helps to create the pattern that audiences need.

4. *Suspense*   The dramatic "chase technique" where the "good guys" pursue the "bad guys" also sustains interest. If the listeners are tantalized, they are likely to stay with the speaker, even if they know how the presentation will end.

5. *Concreteness*   Reducing the complex to the simple makes any persuasive message seem more concrete. Less effort is required to stay tuned in to what is being said. Reducing expansive ideas to

---

[32] This testimony before the Senate Commerce Committee, July 22, 1963, was part of the struggle by civil rights leaders for the adoption of effective legislation. The Civil Rights Act of 1964 made the discrimination that Wilkins asked the senators to imagine illegal. Reported in J. Jeffrey Auer, ed., *The Rhetoric of Our Times* (New York: Appleton-Century-Crofts, 1969), p. 370.

related small ones and vague terms to recognizable ones will help, as will using facts to make the vague concrete. The data of the Opinion Research Corporation have demonstrated over and over again that people try to be fair—that they come to reasonable conclusions when they have the facts.[33]

6. *Humor*   When all else fails to maintain interest humor shouldn't. Public officials, who are constantly called on to give speeches, are acutely aware of how a funny situation can perk up a sleepy audience. However, a clever way of putting something or a witty comparison can frequently be more humorous than a well-worn story or joke. The frequent absence of such well-worn humor in the speeches of successful politicians seems to reflect this. Speakers are beginning to recognize the tendency to remember the joke or story rather than the main point.[34]

Whether the persuasive speech is designed to convince or to go beyond that and activate, attracting attention and maintaining interest is important. As can be seen from the previous discussion, there are many approaches. The particular device selected, however, should depend on the audience as well as on the goal and talents of the speaker.

What if the group seeking to mobilize support has to reach large numbers of people and has the resources to do it? If that is the case, and it is for many state and national citizens' organizations, those involved are likely to combine the direct methods of communication with *indirect methods*. These will be explored in Chapter 6.

Key Words

Audience analysis
Motivational analysis
Media analysis

Suggested Activities

1. Using the questions on pages 130 and 131, do an audience analysis of different community groups.
2. Using Ernest Dichter's approach to in-depth interviews, determine the likely motivations of the members of one community group.

---

[33] See Lerbinger, *Designs for Persuasive Communication*, p. 67, for a summary of the relevant literature.
[34] These and other points related to maintaining interest are in Eisenson et al., *The Psychology of Communication*, pp. 291–293.

3. Select a cause for which you would like to enlist the support of a prestigious person. Following the rules for prestige conversations, attempt to persuade a fictitious person (class member) to join your campaign.
4. Again select an issue. Practice how you would communicate in the following settings:
   a. Canvassing
   b. Small group meetings
   c. Large group meetings

6
Indirect Techniques of Persuasion

Choosing Indirect Techniques

While frequently expensive, time-consuming, and requiring special expertise, indirect methods of communication can get a message out more quickly than direct methods. However, the probability that people will pay attention to the message and stay interested—let alone be persuaded—is less than through the use of direct methods. Still, what is the choice? The *print media* to consider include newspapers, pamphlets, books and articles, and even billboards and posted information. Then, of course, there are the *broadcast media*—radio and television. While indirect techniques have the drawbacks mentioned, when they are used effectively, particularly in combination with direct methods of communication, they can result in persuasion.

Newspapers

Thomas Jefferson said, "I would rather live in a country with newspapers and without a government than in a country with a government and without newspapers." Jefferson's feeling about the importance of newspapers was based on a particular view of the citizen. For him, the citizen makes rational judgments based on factual information. While this view of the citizen rarely corresponds to reality, newspapers do play an important information role for some people, and an indirect one for many. Those who followed newspaper accounts of the energy crisis and Watergate closely were already the best informed, but that didn't prevent their attention and comprehension from increasing. Eventually, through personal communication, newspaper information was received by others. Had Jefferson been one of those observing the role of the press in uncovering abuses of power in the Nixon administration, his feelings about the importance of newspapers (and he certainly would include the broadcast media if he were around today) would have been strongly reinforced.

In recent years much has been said about the decline of newspapers. Most people now say they acquire news from television. Still, as of 1970, there were 1758 daily newspapers in the United States, with circulations totaling more than 62 million copies. While some metropolitan newspapers have in fact died, newspaper circulation is still climbing, and suburban newspapers seem to be thriving.[1]

Quite obviously not all newspapers are alike, and their differences will influence whose message is likely to get printed. Most dailies are monopoly newspapers,[2] but small dailies of 3000 or so circulation abound. In 1970 there were 7612 weekly and semiweekly community papers with an estimated readership of 111 million people. These provide a particularly effective and intimate means of reaching the people living in suburbs, small towns, and farms, and those are the people who are often the source of grass-roots opinion. Indeed, most experts agree that the weekly newspaper exerts a far greater impact on opinions in relation to its circulation than does the average daily newspaper.[3]

The size and frequency of publication only partially influence what gets printed. Also important are the attitudes of those people who are particularly well placed in the organization—in this case, in the newspaper company hierarchy. Kurt Lewin called these strategically located people *gatekeepers*. To understand this concept, think of a channel

[1] Scott M. Cutlip and Allen H. Center, *Effective Public Relations*, 4th ed. (Englewood Cliffs, N.J.: Prentice-Hall, 1952), p. 382.
[2] According to University of California law professor Stephen R. Barnett, newspaper chains now control more than half the nation's daily newspapers. In addition, there are 93 instances in 85 cities where the owner of a daily newspaper also owns a local television station. There is also a one-publisher monopoly in 96 percent of the daily newspaper cities in the country. See "Merger, Monopoly, and a Free Press," *The Nation*, January 15, 1973, pp. 76–79.
[3] Cutlip and Center, *Effective Public Relations*, pp. 382–383.

flowing from the outside world to the newspaper. The gatekeeper controls an important portion of that channel and may prevent something or someone from entering. Gatekeepers in newspapers may, among other things, accept, distort, or reject stories.[4]

Who are these strategically located people? While the gatekeeper may be a particular receptionist or secretary, one study involving 17 Kentucky evening newspapers indicated that the most important gatekeeper was the publisher. The publisher's attitude toward an issue was found to be strongly related to decisions on news coverage.[5] Another study found the wire editor to be the gatekeeper in a particular nonmetropolitan newspaper. The wire editor controlled the flow and selection of information by selecting stories from the various press services for exclusion or inclusion.[6] The wire editor gatekeeper, however, may merely be reflecting the coverage decisions of the publisher. Understandably, locating the one or more people in a particular newspaper who control what gets accepted and understanding their news predispositions will help an individual or group to gain access. They are key players.

The problems associated with trying to penetrate the gatekeeper, particularly in a large daily newpaper, cannot be underestimated. Most stories that *someone* considers news never appear in print. A University of Wisconsin study found that:

1. Out of approximately 300 releases received in a five-day period by a typical morning newspaper, 242 were rejected.
2. Out of 339 publicity releases received in a five-day period by a typical evening newspaper, 218 were rejected outright, 32 were used as received, and 42 were rewritten and used.
3. Out of publicity releases totaling 363 pages received in one week by a typical weekly newspaper, exactly 3 were used.

In another study of urban, suburban, and rural weekly newspapers, it was found that only 18.5 percent of the 1072 releases received in 12 offices in one week were used. Most of these came not from private

[4] See Elihu Katz and Paul Lazarsfeld, *Personal Influence* (Glencoe, Ill.: The Free Press, 1955), p. 119.
[5] See L. Donohew, "Newspaper Gatekeepers and Forces in the News Channel," *Public Opinion Quarterly*, Spring 1967, pp. 61–68.
[6] David Manning White, "The 'Gatekeeper': A Case Study in the Selection of News," in *People, Society and Mass Communication*, eds. Lewis Anthony Dexter and David Manning White (New York: The Free Press of Glencoe, 1964), pp. 160–172.

citizens or citizens' groups, but from educational institutions, government agencies, trade and professional associations, and business firms.[7]

Ultimately what gets accepted for print is news as defined by the crucial gatekeeper. A study of what editors think is *not news* provides some help. After interviewing 61 editors to determine *wastebasket criteria*, Professor James Julian discovered these, in order of frequency:

- Limited local interest
- No reader interest at all
- Story poorly written
- Reasons of policy
- Disguised advertising
- Material obviously faked
- Apparent inaccuracy in story
- Duplication of release
- Material stretched too thin[8]

Given the difficulty of getting a story printed, are newspapers really all that important tactically? We know from Chapter 3 that, for local and state news particularly, people say they are. In addition, research indicates that *under certain conditions*, the media (newspapers included) are successful at conveying information and even persuading. To put it succinctly, "Some kinds of *communication* on some kinds of *issues* brought to the attention of some kinds of *people* under some kinds of *conditions*, have some kinds of effects." [9] These points, of course, have already been discussed. But one thing is clear: The influence of media is usually indirect and subtle. Justice Felix Frankfurter, speaking specifically about newspapers before the advent of television, put it this way:

> The unconscious, and therefore, uncritical absorption of print is much more powerful than any skeptical alertness which most readers bring to print. To an extent far beyond the public's own realization, public opinion is shaped by the kind, the volume, and the quality of the news column.

Of course, a great deal in newspapers doesn't get absorbed at all, even "uncritically." The average reader reads only a portion of any one paper. In fact, typically a reader spends only 30 minutes reading one-fifth to one-fourth of the editorial content. So even if an article

[7] See Cutlip and Center, *Effective Public Relations*, pp. 382–385.
[8] *Ibid.*, p. 385.
[9] Bernard Berelson, "Communications and Public Opinion" in *Mass Communications*, ed. Wilbur Schramm (Urbana: University of Illinois Press, 1960), p. 531.

makes it past the gatekeeper, there is only a slight chance that it will be read.[10] This is one of the reasons for using other indirect forms of communication and direct forms at the same time.

Thus far the *news* aspect of newspapers has been the focus of this discussion. Yet there is another kind of newspaper content that can also be important to citizens seeking to inform and persuade. It consists of *letters to the editor*. This is a far easier way of gaining access, which can give an individual the opportunity to share a point of view, perhaps generating other letters.

More individuals seem to be taking advantage of this communication opportunity. The number of letters newspapers are receiving is growing at a remarkable rate. For example, in 1969 the *New York Times* received 37,449 letters, nearly double the 19,885 received five years earlier. Only 2622 letters were printed in 1969, however.[11]

Perhaps more effective than individual letters are those that are promoted by organizations as a persuasive tactic. Organized letter-writing to newspapers was a particularly important tactic in the 1962 re-election campaign of Charles McC. Mathias, Jr. (R., Md., 6th District). This has been described as a model campaign that would delight any strategist. In fact, Mathias's approach *had* to be good. He was running in a district consisting of five counties that were extremely diverse geographically, culturally, and economically.

Although they were not really sure of the value of the tactic, Mathias's strategists saw organized letter-writing as a top project, and they acted accordingly. It started with a memo from the Mathias camp carefully defining the responsibilities of key writers assigned to cover each newpaper.

> These astute persons must keep abreast of the news in the paper assigned to each of them. When they read an item which favors the candidate they should register approbation and support; if it attacked the candidate, they should rise to his defense. They should take diametric actions on items concerning the opposition candidate. The key writer of each paper should contact the campaign manager or his delegate in this area of activity and check on the policy line to be considered. Once this is clear the letter should be written—in long hand—and mailed.[12]

10 Cutlip and Center, *Effective Public Relations*, p. 381.
11 A. Kent MacDougall, "Dear Sir: You Jerk!," *Wall Street Journal*, August 31, 1970.
12 The American Institute for Political Communication, *The New Methodology: A Study of Political Strategy and Tactics* (Washington, D.C.: American Institute for Political Communications, 1967), pp. 81–88.

While this was not the only tactic used, Mathias's strategists considered it an important one. He won in all five counties.

In the case just described, the letters to the editor were designed to generate support for and discussion about a particular candidate, but they could be used equally effectively to promote an issue. When they are written by a recognizable, credible, and/or prestigious person in the community or state, their impact is likely to be even greater.

Generally they do not result in attitude change. At best they attract attention and trigger a favorable reader response. In fact, surveys indicate that letters are among the best-read newspaper features, and publishers have long valued them for their circulation pull.[13]

Access rules.   If the tactics selected include organized letter-to-the-editor campaigns and/or newspaper advertising, and articles, there are *two relevant kinds of rules.* One type pertains to *writing* effective letters, ads, and articles. If followed, they help activists gain access. The rules to follow in this case will be influenced by the particular newspaper's norms. That is, what kind of letters, articles, or ads does the newspaper usually accept? In addition, there are more general guides to writing effective press releases, advertising copy, articles, and letters. These can be found in any public relations manual.[14]

A second type of rule has to do with *access* rights. These would be the rules that specify the rights citizens have to use the medium of newspapers, and the rights newspaper owners and publishers have to control access and content. There are two important points to be made about this second type of rule. First, such rules are few in number, unlike those pertaining to the broadcast media. Citizens do not have a basic right to get their message out through newpapers. Second, those access rules that do exist give the advantages to newspaper owners and publishers. They are their resources.

For example, newspapers generally need not accept particular articles or advertisements in order to present a "balanced" picture of a situation. The judgments of owners, publishers, and editors regarding balance or imbalance prevail. This is true even when people are willing to pay for the space.[15]

---

[13] MacDougall, "Dear Sir: You Jerk!"
[14] Some rule suggestions are in the O. M. Collective, *The Organizers' Manual* (New York: Bantam Books, 1971), pp. 155–159.
[15] This rule may not be absolute, however. There is a 50-year-old decision of an inferior Ohio court that holds that a newspaper has a duty not to discriminate against a potential commercial advertiser. For details of this decision and other

A second access rule that reaffirms the rights of the owner deals with copy accuracy. When newspaper advertisements that don't involve products are inaccurate, citizens do not have a right to force a correction. For example, during the 1974 energy crisis, some oil and power companies took out full-page ads describing either the good qualities of the industry or more ways of consuming energy. For example, American Electric Power, Inc., a holding company for seven big midwestern utilities, developed a widely circulated advertisement that contained a cartoon. At the top of the page a modishly dressed young man with curly hair, eyeglasses, and beady eyes holds a placard that reads, "Generate Less Energy." In bold type at his feet the American Electric Power Company replies, "Sure. And generate galloping unemployment!" The ad continues by urging Congress to modify the Clean Air Act so that more coal may be burned. In addition, it urges the release of the reserves of U.S. government–owned low-sulphur coal in the West.

Environmentalists, angered not so much by the self-serving nature of this and similar ads as by the half-truths cited as fact, could not respond in kind. A full-page advertisement in the *New York Times* costs about $10,000. There was no rule guaranteeing them comparable access unless they could pay for it. Newspaper owners have certain property rights.

To try to change this situation, which obviously gives an advantage to both newspaper owners and interests with substantial financial resources, two things are being done. Environmentalists have asked the Federal Trade Commission to apply to such advertisements the rules of proof that ordinarily apply to product advertising. Those who advertise products must be able to substantiate their claims. While the application of this rule wouldn't have given environmentalists free newspaper access, it would have reduced the possibility of future advertising inaccuracies. It would have made access on this issue unnecessary. The FTC has not responded.

In addition to the environmentalists' approach, the Media Access Project, through its lawyer, Harvey Shulman, tried to get Congress to force the Internal Revenue Service to apply one of its rules. The IRS code forbids companies to deduct as business expenses any money spent for "lobbying purposes, for the promotion or defeat of legisla-

related ones, see John De J. Pemberton, Jr., "The Rights of Access to Mass Media," in *The Rights of Americans*, ed. Norman Dorsen (New York: Pantheon Books, 1970), p. 290.

tion . . . or for the carrying out of propaganda relating to any of the foregoing purposes." Shulman, testifying before the Senate Environment Subcommittee, argued that corporations have been buying space for political advertisements and treating them as a tax-deductible, nonpolitical business expense. The companies involved responded that their advertisements were "informational and institutional." If the IRS rule were enforced, the financial advantages corporate interests have in such promotion would be somewhat reduced. Without the tax deduction, opportunities for newspaper access would be slightly more equal. Congress took no action.[16]

Not only did the inaction of the FTC, IRS, and Congress reaffirm the right of newspaper owners to control access and content, but a U.S. Supreme Court action did the same. In 1974 the Court struck down a Florida law requiring newspapers to print replies from political candidates attacked in a particular newspaper. Such laws, the Supreme Court said, were an unconstitutional restriction on freedom of the press. In the words of Chief Justice Warren E. Burger, the government cannot require "a newspaper to print that which it would not otherwise print," and compelling the inclusion of some news is the constitutional equivalent of censorship. So much for any inherent right of public access to the press.[17]

One final point about the rules governing newspaper access has to do with monopoly ownership. Some people feel that diversity of media ownership and operation would make citizen access easier and would promote the First Amendment right to free speech. Congress apparently disagrees. After a joint newspaper operating agreement was declared in violation of antitrust laws by the courts, Congress passed the Newspaper Preservation Act (July 24, 1970). Exempting joint ownership agreements from antitrust action, supporters in Congress claimed, was necessary to prevent a *reduction* in the number of daily newspapers.[18] The evidence for this claim is not entirely convincing. The rule advantages for newspaper owners persist.

Pamphlets and Brochures
Newspapers, however, aren't the only print vehicle for communicating information. Most issue and candidate campaigns also distribute pamphlets and brochures.

[16] "Energy Advertising," *The New Republic*, May 25, 1974, pp. 8–9.
[17] Warren Weaver, Jr., "Justices Void Florida Law on Right to Reply in Press," *New York Times*, June 26, 1974, p. 1ff.
[18] Pemberton, "The Rights of Access to Mass Media," p. 292.

One of the most intensive and successful campaigns ever carried out used leaflets and other printed material extensively. In 1909, the Anti-Saloon League established a printing plant of its own in which it printed, until 1923, 157 million copies of temperance papers, 2 million books, 5 million pamphlets, 114 million leaflets, 2 million window placards, and 18 million small cards. The result was a tremendous body of legislation, including the Prohibition Amendment of 1920 (subsequently repealed in 1933).[19] Obviously the Anti-Saloon League didn't have to contend with the diversity of mass media that exists now, which could have been used to counteract the effects of a relatively less expensive publication campaign.

The problem of assessing the merits of pamphlets and brochures in an educational campaign is that so many other methods of communicating are being used simultaneously. Certainly in the case of Prohibition, in churches and on street corners across America people were engaged in direct personal attempts to influence the public toward temperance legislation. Sympathetic newspapers and magazines also carried the message. Still, Prohibitionists felt that their print operation was particularly effective.

Many brochures, pamphlets, and letters now get distributed by mail. So in order to evaluate their effectiveness, the mail factor should also be examined. In the 1950s a group of political scientists attempted to do just that. They wanted to determine the relative merit of mailed literature—letters, pamphlets, etc. Specifically, they wanted to compare the relative effectiveness of two different methods of urging people to vote a particular way on a city proposition. The people selected for the experiment had been, in the year preceding the election, either apathetic, uninformed, or opposed to the measure (a modification in the city charter). A control group of citizens selected at random was used as a basis of comparison.

Preceding the election, one-half of the experimental group was sent pro-proposition literature (letters). There were four mailings in all. The other half of the experimental group was contacted personally and urged to vote for the measure.

The results *seemed* clear. In the control group only slightly more than one-half of those who voted in the election voted for the proposition. Among the voting members of the experimental groups, 76.9 percent of those contacted by mail voted for the measure and 100

19 J. A. C. Brown, *Techniques of Persuasion* (Baltimore, Md.: Penguin Books, 1963), p. 77.

percent of those contacted personally did so. Direct personal contact again prevailed, but mailed literature was also effective. As clear as these results seemed, the researchers realized they were still contending with the same problem. All voters had been simultaneously exposed to other sources of campaign information. Hopefully, that exposure was random, and the differences between the behavior of the experimental and control groups were related to the methods used.

At a minimum, however, the two methods did mobilize voters who might, during the course of the experiment, have developed favorable attitudes toward the proposition. While only one-third of the potential voters in the control group went to the polls, nearly 60 percent of those contacted by mail and three-quarters of those contacted personally voted. Both of these seem to be techniques worth using.[20]

If pamphlets, brochures, and letters sent through the mail can get people to vote and perhaps even be persuasive, increased exposure enhances the effect. An experiment involving undergraduate men residing in a dormitory who received nonsense messages (unintelligible messages) through the mail suggests that repeated receipt of literature is important. Those who received the nonsense messages more frequently actually developed more positive attitudes toward the material.[21]

Clearly, if the messages had obtained controversial or disagreeable material, the outcome would have been different. Still, given how little most voters actually know about issues, and given the number of noncontroversial issues on the ballot in some states and cities, information mailed with some frequency can work.

Billboards and Posters

Other printed methods of communicating information are billboards and posters. In November 1970, a very controversial proposition, called Proposition 18, appeared on the ballot in California. It was designed to fight auto pollution and improve mass transit by diverting some gas tax and license fee revenues to mass transit needs. Billboards were used extensively by the opposition.

Approximately one month before the election, the state was

[20] For details of the experiment, see Samuel J. Eldersveld and Richard W. Dodge, "Personal Contact or Mail Propaganda," in *Public Opinion and Propaganda*, ed. Daniel Katz et al. (New York: The Dryden Press, 1954), pp. 532–542.
[21] D. W. Rajecki and Charles Wolfson, "The Rating of Materials Found in the Mailbox: Effects of Frequency of Receipt," *Public Opinion Quarterly*, Spring 1973, pp. 110–114.

saturated with opposition billboards reading, "More Taxes? No. No. 18." The 700 billboards were placed to achieve a "100 percent showing"; that is, every person in the state should theoretically have seen the billboard at least once before election time. The fact that taxes were not to be increased, only diverted, was never a part of the message.

While the opposition used other methods of conveying its message as well, and the underfinanced proponents offered less message competition than had been expected, the billboards had their effect:

About four months before the campaign started, a statewide attitudinal survey found that 77 percent of California adults favored "spending some of the state gas money (i.e., that currently spent for highways) for smog or air pollution research." Only 17 percent expressed disapproval. About five months later, just before the billboards of the anti-18 forces were erected, the Field poll discovered that only about one in three voters in the state had heard of Proposition 18. However, when they were given a copy of the measure as it was to appear on the ballot, 64 percent said they would vote yes; twenty-two percent opposed. It looked as though 18 would pass. Another Field poll was taken a week before the election, after the measure had been more publicized. Still, only 57 percent had seen or heard about Proposition 18. The ballot statement was read to those who had not heard anything about the measure, and 56 percent of the group were in favor. Twelve percent were opposed. On the other hand, 53 percent of those who were previously aware of the issue said they would vote yes, while 29 percent said they would vote no. Among all voters, potential support for the amendment had declined to 52 percent, a drop of 12 percentage points in approximately one month. Since the main voices for and against the measure had been, up until that time, the major newspapers and the billboards, respectively, it must be assumed that the disingenuous message of the laconic billboards was having the greater influence.[22]

The estimated expenditures of both sides give some indication of how the opposing players believed their money would be most effectively spent. Clearly, for the opposition, billboards were the important medium (Table 6–1).[23]

Activists involved in a citywide campaign (or any campaign, for that matter) where financial resources are limited might think about *posters*. While it takes a number of people to prepare and distribute

22 J. Allen Whitt, "Californians, Cars, and the Technical Death," *Society*, July–August 1973, pp. 30–38.
23 *Ibid.*, p. 34.

Table 6–1
Proposition 18 campaign

	Opponents	Proponents
Billboards	$123,000	$ —
Television	60,000	1,400
Newspaper	17,000	1,456
Radio	15,000	2,401
Total	$215,000	$5,257

Source: J. Allen Whitt, "Californians, Cars, and the Technical Death," *Society*, July–August 1973, p. 34.

them, they can attract particular groups of citizens—those likely to be walking. Neighborhoods that have a great deal of foot traffic (i.e., tourist areas) or neighborhoods where few people own cars (i.e., sections of large metropolitan cities) are good possibilities. However, if they are to work, like other forms of communication, they have to attract attention and hold at least momentary interest. Three rules are: (1) Include only the essential information, (2) leave lots of empty space around the copy, and (3) post them, if possible, in familiar places—windows of private homes or popular merchants. Again, personal influence can enhance their impact.[24]

Most cities and states have rules about posting material. In some areas, for example, notices and posters cannot be placed on public utility poles. Some state supreme courts, however, have struck down as unconstitutional local ordinances limiting this right. Judges have concluded they are violations of free speech.[25] Government buildings, however, are still off limits for political literature.

Books and Articles
Major motivators of political change, historically, have been books and articles. The goals of the Progressive movement, for example, gained widespread popular support largely through the writings of reformist philosophers and journalists. These writings probably would not have inspired anyone if it had not been for earlier radical writings. Edward Bellamy's *Looking Backward*, showing an attractive picture of a socialist commonwealth, was one such work. It sold over 500,000

[24] The O. M. Collective discusses these and other rules, *The Organizers' Manual*, pp. 50–51.
[25] "Significant Court Actions," *California Journal*, May 1974, p. 171.

copies, indicating wide popular acceptance. Another was Henry D. Lloyd's *Wealth against Commonwealth*, published in 1894. Both Lloyd's writings and his speeches helped to spread non-Marxist socialist ideas among other writers and reform politicians and among workers, farmers, and members of the middle class. Their ideas, combined with traditional populist humanitarian and antimonopoly sentiments, formed the basic ingredients of Progressive doctrine.[26]

Magazines soon began to take advantage of the growing interest. Publishers found that stories of fraud and corruption made exciting reading. Contributors included Ida M. Tarbell, who told an amazed America about the abuses of the Standard Oil giant; Lincoln Steffens, who exposed city corruption; David Graham Philips, who revealed the business connections of U.S. senators; and Samuel H. Adams, who wrote about fraud in medical practices and advertising.[27]

The impact of books and articles on political reform has continued to the present. Ralph Nader's *Unsafe at Any Speed* (1965) prompted concern about automobile safety and contributed to stricter safety standards. Michael Harrington's *The Other America* (1962) helped to awaken American citizens to the depth and pervasiveness of hunger in this country. Legislative results followed. The publication of Rachel Carson's *Silent Spring* (1962) was considered an extremely important impetus to the environmental movement. The awareness of the harmful effects of pesticides that it generated was only the first step. The list of these books and articles is long, and their importance, although difficult to measure, should not be underestimated. If book sales, subsequent magazine reviews and articles, broadcast interviews with authors, and references to such books in the *Congressional Record* and other government publications are some measures, their impact was significant indeed.

Usually citizens seeking political change, particularly at the local level, do not have a Nader, Carson, or Harrington at their service. Still, the climate of opinion generated by books and articles directed at national problems can be advantageous locally. Paul Ehrlich's *The Population Bomb* (1968) must have aided the development and use of many local birth control and education centers. In addition, articles need not be circulated nationwide to be effective. A well-written exposé about the failures of the local housing authority can also have

---

26 Thomas H. Greer, *American Social Reform Movements* (Port Washington, N.Y.: Kennikat Press, Inc., 1949 and 1965), p. 104.
27 *Ibid.*, p. 105.

the desired impact. It is surprising how many local writers, sympathetic to a particular cause, will assist.

So the choice of indirect forms of printed communication is vast. Those identified—newspaper articles, pamphlets, billboards, posters, books, and magazine articles—are only a few. Each requires particular resources and has rules to observe, but they all can reach a large audience. Communication through print is unique in that it can be repeated precisely and indefinitely. The challenge, with print, is gaining the attention and interest of readers.

Broadcast Media

Gaining and holding attention is easier when broadcast media are used. Although they are not direct communicators, radio and television personalities are often perceived very personally. They can become familiar and trusted sources of information. Attention, of course, is easily diverted, and unpleasant messages can be turned off or tuned out, but broadcast communicators frequently do reap *some* of the benefits of direct face-to-face contact.

While each broadcast medium is unique in a variety of ways, access to both is *generally* governed by the Federal Communications Commission. The FCC enforces the rules passed by Congress, and the rules, in turn, distribute advantages and disadvantages.

Most of the formal rules governing broadcast operations were established through the Federal Communication Act of 1934. As a response to the increasingly untenable broadcast-interference situation and the ineffectiveness of the Dell-White Radio Act of 1927, President Roosevelt sent a message to Congress calling for new legislation and for the establishment of a Federal Communications Commission. More than one member of the House of Representatives was upset by the implications of the bill. Louis T. McFadden (R., Pa.) addressed his colleagues in the House thus:

> I believe that this bill was written, or at least the controlling and important part of it, in conformity with the wishes of the people who control this industry, and propose to control it as a monopoly, to control public sentiment in the United States, to control it now immediately for political purposes....[28]

Without a quorum present or a roll call, the act was passed.[29]

[28] *Congressional Record,* June 9, 1934.

[29] According to Harry J. Skornia, "the 1927–1934 structure stands today in all its anachronistic glory, as a tribute to the power of the networks and other large industry-owned stations to prevent effective regulation." *Television and Society* (New York: McGraw-Hill Book Company, 1965), p. 72.

"Out, Damned 'Spots'!"

From *Herblock's State of the Union* (Simon & Schuster, 1972)

Access rules.   What is the concern? What are the rules of access that purportedly give the industry rather than the public the advantage? One is known as *the fairness doctrine*. Reversing an initial disinclination to allow broadcasters to editorialize, the FCC ruled in 1949 that stations could editorialize provided they maintained an overall fairness. This was one way of implementing the public-interest requirement of the Communications Act. However, the commissioners warned, "the opportunity of licensees to present such views as they may have on matters of controversy may not be utilized to achieve a partisan or one-sided presentation of issues." [30]

Specifically, through the fairness doctrine, the FCC imposes several obligations on licensees. First, it affirmatively requires that some discussion of "matters of public importance" must take place. Second, it gives the right of reply to a particular person or group who may be attacked "during the presentation of views on a controversial issue of public importance." The same right is extended to candidates editorially opposed.[31] Third, it requires the broadcaster to seek out and present a speaker for "all responsible positions."

However, there are a few potential problems. For examples, what if one side of an issue is presented by someone who has purchased the time and no opposing side can afford to purchase comparable time?

In 1969 the Supreme Court tried to strengthen citizens' right of access to the broadcast media. The decision involved the Red Lion Broadcasting Company, which permitted a sponsored attack on an author. Fred Cook, the person attacked, demanded a *free* opportunity to reply. The broadcasters refused. In one of the most famous communication decisions, the Supreme Court ruled in favor of Cook, upholding an earlier FCC decision.[32] In this case the rule was clear: "It is the right of the viewers and listeners and not the right of the broadcasters which is paramount." [33]

But that was 1969. Rules change, and advantages get distributed differently. In 1973, the Supreme Court emphasized the rights of the station owners. In answer to a suit filed by the Democratic National Committee and Business Executives' Move for Vietnam Peace, an antiwar group, the court ruled that broadcasters are not obligated to accept *paid* commercials dealing with controversial issues. Chief Jus-

[30] Edward W. Chester, *Radio, Television and American Politics* (New York: Sheed & Ward, 1969), pp. 183–184.
[31] Pemberton, "The Rights of Access to Mass Media," pp. 283–286.
[32] *The Red Lion Broadcasting Co.* v. *FCC* (1969).
[33] Pemberton, "The Rights of Access to Mass Media," pp. 287–288.

tice Warren E. Burger had a different point of view this time. He said, essentially, that providing unlimited access to broadcast advertising would give an unfair advantage to those best able to pay.[34] While this was not precisely the same issue, the Court seemed to be distributing access advantages differently from the way it had in 1969—taking them away from those with a controversial point of view and giving them back to station owners.

To summarize the fairness doctrine, one rule governing access to broadcast media, citizens generally have the right to reply to an editorial when they are attacked on the air or when they are opposed editorially as a candidate. They need not pay for the response. They do not, however, have an inherent right to promote a point of view, even if they are *buying* commercial air time. It is the station owners who can decide to whom to sell time, to whom to give free time to respond, and generally how their public service obligation shall be fulfilled. They have still further advantages. They know the rule is more bark than bite. Of 4300 fairness complaints filed with the FCC in 1973 and 1974, 97 percent were dismissed without a hearing.[35]

The *equal time provision*, a far more controversial access rule, distributes advantages in a different way. As Section 315 of the Communications Act, the equal time requirement provides that whenever a broadcaster permits any qualified candidate for public office to use facilities, that broadcaster shall afford all other candidates for the same office an equal opportunity to use the same facilities.[36]

Some of the questions that contribute to the controversy surrounding this rule are:

1. Do write-in candidates qualify?
2. Are presidential addresses political or nonpolitical?
3. Does equal time mean an equal share of prime time?
4. Can there be restrictions on time sales; is it legal to sell any time at all for political purposes? [37]

Some of the exceptions to the rule begin to indicate who has the advantage—the incumbent office holder. A 1959 congressional amendment exempted candidates who appear:

---

[34] The defendants in this case were the American Broadcasting Company, Columbia Broadcasting System, National Broadcasting Company, and the Washington Post–Newsweek Stations.
[35] "TV's Fair Game," *Newsweek*, May 12, 1975, p. 110.
[36] Pemberton, "The Rights of Access to Mass Media," p. 281.
[37] Chester, *Radio, Television, and American Politics*, p. 220.

- In a "bona fide newscast"
- In a "bona fide documentary"
- In a "bona fide interview"
- As a participant in "on-the-spot coverage of bona fide news events"

In addition, a 1975 FCC decision made exempt candidates who are part of press conferences and those who appear in debates. It is important to note that a person is not a candidate until he or she has announced candidacy.[38]

Something to think about
How could an incumbent systematically take advantage of the exemptions? How do they affect minor-party candidates?

How do these exemptions benefit the incumbent? If an incumbent President, senator, or representative running for re-election is able to generate news, opponents may not be able to respond. In the 1964 presidential campaign, for example, Lyndon Johnson went on the air October 18 to announce the ouster of Khrushchev in the Soviet Union and the first nuclear test by Communist China. Senator Goldwater, his opponent, filed a complaint with the FCC, but it was rejected on the grounds that Johnson's announcement constituted "on-the-spot coverage of a bona fide news event." The commission made much of the fact that President Johnson's delivery "had been recommended by the National Security Council." It brushed aside evidence that the Johnson for President Committee had first sought to purchase network time for the address. The Court of Appeals affirmed the decision.[39]

The question is, couldn't almost any presidential message during an election be declared a bona fide news event? The FCC test seems to be whether the events discussed are "specific, current, international events affecting the country's security," or "news events of an extraordinary nature." This test seems wide open.

If a particular candidate has formally declared an intention to run for election or re-election, does the equal time provision guarantee opponents a chance to be heard? Not at all. Section 315 only requires

[38] S. R. Barnett, "Equal Time and the Nixon Style," *Nation*, June 26, 1972, pp. 807–811.
[39] *Ibid.*

that opponents be given the *right* to buy time at the same rates. Of course, challengers have a more difficult time raising funds. Nor does the equal time provision obligate a broadcaster to provide *any* time, either free or paid, to *any* candidate. If no candidate is put on the air in the first place, there is no condition requiring equal time.[40] Obviously, this also aids the incumbent. In a congressional district where a seat is considered "safe," broadcasters might not sell any time.

So what may we conclude about Section 315? Clearly it does give an advantage to incumbents, but minor-party candidates who might not otherwise get heard also have an advantage. In addition, it gives unknown citizens entering a primary race the opportunity to become politically known. Some issue-oriented candidates have in fact used this provision strictly to gain exposure for their point of view. They may have had no intention or hope of winning the race.

The power to enforce the fairness doctrine and equal-time provision comes from the FCC's right to grant, renew, or deny broadcast licenses. This is its major resource. Traditionally, when station owners applied for license renewals, they were automatic. There was no public hearing, and the broadcaster's assessment of how well the public-service obligation was being fulfilled was the only one formally heard. A court decision stopped this practice. In *United Church of Christ v. FCC* (1966), the Court of Appeals for the District of Columbia ruled that "the Commission must allow standing to one or more of the petitioners as responsible representatives to assist and prove the claims they have urged in their petition." Finally representatives of the listening public could be heard. A means of greater citizen access was established.[41]

Recent legislative action, however, may be undermining this move toward citizen input and access. A media-inspired measure, overwhelmingly passed by the House of Representatives and Senate, would have extended the duration of licenses from three to five years, established a performance criterion of "substantial" rather than "superior" service for renewal applicants, eliminated considerations of media concentration and monopoly from license applications or challenges, and taken jurisdiction over FCC matters out of the hands of the consumer-minded District of Columbia Circuit Court of Appeals. Although conference committee agreement was not forthcoming, the

---

[40] Pemberton, "The Rights of Access to Mass Media," p. 282.
[41] *Ibid.*, p. 285.

shift to five-year licensing continues to be broadly supported in Congress.[42]

Access opportunities.   While the rules discussed thus far are crucial in determining the ease of gaining access to broadcast media, the *number and diversity of stations* is another factor. As of 1972, there were more than 4273 commercial AM stations and 2229 FM stations. They blanket the nation and are almost as common in small towns as in larger cities. The potential radio audience is suggested by the fact that 98 percent of American homes have radios. As of 1970, 75 million radios were also in use in automobiles. One estimate is that an average person spends 17 hours a week listening to radio.[43] In addition, while they are not quite as numerous as radio stations, there were 694 television stations in 1972. There were nearly 100 million television sets in operation in the United States, one-third of these color.[44]

On the basis of sheer numbers, there would seem to be no problem. Citizen access should be easy. However, the pervasiveness of monopoly ownership, identified earlier, poses some problems.

Still, although the rules and limited ownership do restrict access, the diversity in broadcast content offers different avenues of access. These are the main possibilities:

1. Special programs based on interviews, group discussions, demonstrations, etc., in either a series or one-time-only presentation
2. Similar but shorter presentations inserted as "participating" features of other programs
3. Brief spot announcements made at various times during a broadcast day
4. Personality spots made by (sympathetic) on-the-air personalities, such as disc jockeys, directors of women's shows, or consumer-affairs broadcasters
5. News items sent directly to the station or fed in by way of the station's news service
6. Editorials prepared by the station endorsing a program or campaign

---

[42] For a discussion of this legislation and its implications, see Andrew Kopkind, "TV Guide," *The New York Review of Books,* August 8, 1974, p. 34.
[43] Cutlip and Center, *Effective Public Relations,* p. 395.
[44] *Ibid.,* p. 398.

Remember, except for bona fide public-service announcements, the broadcaster ordinarily cannot afford to air *free* advertising. The activist must be sure to send only genuinely newsworthy releases or use nonnews programming.[45]

The degree to which the broadcast media are effective in the communication process was discussed in Chapter 4. We know from that discussion that effectiveness varies with particular conditions. Still, illustrations of apparently successful media techniques might be helpful.

For the Democratic party, the most successful use of the broadcast media occurred on September 26, 1960. On that day, 75 million people watched what was to become the major political event in broadcast history—the first of four debates between two men running for the office of U.S. President. Halfway through a rigorous campaign, John F. Kennedy and Richard M. Nixon faced each other in a television studio. At that point, the race was close. Before the first debate, George Gallup revealed that Richard Nixon had a one-percentage-point lead (47 percent to 46 percent).

What did this television encounter and the three subsequent ones do? Most studies conclude that the first debate was the turning point for Kennedy. Of those who watched or listened that first evening, 89 percent believed Kennedy had outdone Nixon, or at least fought him to a draw. According to George Gallup, after the debate, Nixon had lost his lead to Kennedy, 49 percent to 46 percent.[46]

Pollster Elmo Roper claimed that ultimately over 4 million people (6 percent of the voters) made their decision on the basis of the first debate *alone*, but most researchers discount this view. Where the debates had their greatest impact was among the undecided voters. According to the Gallup Poll, for example, the regular Democrats were slightly more impressed by Kennedy's performance than the regular Republicans were by Nixon's. However, among "the waverers" Kennedy picked up 16 percent during the debate, while Nixon gained only 4 percent.[47] When the most closely contested presidential race in American history was over, Kennedy's margin of victory was only 100,000 votes out of 68.3 million cast. These televised debates might have provided the advantage.

[45] These programming opportunities as well as suggestions on writing broadcast material are from Cutlip and Center, *Effective Public Relations*, pp. 396–397.
[46] For a summary of the various studies associated with the debates, see Chester, *Radio, Television and American Politics*, pp. 120–125.
[47] *Ibid.*, p. 122.

Something to think about
Who had the advantage in the 1976 presidential election debates?

Election debates or speeches can have an advantage over other forms of political communication transmitted through the broadcast media if there is what G. D. Wiebe has called a *social mechanism*. This is some vehicle through which people can act immediately on whatever they feel. If listeners and viewers can go to the polls, a social mechanism exists.

Frequently political announcements or documentaries do not contain a social mechanism. Strong feelings may be generated, but the broadcast has probably not included a way for the audience to act on those feelings. Activists using the media should think about including this kind of mechanism. Including a number to phone, a meeting to attend, or an address to write to would help.[48]

If the goal of the broadcast is not action but increased awareness, however, a social mechanism isn't necessary. For example, a 1974 media campaign by the New Mexico Civil Liberties Union did not include such a mechanism, but this group could achieve its objective without one. The group wanted to make citizens conscious of the fact that their right of privacy was being seriously eroded. Action-oriented communication was designed to follow this period of consciousness-raising.

Media messages, in this case, were directed to the 400,000 residents of Albuquerque. The idea was to subject them to a month-long "media blitz" to make them aware of growing, sophisticated assaults on their privacy and other civil liberties.

The campaign involved almost every medium available—not only radio and television. Billboards filled border to border with a single human eye suddenly sprang up along heavily traveled freeways. Tiny eyes, one column by one inch, sometimes as many as a dozen in each edition, started out at readers of the two Albuquerque daily newspapers. One-minute spot announcements cropped up frequently on prime-time television.

---

[48] For a discussion of the social mechanisms in broadcasting, see G. D. Wiebe, "Merchandising Commodities and Citizenship on Television," *Public Opinion Quarterly*, Winter 1951–1952, pp. 679–691.

One spot announcement opened with school children playing in a park. In slow motion, a blond little girl ran happily toward the camera—closer and closer, until the action froze and the color changed to black-and-white. The little girl stared blankly forward in a prisonlike pose with a Social Security number on a placard around her neck. In addition, the New Mexico news media covered appearances, nearly every day, of nationally recognized authorities speaking on privacy issues.

Did it work? Did the citizens of Albuquerque become more aware of the problem? To measure the effectiveness of the campaign, the New Mexico Civil Liberties Union commissioned a prior poll by University of New Mexico polling experts; it showed that 83 percent of the Albuquerqueans didn't think invasion of privacy was a very important issue. After the media blitz, things had changed: 52.5 percent believed privacy was important and that political and legal steps should be taken to protect it. This carefully orchestrated educational campaign, a year in the making, obviously worked. Precisely how isn't known. Which media were more influential is unanswered. But a campaign geared toward action, one with a social mechanism, would be an obvious next step.[49]

Regardless of how potentially effective the broadcast media can be in the education-persuasion process, and regardless of how the rules *try* to guarantee citizen access, a glaring problem persists. Those with the fewest financial resources are most disadvantaged. Of all the techniques possible, unless free public-service time is forthcoming, the broadcast media cost the most to use. That is perhaps one of the major reasons why protest tactics have become so prevalent. Herbert Alexander says protest makes economic sense. If a comparison is made between getting 25 signatures on a petition that receives little or no public attention and gathering 25 people on a street corner to protest, the pay-off from the second tactic would appear to be much greater. Buying that amount of exposure would be impossible for most groups.[50]

Using protest techniques to draw the media can be expensive in nonfinancial ways, however. The cost may be the message that protestors want to convey. Reporters are most interested in news. After

---

49 This campaign description is from Carol W. Cagle, "Privacy Campaign: Eye on the Spies," *Civil Liberties*, May 1974, p. 1.
50 Herbert A. Alexander, "Communications and Politics: The Media and the Message," *Law and Contemporary Problems*, Spring 1969, p. 276.

that they want evidence, accuracy, and reliability. Sometimes these two requirements become incompatible.

The Harlem rent strikes of 1963 and 1964 illustrate the problem. Jesse Gray, a black leader with 15 years experience in the fight against slum housing, had developed an almost symbiotic relationship with reporters. They wanted fresh, dramatic news on the growth of the strike; Gray wanted the coverage. He was happy to give them progress reports he did not and could not substantiate. Gray was convinced that if they believed him, they would help pressure city officials. So, encouraged by sympathetic reporters, he continued to report that the strike was spreading. However, almost as an afterthought, reporters began to ask for documentation. It was not forthcoming. As a result, instead of reporting the inflated claims, reporters began to deflate them, and ultimately to deny Gray media coverage. The clash between the needs of the media and the needs of the protestors resulted, finally, in the loss of the message.[51]

Some groups that rely on protest are learning. They are beginning to identify certain broadcasters as allies or opponents. To guard against any possibility that messages will be distorted, groups are establishing the terms of their own coverage. The 1974 kidnaping of Patricia Hearst is an example of this trend. The kidnappers controlled the coverage almost entirely. The Symbionese Liberation Army decided who would receive the initial messages, dictated how they should be distributed, and even seemed to stage minor events to retain media interest. News broadcasters had no choice, apparently, but to comply with their rules. The SLA had the crucial resource—Patricia Hearst.

Quite obviously it does not take a kidnaping to get media coverage. There are many developments increasing media access. More and more radio and television stations are instituting *free speech messages* where citizens and groups can have a 100- to 150-word message heard on the air. *Cable television* is providing still more access. In February 1972, the FCC ruled that cable stations would have to provide at least one channel for the public to present what it wants, and more than that if one could not accommodate everyone.[52]

Then too, *public-interest advertising agencies* are beginning to

---

[51] This incident is described by Michael Lipsky in "Rent Strikes: Poor Man's Weapon," *Transaction*, February 1969, pp. 10–15.
[52] See Thomas Meehan, "Coming Up Next on Channel C: You," *Saturday Review*, September 9, 1972, pp. 14–20.

provide some of the technical expertise that makes whatever access is gained effective. One group, Public Interest Communications Inc., located in San Francisco, is staffed by professionals. This agency, which has foundation financing, will accept as clients only those who can be defined as disadvantaged or serving the disadvantaged. The list is long—environmentalists, minority and prisoner groups, poverty programs, women's and consumer groups, and government agencies that serve the disadvantaged. The agency's services include the development of newspaper and magazine advertisements as well as television and radio spot announcements.[53]

Finally, and this is only a sample, a *ghetto wire service* has been established. Initiated by New York's New School for Social Research and funded jointly by the Ford Foundation and the New York Urban Coalition, this wire service uses only black and Puerto Rican reporters and editors. Called the Community News Service, its job is to give the media accurate information concerning blacks and Puerto Ricans, to carry messages from one ghetto neighborhood to another, and generally to tell the mass media about a world they rarely see.[54]

So access to broadcast media, while difficult, is possible. When broadcast media are combined with print media, as illustrated by the New Mexico Civil Liberties Union campaign, the results can be remarkable. Even for groups without many financial resources, new organizations and rules are providing a way. Activists should also not forget to consider the less expensive direct methods discussed in Chapter 5. When people are available, they can be even more effective, as long as the rules are followed. However, whether it is direct or indirect, short-term or long-term, any campaign to educate or persuade, as we've seen, involves communication. The principles of communication and research on attitude formation and change become relevant tactical information. Unless both are considered, the probability of success is reduced.

Key Words

Gatekeeper
Fairness doctrine
Equal-time provision
Social mechanism

[53] Carolyn Anspacher, "Ad Agency for the Poor," *San Francisco Chronicle*, April 16, 1973.
[54] "Ghetto Wire Service," *Newsweek*, July 7, 1969, p. 86.

Suggested Activities

1. See if you can identify the major gatekeeper(s) in your daily newspaper(s). Interview those who use the press frequently as well as reporters in order to get some consensus.
2. Interview the public service directors of local radio and television stations. Determine their rules for giving public service coverage as well as the amount of time they usually devote to public-service announcements and programming each week.
3. Interview the assignment editors in the news departments of local radio and television stations. How do they select which stories to cover? What are the essential criteria used?
4. Investigate the public-service opportunities provided by cable television in your area.

IV
Legislative Games

7
The Legislative Arena

About Legislative Games

The issue? The eighteen-year-old vote. The problem? How to establish it by legislation and avoid having to use the constitutional amendment procedure—a procedure that is both long and likely to fail. The tactic? Surprise the Senate and circumvent the power of congressional committees by offering an amendment to the 1970 Voting Rights bill. It was being debated at that moment.

The timing was right. Eighteen-year-olds were being killed in an unpopular war in Vietnam. Campuses were in an uproar over the invasion of Cambodia and the Kent State University shooting. Of course, except among student groups, there was no visible public support for the change, and referendums had been voted down in states where the issue was on the ballot. Still, this seemed the only way open to Edward Kennedy and the other liberal senators supporting this extension of the vote. They wouldn't be able to overcome the opposition of the Senate Judiciary Committee in any other way. Kennedy moved.

The rules were with him. Even though the bill being debated simply extended protection of the voting rights of southern blacks for five more years, he could offer an extraneous amendment, and he did.

Over the objections of the administration, which maintained it was unconstitutional, the vote on the amendment was taken. It passed, 64 to 17.

The anticipated southern opposition to the original bill had collapsed. Only a handful of intense civil rights opponents attempted to keep the Senate tied up through another rule—the filibuster. At the end of two weeks the talking was over.

Skeptical about their constitutional right to regulate suffrage standards, yet feeling that protecting the rights of Southern blacks was important, the House then acted. First, the bill went to the Judiciary Committee. Chairman Emanuel Celler didn't like some of the provisions: banning literacy tests, liberalizing residency requirements, and particularly the 18-year-old vote. Still, he considered other provisions crucial. He consented to it.

The next round was the House Rules Committee. Its members had been siding with the civil rights opponents. Surprisingly, the committee allowed the bill to be sent to the floor for debate under a rule that was advantageous to its supporters. No amendments could be added. House members had to accept all the provisions or none. That was the key decision. The House game could also be won, and it was, 224 to 183.

Reluctantly, President Nixon signed it. He still had doubts about the voting-age provision, but that conflict could be dealt with else-where—in the courts.

In a divided and confusing decision, the Supreme Court spoke. Congress did indeed have the authority to lower the voting age for federal elections, the majority said, but not for state and local elections.

So the amendment process had to be initiated anyway. To avoid the electoral chaos that would result from different voting-age requirements at the federal and state levels, Congress and state legislatures acted unusually quickly. On June 30, 1971, the Twenty-sixth Amendment to the U.S. Constitution was declared ratified. One of the more interesting legislative games was over.[1]

All legislative games are similar to the one just described. Whether they are played at the local, state, or national level, the *major* object of each is to make a law. The necessary implements and the acceptable

---

[1] Gary Orfield describes these and other details of the 1970 voting rights battle in *Congressional Power: Congress and Social Change* (New York: Harcourt, Brace Jovanovich, 1975), pp. 99–103, 270–271.

procedures, or "moves," are specified for legislators just as they are for the football player. In their study of state legislative systems, John C. Wahlke and his coauthors developed the analogy in this way:

> Writing agreed-on words on certain paper in certain forms (as Acts, Resolutions, etc.) and delivering them to certain non-legislative officials constitutes a Legislative "score" just as pushing a football across a line constitutes scoring in athletics. There is an accepted length (or range of length) of legislative sessions as there are innings and quarters in athletic contests.[2]

While the rules of legislative games vary depending on where the game is played, they are usually profuse and complicated. They say how bills are to be introduced and processed, who is responsible for what part of the procedure, how the votes are counted, what "moves" are acceptable, etc.; and they always distribute advantages and disadvantages. Winning the game, as Kennedy and his liberal colleagues in the Senate did, requires knowing both the content of those rules and how to use them to your advantage.

Legislative Arenas

So far most of this discussion has focused on Congress. While it is the one legislative arena we all have in common, others are more frequently the target of citizen efforts. Because the problems legislative players on the state and local levels deal with appear to be more directly related to people's lives and seem more approachable, these legislative players at least need to be introduced. An introduction is the only possibility, for these players vary considerably from location to location. Citizens seeking access to them will have to do their own more thorough analysis of the distribution of power and relevant rules. Still, some generalizations about local and state legislative arenas are possible.

State Arenas

On the state level, as at the national level, legislatures are *bicameral*.[3] That is, they contain two legislative houses. While groups like the National Municipal League argue that these are less efficient than unicameral bodies, having two houses provides one more opportunity for citizen access.

[2] John C. Wahlke, Heinz Eulau, William Buchanan, and Leroy C. Ferguson, *The Legislative System* (New York: John Wiley & Sons, 1962), p. 136.
[3] Nebraska has the only unicameral legislature.

Something to think about
What would be another "action" implication of a bicameral legislature?

However, unlike the houses of Congress, the two houses at the state level are both based on population. This is the result of a 1964 Supreme Court decision, *Reynolds* v. *Sims*. Before that, sparsely populated areas were given an advantage by state constitutional requirements that in at least one house each county should have a minimum of one representative and that no county should have more than three.

Terms vary in the two houses. In approximately three-fourths of the states, upper house members, senators, are elected for four-year terms. Except in four states, the lower house term is two years. This compares with the six-year terms of U.S. senators and the two-year terms of members of the U.S. House of Representatives. At both the national and state levels, terms of upper house members are usually *staggered*. We vote for one-third of the members of the U.S. Senate every two years; on the state level, we usually elect half every two years. The smaller numbers and longer terms of senators seem to add to their prestige and influence, but it is in the lower house that electoral politics gives citizens more frequent influence.

Local Arenas

Thus far we've been talking about national and state legislative arenas. The fact that there are so many similarities between the two levels makes the description easier. For the observer, the local level is extremely confusing, primarily because so many institutions get into the act. To perceive the problem, examine this information. In 1972 the Bureau of the Census reported that there were 78,218 local governments, including 3044 counties, 18,517 municipalities, 16,991 townships, 15,781 school districts, and 23,885 special districts. Within each type of local government, legislative activities occur. Each type has autonomy in certain policy areas, and each has the power to raise funds through taxation or by issuing bonds. Jurisdictions, however, are confined to a specific geographic area.

In order to avoid being overwhelmed completely, we will examine only the major legislative bodies at the local level. These indicate clearly the *decentralization of power* that exists.

In *cities*, at least in those with over 5,000 people, the legislative body is usually called the *council*. In the largest cities they are often bicameral. More generally the council is small, often with only five or seven members. Council members typically are elected from wards or districts, but they may be elected at large and even by proportional representation.[4]

The power of the council will depend on the structure of the local government. In *weak-mayor* structures, councils not only make laws but have control over some of the administrative apparatus. This may include making appointments and preparing as well as approving the city budget. Further, contrary to the situation with *strong-mayor* structures, the council need contend with only a limited veto power, and sometimes with none at all.

An interesting comparison can be made between the strong-mayor, weak-council structure and the legislative-executive relation at the national level. Those who like consistency and neatness in government as well as efficiency like the reduced role of the council. The strong mayor, like the President, can directly confront the legislature and frequently force it to capitulate. On the other hand, those people who are alarmed by the growth of executive power at the national level see little cause to rejoice in the increasing development of the strong-mayor, weak-council structure at the local level.[5]

One point should be made about categorizing local governments in terms of the legislative-executive distribution of power. Most mayor-council cities today do not have either the pure weak-mayor or pure strong-mayor form, but a compromise or blending of the two types. However, in cities of over 500,000 population, something approximating the strong-mayor, weak-council form predominates.[6]

Still another arrangement is evolving at the local level that tends to diminish the power of the city council. This is called the *council-manager system*. Used now by approximately half the cities with 10,000 to 500,000 population, this structure places all administrative authority in the hands of a professional manager. The council does give the manager overall policy direction.

In one variation of the council-manager system, the council retains

[4] Henry A. Turner, *American Democracy: State and Local Government* (New York: Harper and Row, Publishers, 1968, 1970), p. 73.
[5] John H. Baker develops this comparison in *Urban Politics in America* (New York: Charles Scribner's Sons, 1971), p. 177.
[6] For an illustration of how these structures manifest themselves, see Edward C. Banfield and James Q. Wilson, *City Politics* (Cambridge, Mass.: Harvard University Press, 1963), pp. 80–81.

some of its administrative power. It formulates the city budget and appoints and removes department heads. However, the council relies heavily on the advice of a professional, called a *chief administrative officer* in this case. The chief administrative officer is expected to supervise and coordinate the executive apparatus.

Whether or not the legislative game is even worth playing at the local level depends in part on which structure of government the city has. The authority of the city council relative to other local institutions must be carefully assessed. Does the council really have the authority to do what you want?

It is not only the council's authority relative to that of the mayor or manager that must be examined. In most sizable cities and many small ones, there are other legislative institutions: boards, commissions, single officers, and special districts. They have little or no formal connection with the city government proper—mayor and council. As a nineteenth century reaction to the power of party machines at the local level, these independent units were created to redistribute and decentralize authority. While some of them ultimately became city departments under the mayor and council, many are still loosely tied or not tied at all to the traditional structure.

In their study of New York City government, Wallace Sayre and Herbert Kaufman described one particular board, a unit authorized to deal with public health:

> The Sanitary Code is enacted by the New York City Board of Health, a body appointed by the Mayor and invested by State legislation and the Charter with authority to adopt regulations on all matters of health and sanitation.... The regulations of the Board—that is, the Sanitary Code—have the effect of state or city legislation within the city; the Board is then really a unifunctional legislative organ. The Board of Education and Board of Hospitals are somewhat similar institutions.[7]

Special districts administered by boards, such as those described by Sayre and Kaufman, number around 45,000. Half of these are school districts. Others include transit authorities, water districts, park districts, and port authorities. Generally the governing boards are appointed by the state or local government, appointed by the several governments served by the district, or, less commonly, elected by the voters. Performing both legislative and executive functions, they fi-

[7] Wallace S. Sayre and Herbert Kaufman, *Governing New York City* (New York: Russell Sage Foundation, 1960), pp. 97–98.

nance their activities by taxing, selling bonds, or charging directly for their services.

So the legislative arena in cities may not be a city council chamber at all. It is just as likely to be a board room. The activist at the local level will have to study the city charter carefully as a *first step* in locating the source of legislative authority. The activist will have to realize that while these many legislative bodies give opportunities for access, they can also create problems for citizen control. Knowing the key players within each, how they usually play the game, and the special rules operating would challenge any informed citizen.

Before we leave the local level, one more legislative unit needs to be identified, this one existing at the county level. It is called a *county board*, or sometimes a board of supervisors or county court. Usually it has both legislative and executive functions.

One type of county board is the *commissioner* type. Used in two-thirds of all counties, a board of this type has between three and seven members elected either by the county at large or, in some states, by districts.

A second type of county board is the *supervisor* type. Here the board members are first chosen as township trustees or city councilors. They serve on the county board in an ex officio capacity. Since a board of this type is much larger than one of the commissioner type, a board of the supervisor type must have a committee system. As on the national and state levels, it is in committee meetings that important legislative matters are screened, defined, and formulated for full board consideration.

Something to think about
Which method of electing county boards would give citizens greater access? Which type would promote more effective representation?

What Do All These Legislative Arenas Have in Common?
Essentially they involve games where there is more than one winner and where the precise payoff is the result of intense negotiation. Compromise is required. In their study of the American legislative process, William Keefe and Morris Ogul explained compromise in this way:

> The process of winning support calls for tapering demands from the optimal down to the acceptable—ranging from what is desirable to what, if necessary, will do—and (referring to the national

and state levels) it may begin as early as the initial drafting of the bill and run through the final negotiations in a conference committee between the houses.[8]

Some people call compromise "selling out," but others say that given the distribution of power in this country and the general commitment to democratic norms, it is the only way to win. Rarely, except during times of crisis, does the payoff involve a major win for any *one* group. Instead, certain groups get something during each legislative session. Certainly not everyone wins or loses to the same degree, but there are usually no major upsets *for those who play*.

What Legislators Do

So far the discussion of legislative arenas has been very general, but understanding legislative games requires an appreciation of the variety of things legislators do. Each implies a different kind of win. The major battle is not always over the approval of a certain program. It might be over the size of an appropriation. While these are the two major legislative activities, other activities involve surveying the activities of the executive branch, providing assistance to individuals and groups with specific problems, amending constitutions, helping to select other public officials, and generally educating the public.

Lawmaking

Two legislative activities are uniquely interrelated. They are part of lawmaking. The first involves *authorizing* new or amending existing programs. Aid to education, stricter air pollution standards, and tax reform are examples. Once these programs are authorized, however, they have to be financed. At a minimum it will cost something just to administer them. Thus, the second part of the lawmaking process involves *appropriations*.

It seems strange, doesn't it, that programs could be created but no money appropriated for their implementation, and yet it happens. In 1968, the House Appropriations Committee tried to alter a national housing policy meant to break up ghettos by not appropriating any money at all to enforce the fair-housing law. In addition, they tried to kill a program of federal rent supplements designed to let poor people live in standard new housing. The committee members eventually

---

[8] William J. Keefe and Morris S. Ogul, *The American Legislative Process* (Englewood Cliffs, N.J.: Prentice-Hall, 1964), p. 10.

gave in, but not without a struggle—and what they finally agreed to was only a fraction of what was initially authorized.[9]

At the national level the appropriations committees seem to be growing more accommodating. The program committees are less often thwarted. Or to put it another way, on sensitive social issues that have attracted a great deal of attention, committee members are now tending to yield in advance rather than face the humiliation that comes from a loss after a showdown.

Still, the fact that citizens read in the newspaper that so many millions of dollars have been authorized for mass transit systems can be a delusion. Only a fraction of that might get appropriated. Then, of course, once the appropriation is approved by Congress, the President might veto everything or approve the measure but *impound* some of the funds.[10]

As activists follow both the authorization and appropriation processes, they have to watch for wavering legislators who might try to camouflage their actions on a bill. A congressman, for example, might vote to authorize a program, and then, when no one is looking, quietly oppose it by voting for a low appropriation. Lawmaking can be devious.

State and local legislative bodies also get involved in these two aspects of lawmaking—only the policy substance and the amount of money are essentially different. State legislatures, for example, are concerned with such subjects as marriage and divorce, private property, deeds, mortgages, contracts, and laws protecting the people by specifying and defining the punishment for various crimes. Particularly important on the state level are laws enacted under the states' police powers. These include laws to protect the safety, health, morals, convenience, order, and general welfare of the people. Examples are laws that regulate the production and sale of intoxicating liquor; laws regulating various professions, trades, and industries; and laws author-

---

[9] Orfield, *Congressional Power*, p. 265.

[10] As of February 4, 1974, funds withheld by President Nixon amounted to $11.8 billion. He claimed the right to withhold them on the basis of the Anti-Deficiency Act of 1905, which allows the executive branch to "create reserves" for a number of reasons: among others, to provide for contingencies and to effect savings made possible by developments that occur after the funds were originally appropriated. By going to court, however, Congress and special interest groups had specific impoundments declared illegal. For details, see Harry B. Ellis, "Nixon 'Impounds' $11.8 Billion, but Few Congressmen Protest," *Christian Science Monitor*, April 11, 1974.

izing cities and counties to enact ordinances related to sanitation, health, zoning, traffic, and so on.[11]

Take another look at that last activity, "laws authorizing cities. . . ." *The state defines what local lawmakers can do,* just as the U.S. Constitution, much more implicitly, defines what states can do. Let's clarify these *lawmaking relationships.* Concerning the states, the Tenth Amendment to the U.S. Constitution says: "The powers not delegated to the United States by the Constitution, nor prohibited by it to the States, are reserved to the States respectively, or to the people." So unlike the national legislature, state lawmakers are not limited to doing those things expressly granted or implied by their constitutions. They can make laws on a variety of subjects.

The U.S. Constitution not only gives states all those powers it has not kept for itself, but, more specifically, it reserves to the states the authority to create local governments. They can create any number and type of local governing units and grant them any authority they wish. The subservience of the position is quite clear, and it was stated emphatically in a 1923 Supreme Court decision (*Trenton* v. *New Jersey*).

> The city is a political subdivision of the state, created as a convenient agency for the exercise of such of the governmental powers of the state as may be entrusted to it. . . . The state may withhold, grant, or withdraw powers and privileges as it sees fit. . . . In the absence of state constitutional provisions safeguarding it to them, municipalities have no inherent right of self-government which is beyond the legislative control of the state.

This definition of the local-state relationship also applies to other local units of government—counties, townships, and special districts. In fact, they are all really subdivisions of the state acting in legislative-executive capacities.

Does this mean local governments have none of the lawmaking autonomy of state governments? Local governments have autonomy only if the state gives it to them, and the state does this through a *charter.* The charter not only incorporates a city but specifies its form and powers. Charters vary considerably.

Along with the charter, money defines the power of local legislative units. The state has financial as well as legal supremacy. While national lawmakers and state lawmakers raise most of their money

[11] Henry A. Turner identifies these policy areas, *American Democracy,* p. 24.

through the income tax, city officials must generally rely on the property tax. In fact, 40 percent of most municipal revenue is raised in this way. The county or township is usually responsible for assessments and collections. However, taxing property and taxing sales (used in 17 states) are often inequitable and certainly limited forms of taxation. They fail to take into consideration people's ability to pay, for they are not directly related to income. Middle- and lower-income homeowners end up paying a larger proportion of their income for these taxes than do more affluent individuals.

So what do local lawmakers do? More and more they are turning to state and national government for help. Through *grants-in-aid*, revenue derived from taxes is returned to cities. (Both local and state governments have been the recipients of federal grants-in-aid.) These grants have been the major response to the inability of the property tax to adequately support local government.[12] The problem with grants-in-aid is that while they provide revenue, they further limit the independence of local lawmakers, for what the money is to be spent on is determined by who is giving the money. Also, to get the money, the recipient must provide matching funds. In a sense, the grant-in-aid priorities set at the state and federal levels determine local spending priorities.

The answer? Give cities the money without strings. In 1972 this happened. It was called *revenue sharing*. National lawmakers provided for the distribution of $5.3 billion in the first year and a total of $30.1 billion over five years. Local governments, according to a particular distribution formula, get two-thirds of this money. State governments get the rest. The only major spending restriction for local governments is that the money is to be used for public safety, environmental protection, public transportation, health, recreation, social services, financial administration, and libraries.

So the funding problems faced by local lawmakers have been eased slightly by federal assistance. Only legal limitations established by state legislatures and state constitutions remain to be resolved. In the meantime, these continue to limit and define the local lawmaker's role, just as the U.S. Constitution more broadly limits the state lawmaker's role.

Lawmaking has several critical steps. They are similar at each level of government, but they are likely to be far simpler on the local level,

[12] Baker, *Urban Politics in America*, p. 263.

where committees may not be involved. Each step involves a different opportunity for citizen influence. Below is a *generalized* version.

1. *The bill is originated* by an executive agency, an interest group, or an individual legislator.
2. *The bill is introduced* by a legislator.
3. *The bill is referred* to a standing committee by the leadership.
4. *The committee acts,* and the bill is referred to a subcommittee or hearings are scheduled.
5. *The committee decides,* and the bill ʾis disregarded, defeated, accepted and reported out, or amended or rewritten and reported out.
6. *A second committee examines and acts on the bill* (i.e., a rules committee), or the bill is placed directly on a calendar for house consideration.
7. *The house considers and votes on the bill,* and it is debated, amended, rejected, or accepted. The procedure thus far is repeated in the second house.
8. *Differences in the two house versions are worked out* in conference committee, and an agreed-on version is returned to the two houses.
9. *A final vote is taken in the two houses,* and, if it is approved, the bill is forwarded to the chief executive (President, governor, mayor).
10. *Action is taken by the executive,* who may approve the measure, veto it, "pocket veto" it, or permit it to become law without a signature.
11. *Veto review action is taken by each house* if the executive has vetoed the bill.
12. *The bill becomes law* if it was acted upon positively by the executive or if a veto is overridden by both houses.

Citizen lawmaking.   The one type of lawmaking at the state and local levels that departs entirely from this generalized version involves direct citizen action. Through the *initiative* a specified number of voters may propose a statute or constitutional amendment by petition. If it qualifies, the proposal is submitted to the voters for approval or rejection.

In thirteen states citizens may use this method to propose amendments to the constitution; in seven others the method can be used to directly pass laws. Five states use the indirect statutory initiative. Here citizens present the proposition to the legislature, which has the option of passing it without change or submitting it to the voters in the succeeding election. In some states, if the legislature refuses to enact the proposed measure, if additional signatures are collected it is submitted to the voters.[13]

The other departure from the previous generalized version of law-making is the *referendum*. Here, if citizens don't like what the state lawmakers have done, they can again circulate a petition. If they get the required number of signatures, the act is submitted directly to the voters, and the voters decide.

Many local governments also allow the initiative and referendum. In addition, over half the state constitutions prohibit cities from in-curring debts without the approval of a majority of the voters. So, even in the largest cities, crucial matters, especially those concerning capital expenditures, are put before the voters.[14] In this case the order gets reversed. Instead of citizens trying to influence public officials to approve a measure, public officials become busy persuaders. These are the unique constitutional provisions distributing lawmaking authority to citizens that are not available on the national level.

Amending Constitutions

Before we end this general examination of lawmaking, there is another procedure that it is important to understand—how one amends con-stitutions. The discussion of the establishment of the eighteen-year-old vote covered the general procedures at the national level. At this level they are precisely spelled out in the Constitution. An amendment may be *proposed* by a two-thirds vote of both houses of Congress or by a national convention called by Congress in response to an application by two-thirds of the states. Only the first method has ever been used, although some states have attempted to use the second method. There are also two methods of *ratifying* an amendment to the U.S. Constitu-tion. While ultimately the amendment must be approved by three-quarters of the states, this approval can come from state legislatures or special state conventions established for the purpose. The state convention method has been used only once. The newest amendment, proposed and ratified in the traditional manner, is likely to be the Equal Rights Amendment, sponsored by women's groups across the country.

The same two-step procedure that exists at the national level exists at the state level. In all states except New Hampshire, constitutional

---

[13] Turner, *American Democracy*, pp. 43–44.
[14] Banfield and Wilson, *City Politics*, pp. 76–77.

amendments may be proposed by the state legislature. In two-thirds of the states only a single legislature must approve the amendment, but in the others an amendment must be acted upon by two successive legislatures. The vote required in each house to approve it ranges from a simple majority to a three-fifths majority. Except in Delaware, ratification is by the electorate, usually by a majority of voters.

Thirteen states allow citizens to propose amendments directly. Using the initiative process, signatures are collected on a petition, then the measure is put on the ballot. Usually the number of signatures is greater than it would be for a proposed statute.

On the local level, state law indicates who is responsible and how to amend city charters. Generally, only a home rule charter[15] allows local citizens to draft and amend their own charters. The process usually begins with the formation of a municipal charter commission. Once the commissioners propose an amendment, it is submitted to the voters for their approval. Ordinarily a majority vote is needed. In those cities where the direct initiative is used, a required number of signatures can also get an amendment on the ballot.

From all this discussion of lawmaking, it sounds as if this is the only thing legislators do. As the introductory comments indicated, however, the legislative game involves pay-offs other than programs adequately financed or constitutions amended. These are not quite as complex. Nor are the stakes usually as high.

Keeping an Eye on the Executive Branch

The pay-off from this is having laws administered effectively—or at least in the way lawmakers intended them to be. Some people call this *legislative oversight*, but it boils down to keeping an eye on the executive branch of government. In a sense, the legislative branch supervises the executive branch by questioning, reviewing, assessing, modifying, and rejecting administration policies. This "nosiness" is justified because legislators need to know whether their laws, as written, are working, whether or not they are being implemented as they were intended to be, or whether, indeed, new laws in a particular policy area are necessary.

Of course, not every legislator oversees everything. Usually the job is delegated to committees. Different kinds of committees are supposed to deal with different aspects of administrative activity. On the na-

[15] This type of charter allows a city to make changes in its form of organization and powers without constantly going to the state legislature.

tional level, for example, appropriations committees are asked to exercise financial control before money is spent, government operations committees are asked to review the administrative structure and procedures, and program committees are asked to oversee the actual substance of what is being implemented.[16]

To help Congress do what seems to be an unmanageable job, there is a staff of investigators called the *General Accounting Office*. This department offers Congress at least the opportunity to do its job. Whenever Congress asks, the GAO will make studies of specific problems.

So when it comes to keeping an eye on the executive branch, how is Congress doing and what is it doing? Let's take the "what" first. In his study of Congress, John Saloma says that since the Legislative Reorganization Act of 1946, formal and informal techniques of administrative control have expanded.[17] For example, by replacing open-ended authorizations for certain programs with annual authorizations, Congress has seen to it that about 35 percent of the programs are examined each year. These include programs in the areas of foreign aid, space, atomic energy, and defense and weapons systems. Congressional investigations, which averaged slightly over 30 per Congress between World Wars I and II, rose to over 200 per Congress by the early 1950s. In addition, while each committee was only authorized to spend $10,000 to conduct investigations, by 1960 congressional committee budgets totaled $15.5 million. In terms of sheer volume, something is happening.

Still, how legislative oversight is performed has been strongly criticized. The criticism includes these points about investigations:

1. They are often begun for partisan reasons—skip the facts, just embarrass the opposition.
2. They are expensive and disruptive, and fail to bring about needed improvements.
3. They are inefficient—the members of Congress conducting the investigations are uninformed, and they don't have the time to conduct a thorough inquiry.[18]

[16] For details of this obligation, see the Legislative Reorganization Act of 1946, Section 136.
[17] John S. Saloma III, *Congress and the New Politics* (Boston: Little, Brown and Company, 1969), pp. 137–138.
[18] Joseph P. Harris, *Congress and the Legislative Process* (New York: McGraw-Hill Book Company, 1963, 1972), p. 173.

This criticism does not negate the fact that national legislators can *potentially* fulfill this statutory obligation, which is an important one for citizens. For it suggests a way of focusing attention on national problems as well as prodding the executive to do its job. It is an opportunity for citizen access.

Seymour Scher identifies several conditions under which this oversight responsibility is taken seriously. Activists can either take advantage of these conditions or create them.

1. When the leadership of the majority party in Congress believes it can cause sufficient embarrassment, with accompanying profit for itself, to a past or current opposition President who is held responsible for the performance of agency appointees, committee oversight tends to be used for this purpose.
2. When the committee leadership or powerful committee members believe that constituent or group interests cannot be satisfied by the routine personal interaction between Congress and the agency, committee review tends to be a substitute.
3. When Congress perceives a threat, particularly from the President, to traditional prerogatives in relation to regulatory agencies, committee interest in the agencies is a likely response.
4. When, periodically, Congress becomes interested in revising regulatory policy, committee attention to the regulatory agency tends to occur as a byproduct.... An examination of agency conduct frequently is used ... as a screen behind which new legislation is built.
5. When the committee leadership becomes convinced that interests to which it is opposed can be substantially advanced by the exposure of dramatic evidence of agency failure, it can be expected to move first to neutralize or minimize these gains by initiating its own inquiry.[19]

When one or more of these conditions are present, some exciting pay-offs can result. For example, L. H. Fountain of North Carolina is chairman of the Subcommittee on Intergovernmental Relations. The parent committee is the House Governmental Operations Committee. Representative Fountain has few of the traits of an agitator, but this is what he has turned out to be. In the 1960s he became obsessed with the Food and Drug Administration. He was concerned about its failure to fulfill its statutory responsibility. So he acted. For

[19] Saloma, *Congress and the New Politics*, pp. 153–154.

the last six years his subcommittee has grilled a succession of FDA commissioners on an impressive range of topics. This has forced the agency to defend its policies on the sale of birth control pills, on control of pesticides, on recalls of poisonous foods, on removal of cyclamates from the market, and most recently, on its approval of the cattle-fattening but cancer-causing hormone DES. With the help of two committee staffers, Fountain's committee is doing its job. It is the public that wins. Those involved in the Nader Congress project say that this committee has come closer than any other to exercising good oversight.[20] So it can happen.

Keeping an eye on the executive branch also occurs on the *state and local* levels. On the state level the resources that make control theoretically possible are like those that exist on the national level. State lawmakers, for example, have the power to create administrative agencies, define their tasks, appropriate funds for their activities, and specify their procedures and organization. So one would imagine that administrators would want to do their jobs effectively, if for no other reason than to please their creators and sustainers. Of course, most try to do their jobs effectively for other reasons.

Depending on the size of the local legislative body and its constitutional and statutory authority, legislators on the local level may also be players in this kind of game. Their scrutiny is sometimes closer, for local taxpayer organizations, particularly sensitive to the limits and inequities of the property tax, demand efficient administration. They hold elected officials responsible. Still, whether national, state, or local legislators are involved, keeping an eye on the executive branch is not the number one priority. As one congressman put it, this is a "time expensive, low-priority concern except when there is something 'big in it.'"[21] Only when political gains valued by legislators are seen to outweigh prospective losses will they become seriously involved. Citizens at any level should think about ways of communicating potential political gains and losses more vividly. For "wins" from executive-watching can be big ones.

Serving Constituents

Theoretically, everything a legislator does directly or indirectly serves constituents, but one aspect of the legislative job is called just that.

[20] Mark J. Green, James M. Fallows, and David R. Zwick, *Who Runs Congress?* (New York: Grossman Publishers, Bantam Books ed., 1972), pp. 120–121. © 1972 by Ralph Nader.
[21] Saloma, *Congress and the New Politics*, p. 153.

Serving constituents differs from lawmaking, generally, in that the request is personal. It usually does not require legislation that would affect many people. A student writes that he isn't receiving his veteran's checks. A mother complains that she was told she is ineligible for food stamps. A widow explains she is not receiving survivors' benefits. Frequently answering these appeals entails explaining the problem to the appropriate executive-branch agency. Aides to one New York Representative said 60 percent of staff time in 1969 was spent in that way.[22]

While many citizens feel intimidated by their representatives, even state or local ones, those who rely on them for help with particular problems are pleasantly surprised. As a means of cutting through red tape or the maze of bureaucratic information, contacting a legislator or a staff member directly works, because legislators take serving constitutents seriously.

Something to think about
What are some other ways in which legislators could assist students with problems?

Selecting Public Officials
At all levels of government, legislators help appoint some public officials. Generally these are top-level administrators, but they also may be judges. Nationally, it is Article II, Section II of the U.S. Constitution that provides the authority. Spelling out the powers of the President, the Constitution says:

> . . . and he shall nominate, and by and with the advice and consent of the Senate, shall appoint Ambassadors, and other public Ministers and Consuls, Judges of the Supreme Court, and all other Officers of the United States, whose appointments are not herein provided for, and which shall be established by Law; but the Congress may by law vest the appointment of such inferior officers, as they think proper, in the President alone, in the Courts of Law, or in the Heads of Departments.

For citizens this appointment authority is important because winning this game has formidable policy implications. The idea is to use influence to obtain the appointment of those sympathetic to a par-

---

[22] "Bumper Mail Crop Keeps Congressional Staffs Busy," *Congressional Quarterly*, November 14, 1969, p. 2282.

ticular point of view and, of course, to work for the defeat of the unsympathetic. The second approach was used by interest groups who objected to two Nixon nominations to the Supreme Court.

Almost as a matter of course, Presidents have come to expect confirmation of Supreme Court nominees. President Nixon experienced no difficulty when he named a new chief justice, and he expected none in filling the seat vacated when Justice Fortas resigned. He was mistaken, for the first man he nominated, Clement F. Haynsworth, Jr., was strongly opposed by both civil rights and labor groups.

What were their objections? Haynsworth, a conservative member of a southern court, had generally decided cases in ways that were disadvantageous to both labor and civil rights interests. The evidence was communicated to senators individually and through hearings. In addition, a barrage of critical mail from both groups flooded Senate offices.

President Nixon refused to withdraw the nomination, even when asked by such prestigious Republican senators as Margaret Chase Smith (Me.) and Barry Goldwater (Ariz.). Instead, the White House drive for confirmation became intense. Senators who privately told the President of their opposition to the nominee were pressured both directly and indirectly. Former Senator William Saxbe (R., Ohio) reported on the tactics used: "Businessmen and defense contractors I'd never heard of began calling me. . . . And some would add a reminder that they contributed to my campaign."

The final vote came on November 21, 1969. After three months of intense political warfare, it was over in an 11-minute roll-call vote. By 10 votes (45 to 55), the nomination failed. Seventeen Republicans opposed the President. On an issue where Presidents are rarely defeated, defeat came. This was not just a win for labor and civil rights groups, it was also a win for Senate players. An almost forgotten power was revived.

As if to remind themselves that their action was not a fluke, in April 1970 the Senate defeated a second Nixon nominee to the Supreme Court, G. Harrold Carswell. Civil rights groups were again active, particularly after a 1948 speech by Carswell before the Georgia State legislature was made public. As a Florida reporter revealed, Carswell had said:

> I am a Southerner by ancestry, birth, training, inclination, belief, and practice. I believe that segregation of the races is proper and the only practical and correct way of life in our states. I have always so believed, and I shall also so act. . . . I yield to no man as

a fellow candidate, or as a fellow citizen, in the firm, vigorous belief in the principles of white supremacy, and I shall always be so governed.

The fact that the remarks were made in the heat of a political contest 20 years earlier made little difference to many people. His more recent courtroom behavior seemed to reaffirm this position, at least according to the testimony given.

Aided by increasing criticism of the nomination from lawyers who believed it was an affront to the Court, civil rights groups began getting through to key senators. The vote was 51 to 45. Carswell, like Haynsworth, was defeated. Again, a traditionally insignificant power acquired new life. So did the Senate, for a while.[23]

While these were national legislative games involving high stakes, similar games occur on the state and local levels. In most states many of the governor's appointments to administrative posts, boards, commissions, and in some states the judiciary, must be approved by the senate. In other states, legislative power is even greater. In certain southern and New England states, for example, the legislature elects some of the judges and administrative officials.[24]

The opportunity for local legislators to help select officers depends on the authority granted them by the state. In the weak-mayor, strong-council cities, the opportunities are many. The same is true at the county level. Members of county boards often appoint nonelective officials without involving the local executive.[25]

At the county level in many states, the National Women's Political Caucus is taking advantage of this authority quite systematically as another opportunity for access. The Caucus is petitioning county boards to institute the practice of posting and publicizing in local newspapers all appointments to be made. They would like this to occur 30 days before a vacancy is anticipated. This move should give more citizens an opportunity to apply for posts and/or to scrutinize the names of those recommended.

Educating the People

The cynic would say it doesn't happen. Just listen to the campaign rhetoric and you know public officials aren't interested in educating

---

[23] This description of the Haynsworth and Carswell defeats relies strongly on Orfield, *Congressional Power*, pp. 103–116.

[24] Turner, *American Democracy*, p. 25.

[25] This power is limited by the practice of electing most county officials, a practice that evolved in the first half of the nineteenth century.

their constituents. In addition, why have legislators kept their proceedings secret for so long if they really care about this obligation? Any attempts at education are strictly political.

Whether the intention is political or educational, there is a national law that bestows substantial benefits on incumbent members of Congress who say they are educating the public. Similar laws exist at the state level and in some cities and counties. The laws allow legislators to communicate with their constituents without paying postage, a privilege called the *franking privilege*. The rules state that members of Congress are not to use the privilege to communicate as a friend or candidate, but only as a representative communicating with a constituent. In a 1968 advisory opinion, the U.S. Post Office spelled out *what is frankable*:

- A tabulation of the member's voting record
- A letter furnishing official information on a federal election
- A letter of congratulations to a naturalized citizen urging him or her to register and vote
- A notice to residents of a redistricted area notifying them that the member is now their Representative or Senator

The U.S. Post Office, which bills legislative bodies for franked mail, believes the privilege is abused. In 1966, for example, they charged that Sen. Robert Griffin (R., Mich.) was using the franking privilege to mail campaign literature to his constituents under the pretext that it was part of a regular newsletter. For the abuse, the Post Office sent Griffin a bill for $25,000. It had no way of enforcing its collection, however, and the bill was never paid. Griffin denied the charge.[26]

Used legally, franking can also be a way for interest groups to educate voters. If a sympathetic legislator includes information about a pending bill in a newsletter, this may generate support for the group's position. Think of the potential. On the national level, in one year alone (1966), the Post Office estimated that 197 million pieces of franked mail had been sent.[27]

So these are the kinds of things legislators do: make laws and appropriate funds, amend constitutions, keep an eye on the executive branch, help select other public officials, and educate the public. Each of these functions, we've seen, gives citizens an opportunity to play

[26] See "Franking Privilege," *Congressional Quarterly*, November 14, 1969, p. 2284.
[27] *Ibid.*

the legislative game. Each involves a different kind of win, but they all involve the distribution of advantages and disadvantages.

Legislators as Players

How Legislators Get to Be Players

In terms of *formal, constitutional requirements,* it's quite easy to become a legislator. Nationally, to be a representative, you must be at least 25 years old. Thomas J. Downey, elected to Congress in 1974, barely made it. He had just turned 25. In addition to the age requirement, a representative must have been a citizen for seven years, and must be an inhabitant of the state in which he or she is running. The qualifications for being a U.S. senator are somewhat more rigorous: one must be at least thirty, have been a U.S. citizen for nine years, and be an inhabitant of the state that he or she hopes to represent.

Requirements vary at the state and local levels, but again they are described constitutionally. They are generally based on age, citizenship, and residency.

On the surface, given the ability to mobilize voter support, it would seem that everyone has an equal opportunity to become a legislative player. Not true. Certain rules, practices, and circumstances have biased the selection process. Let's look at two: *apportionment* and *incumbency.*

Apportionment refers to the allocation of legislators on the basis of population, in order to achieve proportional representation. The U.S. Constitution says people are to be counted every 10 years. This implies that representation in the lower house must be changed in order to accommodate changes in the population. Until 1929 this was done by increasing the number of representatives to reflect the growing population.

However, things were getting out of hand. The House was becoming too large. So, in 1929, Congress established a "permanent" system of reapportionment that would discourage any further growth in its own membership. The size of the House was fixed at 435. Administratively, the Bureau of the Census counts the number of inhabitants in each state every 10 years and determines the number of representatives each state should have. This information is transmitted to the President, who, in turn, transmits it to Congress. The proposed distribution is supposed to become effective within 15 days.

Complicating the procedure are districts. In 1842 Congress required every state entitled to more than one representative to divide

DOONESBURY   by Garry Trudeau

Copyright 1975, G. B. Trudeau/Distributed by Universal Press Syndicate.

the state into districts of contiguous territory. Each district is entitled to elect one representative. Since 1929, districts no longer have to be contiguous or compact. The complications arise in determining how districts are to be established. Historically, they have been drawn by state legislatures to give an advantage to a certain party or a certain interest. Consistently, rural-dominated state legislatures would draw district lines to protect rural power, in spite of the population shift away from agricultural areas to cities and suburbs. Distortion of districts for political reasons is known as *gerrymandering*.

Several Supreme Court decisions have removed one kind of representational bias. Where districts are numerically so out of balance that a person's vote in one district does not equal another person's vote in another district, this is a denial of equal protection of the law. Until 1964 (*Westberry* v. *Sanders*), some congressional districts had four or five times the population of other congressional districts. After the decision, every state with more than one district had to redistrict so that the populations were roughly equal. No longer could formal rules of this kind give rural interests an advantage.[28]

Two years earlier, the U.S. Supreme Court had made this point relative to *state* legislatures. In *Baker* v. *Carr* (1962), they said that the equal protection clause of the federal Constitution could be used to test the fairness of state legislatures. In 1964, more precisely, they said that *both houses* of state legislatures must be apportioned on a population basis, with districts having populations as nearly equal as is practicable (*Reynolds* v. *Sims*).

What are the *implications* of this bias being declared unconstitutional? A particularly important result is that gradually more legislators are coming from urban or suburban districts than from rural ones. The result? More legislative players are interested in working for the pay-offs sought by metropolitan areas: mass transit, low-cost housing, reduced pollution, welfare, etc.[29] The rule change distributed advantages differently.

A second source of bias in legislative representation has to do in

---

[28] Gerrymandering of another kind has not been declared illegal. State legislatures may still distort the shape of districts to protect certain interests.

[29] One study of state legislatures concluded this by looking at differences in spending patterns before and after the key Supreme Court decision. These researchers found that the longer a state's experience with reapportionment, the greater its propensity to spend in favor of urban needs. For a discussion of this and other conclusions, see H. George Frederickson and Yong Hyo Cho, "Legislative Apportionment and Fiscal Policy in the American States," *Western Political Quarterly*, March 1974, pp. 5–37.

part with rules and in part with circumstance. It is the extraordinary difficulty of *defeating legislative incumbents*. During the 1950s and 1960s, for example, when the country was experiencing enormous changes and international crises, there was rarely an election when even a tenth of the incumbents in the U.S. House of Representatives were defeated. According to Gary Orfield:

> When Woodrow Wilson became President in 1913, he faced a Congress where only one Representative in forty had won election ten or more times. By 1971, a fifth of the members had accumulated this vast seniority, doubling the level of the 1950's.[30]

Incumbents are currently reelected 95 percent of the time. Defeat is just as rare at the state level.

One rule that helps to account for this bias toward incumbents at both the state and national levels is the rule just discussed, apportionment. State legislators have a habit of distorting the shape of districts to protect incumbents at both levels.

Circumstances also protect incumbents, and the circumstances are influenced by other formal and informal rules. For example, the U.S. Constitution says that each House may determine the rules of its proceedings (Article I, Section 5), and each House has. For example, members of Congress have staffs to help them do their jobs. These staff members can work on constituent problems and build constituent loyalty simultaneously. In addition, there is the franking privilege previously discussed. Through "official" communication with constituents, members of Congress keep constituents aware of their names and activities. To assist in this endeavor, Congress allows its members to use the congressional radio and television studios to produce low-cost reports for broadcast in their home states and districts. A 1970 study estimated that these and other privileges gave an incumbent member of Congress at least a $16,000 campaign advantage.[31] But there is more: A recent study by Americans for Democratic Action placed the financial benefits accruing to congressional incumbency even higher— $488,505 annually.

So you've been sent to Congress . . .
The combined cost of congressional offices and support services totals more than $500,000 for each member of the House. What follows is a partial listing of these benefits.

[30] Orfield, *Congressional Power*, p. 307.
[31] *Ibid.*, p. 308.

Personal salary, $44,625 per year.
A *personal staff* of 18, paid up to $227,220.
Four furnished offices, one in Washington, three in the district.
Twenty-six round trips home plus six such staff trips, first-class air fare authorized.
A *stationery allowance* of $6,500, which may be used for personal expenses.
Free mail and telephone services, including up to 480,000 "public document" envelopes per year.
Seventy-one subscriptions to *Congressional Record*.
Two Thousand wall calendars.
Four hundred Agricultural Yearbooks.
Five hundred copies each of *Our Flag, The Declaration of Independence* and *The Constitution of the United States*.
Use of congressional broadcast studios at reduced rates.
An unlimited number of free potted plants.[32]

Then there are those circumstances that benefit incumbents not because of any formal rule, but because of their status. They are easily able to generate publicity both in the mass media and in the newsletters of interest groups they assist. In addition, according to a 1972 Common Cause study, their status and the accompanying power give them an enormous campaign contribution advantage. In 1972 incumbent members of Congress received almost three times as much money as their election challengers ($3.9 million versus $1.4 million).

If rules, practices, and circumstances favor incumbents to such a great extent (and the same is true on the state and local levels), the implications are clear. Winning legislative games through electoral politics is difficult. Since most incumbents are likely to win re-election, the challenge is to get incumbents running for re-election to take a problem seriously. How does a group get a problem turned into an election issue? Incumbency has a second implication. That is, because the composition of most legislative bodies changes very slowly, stagnation is common. There is little opportunity for new groups to have representation, little opportunity for significant policy change, little opportunity for change in the internal distribution of power.

So far, the discussion has revealed several things about legislative players:

1. They are not hindered from running for office by rigid constitutional rules.

[32] Gil Bailey, "The Taxpayers' Gifts to Members of Congress," *California Journal* (March 1976), p. 84.

2. More and more they are reflecting the interests of urban and suburban constituencies.
3. Once elected, they are relatively safe politically. Few incumbents get defeated.

What Influences the Moves of Legislators?

What we know about legislators thus far is of general interest only. What needs to be discovered specifically is, *what motivates a legislator?* What makes a legislator make one move as opposed to another? If winning requires influencing these players, then this is crucial information. It is tactical information. This information can be determined through three questions:

1. How does the legislator view the job and how does that view influence moves?
2. What are the rules of the game in the legislative arena, and does the legislator consider them important enough to follow?
3. How does the legislator view other players—those directly and indirectly involved in the game? Who influences the legislator's moves?

Emanuel Celler represented Brooklyn in the House of Representatives for 50 years. He was defeated in 1972. During that period of time, however, given the advantages of seniority, he had become one of the most powerful men in the House, and he knew it. As chairman of the House Judiciary Committee, he had a variety of resources. Someone asked him in 1958 for his stand on a certain bill. He answered, "I don't stand on it. I am sitting on it. It rests four-square under my fanny and will never see the light of day." He was usually right. Of the 17,728 bills and resolutions introduced in the House in 1969, for example, only 706 were reported from his committee.[33]

Emanuel Celler was obviously a key legislative player. The question is, what motivated him? What made him make the legislative moves he made? If Celler were the crucial player, it would be important to try to look at his past legislative behavior and answer the three previous questions. Then, at least, the activist might know who could influence him and how. Or he would know that he couldn't be easily influenced, that his power would have to be circumvented.

So let's talk about the three questions designed to help citizens understand legislative behavior. First, *how does the legislator view the job?*

[33] Green et al., *Who Runs Congress?*, p. 265.

Role perceptions.　In their study of American state legislatures, John Wahlke and his colleagues found that some legislators see their job as that of a *trustee*. These representatives are guided solely by their personal judgment and conscience. In a sense, they are free agents. Others view their job as that of a *delegate*. These legislators are guided primarily by the instructions or wishes of their constituents. As one "delegate" legislator put it:

> What the district wants me to do is my most important job. I carry out their decisions. I'll put any bill in the hopper they give me. If they want me to move this Capitol, I'd break my neck to do it. (*Wahlke, et al., The Legislative System.*)

Finally, there are the *politicos*. These legislators tend to vary their views depending on the circumstances. They are very flexible.

Among members of the four state legislatures studied, the trustee role was found to be most common. The next most frequent was the politico orientation. Trailing the other two is the delegate view (Table 7–1).

Understandably, most legislators do not fit entirely into any one category. While one type of orientation may predominate, there is usually a role mix. For example, when local matters are involved, a legislator may act as a delegate, but on all other matters that legislator may act as a trustee. Or the legislator may be the delegate in party matters, but the trustee in less political matters.[34]

So how does all this help the activist? By reading the public statements of key legislative players and analyzing how they vote, the way in which these legislators view the job can be determined. Then, for persuasive purposes, it is easier to determine to whom the legislator is likely to look for information, advice, etc. For example, trustees seem to rate the recommendations of legislative committees, the state legislative council,[35] special commissions, and administrative agencies more highly than do those in the other two categories. Delegates, logically, place greater emphasis on word from people in their district. Politicos seem to give more emphasis to the views of interest groups, although depending on the situation, they rate other sources of information as important as well.

Even at the local level role perceptions influence the behavior of

---

[34] Green et al., *Who Runs Congress?* pp. 272–284.

[35] Consisting of selected state representatives and a professional staff, these councils investigate policy problems and make recommendations for solutions to the state legislatures. They exist in approximately 40 states.

Table 7–1
Distribution of representational-role orientations

Role Orientation	Calif. $N = 49$	N.J. $N = 54$	Ohio $N = 114$	Tenn. $N = 78$
Trustee	55%	61%	56%	81%
Politico	25	22	29	13
Delegate	20	17	15	6
Total	100%	100%	100%	100%

Source: John C. Wahlke, Heinz Eulau, William Buchanan, and Leroy C. Ferguson, *The Legislative System* (New York: John Wiley & Sons, 1962), p. 136.

legislators. In one study of city councils in 89 different cities the researchers found that councilors who take the view that they are merely performing a set of legally determined tasks are likely to rely heavily upon executive leadership and public hearings and to take little part in policy-making. However, if they view themselves as community leaders, or as arbiters of community conflict, they will be much more active. They will attempt to develop support for a particular policy position both among other councilors and in the community at large. These predispositions, then, act as filters through which interest-group efforts to influence policy must pass.[36]

So, if the strategy involves a legislative arena, these role perceptions can be important tactical information. It should help to determine whether persuasive efforts should be direct or indirect.

Knowing the way legislators view their job is only one aspect of understanding how they are likely to behave politically. A second guide to their legislative moves is *knowing how they view the rules* of the arena.

> "In the ghetto," explained Ron Dellums on his arrival as a freshman congressman in the Washington of 1971, "it's what's out front that counts. When you don't know a new dance, you stand along the wall, looking very cool, and you watch the steps of the best hustler on the floor. Then you get into the men's room, practice those steps and make it out onto the floor yourself."
>
> In the dance of congressional politics, Dellums said: "Right now, I'm in the bathroom getting it together."

[36] See Betty H. Zisk, Heinz Eulau, and Kenneth Prewitt, "City Councilmen and the Group Struggle: A Typology of Role Orientations," *Journal of Politics*, August 1965, pp. 618–646; and Heinz Eulau and Robert Eyestone, "Policy Maps of City Councils and Policy Outcomes: A Developmental Analysis," *American Political Science Review*, March 1968, pp. 124–143.

Five years later, Dellums, 41, has it together—he's one of the best hustlers on the floor.

Dellums is arguably the most powerful black politician in the Bay Area and among the most powerful in the country.[37]

Legislative norms.   Ron Dellums is talking about the rules of the legislative game. Rules, remember, are norms. Whether they are written down or merely accepted informally, they define what a person in a certain position should do. In part, whether legislators see themselves as delegates, trustees, or politicos suggests their personal decision-making norms—how they *should* make their decisions, to whom they *should* look for advice. Apart from these personal norms, there are institutional norms—the "shoulds" that operate in a given arena. They become rules for that game.

Legislative norms are abundant. More important, they are widely shared by legislative players at all levels of government. In their study of state legislatures Wahlke and his fellow researchers discovered that the most frequently mentioned informal rule was that a member must *always keep his or her word*—live up to any obligation made. Almost as important was the rule, *respect other members' legislative rights.* This means that when a bill concerns only the affairs of a particular county, you support it if the legislator from that county wants it, even if you think it is an outrage. The third rule most frequently mentioned was that members are to remain *impersonal* in all their legislative actions—never use any personal information you have about a member (e.g., she is an alcoholic or he is carrying on with a stripper). Table 7–2 conveys the vast number of legislative rules as well as the degree to which they are shared in each of the four states studied.

Something to think about
How do some of these legislative rules conflict?

On the national level, many of the same norms prevail, and over 80 percent of all members of Congress consider learning them important. Among them are the following:

1. Members of Congress should *specialize* because of the heavy and varied workload.

[37] James A. Finefrock, "Dellums Shows Colleagues New Steps," *S.F. Sunday Examiner & Chronicle* (June 6, 1976), p. 12, Section A.

Table 7-2
"Rules of the game" perceived by legislators in four states*

Rules of the Game	Percentage of Respondents Naming Rule			
	Calif. $N = 104$	N.J. $N = 78$	Ohio $N = 160$	Tenn. $N = 119$
1. *Performance of obligations:* Keep your word; abide by commitments.	64%	47%	28%	24%
2. *Respect for other members' legislative rights:* Support another member's local bill if it doesn't affect you or your district; don't railroad bills through; don't appear before another committee (than your own) to oppose another member's bill; don't steal another member's bill; respect the rights of a bill's author; accept author's amendments to a bill.	32	26	24	47
3. *Impersonality:* Don't deal in personalities; don't make personal attacks on other members; oppose the bill, not the man; don't criticize the moral behavior of others; address other members through the Chair; don't refer to another member by name; observe the "Golden Rule."	30	27	32	31
4. *Self-restraint in debate:* Don't talk too much; don't speak about subjects on which you're uninformed.	17	9	18	59
5. *Courtesy:* Observe common courtesies; be friendly and courteous even if you disagree, even if you are of opposite party to opponent.	19	19	24	26

* Percentages total more than 100 since most respondents named more than one rule.

Source: John C. Wahlke, Heinz Eulau, William Buchanan, and Leroy C. Ferguson, *The Legislative System* (New York: John Wiley & Sons, 1962), pp. 146–147. Reprinted by permission.

Table 7-2 (cont'd.)

| | Percentage of Respondents Naming Rule | | | |
| | Calif. | N.J. | Ohio | Tenn. |
Rules of the Game	N = 104	N = 78	N = 160	N = 119
6. *Openness of aims:* Be frank and honest in explaining bills; don't conceal real purpose of bills or amendments.	24	8	22	12
7. *Modesty:* Don't be a prima donna, an individualist, or a publicity-hound; don't talk for the press or galleries.	9	19	23	21
8. *Integrity:* Be honest, a man of integrity, sincerity.	13	19	18	11
9. *Independence of judgment* (Being independent of outside control): be objective; don't be subservient to a political organization, a boss, a machine, an interest group, lobbyists, or clients.	16	19	11	14
10. *Personal virtue:* Exhibit high moral conduct, no drunkenness or immorality.	13	0	24	8
11. *Decisiveness:* Take a stand; don't be wishy-washy; don't vaccilate.	10	8	11	15
12. *Unselfish service:* Don't be a careerist, an opportunist, or overambitious; don't use your legislative position for your personal advantage.	5	19	14	4
13. *Advance notice of changed stand:* Notify in advance if you are going to change your stand or can't keep a commitment.	26	9	6	1
14. *Openness in opposition:* Don't conceal your opposition; notify in advance if you're going to oppose or introduce amendments.	17	4	13	2
15. *Sociability:* Be sociable; develop and maintain friendships with other members.	6	6	9	11
16. *Conciliation:* Be willing to compromise; don't be a perfectionist; accept half a loaf.	7	12	10	5
17. *Agency for party or administration:* Support the governor, adminis-				

tration, party leaders (of own party); don't vote to over-ride a veto by governor of your own party.	1	6	20	0
18. *Restraint in opposition:* Don't fight unnecessarily; don't be opposed to everything.	4	1	11	13
19. *Application:* Be punctual and regular in attendance at sessions, caucuses, committee meetings; don't leave after your own bill has been considered.	5	3	13	5
20. *Respect for other members' political rights:* Respect the incumbent status of other members; don't campaign against a member in his district; don't do anything that would embarrass him in his district; build him up before his constituents.	23	5	3	1
21. *Objectivity:* Be fair, show good judgment, maturity, responsibility.	4	5	13	4
22. *Agency for legislative party:* Follow caucus or conference decisions; go along with majority of your party.	1	23	7	0
23. *Gracefulness in defeat:* Keep your temper; accept defeat gracefully, learn to take a licking; don't take opposition personally.	10	4	4	9
24. *Ability and intelligence:* Show ability, intelligence; not ignorance, stupidity.	2	8	9	5
25. *Non-venality:* Don't sell vote; don't take money; don't introduce cinch bills, shake-down bills.	6	4	3	13
26. *Restraint in bill-introduction:* Don't introduce too many bills or amendments.	2	1	5	2
27. *Maintenance of confidences:* Don't divulge confidential information; don't violate confidence of caucus committee, executive session.	1	19	5	3
28. *Avoidance of trickery:* Don't engage in parliamentary chicanery, tricky maneuvering.	8	4	6	4

Table 7-2 (cont'd.)

Rules of the Game	Percentage of Respondents Naming Rule			
	Calif. N = 104	N.J. N = 78	Ohio N = 160	Tenn. N = 119
29. *Apprenticeship:* Respect older members; (new members) don't try to accomplish too much too soon.	5	10	8	1
30. *Caution in commitments:* Don't commit yourself too soon; be cautious about making promises; study bills before you decide how to vote.	4	0	3	8
31. *Commitment to job:* Take the job seriously.	4	6	1	7
32. *Institutional patriotism:* Defend legislature and members against outsiders; don't do anything to reflect on the legislature as a body.	12	1	3	0
33. *Respect for opposition groups:* Don't be too partisan; be considerate of minority members.	6	8	3	0
34. *Negotiation:* Recognize the necessity and/or acceptability of log-rolling, horse-trading, swapping-out.	0	0	3	7
35. *Limits to negotiation:* Vote according to the merits of the bill; don't horse-trade, log-roll, or swap-out.	0	3	1	6
36. *Seniority:* Respect seniority-system.	3	1	3	1
37. *Acceptance of committee system:* Respect committee jurisdiction; don't vote to discharge a committee, withdraw a bill; don't vote to amend budget on floor.	7	3	1	0
38. *Self-restraint in goals:* Don't be overeager; don't try to accomplish too much at one time.	2	4	2	1
39. *Senatorial courtesy:* Observe senatorial courtesy (in a narrow sense—control of appointments, etc.)	0	9	0	1

40. Compliance with group: Go along with majority when ⅔ vote is necessary; don't refuse unanimous consent.	2	5	0	0
41. Limits to partisanship: Don't delay by being too partisan, too political.	3	0	2	0
42. Abstinence from dilatory actions: Don't call attention to absence of a quorum; don't demand call of house at inconvenient times.	2	0	1	0
Miscellaneous others	3	28	11	30

2. The most important work in Congress should be done in *committee.*
3. Do not personally criticize a fellow representative.
4. Be willing to trade votes (*reciprocity*).
5. Spend time on the house floor.

An interesting aspect of the pervasiveness of these norms is the degree to which they are shared both by new and existing members of Congress. This seems to suggest that they are so much a part of the political process that they are known even before a legislator is elected.[38]

Sometimes a rebel slips in. In her early legislative years, Congresswoman Bella Abzug observed few of the legislative norms. She didn't see them as important to her job. But that judgment presented problems. The Ralph Nader Congress Project researchers described her early legislative life in this way:

> She has followed few of the codes of etiquette, tongue-lashing the House ("I'm tired of listening to a bunch of old men who are long beyond the draft age standing here and talking about sending our young men over to be killed in an illegal and immoral war.") and tongue-lashing Speaker Carl Albert ("Now you listen to me, Carl. I'm sick and tired, because it's about time this Democratic Caucus went on record against the war.... What's the matter with you?"). She so dominated the proceedings of the Democratic Caucus with her views that it soon became difficult to find a quorum. Congress stores up its vengeance silently. Whenever Abzug offers a measure it gets 20–30 fewer votes than the same bill would under someone else's name. On September 30, 1971, she learned about more blatant retaliations. Shortly before noon, she began walking to the House floor, ready to present a resolution to force the State Department to reveal how deeply the United States was involved in South Vietnam's presidential elections. Although the House formally convenes at noon, routine trivia usually postpone the serious business till 12:30 or later. But on this day, at 12:01, Albert cracked his gavel and quickly called on Tom Morgan. Fighting hard to suppress guffaws, the House listened to Morgan say, "Mr. Speaker, I intended to yield to the gentlewoman from New York for ten minutes for debate only, but I do not see the gentlewoman on the floor." Within seconds, Albert and the House agreed to table the motion. It was all over by the time Bella strolled in at 12:03.[39]

---

[38] These norms and their acceptance by both new and existing members of Congress were identified in a study by Herbert B. Asher, "The Learning of Legislative Norms," *American Political Science Review*, June 1973, pp. 499–513.
[39] Green et al., *Who Runs Congress?*, pp. 172–173.

So the few legislative players who do not observe the institutional norms face aggravating sanctions. This fact, coupled with the more pervasive tendency to accept the norms, tells the activist they are important. They help predict *generally* acceptable and unacceptable legislative moves.

The way legislators view their job and the rules operating in legislative arenas influence another component of legislative behavior. This has to do with *individual and group influence.* The question is, in legislative games, who is likely to influence whom when?

The party.   On the national and state levels, the most influential group is the party. In fact, the party a legislator identifies with is the single most important factor in explaining that legislator's votes.

A legislator reluctantly votes against the party only when the party position is contrary to deeply held convictions or to the public opinion in the state or district, and this isn't often. Various studies of legislative voting behavior indicate that on partisan issues, members of Congress vote with the party between 70 and 90 percent of the time.[40] Moreover, on all issues, they vote with the party over 60 percent of the time (Table 7–3).

The same is true on the *state level,* although state party organization and strength vary considerably from state to state.[41]

The extent to which the party will influence voting in state legislatures depends on a variety of factors. One factor is the degree of party *competition* existing within the state as well as within the legislator's own district. In those states that are very partisan, where party competition is keen, the legislator's feeling about the party is likely to be strong and positive.[42] This is particularly true if the legislator is from the majority party. It is less true for those from the minority party. In this case, unless the minority party controls the governorship, party membership and party voting may be perceived as an obstacle.[43]

Party competition in the district, however, seems to weaken party

40 Harris, *Congress and the Legislative Process,* pp. 68–69.
41 See Hugh Le Blanc, "Voting in State Senates: Party and Constituency Influences," *Midwest Journal of Political Science,* February 1969, pp. 33–39.
42 Wahlke et al., *The Legislative System,* p. 346.
43 As of now, only about half the states are highly competitive. The trend is, however, toward greater competition. See Turner, *American Democracy,* pp. 15–16 for specific states categorized according to party competition.

Table 7–3
Congressional votes on roll calls that produced party division, 1971

	House		Senate		Both Houses	
	Demo-crats	Repub-licans	Demo-crats	Repub-licans	Demo-crats	Repub-licans
With party	61%	67%	64%	63%	62%	66%
Against party	24	21	22	21	24	21
Not voting	15	12	14	16	14	13
Total	100%	100%	100%	100%	100%	100%

Source: Recomputation of data from the *Congressional Quarterly Weekly Report*, 30 (January 15, 1972), pp. 86–87.

loyalty, and ultimately the party's influence on behavior. Legislators elected from safe districts generally show greater party loyalty on roll-call votes than legislators elected from highly competitive districts. A legislator from a highly competitive district is more likely to reflect the socioeconomic interests of the district rather than those of the party.[44]

Along with party competition within the state and district, another factor affecting the degree of party influence is the *issue*. If the issue is *organizational*, the party is likely to be influential. What does that mean? If a proposed bill would establish a new agency, for example, or transfer authority from one office to another, the party intervenes and acts much as an interest group would. Parties, remember, have a stake in personnel. If a bill would reduce their power because a particular office is controlled by one party, or if a bill would increase their power by abolishing a civil service requirement for the job, party leadership will take a position and encourage support.

The appropriation of large sums of *money* also seems to bring out partisan instincts. The party is generally more influential around budget time when decisions involving social welfare and class interests are being made.[45]

Finally, the influence of the party depends on the social and economic character of the state. On major issues, party members are more likely to vote together in an urban industrial state in which each party really does represent a separate socioeconomic constituency.[46]

[44] Thomas R. Dye, "State Legislative Politics," in *Politics in the American States*, 2d ed., eds. Herbert Jacobs and Kenneth Vines (Boston: Little Brown and Company, 1971), p. 199.
[45] *Ibid.*, pp. 194–196.
[46] *Ibid.*

It is difficult to generalize about the influence of the party on legislative behavior at the local level. One reason is that most cities and counties call themselves *nonpartisan*. This means that in their system of election, no candidate is identified on the ballot by party affiliation. This designation has little to do with the population involved. For example, 61 percent of cities over 5,000—regardless of size—are nonpartisan.

A "nonpartisan" label, however, doesn't always say much about party influence. In some nonpartisan elections a party is quite influential. The Democratic party's dominance in Chicago is an example.[47] Still, determining party influence at the state and local levels should not be that difficult. Newspaper accounts of party activities, formal party ballot designations, and roll-call votes in which there may be a pattern of party voting are clues. If the party indeed turns out to be as influential as it is on the national level, then using that institution as one means of access makes sense.

Something to think about
How would an activist use the state party organization to influence a state legislator?

Constituents.   What about *constituent influence*—doesn't that influence the moves of legislative players? It depends. The undeniable resource that voters have is the ability to remove or retain their representatives. For that reason, in an all-out conflict between party and constituency, the constituency is bound to win. This conflict is rare, however, primarily because voters are uninformed about or uninterested in most legislative issues, and because they know almost nothing about their representatives' positions—or even their names.

So how can one say that constituents are ever influential? They are influential primarily through those who play the game for them. Those legislators who are delegates or politicos pay attention to what interest groups and polls are saying. While this is imperfect information and is distorted by a legislator's own orientations, legislators are

---

[47] For a discussion of the various types of partisanship, see Charles R. Adrian, "Some General Characteristics of Nonpartisan Elections," *American Political Science Review*, September 1952, p. 767.

likely to consider *their perception* of the dominant constituent point of view seriously.[48]

The influence of the constituency can be understood by looking more closely at its recognizable parts—interest groups and public opinion. Are legislators at different levels of government influenced very directly by either?

Let's first examine *interest groups.* Determining systematically the influence interest groups have on legislative behavior is difficult. It's more difficult than determining party influence because we are not able to turn to roll-call votes for part of the answer. Furthermore, the factors motivating a legislator are frequently interrelated. Examine, for example, the record of U.S. Senator Henry Jackson (D., Wash.) on defense policy. He comes from a state that relies heavily on defense contracts. Washington is the home of Boeing Aircraft. When Senator Jackson speaks on behalf of that industry in Congress, is he responding to organized interests? It is difficult to say. The loss of a large defense contract by Boeing might mean thousands of people unemployed in his state and a slide in the economy of the entire state. So he may be responding to organized interests or be acting out of compassion for his constituents in general. Probably both factors influence his behavior.

Still, on some issues the influence of interest groups cannot be ignored. One of the most interesting issues in recent years involved federal funding of an 1800-mile-per-hour Supersonic Transport (SST).

This was the game, essentially. In 1970 and 1971 Congress was expected to approve easily the continuing development of the SST. After all, the U.S. government had already invested $1.1 billion in it, and it had the support of three presidents (Kennedy, Johnson, and Nixon), labor, and the aerospace industry. How could the proponents lose with the administration and major interest groups working for the measure?

However, there were other players—opponents. The opposition was concerned about the effect the SST might have on the atmosphere and people's health. Also, they argued, its development would divert federal tax dollars from more pressing needs like housing, health, and education. These players formed a coalition. It included

[48] For a study of the relationship between constituents' and legislators' points of view, see W. E. Miller and D. E. Stokes, "Constituency Influence in Congress," *American Political Science Review,* March 1963, pp. 45–56; and Ronald D. Hedlund and H. Paul Friesema, "Representatives' Perceptions of Constituency Opinion," *Journal of Politics,* August 1972, pp. 730–752.

29 interest groups. They called themselves the Coalition against the SST.

Their tactics were varied. They enlisted the support of sympathetic scientists and economists and prepared a thoroughly researched case against the SST. Then they moved in on the "swing" votes—new members of Congress, members who had voted inconsistently on the SST the previous year, and the undecided. Sympathetic constituents were asked to visit these key players, and experts were asked to testify at hearings.

Each group had a different job to do. Member organizations like the Sierra Club had major campaign contributors call, write, and visit legislators, urging opposition. Common Cause compiled and mailed a press kit of information about the SST to 3000 editorial writers. Anti-SST editorials soon appeared in newspapers all across the country. The coalition also used media advertisements, TV talk shows, and any other method that would arouse public opinion and Congress against the SST. It was a major persuasion campaign. It had to be because of the resources of the proponents. They appeared to be over-whelming.

The organized activity of the opposition coalition worked. After four successful floor votes were nullified by political and parliamentary maneuvers (the proponents knew the rules well), a final and decisive vote was taken. In May 1971, the continuing appropriation for the SST was defeated. Legislative players like Senator Clinton Anderson, chairman of the Aeronautical and Space Sciences Committee, had felt the impact of interest-group effort. In a surprise move, he switched his position and voted against the SST. His comment? "I read my mail." That morning his letters and telegrams had opposed the SST by a lopsided 78 to 8 margin.[49]

This was organized interest-group activity that worked. It doesn't always. Whether it will or not seems to depend on a number of factors—including the issue, legislators' and expressed contituents' feelings about the issue, and legislators' perceptions of particular interest groups and their activities.

Strangely, legislators at the national, state, or local levels do not *perceive* interest groups as particularly important in influencing their moves. However, the issue makes a difference.[50] Generally, if the

[49] This particular account of the SST congressional fight is from Green et al., *Who Runs Congress?*, pp. 250–251.
[50] See Lester W. Milbrath, *The Washington Lobbyists* (Chicago: Rand McNally & Company, 1963), pp. 328–354; Harmon Zeigler and Michael Baer, *Lobbying:*

issue is specialized and affects only a small segment of the population, interest groups, through their lobbyists, are likely to play a larger role. For example, a member of the House Ways and Means Committee told the Milbrath researchers about representatives of two large whisky distilleries who came before the committee. They were concerned about when the tax on whisky should become due and payable. There was no governmental or public interest to be served or disserved. The issue received no attention in the press. The committee merely listened quietly to the pleas from both sides and then made its decision. In this case lobbying was important, but for most people the bill wasn't. This comment seems to explain the traditional view:

> It is the demands of the people that start the country on a certain broad road policy-wise. Lobbyists may affect the language of the bills and legislation that come out in conformity with this broad policy, but they have little influence on the general outcome. They may not have any influence about the choice of the road to drive on, but they have something to say about the way we drive on the road once we are on it.[51]

On the state level the issue is also an important factor in determining the degree of interest-group influence. In a 1963 50-state survey, legislators identified seven issue areas where interest groups were important: liquor, labor, business, agriculture, water resources, gambling, and social welfare. In these areas legislators tended to rely on the advice of interest groups.[52]

What these studies seem to be saying about issues and legislative games is that when policy affects particular *economic interests*, economically oriented interest groups become active players. Since they have traditionally been the only major players, if no one else stands to lose a great deal, they will usually get their way. At least legislators will listen to them and consider their position seriously. However, we know from the SST story, the Equal Rights Amendment battle, and the struggle for campaign reform that some key issues involve an obvious public interest. We also know that more interest groups attempting to serve that broader point of view are becoming serious

---

Influence and Interaction in American State Legislatures (Belmont, Calif.: Wadsworth Publishing Company, 1969); and Zisk, et al., "City Councilman and the Group Struggle," p. 644.

51 Milbrath, *The Washington Lobbyists*, p. 344.

52 Wayne L. Francis, "A Profile of Legislative Perceptions of Interest Group Behavior Relating to Legislative Issues in the States," *Western Political Quarterly*, December 1971, pp. 702–712.

players. So certain groups that were previously considered unimportant by default or because of inexperience may now be considered more important by legislators. We will have to see.

When interest-group interests coincide with constituent interests as expressed through *public-opinion polls,* their importance is enhanced. Of course, interest groups frequently spend time using educational tactics to mobilize that opinion. However it develops, what effect does public opinion have on legislators? Taken alone, legislative studies reveal that public-opinion polls are not among the most influential factors in determining how the legislative game is played or who wins what.[53] Opinions on two different policy issues illustrate the relationship.

One policy issue is the reform or elimination of the Electoral College. For years the Gallup Poll has reported that majorities favor a reform. In 1968, after a very close presidential election, 80 percent of the population favored abandoning the Electoral College. There seemed to be an increasing public awareness that a three-way contest could prevent any one candidate from receiving a majority vote. The decision would then be up to the House of Representatives, not the electorate. Not until 1969 did the House finally vote to amend the Constitution. Public opinion was not enough, however, to get senators to stop a filibuster so that a vote could be taken. So in spite of a very clear indication of public sentiment, the Electoral College remains.

The same situation exists in another policy area—gun control. Repeated surveys since 1959 have shown decided majorities in favor of stricter gun-control laws. Nevertheless, organized opposition, primarily from the National Rifle Association, has been far more effective in influencing the legislative process than have public opinion surveys.[54]

Something to think about
In the two situations just described, why do you think public opinion didn't influence the legislative outcome?

---

[53] Lewis A. Dexter, "Communications—Pressure, Influence, or Education," in *People, Society, and Mass Communications,* eds. Lewis Anthony Dexter and David Manning White (New York: The Free Press of Glencoe, 1964), pp. 395–409.
[54] The supporting data are summarized in Harold Mendelsohn and Irving Crespi, *Polls, Television, and the New Politics* (Scranton, Pa.: Chandler Publishing Company, 1970), pp. 34–38.

If the discrepancy between public policy and public opinion is partial evidence of the negligible influence of opinion, what members of Congress say supports this. In one survey of U.S. senators, the primary use of polls cited was to help them determine what problems their constituents felt needed action and how they and their positions were being evaluated by constituents. Voter opinion on the details of legislation was significant to only 1 out of every 3 senators. It appears that public-opinion polls are used primarily to select effective campaign issues, not to determine what bills should be enacted.[55]

Other public officials.   Particular individuals in a legislative house can be singled out as being uniquely influential. They include committee chairpersons, the majority party leadership, designated specialists, and in the case of Congress, other members of a legislator's state party delegation. The influence of committee chairpersons and house party leadership is in part related to the resources that accompany the offices and in part the expertise that each type of leader develops the longer in the office. A study of state legislators revealed that 65 percent of those identified as experts also occupied the chair of one of the committees in that field. But expertise is also associated with the nonchairperson. In their study of state legislators, Wahlke and colleagues found that 91 percent of the legislators interviewed named one or more members as specialists. More than half seeking a particular kind of expert picked the same person, and more than four-fifths picked the top three persons most frequently mentioned.[56] The word does get around.

But interestingly, topping the list of those with influence in Congress are the other members of a congressperson's state party delegation.[57] Whether because of a common geographic association, common constituent concerns, or greater personal interaction, the influence is particularly strong. These legislative players are the logical allies of activists, if they can be influenced. If they were to become allies, they might work for interest groups as "inside lobbyists." [58] However, their influence decreases when an issue is highly publicized,

---

[55] *Ibid.*, p. 33.
[56] Wahlke et al., *The Legislative System*, pp. 195–202.
[57] Donald R. Matthews and James A. Stimson, "Decision-Making by U.S. Representatives: A Preliminary Model" in *Political Decision-Making*, ed. S. Sidney Ulmer (Cincinnati: Van Nostrand Reinhold, 1970), p. 31.
[58] Keefe and Ogul, *The American Legislative Process*, pp. 334–371.

and when it is clear that constituent opinion is different from the legislative colleague's point of view.[59]

Turning to *executive influence*, we already know from the Milbrath study that for members of Congress, the influence of the executive branch was identified as paramount. The chief executive's influence, however, will vary according to whether or not his party is also the majority legislative party, whether his election was a landslide or a squeaker, and his personal skills. Power, remember, is determined not only by resources but by one's ability to use them skillfully.

Apart from the chief executive, other administrators are key legislative players. They have resources independent of the chief executive's, and legislators are easily placed in debt. For example, administrators can provide certain legislators with "ready-made" legislation, enhancing their prestige; do research and speech preparation; provide lobbying services that are mutually beneficial; and provide key witnesses for legislative investigations. Then there are those favors involving the legislator's constituency. Agency heads can locate a governmental office in a legislator's district, providing constituent jobs. Or they can modify regulations to assist an urban redevelopment project, creating more low-cost housing.[60] These are their resources.

More than any other administrative influence, however, their expertise and information is their most important resource because of the complexity of decision-making, volume of legislation, and lack of information of legislators. In a survey of member complaints within Congress, the decision-making, information-deficiency problem was cited by 62 percent of those interviewed—it was the complaint reported most frequently.[61]

This reliance on administrators for information and expertise is not unique to the state and national levels. In a study of the role of administrative agencies in the legislative process in Los Angeles, California, these agencies were indeed dominant. Career administrators were the predominant source of substantive legislation introduced in the city council, as well as the predominant source of amendments and revisions of legislation introduced from other sources, including the city councilors themselves. They were successful. They demonstrated

[59] Milbrath, *The Washington Lobbyists*, p. 142.

[60] Totten J. Anderson, "Pressure Groups and Intergovernmental Relations," *The Annals of the American Academy*, May 1965, p. 122.

[61] Rogert H. Davidson, David Kovenock, and Michael K. O'Leary, *Congress in Crisis* (Belmont, Calif.: Wadsworth Publishing Company, 1966), pp. 75–78.

a high measure of political talent and skill at playing the game. They usually got more than they gave up.[62]

So relevant executive players should be considered seriously. Because of their resources and skill, they can be a means of access to legislators as well as an important influence on legislative moves.

Staff.   Not to be overlooked in the area of legislative influence is the role of legislative staff—those selected by legislators to assist in all aspects of the job and those assigned to legislative committees. Most lobbyists would prefer to contact staff assistants than to reach the decision maker directly for a variety of reasons, one of which is certainly influence. That influence evolves from the shared philosophy, the day-to-day contact, and the expertise the assistant develops in a given area, and from the information the staff can give legislators about constituent needs, feelings, interest-group demands, etc. According to lobbyists, legislators and their assistants are so interdependent that talking to staff is almost equivalent to talking to the official.[63]

The influence of the professional staff serving committees is also significant. In one study of the Eightieth and Eighty-second Congresses, committee staff members (1) selected the witnesses for hearings, for all practical purposes; (2) briefed committee members prior to hearings on major issues; (3) interrogated witnesses in subcommittee and certain select committee hearings; (4) assisted in bill drafting by negotiating with key players to remove major objections; (5) prepared committee reports that were sent to all members of the House; (6) participated in the executive session of the standing committee when a bill they had worked on was under consideration; (7) assisted on the House floor prior to the vote by analyzing proposals and arguments advanced and gathering additional information; and (8) attended conference committee meetings to explain key provisions and keep track of the decision.[64] Each of these tasks provides an opportunity to influence legislative moves and legislative outcomes. To be unaware of the predispositions and patterns of behavior of key staff members is to fail to comprehend the importance of the positions.

---

[62] See H. W. Reynolds, Jr., "Career Public Servants and Statute Lawmaking in Los Angeles," *Western Political Quarterly*, September 1965, pp. 621 639.
[63] Milbrath, *The Washington Lobbyists*, p. 269.
[64] Kenneth Kofmehl, *Professional Staffs of Congress* (Lafayette, Ind.: Purdue Research Foundation, 1962), pp. 110–125.

Money.   Not the least important influence, although the degree of its influence is difficult to measure, is *money.* As long as groups and individuals can contribute to the campaigns of legislators, it will be a part of the decision-making environment.

Most interest groups can only buy access—the opportunity to have their point of view heard once the legislator is elected. They get their money from small voluntary donations from carpenters, machinists, doctors, dairy farmers, bank executives, and teachers, to name a few. There are hundreds of political action committees registered. Only a handful ever raise as much as $100,000. Then there are those thousands of small contributors who give directly to the candidate.

The trouble begins when a special-interest group has huge assets and a particular interest in a piece of legislation. Then the influence cannot be ignored. The American Medical Association, for example, wants to influence a national health insurance bill. Morton Mintz of *The Washington Post* says that the AMA's state and federal arms have distributed $1.5 million to 300 congressional candidates since the 1972 election. This money is frequently given in chunks of $5,000. It appears to be going to supporters of the AMA bill at twice the rate it is going to nonsupporters. Sure, there is money on the other side. The United Auto Workers, for example, want a more liberal bill, but the $862,000 they spent on politics in 1974 promoted a range of interests, not just health care legislation. So the resources of the AMA are magnified—as are the opportunities for influence.[65] And clearly when estimating the influence of money, activists must not only look at the amounts spent each year by potential allies and opponents. They must also look at how concentrated or diversified the spending is and, obviously, who gets it.

To arrange all these influences on legislative behavior hierarchically is impossible. We've seen that influence depends on how legislators perceive their role, certain structural and cultural factors, the issue, etc. What can be said is that *potentially* the greatest single influence is constituents—through interest-group action, public opinion, or other methods. In reality, because citizens are ill-informed, disorganized, and uninterested, or because much legislation doesn't directly affect all constituents, it is the party that dominates. Party identification is the best single predictor of legislative moves. However, understanding the

[65] Brooks Jackson, "Bribery and Contributions," *New Republic*, December 21, 1974, pp. 13–15.

perceptions of legislators and the conditions under which certain groups and individuals are likely to be successful is tactical information of the utmost importance. It is preparation for the game and perhaps the win.

Additional preparation for the game is understanding the rules— how they distribute power within the legislative arena, how they promote or block access, and how they guide tactical moves. On to that information.

Key Words

Bicameral
Charter
Grants-in-aid
Revenue sharing
Initiative
Referendum
Legislative oversight
Franking privilege
Apportionment
Gerrymandering
Trustee
Delegate
Politico
Nonpartisan

Suggested Activities

1. Determine what authority your local legislative bodies have. How does it compare with the authority of the mayor?
2. Develop methods of citizen access appropriate to each of the law-making steps.
3. Locate the legislative offices of local, state, and national representatives. To whom would you go for what kinds of help?
4. Focusing on one representative, analyze how he or she perceives the job.

8
Rules of the Legislative Game

W. R. Poage, Wright Patman, and F. Edward Hébert are members of the U.S. House of Representatives. As of 1975, their years of service in Congress totaled 121. Most people wouldn't recognize their names, but they have indeed become famous. They were removed as committee chairmen because of the way they performed their official duties. It happened at the beginning of the Ninety-fourth Congress (1975), a Congress particularly bent on reform.

So why is that worthy of fame? Aren't people frequently removed from a position for failure to do the job adequately? What does this have to do with rules? What is unusual about this situation is that in the U.S. Congress members are *not* removed from positions of leadership for incompetence or misuse of power. The only grounds for removal have been personal or partisan. Just a month before Hébert, Poage, and Patman were ousted, Wilbur Mills, the powerful chairman of the House Ways and Means Committee, was compelled to resign for socializing publicly with an Argentine stripper, and after the 1964 election two Democratic chairmen were removed for supporting the Republican presidential nominee. However, removing such a leader even for personal or partisan reasons is rare.

Traditionally, those who chaired committees have been protected by the seniority rule. The idea that these positions were to go to and be retained by the most senior committee member from the majority party was unquestioned. Now the rule that had given them such authority was being questioned.

How did it happen, and what are the implications? Apart from the liberal complexion of the Ninety-fourth Congress, a rule was responsible. In January 1971, both Democrats and Republicans in the House adopted rules permiting *caucus* votes on these committee positions. (A caucus is simply a formal meeting of party members within a given legislative body.) No longer were they to be awarded strictly on the basis of seniority. Yet they continued to be until January 1975. Attempts to challenge the traditional way of distributing power failed. But increasing citizen cynicism toward the legislative process, 75 new representatives to whose advantage it was to weaken the seniority system, and a domestic economic crisis bordering on that of the 1930s produced a shift away from "business as usual."

Most legislative game-watchers predicted that this rule change, once implemented, would distribute more advantages to the elected party leaders—the speaker and the majority leader. For it was they who could now recommend to their caucus other legislative leaders. No longer would they have to bow to the seemingly absolute power of those who chaired committees. *They* would have the ultimate resource.

Things didn't quite work out that way. During the organizational days of the Ninety-fourth Congress, the Democratic leaders proposed the re-election of all chairpersons except Wilbur Mills. In effect, they were proposing the continuation of the seniority rule. But the 24-member Democratic Steering and Policy Committee wouldn't go for it, even if their leaders were recommending it—and it was they who were given the authority by the full caucus to make the nominations.

By secret ballot, the Steering Committee decision was made: Poage (Agriculture) and Hébert (Armed Services) should stay, Wayne L. Hays (Administration) and Wright Patman (Banking and Currency) should go. The committee was challenging not only the authority of the senior leaders but, it seemed, that of the elected party leadership as well.

Then an interesting thing happened. The Democratic Caucus rebuffed even the Steering Committee. They rejected three of the four chairmen in question. The only one allowed to remain was Wayne Hays.

What had gone wrong? The old pattern of power had been seriously disrupted. A rule change plus a new Congress had weakened senior leadership as well as elected party leadership. The party caucus —never before known to have any significant power—was strengthened.

Whether or not this challenge to traditional legislature power would persist, no one knew, but it had occurred, and that was important. It was a warning.

Several points about power emerge from this story of the 1975 leadership challenge in the U.S. House of Representatives. They apply to legislative bodies in general. First, rules help to define the *internal distribution of power*. Second, *legislative power is decentralized*; no one person or faction or leadership category holds power all the time. Third, the rules usually *promote inaction*; they favor the status quo. Each of these rule functions has important implications for citizens trying to understand as well as play the legislative game. Let's see what they are.

Rules as Determinants of Power

Committees

The U.S. Constitution says that each house may determine the rules of its proceedings. State constitutions have similar provisions. These rules distribute advantages and disadvantages. One of the earliest procedural rules at both levels established committees to work out the details of bills introduced. On the national level they were temporary at first. At least 350 were born and died during the Third Congress. By the early 1820s, however, permanent committees, called *standing committees*, had become the automatic recipients of legislative proposals. Subsequently, they became the focal point of legislative power.

Not all standing committees have equal power, or at least, they are uneven in prestige. Their jurisdictions, specified by law, are the substance of that prestige.

The most important committees at each level of government are those directly concerned with money. For example, on the national level, the House Ways and Means Committee, House Appropriations Committee, Senate Finance Committee, and Senate Appropriations Committee have the greatest prestige. Together they have power over our tax structure and the federal budget—not unimportant matters.

The *Rules Committee* in the House of Representatives deserves special attention. While it is not a money committee, it is important because it controls the flow of legislation to the floor. It does this by setting the agenda for debate, specifying how much time will be allowed for debate and what motions will be considered, determining whether or not members can offer an amendment, etc. Without a *special order* from the Rules Committee, a bill must simply wait its turn to be considered. That turn may never come. The Rules Committee on the state level is also one of the most important committees, since it frequently has the same functions and resources.

The negative power of the Rules Committee is enormous. Nationally, it has tended to promote the status quo. If the members of the committee don't like a bill reported from a standing committee, they can refuse to issue a rule. In addition, they can issue an "open" rule that allows amendments to be added from the floor.

The result? The entire nature of the bill, as reported, can be altered. Or, the sponsoring committee may negotiate. Certain provisions of the bill will be eliminated in exchange for a favorable set of rules. Oh to be a member of the Rules Committee and have those resources!

Obviously the importance of various committees changes with the nature of affairs. While the United States was militarily involved in Southeast Asia, the activities of the Senate Foreign Relations Committee were always in the news. So were the activities of the House Judiciary Committee after impeachment proceedings were initiated against President Nixon. Such events, and the accompanying publicity, give particular committees added leverage.

How is the power of a committee expressed? How does it manifest itself? First, of the thousands of bills introduced during each legislative session, only a few are considered seriously by committees, and fewer still are reported out. Only those of special interest to the committee chairperson, the house leadership, and/or the Chief Executive have the highest probability of being reported to the full house for a vote. This negative power to reject bills, to preserve the status quo, is great indeed.

Apart from preventing bills from being voted upon, the power of committees is manifested in another way. Their recommendations are considered very seriously. In his study of the Eighty-fourth Congress, Donald Matthews found that if a proposal was supported by 80 percent or more of the committee members, it passed every time; if 60 to 79 percent of a committee supported a proposal, it would pass 90 percent of the time. On those rare occasions where a bill is reported out with the support of only 50 to 60 percent, however, it passes the full house only 56 percent of the time. So for the activist trying to get the legislative branch to move, committee support is crucial.[1]

Committee Chairpersons

However, committee support, where important, doesn't usually come without the support of *those who chair the committees*. In the U.S. Senate, there are 17 such leaders of standing committees, and there are 21 in the House. On the state level, there are usually 20 chairpersons of standing committees in upper houses, and 18 in lower houses.[2] Of course there are also a few chairpersons of "select" committees—those established for a limited period of time and for a special purpose. Then, too, there are chairpersons of *joint* committees, those composed of members from both houses.

So what makes a chairperson so powerful? For one thing, the person chairing a committee controls the traffic within it. The chairperson calls committee meetings, sets the agenda, rules on matters of order, and negotiates with other leaders (e.g., the chairperson of the Rules Committee). More important, this individual has favors to hand out. The chairperson decides how staff are to be assigned to committee members, who shall be on what subcommittees, and who shall head subcommittees. These are not unimportant resources, and they provoke kindness and loyalty from committee members.

Something to think about

How can the resources of a committee chairperson be an asset to political activists? How can they be used to aid change?

On the state level, the committee chairperson is not as important in the decision-making process. In his study of state legislatures, Malcolm E. Jewell found that most important bills are guided to key committees dominated by a few legislators. They may be either party or faction leaders, and are not necessarily the chairperson.[3]

---

[1] On this point, see also the study by J. W. Dyson and J. W. Soule, "Congressional Committee Behavior on Roll-Call Votes: The U.S. House of Representatives, 1955–65," *Midwest Journal of Political Science*, November 1970, pp. 626–647.

[2] See Citizens Conference on State Legislatures, "A Report on Legislative Progress from Mid-1970 through 1971," April 1972, p. 7.

[3] Malcolm E. Jewell, *The State Legislature* (New York: Random House, 1962), p. 93.

On the national level, where a chairperson is consistently important, opportunities to abuse resources abound. Graham Barden (D.,
N.C.), for example, was chairman of the House Committee on Education and Labor for eight years. Prior to his 1960 retirement, he
continually professed support for federal aid to education. Simultaneously he continually worked to prevent passage of any such legislation.
His behavior and tactics illustrate clearly the negative power of a
committee chairperson. The resources are many. This is how he used
them in committee and on the House floor:

1. He refused to institute committee rules specifying regular committee procedure.
2. He scheduled committee meetings irregularly, sometimes with
   gaps of two months between sessions.
3. He terminated a committee meeting by declaring the absence of a
   quorum, even when a quorum of the committee was present.
4. He failed to recognize committee members with whom he disagreed.
5. He kept the committee staff small and inactive.
6. He held extensive desultory hearings without any coordinated
   legislative forms.
7. He arbitrarily limited the range of subjects to be considered in
   committee hearings (e.g., to legislation on public schools only).
8. He called a "quickie" vote of the committe to kill legislation when
   an antieducation majority was present.
9. He gave disproportionate time to opponents of aid to education
   while serving as floor manager of an education bill.
10. He resigned as floor manager of a bill during a critical period of
    floor consideration.[4]

Well, you might ask, considering this erratic behavior, how did he
even get to be committee chairman? How did he retain that position
for so long? The answer, previously referred to, is called the *seniority
rule*, which operates in both houses of Congress and in many state
legislatures. The rule is that committee leadership is to be awarded to
the majority party member who has the longest number of years of
continuous service on the committee. Clearly the one given the greatest advantage is not the most competent or most highly regarded

[4] Reported by John S. Saloma III, *Congress and the New Politics* (Boston: Little,
Brown and Company, 1969), p. 120.

member, but the one from the majority party who has been there the longest.

Until January 1975, when Hébert, Poage, and Patman were removed, this late nineteenth century tradition was rigidly observed. A challenge to this power could usually only come from other legislative leaders, and this did not happen often. Who are these other key players, what are their resources, and how can they challenge the power of the senior leaders?

Presiding Officers and Party Leaders

We've said that power in legislative arenas is *decentralized*. That means resources are shared between those who chair committees and elected party leaders. In the lower house, on the state and national levels, the *speaker* is the elected party leader with the greatest resources. Potentially, some of those can be used to challenge the authority of committee leaders. What can the speaker do? Primarily the speaker controls procedures in the full house. Specifically, on the national level:

> He must recognize any member who wishes to speak on the floor; he rules on the appropriateness of parliamentary procedures; he determines the presence of a quorum; he selects the chairman of the committee of the whole; he votes in case of a tie; he counts and announces votes; he decides in doubtful cases to which standing committee a bill will be assigned; he appoints special or select committees; he appoints the House members of each conference committee, and he maintains decorum in the chamber.[5]

As both presiding officer and party leader, the speaker's resources, then, are considerable. Since the 1975 attack on the Ways and Means Committee, he has additional resources. The Democratic Caucus stripped Ways and Means of its power to assign members to the various standing committees and gave it to the speaker. This is a considerable form of leverage.

The influence of the speaker comes from more than just a particular procedural resource, however. It comes also from the scope of the legislative process and from the party. For example, there are so many stages through which a bill must pass before it becomes law, and the

[5] Richard F. Fenno, Jr., "The Internal Distribution of Influences: The House," in *The Congress and America's Future*, ed. David B. Truman, The American Assembly, Columbia University (Englewood Cliffs, N.J.: Prentice-Hall, 1965), p. 59.

speaker has so many *opportunities* to influence it, that this influence is magnified. In addition, the speaker is elected by the majority party and so is looked to for leadership on important legislative matters and serves as the principal broker between the President and the majority party in the House. When that majority is large, as it was during the Ninety-fourth Congress (2 to 1), this role as party leader in the House is enhanced still more.

The power of the speaker at the *state level* is also significant. In fact, it may be greater than on the national level. At this level he or she usually appoints members of all committees in the lower house, refers bills to committees, recognizes members who want to speak, puts questions to vote, interprets rules, and decides points of order. As at the national level, the speaker at the state level is the presiding officer and oversees the total legislative process in that house. However, unlike in the U.S. House, the state level speaker additionally has some of the powers of the Rules Committee. He or she often chairs that committee. Consequently, except for the governor, the speaker is frequently the most important political figure in the state.

The party *floor leaders* on the national and state levels have far fewer resources—at least in the lower house. Elected by each party, the leader is really the chief strategist and tactician on the floor for that party. The leader is assisted by a "whip." Of course the house majority leader has a few more resources than the minority leader. For example, the majority leader helps set the schedule for debate and, along with the speaker, suggests potential chairpersons to the party steering committee. This opportunity has existed only since 1975, however. The minority floor leader's resources are enhanced when the party controls the executive branch.

Unlike the presiding officer in the lower house, the speaker, the person who presides in the upper chamber has very little power. Generally, the presiding officer can only recognize members who desire the floor, decide on points of order, and vote in case of a tie. In addition, this officer doesn't always preside. On the national level, the presiding officer (President pro tempore) acts only in place of the Vice President, and in many states, in place of the lieutenant governor. In the twelve states that do not have a lieutenant governor, however, this leader's prestige is enhanced.

More powerful than the house floor leaders but not as powerful as the speaker are the *Senate* floor leaders. At the state and national levels they are elected by each party. Essentially, their job is to set the Senate's schedule. In doing so, the majority leader will frequently consult with others, including the minority leaders. Why does the majority leader have to ask anyone if he or she has the schedule-setting authority and has been elected by the majority party? It is because of an interesting little rule that operates at the national level, and that also operates in many state legislatures, called *unanimous consent*. This means, simply, that the schedule (and a great many other matters) requires unanimous consent. Obviously, the cooperation of the minority party is required. It is also required in the House. Not designed for controversial measures, unanimous consent is meant to expedite matters. Voting to consider a measure is eliminated. However, one member who objects has the power to prevent action. Other, more time-consuming procedures must then be used. Fortunately, the majority leader's control of the schedule is only infrequently challenged.

So why is scheduling important? It is important because "timing" is. While the majority leader cannot indefinitely refuse to schedule a bill in which a significant number of members are interested, the time chosen can affect its chances.

Scheduling is the floor leader's only *formal* resource. As the leader of the party in the legislative arena, there are also informal resources available. The floor leader has substantial influence on committee assignments, can influence the composition of key committees, and usually has instant access to the President or governor, particularly if the executive is from the same party. Using these and any personal skills, the leader attempts to lead the party in the Senate. With the help of the "whip" (the number two party leader), the floor leader tries to persuade colleagues to act in committee and on the floor according to the wishes of the party leaders.

Something to think about
How could political activists use party leaders to help them get what they want? How could they gain access to them?

Caucus Leadership
Most observers of the legislative process have called the party caucus "impotent." Committee and floor leaders have always called the shots. Well, not quite *always*. During Woodrow Wilson's first term the Democratic party in the national legislature played an important role in controlling legislation brought in by the standing committees and

in passing Wilson's legislative program. Since then, however, it has declined in strength and use on the national level, apparently because of the internal philosophical splits in each party. After all, there is no effective means of enforcing caucus decisions.

Well, that is the way the caucus has generally been described. Certainly in the past it has presented no challenge to senior and floor leadership; but something is happening. In the 1970s it seems to be acquiring new life. The caucus of the majority party in Congress has not only challenged traditional leadership, as indicated by the removal of the three House committee chairmen, but has attempted to set policy as well.

How do they do it? Through rules, of course. For example, according to the rules of the Democratic Caucus, whenever a policy position gets a two-thirds vote, all Democratic members of the relevant committee are to vote that way consistently within the committee. Republicans operate their caucus (called a conference) on a majority basis. They do not seek to bind their members on voting positions, however.

What if someone does not support the position? When the issue involves a constitutional question or a contrary pledge to constituents, no member is bound. However, a member of the party who feels unable to support the position for other reasons tends to oppose it either quietly or not at all. In other words, a member doesn't work actively against the policy. For example, in January 1973 the House Democratic Caucus passed a resolution to end the war—an unexpected decision for that legislative body. Twenty-two members felt they had to go against the party line. Instead of opposing the position, however, they simply did not vote. The result? The House voted on May 10, 1973 (219 to 188) to cut off supplemental funds for bombing Indochina. This act, prompted by the party caucus, was not insignificant.[6]

The success of the caucus in this instance, however, was in part the result of unified leadership support. Committee chairpersons, floor leaders, and the person chairing the House Democratic Caucus were in agreement. Sometimes they aren't. They weren't in the 1975 decision on re-election of House committee chairmen—and the caucus prevailed. A second rule may allow them to prevail more frequently. In 1973 the House Democratic Caucus (the only one showing life) passed a rule that says that any Democrat who persuades 50 colleagues to sign a petition may call a special caucus and ask for a "modified

<hr/>

[6] "Congress and the War," *New Republic*, May 26, 1973, p. 9.

closed rule." This would permit the full House to vote on specific amendments *even when a committee chairperson objects.*

The first attempt to apply the rule was a tactical nightmare. It was an affront to the power of the most important committee chairman— Wilbur Mills (Ways and Means). The caucus was trying to force the Rules Committee to accept amendments to the tax bill that were designed to end oil company tax loopholes. Mills had designed the original bill. While the move didn't work[7] the first time, it did the second. The new Ways and Means Committee chairman, Al Ullman, acquiesced in the decision of the Democratic Caucus. When the issue came to the House floor in 1975, repeal of the infamous oil and gas depletion allowance passed, 248 to 163.

The leadership *potential* of the party caucus is even greater in those *states* with a strong party system. In his study of New England state politics, Duane Lockard observed that the majority caucus met frequently and often maintained discipline on behalf of a party program. Positions of leadership went to those legislators loyal to the party.[8] In most state legislatures, however, strong party organization does not exist. In fact, a mid-1950s study concluded that only one-quarter of the state legislatures had strong majority caucuses or conferences.[9]

Still, as an actual and potential center of power the majority party caucus cannot be ignored. It provides a way of democratizing the legislative process and another source of citizen access. It also represents a way of circumventing the power of other leaders.

Let's talk about that some more—*circumventing power*. Ultimately, that is what activists have found they must sometimes do to get what they want in the legislative arena.

Challenges to Legislative Power

As obscure as they may seem, there are ways to challenge the rules, and ultimately the distribution of power. Rule changes providing for the election of committee chairpersons and implementation of caucus policy decisions are examples. Both these changes challenged the authority of congressional committees. Other new challenges include the end of committee secrecy in the House and Senate and the end of conference committee secrecy. As of January 1972, 29 state legisla-

---

[7] For details, see "Oil Depletion," *New Republic*, June 15, 1974, p. 7.
[8] Duane Lockard, *New England State Politics* (Princeton, N.J.: Princeton University Press, 1959), pp. 297–302.
[9] Belle Zeller, ed., *American State Legislatures* (New York: Thomas Y. Crowell Company, 1954), pp. 194–197.

tures had also eliminated committee secrecy in one or both houses.[10] All these actions are new challenges to the established distribution of power.

Challenging legislative power is not new, however. There are traditional devices that can be used, but they ordinarily require a determined majority. For example, a bipartisan effort was responsible for weakening the position of the speaker of the House. Prior to 1910, the speaker appointed all committees and chairpersons and personally chaired the powerful Rules Committee. After he consistently used these resources to weaken the progressives in Congress, Speaker Joe Cannon was stripped of many of them. Progressives in the Republican party (the majority party) joined with Democrats to remove the speaker from the Rules Committee, deny the speaker the power to many committee appointments, and restrict the power of recognition. As powerful as it still is, the office of speaker has never been the same.

Another traditional way of limiting legislative power is through *committee appointments*. During the opening days of the Ninety-fourth Congress, liberal Democrats, enjoying their enhanced power, made sure liberal Democrats were added to key committees that had been blocking various reforms. The House Ways and Means Committee, for example, had its membership increased from 25 to 37. In addition, they further diluted the committee's power by compelling it to establish subcommittees. No longer would the chairperson and conservative members be able to block significant tax reform.

The *discharge petition*, previously referred to, is a method of circumventing committee power that rarely works. The rule states that bills not reported out within 30 days of referral to a committee may be subject to discharge. In the House, the discharge motion must be signed by an absolute majority (218) of the membership. The Rules Committee may be discharged of a bill after it has held it for only seven legislative days. In the Senate, a discharge resolution may be initiated by an ordinary motion. Many state legislatures also use this device.

So why doesn't it work? Because few people want to antagonize power holders, and a legislator who signs a petition is doing just that. The legislator is tampering with the territory of a congressional committee whose support may be needed at some future time. The result? Since 1909, only 24 of the 835 petitions filed in the House have been

---

[10] Citizens Conference on State Legislatures, "A Report on Legislative Progress," p. 7.

approved—not a great success record. Still, if a determined majority is there, and it has been mobilized through publicity, lobbying, and letters, it can act. When Emanuel Celler continued to block the Equal Rights Amendment proposal in the Judiciary Committee, Rep. Martha Griffiths decided to challenge him. In a period of growing feminist militancy and awareness, Congressmen could not risk opposition. She got her majority of signatures in less than six weeks.[11]

While there are many more subtle ways of challenging legislative power, one other major device should be mentioned. It is unique in that it is designed to challenge not the power of a legislative committee or chairperson, not the power of the floor leaders, presiding officers, or caucus, but the power of one ordinary senator. Custom and *Senate Rule 22* give inordinate negative power to any one person or small group opposing the majority. It provides for unlimited debate on a motion before it can be brought to a vote. A *filibuster* is a misuse of this resource. Instead of encouraging debate on the merits and demerits of pending legislation, a filibuster does other things. By "talking uninterrupted," one senator or a team of senators can gain concessions from the majority or even achieve the withdrawal of the bill. It was a major device used by southern senators to forestall passage of civil rights legislation for many years. Senator Strom Thurmond overspoke for more than 24 hours against such legislation.

This power can be challenged, although not easily. *Cloture* is the technique used to end the talk and get to the vote. One-sixth of the membership can initiate action by petitioning the Senate to close debate. If the petition is approved by three-fifths of the members of the Senate, the bill will come up for a vote. Before the final action, more talking is possible, but no one can have more than an hour before the bill is finally considered.

Like the discharge petition, cloture hasn't had much success. The Senate is proud of its freedom of debate. In addition, there is a practical consideration. The filibuster is a powerful minority weapon that each senator may want to use some day. The result? Between 1917 and 1972 there were over 60 cloture votes. Only 11 succeeded. Since 1975, cloture should meet with more success. In that year the Senate voted to change the cloture rule from two-thirds of those senators present to a permanent three-fifths (60 senators). It doesn't sound like much of a change, does it? In fact, prior to 1975 many important bills

11 Gary Orfield, *Congressional Power: Congress and Social Change* (New York: Harcourt, Brace Jovanovich, 1975), p. 301.

failed because senators were unable to acquire just two or three more cloture votes.

On the basis of this discussion it is clear that there are ways to challenge the distribution of power in legislative bodies. Such a challenge can occur through rule changes or through skillful use of existing rules. In each case, however, it requires understanding of how sentiment is likely to be distributed, who the key legislative players are, and what rules can be used to one's advantage and disadvantage. In addition, it requires a realistic assessment of the odds. As we've seen, opportunities for the negative use of power abound in legislative arenas. The status quo is favored to win. Just how favored was indicated by a *Congressional Quarterly* analysis of the 1972 session. On more heavily contested issues the odds were 3 to 1 against the initiators of change. Prevented from passing were bills related to no-fault auto insurance, small business worker safety, an increase in and extension of the minimum wage laws, the establishment of a consumer protection agency, and regulation of strip mining. Whatever the bill, whether it was initiated by groups promoting private economic interests or those promoting broader public interest, the initiators of change were consistently most likely to fail.[12] Still, the odds are not overwhelming. The changing composition of legislative bodies and increasing citizen action have produced both institutional and social reforms.

Rules Relevant to Access

Legislative games have another kind of rule—those pertaining to access. Not every athlete can participate in the Olympics. Not every race car driver can race in the "Indianapolis 500." Legislative games have these rules also, and the action-oriented citizen needs to know about them.

The rules pertaining to legislative access are of two kinds. They have to do with electoral politics and pressure politics. Ultimately each type influences legislative outcomes and who can play.

Rules Relevant to Electoral Politics

If one uses electoral politics, there are several ways to gain access to legislative arenas. They include:

---

[12] See "Lobby Highlights: Foes Score Success in 1972," *Congressional Quarterly*, November 4, 1972, pp. 2917–2923.

"And in this corner, fighting his way out of his robe — "

Copyright 1975 by Herblock in the Washington Post

1. Run for office or help get someone else elected
2. Recall a legislator from office
3. Make a law directly through the initiative process
4. Prevent a law from going into effect through the referendum

Each of these modes of access has formal rules and informal ones. Let's take a look at *getting elected* first. Volumes have been written on the informal rules of elections. They have to do with setting up campaign organizations, developing campaign strategies and tactics, financing, etc.[13] Rather than dealing with those rather complex rules in a short space, we suggest that the activist considering this approach should study that literature.

Some *formal rules*, however, can be specified. A few have already been identified. They pertain to age, residency, and citizenship requirements for legislative office. In each state these can be obtained from the Board of Elections or the Election Commission. Check the telephone book under the name of your county or city. Of course, they are also identified in state constitutions, election codes, and city charters.

These rules are rather easy to comply with, particularly if the candidate will be representing a major party or the office is nonpartisan. For a minority-party candidate, the procedural requirements are more difficult. Those that apply to getting on the ballot are usually to the advantage of the major parties. Just ask George Wallace about the difficulties he had qualifying the American Independent Party in 1968.

The *initiative, referendum,* and *recall* are crucial approaches to electoral politics. In a sense, they give citizens access to themselves as legislators rather than to a legislative arena. Unfortunately they are allowed only in some states and localities. The rules applicable to the initiative explain how citizens can get a legislative proposal on the ballot. Those applicable to the referendum describe the procedures for preventing a law passed from becoming effective. The rules per-

---

[13] A few of the many available sources of information are David A. Leuthold, *Electioneering in a Democracy: Campaigns for Congress* (New York: John Wiley & Sons, 1968); Gerald M. Pomper, *Elections in America: Control and Influence in Democratic Politics* (New York: Dodd, Mead & Company, 1968); Cornelius P. Cotter, ed., *Practical Politics in the United States* (Boston: Allyn and Bacon, 1969); Paul P. Van Ripper, *Handbook of Practical Politics,* 3d ed. (New York: Harper & Row, Publishers, 1967); Frederick Pohl, *Practical Politics, 1972* (New York: Ballantine Books, 1971); and Donald G. Herzberg and J. W. Peltason, *A Student Guide to Campaign Politics* (New York: McGraw-Hill Book Company, 1970).

taining to recall define how citizens may remove public officials from office—either those not doing their job or those who are particularly obstructive or unresponsive.

Generally, the rules for all three approaches indicate the number of signatures needed to qualify for the ballot and the time in which they must be gathered.[14] Although frequently cumbersome and time-consuming, the methods of access they provide give citizens a unique opportunity to be more than just political benchwarmers. If only they existed in more states!

Something to think about
Under what conditions would citizens be most likely to use the initiative? When would it make sense as a strategy?

A final set of rules related to access through electoral politics has to do with *campaign contributions*. If a citizen or interest group is trying to gain legislative access by financially assisting a candidate, there are laws related to contributions at every level of government.

Those on the *national* level have undergone the most sweeping changes recently. The *1971 Federal Campaign Act* says, for example, that each candidate and each committee representing a candidate must file periodic financial reports listing who contributed how much, and what the money was being spent on. These reports have to be filed both in Washington, D.C., and in the home state. For the first time in history this legislation made the records of campaign contributions and spending available to the public. Unlike the old Corrupt Practices Act, which had been in existence since 1925, the 1971 legislation placed no limits on individual contributions. However, it did place limits on contributions made by the candidate and his or her family (i.e., $35,000 for the Senate, $25,000 for the House of Representatives). It continued to disallow *direct* political contributions by corporations or unions. In addition to the disclosure requirement, another new aspect of this law was the limitation on media spending. This was an attempt to curtail overall campaign costs.

Congress wasn't satisfied with the 1971 law. In part as a response to the campaign contribution abuses associated with Watergate, they passed the *1974 Campaign Reform Bill*. This law set *spending* and broader *contribution* limits. Specifically, no individual can give more

---

14 See the appendix for the rules pertaining to each state.

than $1,000 to one candidate in a federal election nor more than $25,000 to all candidates. However, this amount can be given repeatedly in a primary, runoff, and general election. In addition, donating organizations (corporations, unions, public-interest campaign funds, trade associations) can contribute no more than $5,000 to any one candidate. The provision placing limits on the amount a candidate and his or her family could contribute to the candidate's own campaign was declared unconstitutional in 1976.

Also declared unconstitutional were spending limits—$70,000 in House races (both primary and general elections) and a sliding limit in Senate races, depending on the voting-age population of the state. For example, a limit of $150,000 was placed on the race in small states, but a $1.7-million limit applied in California, the largest. Spending in the primary was to be 30 percent less than in the general election. All congressional candidates, under this new law, were allowed an extra 20 percent for fund-raising expenses. In the general election, national and state party organizations were permitted to spend an extra $10,000 for House races and more for Senate campaigns.

Apart from the public financing of presidential (not congressional) campaigns, which remains part of this law,[15] the other major provision is for an enforcement commission. Instead of having employees of Congress responsible for enforcement, as in the past, a *Federal Elections Commission* has been established. Its effectiveness depends on who the commissioners are. Congress was originally able to make some of the appointments. But in 1976 the U.S. Supreme Court said that only the President may appoint members of the six-person commission. All are subject to confirmation by both houses of Congress. Although the commission does not have the power to initiate criminal proceedings (this still must be done by the U.S. attorney general), it does have subpoena and civil action authority. It can move immediately upon receiving a complaint that the law is being violated, even during a campaign.

These new federal election laws have several implications. While they may democratize the election process by giving more candidates who are not individually wealthy or who do not have major financial connections a chance, they have a negative implication also. They give the incumbent a further advantage, since an incumbent usually needs to spend far less to get re-elected. The limit in House races, we know, was to be $70,000, but 1972 statistics indicate that in the few

[15] Discussed in Chapter 10.

races where the incumbent was defeated, the challenger spent more than $100,000.[16]

So, for those seeking to gain access to legislators by contributing to their campaign or helping to organize fund-raising, these are the federal rules. Progress at the *state level* has also been encouraging. As a result of mini-Watergates across the country, 1973 and 1974 were years of reform; 25 states enacted serious campaign finance legislation.

Rules Relevant to Pressure Politics

Some of the access rules previously described are indirectly related to pressure politics. Initiative and recall campaigns, for example, as well as campaign contributions can be mechanisms of pressure as well as electoral politics. However, other rules are more directly related to pressure politics. As one tries to gain access to legislators and influence their behavior, these rules should be observed.

A major set of rules has to do with *lobbying*. On the national level, most of these are contained in the Regulation of Lobbying Act, part of the Legislative Reorganization Act of 1946. The act is misnamed, for under its provisions very little regulating gets done. Theoretically, any person or organization soliciting or receiving money to be used *principally to aid*, or any person or organization whose *principal purpose* is to aid, the passage or defeat of legislation before Congress is required to *register* with the Clerk of the House of Representatives. This is the national definition of a lobbyist. In addition, the person or group must *file quarterly reports* showing all money actually received and expended, including the names and addresses of all persons contributing $500 or more or to whom $10 or more has been paid. It also requires disclosure of the name and address of the person, by whom the person is employed, and in whose interest he or she appears or works. The duration of the employment, the amount of payment, and by whom the person is paid must also be noted. In addition, the person must describe how much is to be paid for expenses and what expenses are to be included.

Sounds like a very compact and thorough set of rules, doesn't it? The problem is, it is vague and poorly administered. Phrases like "principal purpose" allow some active interest groups to refuse to register. They claim lobbying is only incidental to their objectives. So the National Rifle Association can spend $2 million yearly (a Senate subcommittee estimate) to prevent gun control legislation and gen-

16 "Money and Politics," *New Republic*, October 26, 1974, p. 6.

erate half a million letters to members of Congress, and still not register as a lobbying organization.

The Clerk of the House and Secretary of the Senate are responsible for compiling this information. There is no special agency responsible for it. Thus, it may take so long to see the published reports in the *Congressional Record* that the information is no longer useful. The reports for the last quarter of 1971 were not made public until May 25, 1972.[17] As if all this were not bad enough, the law fails to provide any ascertainable standard of guilt, so anyone who wanted to enforce it might find the law in violation of due process. Still, just in case, there are some provisions for violations. Any person convicted is subject to a fine and/or imprisonment and is prohibited from influencing legislation for a period of three years from the date of conviction.

Most of the problems pertaining to the rules of lobbying would be eliminated if Congress were to pass the Common Cause sponsored lobby reform act. The Senate passed that legislation during the summer of 1976: the vote, 82–9. The House will likely follow. The major reform provisions in the Senate bill include a much more precise and all-encompassing definition of a lobbyist and an adequate enforcement mechanism. For example, under the bill, individuals wouldn't be required to register and report, only organizations. But every organization would have to register and report quarterly if it met at least one of the following three tests: If there were 12 direct oral contacts with Congress by paid officers or employees of the organization in any quarter-year, if an outside lawyer or leg-man were hired to lobby and were paid $250 or more in the quarter, or if the organization spent $5000 or more in a quarter promoting letter-writing campaigns on issues before Congress. Lobbying of the Executive branch would also be covered by this bill. The General Accounting Office would be responsible for administering the law, and it would have rule-making and civil enforcement powers. If passed and signed by the President, this would be a far stronger set of lobbying rules than the 1946 legislation.

But there are other kinds of rules pertaining to lobbying. They were enacted by Congress but are enforced by the Internal Revenue Service. By allowing or disallowing deductions for certain kinds of lobbying activity and by conditioning tax status on, among other things, the extent of legislative activity, Congress has supposedly been

[17] Lawrence Gilson, *Money and Secrecy* (New York: Frederick A. Praeger, 1972), p. 25.

able to influence who lobbies, in what way, and how much. Section 501(c) of the Internal Revenue Code describes the organizations exempted from the income tax. Religious, charitable, scientific, educational, and other organizations with similar purposes are exempt provided that "no substantial part" of the organization's activities consists of attempts to influence legislation or participation in political campaigns. Section 501(c) says that contributions to organizations that qualify for the tax exemption are tax deductible.

Congress uses the Internal Revenue Code to regulate lobbying in still another way. Section 162(e), a 1962 amendment to the Code, allows taxpayers to deduct as an "ordinary and necessary" business expense the cost of preparing and presenting testimony, statements, or communications before Congress or other legislative bodies on legislation of direct interest to the taxpayer.

There is a strange inconsistency here. The Senate Finance Committee, which recommended this amendment, apparently did not see the illogic in giving business groups a tax deduction for lobbying expenses while penalizing public-interest groups for the same kind of activity.

A situation involving the Sierra Club illustrates the problem. In June 1966, this environmental organization placed advertisements in the *New York Times* and the *Washington Post* declaring its opposition to legislation proposing the construction of power dams in the Grand Canyon. In addition, the club urged the public to support the fight against the project by writing to members of Congress. Soon after these advertisements appeared (six months), the IRS revoked the Sierra Club's tax-exempt status and ruled that contributions to the Sierra Club would no longer be allowed as deductions. The club revenues fell off by an estimated $5,000 per week. While the Sierra Club was penalized for its indirect lobbying activity, the power companies on the other side of the controversy could deduct their own expenses in lobbying directly for the bill. In addition, they could deduct any dues paid to organizations that were used for similar purposes.

This case illustrates rather clearly the unequal distribution of advantages resulting from these regulations. Still, they are rules that groups must observe.[18]

---

[18] This description of these IRS regulations and their application to the Sierra Club is from Dale C. Freeman, "The Poor and the Political Process: Equal Access to Lobbying," *Harvard Journal on Legislation*, March 1969, pp. 369–392. Mr. Freeman makes several recommendations for dealing with the problems he describes.

If the national situation is bad, the lobbying regulations in states have been worse. However, the legislative reforms sweeping states in 1973–1974 included lobbying. According to a study by Common Cause, nine states strengthened their lobbyist registration disclosure requirements. Others appear ready to act.

So until 1976, it had been the national legislature that most resisted establishing strong lobbying rules. Those given the advantage by this inactivity have been groups that want to hide their lobbying activities and the amount they are spending to influence legislation. Placed at a disadvantage, clearly, have been citizens who seek to discover what is going on in Congress—who is benefiting from what? who is influencing whom?

Something to think about
How does this inaction give legislators an advantage?

We've been talking about the formal rules, however inadequate they may be. There are also informal ones. Interviews with lobbyists reveal that these rules, although not written down, are generally adhered to and accepted as important.[19]

1. *Be pleasant and nonoffensive.*
2. *Convince the official that listening is important.* Since elected officials are nearly always concerned with constituent interests, a demonstration that this is of interest to constituents is one of the best ways to get attention.
3. *Be well prepared and well informed.* Officials require that lobbyists be knowledgeable because they need information and want something in return for the time and attention they give.
4. *Be personally convinced.* While this is important, many lobbyists deliberately present arguments on the other side. They do this partly to suggest fair-mindedness, but mainly to strengthen their own side. A lobbyist who presents both sides leaves the official with the impression that the lobbyist has looked at all sides of the question before arriving at a conclusion.
5. *Be succinct, well organized, and direct.* The lobbyist who keeps an

---

[19] Lester W. Milbrath, *The Washington Lobbyists* (Chicago: Rand McNally & Company, 1963), pp. 220–226.

appointment and then lets the member of Congress get on with other work comes to be liked and respected. This is also true if the legislative assistant is the one being lobbied. William B. Charkasky, assistant to Senator Gaylord Nelson, said, "If someone can't give me a brief oral description of the bill or a note describing it, forget it. I haven't got time to read bills." Robert Sherrill observes that if this is true for Charkasky, it's twice as true for his and every other Senator.[20]

6. *Use the soft sell.* Don't push a case too hard. Recognize the atmosphere of compromise that inevitably prevails in legislative game playing.

7. *Leave a short written summary of the case.* Most officials prefer to have something in writing to relieve them of the necessity of taking notes and to ensure correctness of information and interpretation, *but do make it short!* As Wes Barthelmes, who has worked for two representatives and two senators, put it,

> The primary means of communication is by voice. Usually any memo or any piece of paper that runs more than two pages they balk at. You haven't got a lot of academicians or scholars up here—they want to get it quick and fast.[21]

So these are the informal rules. In the case of lobbying, they are more important than the formal ones. Also, they are just as applicable to the state and local levels. They should make continuing access easier.

Many citizens gain access to legislatures not through organizations that use official lobbyists, but by contacting legislators directly through *letters.* Although this is usually considered an important group tactic, even individual letters can influence legislators. Aides to Senator Miller of Iowa remembered, for example, a 1962 letter that persuaded the senator to introduce an amendment lifting restrictions on defense-contract bidding for small businesses. The aides said that Small Business Administration officials later called the constituent-proposed amendment "one of the most useful we've ever had." And Rep. Morris K. Udall (D., Ariz.) also recognizes the value of a well-written letter. He told his constituents in a 1967 newsletter, "On several occasions I can testify that a single thoughtful, factually persua-

---

[20] Robert Sherrill, "Who Runs Congress," *New York Times Magazine,* November 22, 1970, p. 52+.
[21] *Ibid.*

sive letter did change my mind or cause me to initiate a review of a previous judgement." [22]

So what is a good letter? Clearly there are no formal rules, but here are some *informal* ones.

Writing Tips

Rep. Morris K. Udall (D. Ariz.) and the League of Women Voters provided these hints on how to write a member of Congress:

- Write to your own senator or representative. Letters sent to others will end up on their desks eventually anyway.
- Write at the proper time, when a bill is being discussed in committee or on the floor.
- Use your own words and your own stationery. Avoid signing and sending a form or mimeographed letter.
- Don't be a pen pal. Don't try to instruct the representative or senator on every issue that comes up.
- Don't demand a commitment before all the facts are in. Bills rarely become law in the same form as introduced.
- Identify all bills by their title or their number.
- If possible, include pertinent editorials from local papers.
- Be constructive. If a bill deals with a problem you admit exists, but you believe the bill is the wrong approach, tell what you think the right approach is.
- If you have expert knowledge or wide experience in a particular area, share it with the member. But don't pretend to wield vast political influence.
- Write to the member when he does something you approve of. A note of appreciation will make him remember you more favorably the next time.
- Feel free to write when you have a question or problem dealing with procedures of government departments.
- Be brief, write legibly and be sure to use the proper form of address. Examples:

The Honorable John Doe
United States Senate
Washington, D.C. 20510
(Dear Senator Doe:)

The Honorable John Doe
House of Representatives
Washington, D.C. 20515
(Dear Mr. Doe:) [23]

---

[22] "Bumper Mail Crop Keeps Congressional Staffs Busy," *Congressional Quarterly*, November 14, 1969, p. 2283.
[23] *Congressional Quarterly* (November 14, 1962), p. 2283.

Another major opportunity for citizen access—at all levels of government—is the *committee hearing.* Notice of upcoming hearings on particular national bills is given in the *Congressional Record,* often more than the required one week. States have been more negligent about giving notice, although the situation is improving.[24]

On the national level and in many states and cities, hearings are scheduled on most major bills. Usually they occur during the first five or six months of each year. There are no rigid rules about who may testify. All that is generally necessary is to *send a request to the committee or subcommittee chairperson* as far in advance of the hearing as possible. Also send a written statement to the committee a day or two before the hearing. If the chairperson refuses to schedule someone, a request can be made to the ranking minority member of the committee, who usually can call witnesses for one day. Or, it is sometimes possible to appear at a different committee hearing and achieve the same objective.

Amazingly, *you don't have to be an "expert" to testify,* although this helps. Often personal experience and passion count far more than expertise. For example, an 11-year-old Florida school girl recently testified before the Senate Commerce Committee on a study she had done of the impact of television advertising on her classmates. During hearings on a coal mine health and safety bill, miners with severe black lung disease gripped the attention of members of Congress by showing how they collapsed from lack of breath after jumping up and down just a few times.[25]

As with testifying, whether or not hearings should be held, where they should be held, and what should be the order of appearance of witnesses have no rules. Anyone can initiate hearings—citizens, other members of Congress, or the committee itself. Furthermore, they need not be held in either house office building or even in the capital. A particular citizens' group may successfully bring hearings to their city.

---

[24] For specific information on scheduling and providing notice of meetings in each state, see the Citizens Conference on State Legislatures study of the 50 American legislatures, *The Sometimes Governments* (New York: Bantam Books, 1971), and their update in "Legislatures Move to Improve Their Effectiveness," April 1972, pp. 7 and 8.

[25] Mark J. Green, James M. Fallows, and David R. Zwick, *Who Runs Congress?* (New York: Bantam Books, 1972), pp. 266–267.

Something to think about
How would local hearings benefit a particular political action? How could citizens influence the location of a hearing?

Wherever the hearings are held, a committee chairperson does not have to share hearing time equally among proponents and opponents and does not have to agree to any particular order of appearances. But most try to be fair. Sometimes witnesses try to influence hearing arrangements. For example, an early appearance may be an advantage. It allows a person to testify before the committee becomes exhausted. It also is likely to attract more media attention. On the other hand, a later appearance makes it possible to collect more tactical information. By scrutinizing earlier committee questions and the testimony of other witnesses, a later witness knows the key concerns and how to prepare definitive answers.

In summary, the lack of rules concerning hearings gives committee chairpersons a great deal of discretion. In addition, it gives citizens a chance to influence key decisions. It is an important access opportunity.

Still another set of formal and informal rules of access relevant to pressure politics are those pertaining to the *introduction* of bills. The essential rule is, regardless of the legislative arena, *only a member of the relevant house can introduce a bill*. So even if the chief executive, an executive agency, or an interest group has a bill in hand, they cannot gain access without the sponsorship of a legislator.

There are two types of sponsorship. The first type suggests that the representative will not only introduce the bill, but will take personal responsibility for its progress. This may include answering correspondence on the bill, defending it in committee and before the full house, and discussing it with proponents and opponents. The representative becomes the chief negotiator.

If an interest group is seeking personal sponsorship, it is important to choose not only someone who is sympathetic but the person who has the greatest resources. Hopefully, the representative will be on the committee considering the bill or, better yet, will chair the committee. Party connection is also helpful. Get someone from the majority party. Bills introduced by minority members don't get very far. If a particularly important bill has been introduced by a minority member, a majority member may introduce a similar one just to gain the attention and credit that can come from being associated with a bill bound for success.

A second type of sponsorship is less helpful. When bills bear the notation *"by request,"* it means that the legislator has agreed to introduce a measure for some group or individual. It also means that the legislator will not necessarily work for it and may not be committed to its principles. This label often reflects a legislator's reservations and thus can mean the bill's eventual defeat. If the legislator introducing the bill doesn't take it seriously, why should others?

Sometimes *multiple sponsors* are obtained. This occurs in two ways. A citizen or group may seek sponsors in each house in order to get simultaneous action on the matter, or multiple sponsors may be obtained in one house. This may be bipartisan sponsorship or mass sponsorship (i.e., 20 to 40 members). Both attract attention to the measure and provide added leverage. It's interesting to note, however, that some houses have a rule against multiple sponsorship. The U.S. House of Representatives does, but that doesn't prevent it. Although only one name can be printed on the bill, identical bills are simply introduced by several members. It has the same effect.

Thus far all the access rules discussed have had to do with normal tactics. Yet we know that extraordinary tactics, particularly forms of protest, are also used to gain access. Again, there are both formal and informal rules to consider.

The First Amendment to the U.S. Constitution contains the most fundamental rules. It protects freedom of speech and assembly. Under this amendment and the Fourteenth Amendment (due process clause), neither the national government nor state governments may abridge these rights, even if the speech or gathering is controversial and unpleasant. However, the rights are not absolute. Not all speech and assembly are protected. For example, speech that is slanderous, obscene, seditious, or contemptuous of court is not protected. Nor is either speech or assembly protected when there is the probability of a clear and present danger. In addition, assembly designed to accomplish an illegal purpose or resist lawful authority is not guaranteed. Still, the protective scope is broad. As long as one uses good sense and follows a few basic rules, protest is legal.

Sometimes there are permit rules to observe. The city clerk or agency that has jurisdiction over the place where citizens wish to stage their action usually issues them. Then there are police permits. Different cities have different rules governing the requirements for assembling groups of various size. Permits are not usually necessary for sidewalk demonstrations, but why not check? Street marches almost always require permits. Towns and cities have parade and traffic ordinances. However, permits must be issued impartially. In *Poulos v. New Hampshire*, 345 U.S. 395 (1953), the court ruled that if freedom of assembly is unconstitutionally denied by a licensing agency, the legal remedy is to seek a court order requiring the license rather than assemble without it.

The following *informal rules* are just good sense.

1. Make copies of the necessary permits or the local ordinance permitting you to hold the event. These can be shown to police if necessary.
2. Be considerate toward nonparticipants by leaving room for traffic and pedestrians.
3. Use carefully trained marshals or affinity groups to control the crowd. (Affinity groups consist of four to six people who spread throughout an area and attempt to maintain some cohesiveness.)
4. Just in case, there should be sympathetic lawyers, law students, or legal observers on hand to offer immediate legal advice. In addition, they can act as expert eyewitnesses in court, if necessary.[26]

By realizing both the limitations and the scope of the formal rules and observing these few informal ones, citizens can communicate their message. With the help of the media, legislators can assess the merit of both the organization and the cause.

So the rules of access are many. They deal with electoral activities such as the initiative, referendum, and recall. They also deal with helping a candidate get elected by contributing financially to the campaign or merely being sure the candidate's name appears on the ballot. The major rules pertaining to pressure politics as a means of access include the formal and informal rules of lobbying, the rules governing introduction of bills, and the rule vacuum associated with hearings. Not to be overlooked, if necessary, are those rules associated with protest activity.

Whether legislative rules distribute power or influence access, we have seen that they do much more. They are *stabilizing forces,* so much so that they have made change difficult. They are also predictive devices. To the extent that they are accepted, they communicate likely behavior to others. Finally, they are not neutral. They distribute

[26] These rules and informal rules relevant to other forms of protest are described in the O. M. Collective, *The Organizers' Manual* (New York: Bantam Books, 1971), pp. 112–137.

advantages and disadvantages in a way that ultimately protects those who hold power—people with resources who are willing and able to play the legislative game. The techniques of access described in the following chapter indicate more clearly ways in which some of these rules are used.

Key Words

Seniority rule
Discharge petition
Filibuster
Cloture
Lobbyist

Suggested Activities

1. Identify the particularly important legislative committees functioning in your town and county.
2. Determine what rules and tactics allow activists to circumvent the power of your state legislature committee chairpersons.
3. Simulate a filibuster to prevent a bill you oppose from passing the U.S. Senate.
4. If they are legal in your state, determine the success record of statewide initiatives in recent years.
5. Discover whether your state and city have election rules requiring disclosure of contributions or contribution and spending limits.
6. Select a city issue about which the class is concerned and knowledgeable. Organize a visit with a local legislator. Talk to him or her about the issue, observing the rules of lobbying.
7. Visit a committee hearing in your city. Record who testifies, the nature of the testimony, and any informal rules they appear to be following.

9
Getting Through to Legislators

A former U.S. senator and member of the Oregon state legislature, Richard Neuberger, has some vivid memories of groups getting through to legislators. While he defended people's right to communicate with and persuade their representatives, he sometimes became disillusioned. This was his reaction when a bill that would have limited the number of billboards on state highways was defeated in the state legislature:

> Although I had a perfect voting record on the A. F. of L. score-sheet, the head of the signpainters union called me an "enemy of labor," and claimed that I wanted to throw hundreds of men out of work. Then the "widows and orphans" began to appear: forlorn families which would become public charges if they no longer could rent their roadside property to the signboard companies. The state advertising club sent an impressive delegation, which accused me of being a foe of the Bill of Rights: the advertising men would lose their "freedom of speech" if their billboards were banned from the countryside. Although the bill had been suggested to me by a wealthy old woman who loved the outdoors and did not like to see it defaced, my proposal was denounced by those delegates as being of communist origin. . . . Put to a public referendum, I imagine the bill would have passed by at least 5 to 1. These few small pressure groups were able to induce the legislature to reject it

overwhelmingly. I still marvel at the fact that the billboard owners themselves never once appeared during the entire operation.[1]

Pressure Politics

This is a story of lobbying—people trying to convince public officials to support or oppose a particular proposal. It is *pressure politics.* Clearly, there is no guarantee that "the good side" will win and "the bad side" will lose. Lobbying just describes ways of getting through to legislators. In this case various groups of citizens, not professional lobbyists, were trying to get Oregon state legislators to oppose a ban on billboards. They succeeded. They demonstrated that they had power.[2]

However, power doesn't exist in a vacuum. It exists relative to other players. When other players (e.g., environmentalists) forget to play, or have too few resources, or use their resources ineffectively, the probability that one side will win is magnified. Where were the ban-the-billboard players in this story? What were they doing? Wherever they were, if indeed they were playing, their efforts were not enough. So power is defined by the *resources* one has and is able to control, along with the *ability, opportunity,* and *willingness* to use them.

Lobbying is a major interest-group tactic involving a variety of different activities. Sometimes the activities are *direct* forms of influence. An interest-group representative and/or lobbyist will *personally* present a point of view. This can happen in the legislator's or staff member's office, at a social gathering, in a letter, or at a committee hearing. Usually a combination of approaches is used. Then there are *indirect* activities. In some cases the lobbyist or interest-group leadership will try to generate *grassroots support* for a measure. As many people as possible—particularly major players—are encouraged to send letters and telegrams to representatives. This is called a "shotgun" approach. Protest activity would also be included in this category. On the other hand, indirect lobbying may only entail getting key people to try to influence the legislator—friends, major campaign

[1] Richard L. Neuberger, *Adventures in Politics: We Go to the Legislature* (New York: Oxford University Press, 1954), pp. 102–103.
[2] Robert A. Dahl says, "a measure of the power of an actor—be it an interest group, a legislator, or a governor, is the difference between the probability of a given legislative action occurring when the actor takes no stand, and the probability of this given outcome when the actor has taken a stand." See "The Concept of Power," *Behavioral Science,* July 1957, p. 203.

contributors, legislative or party leaders. This is referred to as the "rifle" approach.[3] The pro-billboard lobby used both indirect and direct activities.

While it is difficult to evaluate precisely whether direct or indirect lobbying activities tend to be more effective, two kinds of evidence suggest the former. First, consider what we already know about personal influence, discussed in Chapters 4 and 5. The empirical data are fairly convincing. Second, lobbyists themselves (65 percent) consider direct personal presentations to be more effective, although indirect forms of communication are growing more common.[4]

Whatever the approach, the specific types of lobbying employed will depend on the *resources* of the group. These include the group's size, prestige, membership cohesion, leadership skills, membership distribution (e.g., nationwide or statewide), support of and experience with other groups, money (e.g., dues, grants, etc.), longevity, and cause and goals (e.g., realistic or unrealistic, popular or unpopular). Obviously a group without money will not try to buy television time, and a group with a small membership or following will avoid door-to-door canvassing.

If a group does have an official or unofficial lobbyist, other resources become significant. At least, legislators think so. For example, in Indiana, about 70 percent of the legislators interviewed said the most important qualities a lobbyist should have are honesty and integrity. Next in importance (53 percent) is *knowledge* of the subject matter. Then they mentioned an *agreeable personality* (38 percent). Less important are helpfulness in conducting research and providing information (16 percent), previous legislative experience (12 percent), and formal education (5 percent).[5] These would be important qualities for a group to keep in mind when selecting a lobbyist.

When a group or lobbyist lacks particular resources, a logical approach is to form a *coalition*. This occurs frequently in legislative games, and when group players join together, that relationship tends

---

[3] V. O. Key describes both "shotgun" and "rifle" forms of indirect lobbying in *Politics, Parties and Pressure Groups*, 5th ed. (New York: Thomas Y. Crowell Company, 1964), pp. 134–136.
[4] See Lester W. Milbrath, *The Washington Lobbyists* (Chicago: Rand McNally & Company, 1963), pp. 209–254.
[5] Kenneth Janda, Henry Teune, Melvin Kahn, and Wayne Francis, *Legislative Politics in Indiana* (Bloomington: Indiana University, Bureau of Governmental Research, 1961), p. 19.

Caucus
by HüGo
Dear Patient:
As you Know
Mal-practice suits
in this state
have grown alarmingly.
many of us in the
medical profession
will have to discontinue
our practice if this
trend continues.
This will result
in inadequate
medical and health
needs for the state
of California.
I urge you to
write to your
legislative
representative.
©1975 HüGo
ALL RIGHTS RESERVED
let him Know of your
concern over the
health of the state
and your wish to
assure
doctors...
...the income to
which we've
become accustomed

to persist over time.[6] As long as the groups share the same policy position, both trust and a way of working together evolve and grow. Each partner in the coalition engages in those lobbying activities that its resources will allow.

How does it all come together—the resources, ability, and opportunity—to create power or influence? The following case studies are examples of pressure politics. The major tactic used is direct lobbying. Each case illustrates a different approach, but the element they all have in common is winning.

Direct Lobbying

Lobbying a sympathetic or neutral legislator is the ordinary approach. Rarely do interest groups try to change a legislator's mind. The American Civil Liberties Union (ACLU), working for the impeachment of Richard Nixon, did the unusual—and they succeeded in this instance.[7]

Richmond (Staten Island) is as conservative a county as there is in New York. In 1972, Richard Nixon received approximately 75 percent of the vote. Even in the spring of 1974, when national polls were showing considerable public disenchantment with the President and his administration, a Staten Island newspaper poll showed that over 60 percent of the local residents still supported him. The total membership of the ACLU—generally a liberal group—in the entire county was only 261, or 0.1 percent of the population.

The plan was to try to convince the local member of Congress to support impeachment. This required making initial contact. Staff member Norman Siegel's letter to Congressman John Murphy was the first step. Although his party affiliation (Democrat) made him likely to support impeachment, Murphy is conservative. In fact, he was nominated by both the Democratic and Conservative parties. He failed to reply to Siegel's letter. Norman Siegel and the local ACLU persisted. Through letters and ads they asked their members and anyone answering the ad to attend a meeting on impeachment. The 150 who attended decided to organize a letter-writing campaign to

[6] In his study of 119 national interest groups operating in Congress during a 16-year period (1945–1960), Robert L. Ross discovered that interest-group clusters emerge and remain stable over a long period of time. Shifting alliances are not very frequent. See "Relations among National Interest Groups," *The Journal of Politics*, February 1970, pp. 96–114.

[7] Ira Glasser, "Grass Roots Campaigning the Key to Success," *ACLU News*, March–April 1974, p. 4. The case, as described, is essentially Glasser's account. He is the executive director of the New York Civil Liberties Union.

Murphy, and to press for a meeting. Requests for the meeting were still resisted—Murphy was in a difficult spot.

After more letters and many telephone calls, the meeting was scheduled. Approximately 100 people came. They pressed him hard on impeachment. The fact that he even came showed that he was vulnerable. He certainly had never previously entered a New York Civil Liberties Union office. By the end of the meeting a change in his position became visible.

Well, that should have satisfied everyone, but it didn't. The people who attended the meeting told him it wasn't enough to come out quietly for impeachment. They wanted him to speak publicly for it. Incredibly, he agreed.

In February 1974 the meeting was held. In spite of a freezing hailstorm, 300 people showed up. Sharing a platform with Civil Liberties Union members, he gave a carefully prepared speech calling for impeachment. The event made page one of the *Staten Island Advance*. Given the background of both Murphy and the *Advance*, the whole thing seemed inconceivable. It was direct lobbying that worked.

What are some of the lessons to be learned from this case? First, membership resources may not be crucial if you know how to use what you have. Murphy didn't know the size of the local membership —all he knew was that a number of informed and committed people were trying to persuade him to change his position. He also knew, in spite of the local poll, that there weren't many equally committed people on the other side. Second, amateurs can do it. While the ACLU did have a small professional staff, most of the planning and work was done by members. They used techniques that required no special expertise—meetings, letters, and telephone calls. They just followed the rules that common sense dictated, and they won. Perceptively, Ira Glasser explained the legislative game and the ACLU's rule in this way: "Intransigent minorities—and not majorities—are what usually make the greatest impact on legislators, and that's what we are."

The struggle over a civil rights bill illustrates how skillfully direct lobbying must be coordinated and planned when *many* legislators are targets.[8] This situation is quite different from pressuring just one person.

The bill was H.R. 7152. It was described as the most sweeping

[8] For these and other details, see "Intensive Lobbying Marked House Civil Rights Debate," *Congressional Quarterly*, Feb. 21, 1964, pp. 364–366.

civil rights measure to clear either house of Congress in the twentieth century. It resulted from "the most intensive and effective behind-the-scenes lobbying in modern legislative history."

Let's first take a look at the *coalition* involved. All the major organizations backing the bill participated through an umbrella organization known as the Leadership Conference on Civil Rights. First formed in 1949 to pull together the efforts of all groups interested in civil rights legislation, the organization grew from the original 20 participating groups to 79 as of 1964. Through their coordination, literally thousands of people associated with affiliated groups poured into Washington for the debate on H.R. 7152. These included not only members of civil rights groups but representatives of labor unions, church groups, citizens' organizations, bar associations, and veterans' groups. The leaders of this coalition effort were Clarence Mitchell (NAACP), Andrew Biemiller and Jack Conway (AFL-CIO), Joseph Rauh [Americans for Democratic Action (ADA)], and James Hamilton (National Council of Churches).

Something to think about

Consider the information provided in Chapter 2. What did the leaders of this coalition have to remember to make it successful?

Judiciary Committee Chairman Emanuel Celler (D., N.Y.) was the Democratic floor manager for the bill. His major organized Democratic assistance was provided by the generally liberal *Democratic Study Group*, consisting of about 125 House members. The DSG set up a special 22-person civil rights steering committee, headed by Rep. Richard Bolling (D., Mo.). This group maintained liaison with the Justice Department on the bill from early summer on. The Civil Rights Division of the Justice Department assisted in several ways.

Republican House members were active as well. Various Republican Judiciary Committee members assisted, led by Rep. William M. McCulloch (R., Ohio), the ranking minority member of the Judiciary Committee. Also active was the Republican Legislative Research Association, a group formed in 1962 to fight for such things as minority staffing. Minority Leader Charles A. Halleck (R., Ind.) agreed to support the bill, but not actively. He was present on the floor for very little of the debate and participated in few of the votes. It was left to McCulloch to line up Republican votes.

The *opposition* appeared unusually weak. After all their previous victories, they seemed to be losing some spirit. The Coordinating Committee for Fundamental Freedoms, a group formed in 1963 for the express purpose of defeating the bill, provided the only organized lobby opposition. While they kept two staff members at the Rules Committee hearings and had representatives on hand to witness the floor debate, they did very little to actually round up votes for weakening amendments or against the bill. Fortunately for the proponents, major business groups did not join the opposition. With more relevant legislation on their minds, they overlooked those provisions of the bill that, under other circumstances, they might have considered a danger to their independent business operations. The southern Democratic effort to defeat the bill was unusually low-toned. Although numerous amendments were proposed to weaken the bill, there was no all-out attack similar to southern efforts in earlier years —in spite of the fact that the 60-member southern caucus held informal strategy sessions.

Not anticipating the weakness of the opposition, the coalition made their plans. Their strategy was called "get out the vote." It entailed making sure that every House member who might reasonably be expected to back the bill was on the floor at crucial times. However, before that strategy could be implemented, they had to deal with the Rules Committee.

The Rules Committee, chaired by a Democrat from Mississippi, would not issue a special rule. Coalition leaders had anticipated that. The DSG spearheaded an effort to force the bill out of the committee through a *discharge petition*. This was one of the rare occasions when this move worked.

Now the floor strategy had to be implemented. This involved careful timing, coordination, and varied tactics. Mostly it involved direct personal lobbying. This is how it worked.

How Supporters "Got Out the Vote" on Key Amendments

Convinced that with proper planning they could produce the votes to beat back crippling Southern amendments during the prolonged House debate and off-the-record voting on amendments, the Leadership Conference decided on a multi-pronged strategy.

First, it was decided to keep careful tabs on every Member who might reasonably be expected to back the bill. As the public galleries opened before each day's House session, in poured numerous representatives of the various Leadership Conference organizations which had come to Washington for the debate. Each one of these persons had a specific responsibility: to watch a certain number (4 or 5) of Congressmen, record their attendance and mark down their votes on all proposed amendments. Under this system, suggested by Clarence Mitchell of the NAACP, an effort was made to pair each "watcher" with Congressmen he knew personally, so that he could also call them off the floor to ask their support on important votes. Frequently, however, the gallery "spotters" had not previously met the Congressmen they were to cover.

When a spotter in the gallery saw that one of the Congressmen he was to watch was off the floor too long, a telephone call would be placed to the central headquarters of the Leadership Conference in the nearby Congressional Hotel. At the hotel, a master chart of office locations in both House office buildings was maintained. The civil rights groups had sought out a friendly Congressman on each floor and arranged to have two representatives stationed at a telephone in his office. Whenever a useful Member's absence on the floor was reported, a call would go to the civil rights workers on his floor. Immediately, a visit would be paid to the truant's office to urge him to be present in the House Chamber.

Persons associated with Negro civil rights groups, labor unions and church groups all participated in the button-holing of Congressmen. When union agents contacted Members about their attendance or actual votes on the floor they had a powerful weapon: the record of past or promise of future union help, both in money and manpower, in election campaigns. But union agents were steered clear of the offices of Republicans or Democrats they had opposed in past elections. In large measure the calling on Republicans was done by church representatives.

About halfway through House debate, the system of calling on Members in their offices to get them back to the floor was largely dropped, both because over-all attendance was good and because some Members had expressed resentment over the close control. Supplementing and eventually replacing the system of agents in the House office buildings was the successful "buddy system" the DSG had first worked out in 1963 voting on the foreign aid authorization bill. Under the direction of Rep. Thompson, each of 20 DSG members was responsible for keeping track of five or six other Members, regarding both attendance and voting. The system worked well, reducing substantially the need for regular DSG whip calls.

In addition, the DSG stationed men at the head of the teller line on the House floor to see if Members voted. Thus careful attendance and voting records, checked both from the galleries and the floor, could be kept on all Members. Some Congressmen reportedly expressed resentment about the close floor teller control system, but Speaker John W. McCormack, who had taken exception to the system when it was first used in 1963, was now reported to be in favor of it. Original authors of the system were two freshmen, Reps. Neil Staebler (D Mich.) and Donald M. Fraser (D Minn.).[9]

The planning paid off. The House passed the bill by an overwhelming 290 to 130 margin.[10] So what are the lessons to be learned from this successful lobbying effort? There are several. First, if you have or can acquire *people resources*, use them. The Leadership Conference included organizations with hundreds of thousands of members. It would have been a mistake to ignore this potential.

If you have or can acquire *expertise*, use it. Members of the Justice Department seated in the House gallery throughout the floor debate were repeatedly called down for strategy sessions with the Democrats leading the fight on the floor.

Once a strategy and tactics have been planned, *continue to reassess* them. Each day, before the House convened, a basic strategy and planning meeting was held. The leaders of the coalition and the DSG were present, as was a White House representative.

Promote bipartisan support. If McCulloch had not been leading the Republican effort, many Republicans might have gone along with the southern wing of the GOP. Under the leadership of Reps. William C. Cramer (R., Fla.) and Richard H. Poff (R., Va.) (Judiciary Committee members), Republicans offered various amendments to modify or curtail parts of the bill. McCulloch, however, had already persuaded the overwhelming majority of House Republicans to support a strong bill.

Use traditional leadership if it is present. In this case it was. Both the majority and minority leaders of the key committee were willing and played an essential role. They had the resources to do it.

Understand opposition behavior. While the moves of the opposition in 1964 did not seem to be a serious threat, they could have been. In preparation, the coalition and Democratic leadership reviewed past battles, assessed likely moves, and were ready.

These, then, were some of the lessons of one of the great games of modern legislative history. They would be referred to frequently in

---

[9] *Ibid.*, p. 365.

[10] Known ultimately as the *Civil Rights Act of 1965*, this law prohibits discrimination in public accommodations and in programs receiving federal assistance. It also prohibits discrimination by employers and unions. An Equal Employment Opportunity Commission was established to enforce that part of the law. It also contains provisions for stronger enforcement of voting laws and school and public facilities desegregation.

subsequent civil rights battles. But whether a major lobbying victory receiving national attention or a lesser victory achieved by persuading one person, combined they convey the importance of several things: members willing to work, coalitions where necessary, strategic and tactical planning, flexibility, timing, bipartisan support, and expertise. In all, they suggest that direct personal lobbying is one form of pressure politics that can work.

Indirect Lobbying

Direct lobbying, however, is only one approach. The second approach is *indirect*. This is sometimes planned by lobbyists, and at other times planned by interest groups directly. The approach may include a petition or letter-writing campaign; contact by the party, a key constituent, or a friend; or reliance on media or other institutions. If the groups involved have the resources, all these indirect tactics may be used simultaneously. They may also be used in combination with direct lobbying.

What distinguishes these tactics from direct lobbying? In indirect lobbying the message sent to the legislator has been systematically influenced or encouraged by a third party. That is, the communication is a direct result of a lobbyist's or interest group's efforts to mobilize support. If a citizen read a news story in the paper and decided to write his or her representative, that would be a spontaneous act. It would fall into the category of direct personal influence. In contrast, if a group to which that citizen belonged were to urge him or her to write that representative, that act would be indirect lobbying. The citizen would be an *intermediary* for the group.

One way to gauge the relative value of various indirect tactics is to ask the people involved. Lester Milbrath did that in his study of lobbying. He questioned lobbyists operating in Washington and in Michigan as well as members of Congress. Using a rating system of 0 to 10, he was able to develop the comparative data shown in Table 9–1.

It's interesting to note that lobbyists and members of Congress don't seem to agree. Lobbyists, for example, clearly rate constituents as the most important intermediaries, whereas members of Congress rate contact by a close friend as most important. Not unimportant, according to most lobbyists and members of Congress interviewed, were letter and telegram campaigns and public relations (media) campaigns. The tactic everyone considered least important was publicizing voting records.

Table 9–1

Ratings of communication through intermediaries by Washington lobbyists, Michigan lobbyists, and congressional respondents

Type of Communication Through Intermediaries	Percentage Selecting Each Rating											Median*	Mean*	Number
	Rating													
	0	1	2	3	4	5	6	7	8	9	10			
Contact by Constituents														
Washington lobbyists	14	3	6	8	2	11	7	4	8	12	24	5.79	5.90	99
Michigan lobbyists	21	3	24	9	0	12	9	0	9	3	9	2.17	3.84	33
Congressional respondents	3	0	7	17	10	21	3	3	17	3	14	5.10	5.62	30
Contact by a Close Friend														
Washington lobbyists	26	5	8	13	3	15	6	6	6	5	5	2.77	3.76	98
Michigan lobbyists	30	15	15	15	0	6	3	0	9	0	6	1.30	2.73	33
Congressional respondents	7	0	7	7	7	11	4	15	11	15	15	6.87	6.19	30
Letter and Telegram Campaigns														
Washington lobbyists	20	6	6	5	7	19	1	7	17	4	7	4.29	4.55	99
Michigan lobbyists	54	12	6	3	0	12	9	0	3	0	0	.92	1.73	33
Congressional respondents	17	10	13	3	27	10	0	0	13	0	7	3.75	3.87	30
Public Relations Campaigns														
Washington lobbyists	21	2	2	3	2	15	2	11	17	5	17	6.14	5.55	97
Michigan lobbyists	24	9	3	3	0	18	3	9	6	9	15	4.58	4.79	33
Congressional respondents	4	0	4	22	19	11	7	7	11	7	7	4.67	5.30	30
Publicizing Voting Records														
Washington lobbyists	49	8	12	5	4	8	2	4	2	2	2	1.00	2.05	98
Michigan lobbyists	78	6	3	3	0	3	3	0	0	0	3	.63	.84	33
Congressional respondents	35	8	4	15	11	11	0	8	8	0	0	2.75	2.73	30

* Neither measure of central tendency is quite suitable. One cannot assume equal distance between intervals as required for the mean, yet the median ignores the distance of extreme ratings from the central point. The full distribution of the ratings is the best guide to the data.
Source: Lester Milbrath, *The Washington Lobbyists* (Chicago: Rand McNally & Company, 1963), p. 240.

Political parties.   Let's take a look at some of these indirect techniques, beginning with the *political party* as an intermediary. Although this is not apparent from the previous data, Milbrath did attempt to determine the influence of party officials. He discovered that members of Congress are rarely contacted by party officials for personal or ideological reasons, but are contacted regularly about constituent problems. In addition, contacts are made for two other reasons —to influence an appointment being considered and to influence a decision concerning the party official's district or state.[11]

Missing from this list of reasons for contact is public policy. Party officials who do not hold public office are simply not perceived as important policy intermediaries. Lobbyists are more blunt. They say they don't use party officials because the party has little influence on governmental decisions and that party platforms are useless as a guide to future decisions.[12]

How do these perceptions square with what we know about the motivations of legislative players? Isn't party identification the greatest single predictor of legislative voting? Yes, it is, but the influence is implicit. It is not usually exerted through contacts by party officials outside the legislative or executive arenas. Party leaders inside those arenas have influence, but *primarily* because of the resources that go along with the positions they hold, not because of their party affiliation. A committee chairperson, for example, is influential because he or she chairs a committee, not because he or she is a Democrat or a Republican. The exception to this seems to be the increasing importance of the party caucus, particularly in the U.S. House of Representatives.

Do citizens and citizens' groups have access to legislative leaders who happen to be affiliated with a party? Is it at all realistic to think of them as potential intermediaries for whatever reason? In their study of parties and citizen influence, John Saloma and Fredrick Sontag were both negative and optimistic (if that combination is possible). They were negative about the present situation at the national level.

> To date, ... the real structure of power in Congress—the congressional party leadership and committee leadership of both parties, the so-called congressional establishment—remains essentially untouched. Probably no other segment of the American parties as they are currently structured has provided less opportunity for

[11] Milbrath, *The Washington Lobbyists*, p. 190.
[12] *Ibid.*

citizen involvement in party affairs and continues to be effectively insulated from political change in the country at large.

. . . The citizen activists who diligently lobby congressmen and testify before congressional committees seem strangely unaware of the power and potential of the party organizations in Congress.[13]

The last line suggests their optimism. As gloomy as the existing situation is, they believe the party *in Congress* can become an important avenue of influence.

For the citizen interested in influencing the course of government, the Congress with its relatively undeveloped party organizations is potentially the most tangible instrument available. Congressmen themselves are the most important party leaders readily accessible to the public, with established offices in their districts and in Washington. They are the most visible group of party officials in continuing contact with one another capable of exercising national party leadership. They enjoy resources that few national or state party leaders can afford—sizable staffs, the franking privilege, telecommunications and a variety of services provided by congressional and party staffs. Compared with the national committee man or committee woman, a member of Congress is an easily reached party leader with power to respond to a wide range of requests from constituents.[14]

Who are these other party leaders to whom Saloma and Sontag refer? How do they fit into the influence picture? Figure 4 might help.

The *National Committee*[15] consists of one man and one woman from each state and territory. The committee is formally elected by the national convention, but in practice the convention ratifies the choices proposed by each delegation. The *chairperson* is theoretically elected by the National Committee, but in practice the party's presidential candidate determines who will hold that office.

Since they are at the top of the organization chart, one would expect the members of the National Committee and its chairperson to be uniquely important in the party. They are not. During their four-year term they offer advice and help during the national election, determine the date and place of the national convention, and some-

13 John S. Saloma III and Fredrick H. Sontag, *Parties: The Real Opportunity for Citizen Access* (New York: Alfred A. Knopf, 1972), p. 121.
14 *Ibid.*, p. 122.
15 This discussion of party organization relies on Kay Lawson, *Political Parties and Democracy in the United States* (New York: Charles Scribner's Sons, 1968), pp. 59–62.

Figure 4
Organization of the parties.

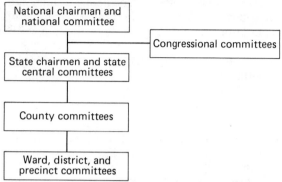

times (although rarely) make policy statements. Their authority is very limited. More and more it is the presidential candidate and his or her staff who run national elections. One need only recall the role of President Nixon's Committee to Re-elect the President to realize how vast that power can be.

If the committee is not very important, the chairperson is somewhat more so. At least he or she has some resources. The chairperson is, after all, the personal choice of the presidential nominee. This gives the chairperson access to the candidate (who, it is hoped, will soon be the President). If the party should win the presidency, the chairperson has another resource—his or her office becomes the clearing house for patronage.

The jobs of the committees and chairpersons in *states* are similar to those on the national level. They too help with elections and arrange conventions. However, since the President and Congress as well as statewide office holders are elected *through the state*, their responsibilities and status are greater. The way to become a state committee member is through an election. That, however, is usually symbolic. More frequently membership is a reward for services (often financial) rendered to the party.

At this level, too, it is usually the party leader holding office, not the party official, who is important. This is true only in those states where parties are strong. In those states, interest groups will use party leaders as intermediaries. They won't appeal to just one party, however. Chances are they will attempt to contact leaders of both parties.

This becomes difficult at times, and some groups have given up and formed alliances with a particular party. On the national level, for example, the NAACP and AFL-CIO alliance with the Democratic party is quite apparent. On the state level, other associations are clear. The Non-Partisan League in North Dakota and the Manufacturers' Association in Pennsylvania have enormous influence in the state Republican organizations. The same could be said about the United Auto Workers' influence in the Michigan Democratic party organization.[16]

Not unexpectedly, Saloma and Sontag see the state party as a particularly important citizen resource—at least potentially.

> As the stakes of state politics continue to rise, the state parties could, because of their particular advantages, provide the means for broader citizen participation and party modernization. State parties, for example, afford the advantages of access. In all but a very few of the largest states, party conventions and meetings are within commuting distance for most residents. Citizens can attend hearings and debates in the state legislature more readily than they can come to Washington. State party officials can be visited in person. State party officials with statewide WATS lines can be only a local telephone call away. Live coverage of state and county committee meetings and conventions will be possible as cable television systems are expanded. Broad-band cable communication will afford many more opportunities for local forms of party organization.[17]

While county committees and chairpersons may coordinate election activities at the local level in some states, it is the *precinct* that has the resources—workers. (In some urban areas, there is a ward organization that separates the precinct and county levels.) They get out the vote. At this level work is organized through a committee whose members are selected in a variety of ways. They may be selected by other active party members through a caucus or convention, or they may be elected in a local primary. In some states precinct committee members are selected by higher party officials.

However they are chosen and regardless of the importance of their job, they are not perceived by the public as being very important. In one study conducted in the Detroit area, only 16 percent of those

---

[16] William J. Keefe and Morris S. Ogul, *The American Legislative Process* (Englewood Cliffs, N.J.: Prentice-Hall, 1964), pp. 354–355.
[17] Saloma and Sontag, *Parties*, p. 155.

interviewed were aware there were party leaders. Only 2 percent could name their precinct leader.[18] In addition, it is even difficult in many places to find someone to run for a precinct position. A Kansas state party chairman noted:

> You will find on the primary ballots in 50 percent of the precincts no candidates at all for precinct committeemen. There may be contests and a choice in 3 percent of them. In the remainder there will be one uncontested candidate for each post.... I was once elected by a landslide of one write-in vote.

The 1968 Party Precinct Participation project of the League of Women Voters confirmed this difficulty in finding candidates.[19]

Stanley Naparst must not have heard about the difficulty of finding local party officials. When he ran in 1974 for a seat on the Alameda County (California) Central Committee, he considered the election serious business. Without any official party support but with a campaign war chest of $70, he traveled the county from one end to the other seeking support. "Are you voting in the Democratic primary?" Naparst asked endlessly. Then a handshake. "I'd like to ask you to vote for me for the County Central Committee." "Why should I?" asked one woman he met at the local PTA carnival. "Because I'm honest and want the party to represent people," said Naparst. She took a handful of his cards (he spent $54 of his budget on 10,000 cards asking for votes). Why did he even bother to run? He expressed displeasure with "the way the world is run," then said, "People make the decisions, and people can change things. The Central Committee is a place to start." [20] Stanley Naparst won the election. If asked, he will probably take the role of intermediary seriously.

Something to think about
For Stanley Naparst to be an *effective* intermediary, what conditions would have to exist and what resources would he need?

So political party organization exists at each level of government, and each level of organization provides the *potential* for citizen ac-

[18] Daniel Katz and Samuel J. Eldersveld, "The Impact of Local Party Activity upon the Electorate," *Public Opinion Quarterly*, Spring 1961, pp. 1–24.
[19] Saloma and Sontag, *Parties*, p. 159.
[20] "Toehold on Trying to Change Things," *San Francisco Chronicle*, June 6, 1974.

cess. However, the structure is *decentralized*. Although organizations at each level work together to win elections, they are autonomous. National party leaders do not dictate to state parties, who do not dictate to local parties. While this decentralization may open the party to citizens, it contributes to its weakness. Without organization *cohesiveness*, office holders are less likely to take the advice of party officials seriously. After all, no one party leader can say he or she speaks for "the party." Thus, while the party has great potential as an indirect source of influence and some *potential* for citizen access, the actuality is quite different.

Letters, telegrams, and petitions.   Other indirect forms of pressure politics are letters, telegrams, and petitions. Those who send them, of course, are the intermediaries. They are prompted to act by an interest group. While petitions weren't evaluated, the Milbrath study did ask lobbyists and members of Congress to evaluate the effectiveness of letters and telegrams. Washington (not Michigan) lobbyists rated them as moderately successful. They considered only personal contact by constituents and public relations campaigns to be more important tactics. Members of Congress, however, rated them as less effective. Except for the publication of voting records, they believed it to be the least effective tactic.[21]

The general idea of a letter-writing and telegram campaign is to convince a public official that a given proposal has strong or overwhelming support. Whether or not the official will be convinced depends, in part, on how the official perceives the role. Some legislators readily conform to the pressure generated, some react strongly against it, and others react mildly or not at all. There are even legislators who react to a deluge of mail by asking opposition groups to produce an equal or greater number of letters on the other side, so that they will be left free to vote their convictions.

So the reaction is mixed, and because of that fact, lobbyists vary widely in their ratings of the tactic. Understandably, it is the lobbyist from a large organization who is most likely to rate it highly. After all, a large membership enables an organization to turn out thousands of letters. However, regardless of the size of the organization, lobbyists seem to agree that letters are better than telegrams. It is difficult to send a thoughtful and reasoned telegram.[22]

[21] See Table 9–1.
[22] Milbrath, *The Washington Lobbyists*, pp. 248–249.

When these tactics are successful, what contributes to the success? The first thing is size. The campaign usually must include many pieces of mail and be weighted to one side of the issue. If a member of Congress gets 30,000 letters on an issue, this is considered a great number, even if it represents the view of less than 10 percent of the member's constituents. At a minimum this deluge is likely to stimulate closer scrutiny of the proposed legislation. Second, letters and telegrams should appear spontaneous. Generating "spontaneous" letters can be tricky business. It becomes a game in itself, as lobbyists try to launch a campaign that does not look like one, and legislators try to spot a campaign and discount it. Smart lobbyists do not prepare mimeographed messages for members to sign and mail, nor do they suggest the wording of messages. It may even be dangerous to supply points or topics to be mentioned in the letters. The best tactic is for groups to teach their members how to write letters to officials and trust them to make relevant points.[23]

Letter-writing was a key tactic used in the Utah campaign to defeat ratification of the Equal Rights Amendment. The organizers called themselves HOTDOGS (Humanitarians Opposed to the Degradation of Our Girls). Their approach was to generate letters to both legislators and the media prior to the opening of the 1972 state legislative session.

They knew their job would be difficult. The proponents had gained ratification in many states very quickly, and in Utah, a poll of all candidates running for the state legislature indicated the amendment was favored by both parties.

Still, HOTDOGS had several things going for them. First, they had the informal support of the John Birch Society. At least, the leaders of HOTDOGS were listed as John Birch Society members, and the April 1973 issue of the JBS monthly magazine, *American Opinion*, made known the connection of the society with anti-ERA groups.

So what did that informal affiliation bring HOTDOGS? First, it brought geographic distribution. While the proponents of the ERA operated primarily from Salt Lake City, John Birch Society chapters exist throughout the state, especially in the southern and rural sections. Thus, there was an established organizational base with which HOTDOG members could communicate and from which they could work. Constituents throughout the state could send letters to legislators.

[23] *Ibid.*, pp. 245–247.

Second, the JBS is tactically experienced. Several of the tactical principles published in *The Blue Book of the John Birch Society* were employed by HOTDOGS. One specifically has to do with letter-writing. It says that an organized campaign of letter-writing and petitions should produce a continuous flood of opinion, sent not just to legislators but to television and radio stations, newspapers, educators, and business and civic leaders. In addition, the *Blue Book* emphasizes that a director should oversee the letter-writing carefully, planning it and evaluating its effectiveness.

In addition to the informal support of the John Birch Society, HOTDOGS shared an ideology with the dominant religious faith of Utah—Mormon (Church of Jesus Christ of the Latter Day Saints). Not only does a large proportion of the Utah population belong to the Mormon Church, but the church's influence penetrates every aspect of life, especially politics. The teachings of the Mormon Church place a heavy emphasis on the importance of the family, the desirability of children, and a patriarchal structure in the home. Women are offered a secondary role in the church's life. For example, they may not become members of the priesthood. Articles in the church magazine, *The Ensign,* and speeches by Mormon Church leaders condemned the leaders of the women's movement as "Pied Pipers of Sin" who lead "women away from their divine role of womanhood down the pathway of error." While the church took no formal position on the Equal Rights Amendment, HOTDOGS had no trouble connecting it with "women's lib"—the movement out of favor with the church.

The main issue in the letters was the fate of the family should the ERA be ratified by 38 states. Women would be forced to give up their preferred way of life. Specifically, according to HOTDOGS, the ERA would (1) inhibit child-bearing and cause youngsters to be put in day-care centers, (2) wipe out a woman's freedom to choose between taking a paying job or being a full-time wife and mother supported by her husband, (3) make every wife in the United States legally responsible for providing 50 percent of the financial support of her family, (4) abolish a woman's right to child support and alimony, and (5) remove from state laws the presumption that the children of divorced parents should remain with their mothers unless overwhelming evidence of neglect, mistreatment, or bad character exists.

Although the proponents of the ERA tried to counter these arguments and publicize the opportunities for women that would result from the passage of the ERA, the issue became too emotional. The proponents had to spend most of their time defending themselves against such charges as "it will require coed public restrooms," or "it will make criminal penalties for rape unconstitutional." The predictions of havoc could not be dispelled in time.

The letters and the press coverage they generated had their effect —even though the letters were sometimes hysterical in tone and had been distributed as form letters. The effect of these letters, even when they were not hysterical, had little to do with their actual content. It had more to do with legislators' perceptions of the ERA coupled with their perceptions of intense constituent feelings conveyed through letters. Ultimately, Utah legislators could see few practical benefits following from the ERA. Many came to the conclusion that the amendment was not crucial to abolishing discrimination on account of sex. In addition, these legislators felt, it would be open to many irrelevant legal challenges. So, given the commitment and organization of the opposition, they could oppose it comfortably, and they did.[24]

Something to think about
How should the pro-ERA activists have conducted their pressure campaign? What did they need to win?

If telegrams are considered less effective than letters because they convey less thought and reasoning, *petitions* should be ranked even lower. That is not to say, however, that they are never used and never considered effective. The problem is that so many names are necessary before they are taken seriously that circulating them is time-consuming. For that reason they are used more frequently on the local level, where fewer names can have greater impact.

Gathering names on a petition is only the first step. The group or individual organizing the petition drive must consider carefully when and how the petitions should be presented to a legislator. Timing is important. Just before an important committee or full house vote seems appropriate. Making the presentation public is also important. Instead of presenting the petition to the legislator quietly, the issue and the petitions can be the occasion for a press conference. If that

[24] The previous description of the ERA struggle in Utah relies on an article by Margaret I. Miller and Helene Linker, "Equal Rights Amendment Campaigns in California and Utah," *Society*, May/June 1974, pp. 40–53.

isn't possible, they should at least be presented publicly—somewhere where the media and the appropriate legislator "happen" to be.

Protest.   So far the discussion has focused on *normal* indirect forms of pressure politics. However, *protest tactics*, we know, have traditionally been a way of getting through to legislators when nothing else seems to work. They are indirect because they usually rely on the media to communicate the message, and they can be employed by individuals or groups. Although neither citizens, public officials, nor lobbyists seem to approve of protest tactics, they have been known to bring results. The conditions must be right, however.

When Mrs. Rosa Parks, a 42-year-old black seamstress, boarded a Cleveland Avenue bus in downtown Montgomery, Alabama, on December 1, 1955, she wasn't thinking about the "right conditions" or even protest. Yet her action, in terms of its ultimate consequences, was the beginning of one of the most famous protests of the twentieth century. The story conveys the importance of both individual and group action, commitment and determination, and training and discipline, as well as the issue involved.[25]

Martin Luther King, Jr., described how it all started. Mrs. Parks was returning home after a regular day's work in the city's leading department store. She had been on her feet all day and was tired. After boarding the bus, she sat in the first seat behind the section reserved for whites. A few minutes later the bus driver ordered her, along with three other black passengers, to move back in order to accommodate boarding white passengers. However, all the seats were taken. If she obeyed, she would have to stand. The white passengers would have the seats. The other three black passengers immediately complied with the driver's request. Mrs. Parks quietly refused. The result was her arrest. She was violating both city and state law.

Mrs. Parks's arrest soon became public knowledge. Black community leaders called a meeting to determine what should be done. The decision was to distribute leaflets with this message:

- Don't ride the bus to work, to town, to school, or any place Monday, December 5.
- Another Negro woman has been arrested and put in jail because she refused to give up her bus seat.

25 The details that follow are provided by Martin Luther King, Jr., in *Stride toward Freedom* (New York, Harper and Row, Publishers, 1958). Copyright © 1958 by Martin Luther King, Jr. Reprinted by permission.

• Come to a mass meeting at 7:00 P.M. at the Holt Street Baptist Church for further instruction.

On that Monday, the boycott was 100 percent successful. Not one black citizen would ride.

Prior to the mass meeting Mrs. Parks was tried. She was found guilty of disobeying the city's segregation law and fined ten dollars plus four dollars for court costs. She decided to appeal.

The conviction of Rosa Parks not only provided the opportunity to test the constitutionality of the segregation law, but served to arouse the black community. On the night of the mass meeting, the church was full, and three or four thousand people who could not get in waited outside. They listened to the proceedings through loudspeakers. Martin Luther King urged nonviolent protest—specifically, a citywide bus boycott. The strategy was to put economic pressure on the bus company, who in turn would put political pressure on the city council—indirect lobbying.

Ralph Abernathy read the demands that the city council would ultimately have to consider. The substance of the resolution called upon Negroes not to resume riding the buses until (1) courteous treatment by the bus operators was guaranteed; (2) passengers were seated on a first-come, first-served basis, Negroes seated from the back of the bus toward the front while whites seated from the front toward the back; and (3) Negro bus operators were employed on predominately Negro routes. The resolution was not only passed unanimously, but cheered.

A strategy committee was organized. Whenever a new emergency demanded attention, the committee met to consider it. One of their constant concerns was arranging alternative transportation. It wasn't easy. At first every black taxi company in Montgomery agreed to help and did. Then, the police commission stopped them. The law said taxi drivers had to charge a minimum fare of 45 cents. In place of this, the committee worked out an elaborate volunteer transportation committee. With 17,500 blacks to consider, it had to be good, and it was.

Despite the success of the system, the spirit of protest had become so much a part of people's lives that some preferred to walk. That simple act was important symbolically. Once a car pool driver called to an elderly woman walking, "Jump in, grandmother, you don't need to walk." She waved him on. "I'm not walking for myself," she explained. "I'm walking for my children and my grandchildren." She continued toward home on foot.

Eventually, the transportation system needed to be expanded. A fleet of station wagons was added, and that took money. Fortunately, press coverage had carried word of the struggle across the world. Contributions came in from as far away as Tokyo. Altogether they added up to nearly $250,000.

However, while the world seemed sympathetic, judging from media coverage and contributions, the city government was not. It couldn't be budged, even after a compromise. Since there were no imminent bus driver vacancies and there were union regulations to consider, the black leaders said they would settle for the bus company's willingness to take applications from blacks and to hire some as soon as vacancies occurred. No luck.

The opposition was nervous, and this manifested itself in several ways. There was an explicit attempt to divide and conquer the black community by announcing in the local press that a "settlement" had been worked out with a group of prominent Negro ministers. This was revealed as a hoax, and the city government lost face.

The city also employed a "get-tough" policy, implemented by the police. Arrests were made for minor and often imaginary traffic violations. Martin Luther King was among those arrested. The violence of the opposition was the major manifestation of weakness. Dynamite was thrown, there were mass arrests, and one blind man was dragged by a moving bus. He had caught his leg in the door. Eventually King was again arrested, this time not for a traffic violation, but for violating the state's antiboycott law.

None of these opposition tactics worked. Black citizens could not be provoked. From the beginning a basic philosophy guided the movement. Although it is formally referred to as nonviolent resistance, the black community called it "Christian love." King put it this way:

> It was the Sermon on the Mount, rather than the doctrine of passive resistance, that initially inspired the Negroes of Montgomery to dignified social action. It was Jesus of Nazareth that stirred the Negroes to protest with the creative weapon of love.

The philosophy was disseminated mainly through the regular mass meetings that were held in the various black churches of the city.

Victory came not from the success of the economic boycott or through the media's influence, but through a different intermediary—

the federal courts. Alabama's state and local laws requiring segregation on buses were held to be unconstitutional. They were contrary to the equal protection clause of the Fourteenth Amendment. A year after Rosa Parks had refused to stand on the bus, the bus integration order reached Montgomery.

It wasn't accepted peacefully. There was a reign of terror. City buses were fired on, a teenage girl was beaten, the Bell Street and Mt. Olive Baptist churches were almost completely destroyed, and black businesses and homes were bombed, but then it stopped abruptly. Victory in fact had arrived.

Some people ask, was all the protest useless? After all, it was the courts that moved the city council, not the boycott. The Constitution was the crucial resource. True, but the simple act of Rosa Parks prompted others to act, and the discipline and humanism that evolved out of the action paved the way for a very different kind of southern black. The Montgomery message was felt everywhere. King called what developed "suprarational," having a divine dimension. Whatever it was, no longer would black citizens be willing to accept injustice.

> There comes a time when people get tired of being trampled by oppression. There comes a time when people get tired of being plunged into the abyss of exploitation and nagging injustice. The story of Montgomery is the story of 50,000 such Negroes who were willing to substitute tired feet for tired souls, and walk the streets of Montgomery until the walls of segregation were finally battered by the forces of justice.

Ultimately, Martin Luther King and other civil rights leaders used a variety of pressure tactics. Protest was only one of them. As we've seen from these illustrations of direct and indirect approaches, both the resources of the group or individual and the openness of the legislative arena help define the choice.

We know there are other ways of getting through to legislators, however. They rely on the electoral system. Let's take a look at some of them.

Electoral Politics

> We seem to be unable to think of change, so we cop out, and go to the polls periodically to vote. Once every two years or four years or more, we fool ourselves into thinking we are saving freedom, protecting democracy, by pulling a lever of a machine. We are so proud, so self-righteous.

But as we vote, we never think that voting does nothing but condemn us to the status quo. To vote is the ultimate act of futility; it is to pretend change while prolonging stability. Our only act of citizenship, our only public act, turns out to be a private farce. As we vote, we simply endorse our own immobility.[26]

Voting: Does It Make a Difference?

Is voting the farce that David Schuman says it is? Is it merely a device to promote the status quo? Can voting ever be considered an effective way of getting through to legislators?

Let's deal with Schuman's position first. In several respects his argument appears valid. Voters are so uninformed about candidates, their records, and issues that elections cannot be considered serious attempts to influence policy. In addition, we need only be aware of the success record of incumbents to realize the extent to which elections preserve the status quo. Then too, there is so little ideological difference between major-party candidates that regardless of who is elected, policy will be essentially the same.

While none of these three points can be denied, they require further comment. The first argument could be linked to the second. People may be so uninformed that they find it easier to simply elect the incumbent. Of course, another explanation is possible—people may be so satisfied with the state of affairs that they don't want to change players. Whatever the explanation, the level of voter ignorance in this country is apparent. Rarely are representatives held responsible for their actions. Only a major crisis (Watergate, serious inflation or recession, war, etc.) provokes voter interest in political players, and that periodic interest is usually as uninformed as the periods of sustained disinterest. In this respect, Schuman is right. Voting is a farce. Voting is not *usually* an effective way of getting through to legislators.

Schuman also makes another point that requires comment. Major parties offer no choice; both promote the status quo. One whose goal is revolutionary change—total systemic and value change—will perceive Schuman's position as correct, for whether they are Republican or Democrat, candidates are not revolutionary. They *generally* accept the importance of private property, the free enterprise system, individualism, separation of governmental powers, constitutionalism, etc. If, however, one's goal is political reform, then Schuman's argu-

[26] David Schuman, *Preface to Politics* (Lexington, Mass.: D. C. Heath and Company, 1973), p. 80.

ment is weak. All one needs to do is check legislative voting records on such issues as welfare reform, secrecy in government, national health care, capital punishment, victimless crimes, and defense spending to realize that there *is* a difference. To behave as though there were not is to ignore the realities of legislative behavior.

In November 1974, only 39 percent of the 145 million people eligible to vote made it to the polls. Perhaps they, like Schuman, felt it doesn't matter. However, it mattered in New Hampshire that year. A handful of votes decided who would be the U.S. senator for the next six years, and there *were* differences between these two candidates, differences that counted. One writer explained the importance of voting in this way:

> To believe that nothing can be accomplished through the political process is to assure that nothing can be. . . . To think that it makes no difference who represents New Hampshire is to think marginal differences don't count, but they do count. All that moves us forward from worse to better is an accumulation of marginal differences. That is the essence of progress in a nation where innumerable accommodations are continually necessary to maintain order and approximate justice. When a sizable body of citizens becomes convinced that such accommodation is worthless or wrong, or that progress can come only through some cataclysm, then it's goodbye to domestic tranquility. Bitter confrontation becomes the order of the day, not reconciliation of differences and a search for common ground on which to advance.[27]

David L. Hurwood also has something to say on the subject of voting, particularly on a subject he calls "creeping noninvolvement."[28] In 1956 he and other reform-minded Democrats joined together to overthrow "boss rule" in their election district. They were working against the traditional Democratic district leaders in Manhattan, New York. Ultimately, they were working against the entire organized Democratic political machine of New York, dominated by Tammany Hall chief Carmine De Sapio.

Their gripe was the quality of leadership. Instead of coming to grips with community problems, particularly adequate middle- and low-income housing, party leaders were concerned with their own power, according to Hurwood. To insure that power, the Manhattan

[27] "Politics as Spectator Sport," *New Republic*, January 18, 1975, pp. 5–6.
[28] For these and other details, see David L. Hurwood, "Grass-Roots Politics in Manhattan," *Atlantic Monthly*, October 1960, pp. 65–70. Copyright © 1960, by The Atlantic Monthly Company, Boston, Mass. Reprinted with permission.

district leaders were preoccupied with the patronage and special favors they could get for themselves and their pals.

The strategy of the reform group, now called the Lenox Hill Club, was electoral. They would challenge the district leadership of the dominant Tammany Hall element in the New York City Democratic party machine.

In 1957 the first opportunity came. In an assembly race the reform candidate lost, but did get 40 percent of the vote. The following year the reform candidate won in the primary, only to be beaten in the general election by a Republican. In 1959 they tried again, and this time they believed they wouldn't lose. After all, the issues were clear; there was a choice.

The work—informing fellow citizens that the election *was* important and their vote crucial—would be exhausting. David Hurwood described what it was like:

> What is it like to canvass in a Manhattan assembly district in the hot summer? Your reporter accepted responsibility for campaigning in his immediate neighborhood and can speak from experience. You hurry home from the office and grab a quick supper in order to be out knocking on doors by six thirty. You pull out the index cards for the enrolled Democrats in the buildings you want to cover, scoop up an assortment of campaign literature, and take off.
>
> In your first tenement house it is so hot and sultry that by the time you climb the third flight of stairs the sweat is rolling down your arms and your short-sleeved shirt is clinging to you. In the semidarkness you study your pack of index cards for names and apartment numbers. When you think you have matched name and dwelling, you knock on the door. (No bells in tenements.) A female voice shouts, "Who is it?"
>
> You squint at the card again (now smudged by your sweaty fingers), and after trying to rehearse the name *sotto voce* call out, tentatively, "Mrs. Lojtkielewicz?"
>
> "Yeah?"
>
> "I'm a neighbor of yours. I'm canvassing for Harry LeBien and Jean Kemble, who are running for district leaders in the Democratic Party. Could I see you for just a minute?"
>
> "I'm not interested."
>
> "But the election is coming up on September fifteenth. It's an important contest, and we're trying—"
>
> "Not interested," says the voice, definitely receding into the apartment.
>
> "Well, I'll slide some literature under the door. Would you just look it over?"
>
> No answer.

The next encounter starts out more auspiciously. The door opens
to your knock, and a kindly middle-aged lady confronts you. "Mrs.
Strcka?"

"Yes?"

"I'm a neighbor of yours—" and you go on with your story.

"Oh, don't worry about me," she interrupts. "I always vote
straight Democratic."

"That's fine," you say. (It's *not* fine.) "But you see, this is a contest *within* the Democratic Party to choose the man and woman
who will be leaders in our district for the next two years."

"Don't worry. I'm a good Democrat. I always vote the straight
ticket," and she gently but firmly starts to close the door.

"But please remember to vote for LeBien and Kemble on the
fifteenth—poll's open three till ten—the school—Here, take this,"
and you hand her a leaflet just before the door shuts and you hear
a final "Don't worry!"

You try another door, and a man answers. "I'm canvassing—
LeBien and Kemble—district leaders—fine candidates—Lenox
Hill Club—"

"Why should I vote for LeBien and Kemble?" he asks stonily.

"Because they are not looking for handouts and favors but will
serve you and me, the rank-and-file Democrats of the district."

"What's your angle in this?"

"My angle?"

"Yes. You getting paid for this?"

"Why, no."

"Then what are you doing it for?"

"We're all volunteers, members of the Lenox Hill Club. We're
fighting for something we believe in, the good of the district, party
reform."

"Yeah?"

"Yes!"

He is not impressed.

There are some encouraging calls; some people say, "I know
all about it, I've followed the campaign, and I'm for you." And
there are memorable times, such as the evening Jean Kemble can-
vasses with you and you see people's faces light up with pleasure
to think that the candidate herself should trouble to call on them.
As the days wear on, you come to feel that perhaps you are getting
through to the voters—convincing those who are on the fence,
raising questions in the minds of those who would have automatically voted the other way. This is politics at the grass roots, an
unforgettable lesson in the democratic process.[29]

The crucial task on the day of the election was to get sympathetic
people to the polls. Hurwood watched people arrive to vote:

[29] *Ibid.*

If you have never thrown yourself into a campaign, urging people day after day to vote your candidate, you can have no idea how gratifying it is to see some of them actually materialize at the polls. You say to yourself: "I had a hand in bringing these people here. I was free to persuade them to support my candidates and my principles, and here they are." It makes the word "democracy" come to life.

The effort wasn't quite good enough. The reform candidates received 47 percent of the vote. They lost by 424 votes. *To win, they would have needed an average of only nine more supporters in each of the 52 election districts.* Hurwood knew that on his list of sympathetic voters alone, 40 had not voted.

Why? In some cases, no one could question a nonappearance—illness, a death in the family, a trip—but for most voting was not important enough an event to warrant a small revision in afternoon or evening plans. Hurwood says that this was a classic example of a crucial election lost by default.

What we tried to do in the Eighth A. D. North, our little piece of America, was something we are constantly exhorted to do, starting with high school commencement: to participate in the affairs of the community, to make democracy work, to put dedicated men and women in positions of leadership, lest that leadership go by default to the self-serving and the cynical. We failed because too many people did not really consider it important to do this. Similar failures have taken place, and will take place, all over the United States for the same reason.

People stayed home, and David Hurwood and his friends were not able to influence the composition of the New York State Assembly. As organized as they were, their attempt at electoral politics was a failure. The opposition had a resource that couldn't be denied—citizen apathy.

While the Lenox Hill Club may have initially failed to influence the legislative game through electoral politics (later they won), others have not. When interest groups are large enough, organized and cohesive, with good internal communications systems, they can have an impact on elections. All they need is an issue that will arouse the membership. What follows is a description of organized voting at its best (although the objective is controversial).

Working for the Defeat or Election of Candidates

• Joe Tydings wears an American flag in his lapel and tells people he owns 11 shotguns.

- Paul Fannin sends a picture of himself toting a shotgun to a gun magazine, hoping they'll print it.
- Gale McGee shows up at a rifle match and poses in a shooting jacket.
- Hugh Scott invites Pennsylvania marksmen to compete for the Hugh Scott Championship Trophy.

What all these U.S. senators had in common was a problem. They all had offended gun enthusiasts with their votes on gun control legislation, and they were all up for re-election. Would conspicuously displaying their own personal devotion to the shooting arts keep them from getting shot down at the polls?

Senator Tydings and others were well aware of the legislative clout of the gun lobby. The pressure activities of the National Rifle Association had effectively been able to prevent any serious federal gun legislation from being enacted. For example, before one particular piece of gun control legislation was considered, Sen. Harrison A. Williams (D., N.J.) reported receiving 50,000 letters opposed to gun control in a three-week period. Senator Jack Miller (R., Iowa) counted 4,000 in a single week during that same period. The office of Sen. James O. Eastland (D., Miss.), the chairman of the committee to which the gun control bill was referred, reported receiving 22,000 telegrams and hundreds of thousands of letters within four days.[30] The question was, would electoral politics work just as well? It had two years previously when Sen. Joe Clark (D., Penn.) had been defeated primarily through the efforts of gun enthusiasts.

The main focus of the electoral attack this time was Tydings (D., Md.). He was the leading congressional sponsor of legislation requiring registration of guns and licensing of gun owners. According to the leader of Citizens Against Tydings (CAT), Michael J. Parker, the successful defeat of Tydings would undoubtedly have an impact on other legislators—particularly gun control advocates. It would serve as another warning.

What were CAT's resources; what allowed it to embark on this effort? The membership was not very large. Three or four hundred people were involved during the peak periods of the campaign, and twice as many over the entire thirteen months that it lasted. How-

[30] For these and other details, see Arlen J. Large, "The Gun Lobby Works to Defeat Lawmakers Who Support Controls," *Wall Street Journal*, September 11, 1970. Reprinted with permission of The Wall Street Journal, © 1970 Dow Jones & Company, Inc. All rights reserved.

ever, they were committed, and they had an issue that generated support in Maryland. People who target shoot, collect guns, or keep guns for their own protection, as well as the many hunters, were all sympathetic. They felt gun control was a violation of their rights. CAT's financial resources were assured through a magazine called *Gun Week*. The estimated $50,000 to $60,000 that CAT spent on the campaign came primarily from subscribers who responded to CAT ads. Most contributions were for $1.00 or $5.00. There were only a couple of $1,000 contributions.[31]

They used their resources in a variety of ways. They passed out 150,000 bumper stickers that read, "If Tydings Wins, You Lose." In addition, they mailed out 35,000 brochures, distributed 150,000 brochures, ran 30 full-page ads, and had radio spot announcements on 26 stations for four days. All this plus two telephone campaigns might have been enough to switch 15,000 votes to Tydings's *victorious* Republican opponent.[32]

Where pressure politics did not work, electoral politics apparently did. Michael Parker put it this way:

> We decided we'd spent enough time talking to Tydings. We made our feelings on his gun control legislation known to him many times. It gets to the point where letter-writing just won't work.[33]

The efforts of CAT certainly wouldn't have worked had several factors not been present. CAT had the resources to run an organized campaign; they had a popular issue and a readily identifiable target associated with the wrong side of the issue; they were working against a candidate who apparently had not generated enough voter support on other issues to survive the attack; the pro-gun control opposition was weak; and they had an alternative—a candidate in another party who would be more sympathetic.

Something to think about

Apart from changing his position on gun control, how might Senator Tydings have resisted this electoral pressure?

---

[31] "Out Gunning," *New Republic*, November 28, 1970, p. 7.
[32] *Ibid.*
[33] *Ibid.*

Many uses of electoral politics are not attempts to defeat particular candidates, but rather attempts to see that certain candidates get elected. Groups do this by supplying campaign workers to see that sympathetic voters are registered and vote, by contributing systematically to campaigns, by publicizing voting records, by endorsing candidates, and even, at times, by running their own candidate. The hope is that if a group helps a candidate get elected, that group's point of view will be consistently represented in the legislative arena, or, at a minimum, that there will be easy access to the legislator.[34]

This is how the National Committee for an Effective Congress does the job:

> Saginaw, Mich.—On a cold March day a year ago a small prop plane landed at the tri-city airport in Saginaw, Michigan. It discharged three campaign workers who had come to back up the bid of a young Democratic lawyer, Bob Traxler. He was trying to win the special election in a district held by Republicans since 1932. Scurrying through the snow, they cast an awed glance at Air Force One and Air Force Two, dominating the runway. President Nixon —confident that a win in this GOP district would bolster his tumbling popularity—had flown in with full entourage to campaign for the Republican Candidate. . . .
>
> The arrival of three workers marked the beginning of NCEC's special 1974 Campaign Services Project, an effort to provide first-rate technical assistance to NCEC-endorsed candidates. The Traxler campaign, it turned out, was a perfect prototype: a bright, committed candidate; a lively corps of local workers; an uphill, underfinanced contest in a solidly conservative district. With three weeks to go, the NCEC team worked with Traxler to define more sharply his campaign's central theme. They arranged for crucial media production and purchasing, a strategic poll and last-minute newspaper rebuttals to counter the GOP's Agnew-like charges against Traxler. On April 16, Traxler won with 51 percent of the vote. The cost to NCEC for what Traxler later called "one of the key factors that added up to my victory" was less than $5000.[35]

Bob Traxler was one of 50 House candidates in 1974 who benefited from the expertise of the NCEC's "flying squad"—a team of 25 political professionals supported by members' dues. Each was selected from a group of 200 candidates interviewed. The criteria for support

---

[34] In those states with a highly competitive party system, interest groups working for candidates are perceived as less important by legislators; they rarely think of them as having sponsored the campaign. See John C. Wahlke et al., *The Legislative System* (New York: John Wiley & Sons, 1962), p. 100.

[35] "NCEC Campaign Role—New People, New Methods," *NCEC Congressional Report* (March 1975), pp. 1–2.

were (1) the candidate must clearly be preferable to the opponent as a national representative (in this instance more than half the opponents were ultraconservative GOP Congressmen, and the NCEC supports liberal candidates); (2) the candidate must need NCEC support; and (3) NCEC support could provide the margin of victory. The result of this selection process and support? Thirty-five of the NCEC supported House candidates won in 1974.

Getting Others to Vote

The various ways of helping a person get elected to the legislature require different degrees of individual and group involvement. Canvassing and voter registration require the greatest effort. Then registered voters must be prodded to vote. Getting out the vote is an automatic part of any campaign.

When John F. Kennedy ran for President, he made an all-out appeal to the stay-at-home vote. His strategists estimated that of the 107 million people old enough to vote in 1960, 40 million had not bothered to register. Since they believed that roughly seven out of ten of these nonregistered voters would vote Democratic if they could be brought to the polls, the strategy board set a goal of 10 million. Ultimately, in 1960 almost 69 million Americans went to the polls, an increase of 6.8 million over 1956. Kennedy workers registered voters, watched the polls on election night, and phoned those in key precincts who hadn't yet voted, urging them to vote.

How many of these normally stay-at-home voters actually voted for Kennedy is hard to say, but tactical information told Kennedy's strategy board that the stay-at-home voter is far more likely to be a Democrat than a Republican. Given this information, getting out the vote became a key tactic.[36]

Something to think about

Once voters are registered, how can political activists get them to the polls?

Using the Initiative

Some direct ways of using electoral politics to promote an issue are

[36] The American Institute for Political Communication, *The New Methodology: A Study of Political Strategy and Tactics* (Washington, D.C.: The American Institute for Political Communication, 1967), p. 48.

the *initiative* and the *referendum*. In those states and counties that allow them, these elections allow citizens as lawmakers to decide the issue.

Bruce Helm, a 32-year-old resident of Seattle, Washington, discovered this. He was a credit manager in a local furniture store. He had never taken an active part in politics, but he was upset. He had read in the local newspaper that the state legislators had voted themselves a salary increase from $3,600 to $10,500. How could they do this when President Nixon's Wage Board was putting a 5.5 percent ceiling on other people's wage increases? This represented a 193 percent pay raise. Furthermore, how could they act without even holding public hearings? When he read that the wage increase had been tied to the entire budget bill, thus preventing any legislator from opposing it without opposing the entire budget, he was even more outraged.

On his first day off, Bruce Helm went to the state capital. To his dismay, he found out from the secretary of state's office that since the raises were part of an "emergency" bill, a referendum was legally impossible.

Still he wouldn't be stopped. He found a law firm willing to work without fee to challenge the illegality of this referendum. The state supreme court ruled against him, however.

Bruce Helm's last strategic option was an initiative drive. He wanted to limit the pay raises to the 5.5 percent ceiling. The question was, could he get the required 117,000 signatures in the one remaining month? The media cooperated. A story in one Seattle newspaper produced 3,000 donors who contributed $17,000. While the largest contribution was $125, most were from $1 to $10. He used this money to have 400,000 petitions run off. Some printers worked free. About 250,000 of these petitions were placed in the Sunday edition of a newspaper that had statewide distribution. As a result, hundreds of volunteers sought him out. Private pilots flew the petitions to remote areas, and ham operators provided a free communication network. The furniture store where he worked was constantly crowded with people who were interested in volunteering, and his home became headquarters. Eight to ten campaign workers were usually there.

The first result of this effort was that he met the registration deadline. Over 700,000 signatures were delivered in 34 cartons. This was three times more than any previous petition effort in the state had produced. One-third of the state's registered voters had signed.

Getting people to sign the qualifying petition is only the first step in an initiative campaign. It is, however, an educational process. In this case it must have been a successful one. On election night, Bruce Helm learned that the initiative had passed by a margin of 4 to 1. Others had felt as strongly as he about the issue.[37]

This story of Bruce K. Helm's introduction to electoral politics tells us several things. First, an individual can use elections to get through to legislators, and not only at the local level. Second, the issue counts. If other people hadn't been as outraged as he, it would have been difficult to get the funds, volunteers, and signatures that he quickly received. Third, citizens need to consider different strategic options. Helm wasn't stopped when the courts issued their negative ruling. (Of course, some states do not offer citizens the option that he ultimately had to use.) Finally, media assistance can be crucial. Since Bruce Helm was not working from an organization he could communicate to and mobilize, he had to have an alternative way of gathering support quickly. Had there been more time, however, he probably would have found several citizens' organizations ready to assist. As things turned out, even though he had no previous political experience, he seemed to use the right approach. Politics, the story suggests, is even for amateurs.

The approaches to electoral politics so far discussed take resources —individual and group. The greatest resource they take is people's time. Frequently, however, individuals and groups want to assist a candidate without expending great effort. Perhaps they don't *have* the time. If that is the case, at least three other approaches can be used: endorsing a candidate, rating candidates, and contributing to a candidate's campaign. The first two are realistically only available to interest groups, while the third can be used by individuals as well. All three, however, are ways of getting through to legislators.

Endorsing Candidates

Interest groups that decide to endorse candidates or rate them have to have *prestige*, at least with a certain sizable constituency. Otherwise, the effort is meaningless. The purpose, of course, is to get voters sympathetic to that group to vote as the group urges.

Endorsements are particularly important at the local level, in elections drawing little citizen interest. These races are likely to be nonpartisan, involve few or no incumbents, and attract many candi-

---

[37] For these and other details, see Herbert G. Lawson, "Is 193% Just Too Big a Pay Raise? You Bet, Say Some Irate People," *Wall Street Journal*, November 5, 1973. Reprinted with permission of The Wall Street Journal, © 1973 Dow Jones & Company, Inc. All rights reserved.

dates. In one such election, a Los Angeles community college board race, the order in which the candidates' names appeared on the ballot was particularly important. However, endorsements by a major newspaper and a conservative campaign group were also found to be beneficial to candidates.[38] This suggests that *low-visibility* races are the ones ripe for endorsement. When candidates have been overlooked by the press and parties, citizens look to other institutions for some guidance.

Something to think about
What local and state offices generally involve low-visibility campaigns?

Rating Candidates
While candidates enjoy being endorsed by groups and actively seek the endorsement of some groups, they don't like to be rated. *Rating* involves selecting several controversial legislative measures and awarding legislators a score on the basis of their votes. These scores are then widely publicized. Some people consider these ratings incomplete information. In addition, while legislators agree that ratings generally have an effect on them, they perceive them as punitive and sometimes unjust. Other legislators, however, may consider ratings too complete, too open.

Even lobbyists are nervous about rating candidates. It may prompt retaliation and limit future access. Only those lobbyists representing organizations with "poll power" are likely to consider ratings an important tactic.[39]

What good does rating candidates really do? Legislators say it has some effect on their behavior, but only when an interest group has *demonstrated* that it can mobilize its members and supporters at the polls. A safe legislator is unlikely to be affected. However, there are legislative seats that are considered "marginal"—where the race will be close. On the national level, in each election, approximately one-third of the Senate seats and from one-fifth to one-fourth of the House seats are considered marginal. In these races the winning can-

---

[38] J. E. Mueller, "Choosing Among 133 Candidates," *Public Opinion Quarterly*, Fall 1970, pp. 395–402.
[39] Milbrath, *The Washington Lobbyists*, pp. 252–254.

didate usually receives less than 55 percent of the vote,[40] and endorsements and ratings become more important.

The trick is getting group members to follow the recommendations of the group leaders. In his study of interest groups, Harmon Zeigler had this to say about the problem:

> A fair assessment of the influence of groups over their members' votes is that it is zero at worst and only minimal at best, for organizations are not wholly impotent in such matters. Although it is doubtful they can change their members' political values, they can publicize particular issues and candidates in an attempt to make them visible. By playing on the basic political orientations of members, groups can have a positive effect on their voting turnout or even cause them to reevaluate candidates and issues.[41]

So as an attention-getting device an endorsement or rating could be marginally useful. Neither is likely to change a member's position, however.

Contributing to Campaigns

What about *campaign contributions?* Do they do anything other than inflate the donor's ego? They do two additional things. Because funds are essential if a candidate is to gain public office in this country, contributions can help a sympathetic candidate get nominated or elected. Then, once a legislator is in office, they are a way of assuring open channels of communication.[42] The reason contributions are unlikely to be able to change a legislator's behavior is that contributions tend to cancel one another out. Groups and individuals on opposing sides of one issue often contribute to the same candidate.

To have any effect at all, an individual contribution must be large or be combined with others through some organized effort. Those organized efforts generally take two forms. First, some groups contribute to the campaigns of sympathetic legislators as one of many pressure and electoral tactics. While this approach is more common, there are also organizations such as the National Committee for an Effective Congress that rely strictly on funding campaigns.

The American Medical Association is an example of the first kind of organization. It uses a wide variety of tactics to get through to

[40] Keefe and Ogul, *The American Legislative Process*, p. 111.
[41] Harmon Zeigler, *Interest Groups in American Society* (Englewood Cliffs, N.J.: Prentice-Hall, 1964), p. 123.
[42] See Milbrath, *The Washington Lobbyists*, p. 283, and Zeigler, *Interest Groups in American Society*, p. 126.

legislators. However, its officials believe the AMA's influence in the last 10 years is due primarily to money. Through its political arm, the American Medical Political Action Committee (AMPAC), the AMA reported spending $3.09 million between 1962 and 1972 in support of sympathetic congressional candidates. Their state and local organizations have probably spent four times as much. Walter C. Bornemeier, 1970 President of the AMA, commented:

> Before AMPAC was formed 10 years ago, we couldn't even get an audience with congressmen or legislators. Now we are heard and respected. AMPAC has helped us buy the right to a dialogue.[43]

Getting through to legislators, we can conclude, is possible—both through pressure politics (direct and indirect lobbying) and through electoral politics. While there are no guarantees, carefully selecting specific tactics on the basis of the individual's or group's resources, tactical information, and opportunities should increase the probability of success.

Games are often lost not because of any deficiency in actual or potential resources, but because planning is inadequate. The pay-offs on legislative games are too great for that to be the reason for a defeat.

Key Words

Direct lobbying
Indirect lobbying
Endorsing
Rating

Suggested Activities

1. Select a controversial issue pending before your town council or county board. Determine how interest groups are lobbying legislators on that issue. This will require interviewing interest-group leaders and legislators as well as analyzing relevant newspaper articles.

2. Attend a meeting of your party's county committee. With what kind of business are they dealing? After the meeting, ask com-

---

[43] Judith Robinson, "American Medical Political Action Committee," in *Political Brokers*, ed. Judith G. Smith (New York: Liveright Publishing Corporation, 1972), pp. 69–70. Copyright © 1972 by National Journal. Reprinted by permission.

mittee members to identify how or if constituents use them to intervene in legislative matters.

3. Plan a letter-writing campaign dealing with a controversial issue.
4. Evaluate the results of the last city or statewide election. Selecting a relatively close race, assess how many votes in each precinct or district would have made a difference.
5. Identify those organizations in your city or state that usually endorse and/or rate candidates. With which types of constituents are they most likely to be effective?

V
Executive Games

10
The Executive Arena

About Executive Games

Mrs. Lillie Gravely suddenly developed a problem that her doctor
told her was caused by a kidney blockage. She was told to have an
X-ray taken immediately and to get herself into a hospital for
further examination and possibly an operation. Mrs. Gravely knew
that she was headed for trouble because she has no health insurance, no savings to speak of and a small income of $15 a day when
she is working. She lives in a house with her daughter, son-in-law
and nine grandchildren, who depend on her for help in paying
bills. Mrs. Gravely has never taken welfare and doesn't want to.
When asked about this by a government clerk, she said, "If my
daughter can feed nine children, she can feed me too." She is far
from the golden age of 65 when she will be able to claim Social
Security and Medicare. But the pain was bad enough to launch
her on the grim odyssey in search of Medicaid, which began in the
emergency room of the Providence Hospital in Washington. She
gained entrance by citing the policy provided to her son-in-law by
his employers. That got her to a cot, where she waited eight hours
before being X-rayed. (Afterward she received a bill for $72—the
cost of the X-ray, painkiller and use of the bed—and a note informing her that she would have to pay the bill herself because
she is not in the "immediate family" of the insuree.)

Now X-rayed, Mrs. Gravely still had to get into the hospital.
Her doctor is on the staff of the Washington Hospital Center,

an expensive private institution. He wanted her to go there for treatment, but the hospital does not accept patients unless they are insured, can post a cash deposit based on the expected length of stay or prove they are covered by Medicaid. Mrs. Gravely did have health insurance at one time, but she gave it up when she discovered that it wouldn't pay hospital bills. She had tried to get Medicaid once before, just in case of emergency. But the clerk had sent her away, saying she shouldn't pester the government for help unless she needed it. She can't afford the cash deposit.

Following her visit to Providence Hospital, Mrs. Gravely went early in the morning to the District of Columbia Human Resources office. She explained that she needed a Medicaid card to get into the Washington Hospital Center at 3 o'clock that afternoon, the time appointed by her doctor. Though sick, she was told she had to apply in person and wait her turn like dozens of others around her. She stayed until 3 o'clock and beyond, and eventually was told to come back with more documents: her life insurance, a copy of her bank statement, a statement from her employer. On her second visit, she was told she needed a more recent bank statement. She rested. On her third visit, a week after her doctor had told her she should be in the hospital, the clerk at the Medicaid office told her she had been approved for a red-and-white card, not a black-and-white card, and that she would receive it in the mail after some other clerks had verified all her documents. Mrs. Gravely protested that she was a week overdue in the hospital. After some negotiation the clerk agreed that if she wished, Mrs. Gravely could have the hospital call the Medicaid office before 3 o'clock and they would vouch for her as a cardholder. But it later turned out that the red-and-white card is good for the municipal hospital only—DC General—and it doesn't pay for doctor bills. Like many others, Mrs. Gravely sees DC General as the place where they "put all kinds of people together, dope addicts and everything." But she is prepared to go there because she sees no other choice. When she called the Medicaid office to get the number on her card, she was told the computer had broken down, and she thinks she still hasn't been approved. Had she been accepted by Medicaid, she would have received a black-and-white card that opens doors but doesn't pay all bills. A black-and-white card would let her choose doctors and hospitals for herself, as others do. But the law reserves that card for families with dependent children (welfare folks), the blind and disabled. Mrs. Gravely says she heard about someone fresh from the country who was asked to pay $100 under the table for a black-and-white card (and got one). No one offered her such a deal.[1]

[1] Eliot Marshall, "When Mrs. Gravely Gets Sick," New Republic, April 20, 1974, pp. 15–16. Reprinted by permission of The New Republic, © 1974 The New Republic, Inc.

This is one person's story of an encounter with governmental bureaucracy—in this case the health bureaucracy operating in Washington, D.C. Probably thousands of similar stories are told each year. Yet dealing with the bureaucracy is not as hopeless as it may sometimes seem. As with any governmental institution, to get it to budge, you have to understand it. That means knowing its unique features as an arena, knowing who does what and what influences their moves, knowing about the distribution of power, and of course knowing the rules. Then too, the citizen seeking access to the institution has to have or acquire some resources and know what to do with them.

The arena that is the focus of this chapter is not just one, but many. Bureaucratic organizations exist at all levels of government. They are part of the executive branch. They are called *bureaucratic* because of the way they are organized: power is arranged hierarchically—the most power is held by those at the top of a pyramid, the least by those at the bottom; jobs and job relationships are clearly defined—each person knows his or her boss, peers, and subordinates; there are rules for dealing with most situations—whether filling out a form or handling a complaint; and information tends to flow from the lower levels of the pyramid to the top. This all sounds rather abstract, but most people deal constantly with bureaucratic organizations. Banks, the army, departments of employment, the post office, schools, and the Internal Revenue Service are just a few of those frequently encountered.

One puzzling aspect of governmental bureaucracies is that they have so many names; the most common are departments, agencies, services, and commissions. Regardless of the name, however, they are organized in basically the same way.

While each bureaucratic organization is headed by only a few people—often only one—the entire executive bureaucracy at each level is headed by a chief executive. Nationally, it is the President; in states it is the governor; locally it may be one of several people—a mayor, a city manager, or a chief administrative officer. The interesting thing about the executive branch at all levels is that it is not neat and tidy—it does not fit the perfect description of an ideal bureaucracy. Whatever the level, bureaucratic organizations have differing degrees of power and independence, and chief executives are not completely in control.

The complexity and confusion that seem to characterize the executive branch shouldn't cloud the fact that all executive games have similar objectives. The major one is implementing policies, but others include making policy recommendations to legislative institutions and making recommendations about how much to spend on what. Also, many organizations do more than someone else's bidding. They also make rules and judgments, particularly as they regulate certain operations in the private sector of the economy.

So winning an executive game means that a player or players have been able to influence how policies get implemented, what policies and budgets get recommended, and/or what regulations or judgments are delivered. The particular win one seeks, however, and the moves one may make depend on the executive organization one is trying to influence. Is it the Veterans' Administration, those dispensing food stamps, or the Department of Motor Vehicles? A brief overview of the executive arenas might at least suggest the possibilities.

Executive Players

Who are they and what do they do; how do they get to be players; and what influences the way they play the game? These are the key questions that activists must answer. Unfortunately, political scientists don't know as much about executive players as they do about legislative ones. In part, this is because there are so many different types of players, recruited in widely different ways, with such different jobs to do. Still, let's give it a try.

Chief Executives

In the spring of 1966, the Oakland City Council chose John H. Reading, a leading manufacturer of tamales, as mayor. The previous mayor had been forced to resign. The city that John Reading governs is located on San Francisco Bay in California. In 1970 its population was 361,561.

Chief executives, such as John Reading, do three kinds of jobs—*administrative*, *legislative*, and *political*. Their ability to do the first two depends very much on their skill at the third. Furthermore, which gets emphasized depends upon how the chief executive sees the job.

Political activists who decide to play executive games need to know the formal resources that help define the chief executives' administrative and legislative authority, but clearly they need to know more. What are a particular chief executive's political skills? A person occupying that office who is able to build support for administrative and legislative decisions will indeed be a formidable ally or opponent. Then, too, the chief executive's strengths as a player will depend on *willingness* to use both formal and informal resources. That willingness cannot simply be assumed, as we shall see.

The administrative job.   Governors and mayors are at a disadvantage, administratively. Unlike the President, these chief executives are not even formally in control of their administrative structures. Administrative authority at these levels is fragmented. For example, many mayors do not have control over the school system, the redevelopment agency, and the housing authority—and these are just a few local organizations with administrative autonomy. Then too, in those cities that have chief administrative officers (CAOs) or city managers, the mayor's administrative authority is even more limited. CAOs usually coordinate the city's administrative departments, and city managers do even more. They can appoint and supervise the heads of city departments, prepare and oversee the implementation of the budget, and make policy recommendations to the city council. Some counties also have chief administrators who have these responsibilities. Generally it is only the chief executive of a city with a strong-mayor structure who manages to retain some semblance of administrative control. Others must be satisfied with more limited appointment and budgetary authority.

Governors, too, have less than complete administrative authority. Many states also have independently elected executives (state treasurers, superintendents of instruction, attorneys general, etc.), appointed executives whose terms do not coincide with the governor's, and executives appointed by boards or commissions rather than the governor. In fact, just over half the major administrative posts in state governments are filled by gubernatorial appointment.[2] If the existence of independent executives were not limiting enough, many governors are not even free to remove those they have appointed without getting the approval of the state senate or demonstrating the official's incompetence, neglect of duty, or malfeasance.

So what are the political implications of this fragmented administrative authority at the state and local levels? First, for citizens seeking to influence state policy through top-level appointments, there are fewer opportunities to go directly through the mayor or governor.

[2] Duane Lockard, *The Politics of State and Local Governments*, 2d ed. (New York: The Macmillan Company, 1963), p. 348.

Other executives may have to be influenced. Second, for governors and mayors seeking to build and maintain political support, *patronage* is less of a possibility. They just don't have as many top-level jobs to pass out to the "deserving." Finally, those activists seeking to influence policy through the executive budgetary process may have to focus on someone other than the *chief* executive. This is particularly true at the local level.

Strictly in terms of formal authority, the President fares somewhat better. The President has greater *appointment* power than most mayors and governors and greater *budgetary authority*—certainly more than chief executives in weak-mayor cities. Let's look at this authority.

The U.S. Constitution gives the President the authority to make some executive appointments (ambassadors and public ministers), with the approval of the Senate, and gives Congress the power to allow presidents to make less important appointments as well. The result is that the President makes all those executive-branch appointments that are outside the civil service system. He directly appoints about 2000 top-level bureaucrats. Of course, the President still needs Senate confirmation for most of these. He or she needs something else as well—the informal approval of the senior senator in the President's party who represents the state in which the appointee will be assigned. This request for approval, called *senatorial courtesy*, has political advantages, but more than that, it is necessary. If the President ignores this informal norm, the senator may declare the appointment "personally obnoxious" and ask the Senate to withhold confirmation. The Senate usually obliges.

While the President is able to appoint, promote, demote, or transfer many top-level bureaucrats, this is not an unlimited resource. He or she can't, for example, just get rid of someone who has been appointed. Formal rules prevent the President from easily removing independent agency heads and civil service appointees, and informal rules (i.e., political obligations) prevent the removal of others.

Like that of mayors and governors, the appointment power of the President often becomes the focus of citizen action. Environmentalists will try to influence the appointment of the secretary of the Department of Interior and the director of the Environmental Protection Agency; business interests will try to influence the appointment of the secretary of the Department of Commerce and members of the Federal Trade Commission. This is not an insignificant focus, for department heads and agency directors have a great deal of independent authority to make decisions.

The second most important administrative resource of the President is *budgetary authority*. Coordinated and screened by the Office of Management and Budget, all departmental budgets and spending must be approved by the President. Sure, Congress has the final say, but what the President asks for is important.[3] So if interest groups can get a particular budgetary request included by influencing either department and agency heads or the President, the chances that the request will be approved by Congress are good.

Thus, in terms of formal authority to oversee the executive branch of government, administratively the President is in the best shape. Governors, strong mayors, and county administrative chiefs have more limited but still significant administrative authority. Mayors in weak-mayor city structures have the least authority over appointments and the budgetary process. Unless they compensate for that factor by building their political clout, they may not be significant players.

The legislative job.   The formal authority of presidents, governors, and mayors to legislate is less than their administrative authority. However, all recommend policy to legislatures, have members of their administration testify before legislative committees, lobby for administration-backed measures, sometimes call special legislative sessions, and ordinarily have the power to veto legislation. Only weak-mayor structures deny or limit the mayor's veto power. The last two activities involve formal authority.

Let's talk about some of these activities and why the chief executive can be an important legislative player. Because he or she has access to so much *information* relative to policy-making, the chief executive's legislative proposals and attempts at persuasion are taken seriously. Legislators just don't have the staff or information-retrieval systems to rival those in the executive branch. Second, no one legislator has a resource as powerful as the *veto*. This allows chief executives not only to reject certain pieces of legislation, but to build support for their own programs. For governors the veto power is magnified because most can *item veto*—delete specific parts of an appropriations bill rather than having to accept or reject the entire measure. Clearly the mere threat of a veto can gain the chief executive important concessions. It's not easy for legislatures to override

---

[3] The funds voted by congressional appropriations committees vary only slightly from executive requests. See Richard Fenno, *The Power of the Purse: Appropriations Politics in Congress* (Boston: Little, Brown and Company, 1966), pp. 410 and 614.

vetoes. At the national level and in most state and local legislative bodies, overriding a veto requires at least two-thirds of the legislature. Usually a legislature must be controlled by the opposition party for this to succeed.

All this is rather abstract. Let's take a more concrete look at the legislative job of one chief executive—the President. It should become clear that the importance of the job has to do with far more than formal resources.

Foreign affairs and the economic well-being of the nation are the subject areas where presidents appear to be particularly strong policy makers. Looking at foreign policy first, we find that presidents get their way about 70 percent of the time (if you discount matters involving refugees and immigration). This compares with a 40 percent win record in domestic areas.[4]

Why are presidential policy initiatives in foreign affairs accepted so often? It has to do partly with their formal authority, partly with circumstances, and partly with congressional default. The President's constitutional authority in foreign affairs gives an edge. The President has *diplomatic* authority to make treaties (with the advice and consent of the Senate), make executive agreements, formally recognize other countries through diplomatic ties, and represent the nation as chief of state. He or she has *commander-in-chief* authority to command the U.S. Armed Forces, appoint military officials, and initiate and conduct war. The *scope* of this authority makes the President different from state and local chief executives, although they too have some formal obligation to preserve peace.

The rapidity, complexity, and unpredictability of international events have created a psychological climate that also contributes to the President's power in the foreign policy area. People seem to sense that some one person needs to be able to act quickly and to be held responsible for dealing with international crises. After all, the President has available a vast intelligence-gathering network and diplomatic team. These provide the President with the information needed to cement control.

The foreign policy leadership of presidents has also resulted from congressional default. Sensitive to the political payoffs that result from being concerned about domestic matters, members of Congress frequently have not asserted themselves outside that area. They are

4 See the Congressional Quarterly Service tabulation of Presidential Initiative and Congressional Response from 1948 through 1964 in *Congress and the Nation, 1945–1964* (Washington, D.C.: U.S. Government Printing Office, 1965).

satisfied with executive agreements instead of treaties that require Senate approval. They seem content to allow presidents to engage in war without a formal declaration from Congress. With some exceptions, Congress has been a pushover when it comes to providing the money to pay for foreign policy decisions made essentially by the executive branch. Oh sure, every now and then Congress shows a sign of life, as it did when it passed the *War Powers Bill* in 1973,[5] but its record of asserting itself in the foreign policy area leaves something to be desired. In May 1975, for example, the Senate seemed satisfied with President Ford's independent action over the Mayaguez affair. The U.S. ship Mayaguez had been seized by the Cambodian government, and the National Security Council decided on a rescue operation. President Ford *consulted* with the Senate through eighteen selective phone calls. The calls were made by midlevel White House staffers *after* U.S. troop movement had been ordered and only 35 minutes before the first shots were fired by U.S. troops.[6]

Congress has not been quite so generous about relinquishing its responsibility to preserve through sound policy the economic well-being of the nation. Still, it has given the President considerable authority. The major authority was granted through the Employment Act of 1946, in which the President is repeatedly singled out as the official who is "to foster and promote free competitive enterprise, to avoid economic fluctuations or to diminish the effect thereof, and to maintain employment, production, and purchasing power." To help do this formidable job, the President was authorized to establish a Council of Economic Advisors. Together, they were asked through this law to make any legislative recommendations necessary to get the job done.

Circumstances too have made the President a major legislative player when economic policy is involved. The formal and informal authority granted to presidents to deal with severe economic crises has led to a gradual acknowledgment that, indeed, the President is responsible for managing the economy. Although most people think of Franklin Roosevelt as the President most responsible for this shift, more recent presidents such as Richard Nixon have contributed too.

---

[5] This law establishes a 60-day limit on the President's powers to commit U.S. troops abroad, unless Congress has declared war or specifically authorized the action. In addition, it permits Congress to end such a commitment at any time by concurrent resolution, without the President's signature.

[6] I. F. Stone, "Conned in Cambodia," *The New York Review of Books* (May 21, 1975), p. 16.

Identifying foreign policy-making and economic policy-making as the major areas in which presidents seem to have a legislative advantage does not mean that their importance is severely limited elsewhere. They seem to have something to say and promote as well as influence in every policy niche. However, if a citizen or citizens' group has established a political goal in either of these two *major* areas, the President's point of view and support are crucial. If the President is an opponent, intense lobbying and probably a veto will have to be overcome. Neither is very easy.

The political job.   Back to John Reading of Oakland. He is a mayor operating in a city that makes his political job difficult. Oakland has been described as nonpolitical.[7] There appears to be little citizen interest in the electoral process and an absence of strong party or interest-group activity. So, if Mayor Reading wanted to mobilize politically oriented groups to help him get his way, to whom would he turn?

One obvious effect of this political vacuum is weakened legislative and administrative leadership. John Reading and mayors in similar political climates are rarely able to get their way with their city councils. Incumbent legislators are re-elected so easily that they do not need to turn to the mayor for political support, nor can they rely on him to assist their own legislative proposals. His only assets are his limited legislative and administrative resources plus the prestige of his office—not much in such cities as Oakland. So when Mayor Reading wants a legislative or administrative recommendation approved by the council, with what can he bargain?

Still, many cities are not nonpolitical, and state and national governments certainly can't be described in this way. In this kind of climate, what is the political job of the chief executive? Generally, it is to build and maintain interest-group, party, and broad constituent support in order to get what he or she wants, both legislatively and administratively.

Let's take a look at the way governors do one aspect of their political job—mobilizing party support. The leadership a governor can exercise in the party is different from that of other chief executives. While the President may be the undisputed party leader, and while

[7] The comments about John Reading's administration are from a study by Jeffrey L. Pressman, "Preconditions of Mayoral Leadership," *American Political Science Review,* June 1972, pp. 511–524.

the mayor may have (in some cities) no party organization to lead, the governor is usually just one of many state party leaders. He or she exerts leadership by negotiating with faction leaders, regional party leaders, and legislative party leaders. In those states where the party is important, the governor *must* do this. The future of the legislative program and the governor's political life may depend on it. So the governor attends party conventions, gives "breakfasts" for party leaders, accepts invitations to help other party members win election or re-election, rewards loyal party members with jobs—*anything* to develop and maintain that support. If this is successful, the governor indeed will become *the* party leader, the one able to influence state party platforms and legislative programs (if his or her party is in the majority).

All chief executives who operate in a strong interest-group climate face a political job that is even more difficult than dealing with party leaders—maintaining interest-group support. Vague campaign rhetoric and promises may have brought a chief executive initial interest-group support, but once elected, he or she has to produce. Some governors, for example, worry about such things as keeping the support of both environmentalists interested in saving trees and the state's lumber interests, who want a quicker way to cut them. Interest-group conflicts abound at every level.

The political job always requires an ability to skillfully negotiate and persuade. This is particularly important in dealing with interest groups. The knowledge each group has of the chief executive's other resources (party, legislative, and widespread public support) helps to determine the terms of any agreement. The chief executive's point of view is likely to prevail when those resources are apparent to each side and the chief executive knows how to use them. However, some interest groups always lose more than others. As this occurs, if the group's support is an important part of the political base, the chief executive may compensate for the loss—perhaps by appointing to public office someone whom the group favors, or by signing another bill for which they lobbied, or by making administrative decisions to soften the blow.

How the chief executive sees the job. These are all the things a chief executive *can* do to be an effective legislative and administrative leader. Whether or not the chief executive *will* do them depends not only on political skills but on the way he or she sees the job. Both these conditions need to be assessed by political activists who seek the chief executive as an ally or have to contend with the chief executive as an opponent.

Here's where John Reading comes in. Not only does the mayor of Oakland operate in a weak political climate, he does little to strengthen that climate in order to increase his political clout. This reluctance must have to do with how he sees his job.

In many cities the mayor is president of the city council. If so, the mayor not only presides over public council meetings and private work sessions, but also appoints council committees. Mayor Reading performs these legislative tasks with little regard for building political resources and, ultimately, getting what he wants. For example, he tends to appoint council committees on the basis of interest and expertise, is generous about allowing time on the agenda, and is unwilling to persuade councilors to see things his way or even count votes to see what support he has. So while he may be fair and conscientious, he cannot exert leadership because he doesn't use these resources politically.

Something to think about
In order to increase council support for his recommendations, how might John Reading use his legislative resources differently?

Mayor Reading can also make appointments with the approval of the majority of the city council. This is another way he could build support for his policies. However, he doesn't usually use this resource in this way. He appoints members to boards and commissions because he likes and admires them personally, frequently discovering after the appointment that they do not share his political preferences. Other chief executives might ask, whom do I like and respect who will help me pursue my goals?

Fortunately for John Reading, he has the support of the major citywide newspaper. Surely that support gives him leverage. Well, it would if he cultivated it, but he doesn't work that way. He prefers quiet, rational discussions to dramatic press conferences and pseudo-events. The result is that he loses many opportunities to use the prestige of his office to build citywide support for his point of view.

So Mayor Reading, the chief executive in a weak-mayor council government, is no major prize as a political ally. In part because of inadequate formal resources, but more because of the underutilization of existing ones, the mayor has a difficult time exercising leadership.

To realize the potential, one need only take a look at another mayor in a seemingly weak-mayor city government. His name is Richard Daley; the city is Chicago. Alan Shank, an observer of mayoral leadership, has this to say about Mayor Daley: "A casual observer examining the formal government structure of Chicago might well conclude that the mayor is only one relatively unimportant actor in an extremely fragmented and decentralized system. In theory, the 'weak' mayor shares power with a host of elected and appointed city and Cook County officials, none of whom are responsible to each other...." [8]

But apart from the formal structure, Daley hardly has a reputation as a weak mayor. He has traditionally been influential, if not the dominant figure, in municipal decision-making. Why? Unlike John Reading, he has been willing to build and maintain political support. He has done this primarily through the Democratic party machinery, although Chicago is a nonpartisan city. By controlling the nonpartisan process for the party (citizens are very aware of the party affiliation of aldermen running for election), and by dispensing favors and patronage in the city's wards, Daley can exert a great deal of pressure on aldermen, individually and collectively. He would be a crucial political ally.

Of course, Reading's view of the job is not unique to mayors. Some governors and presidents have also deemphasized certain aspects of the job—even the political. President Eisenhower was generally in this category. For example, when he was asked whether he personally favored the principle of school desegregation as set forth in the Supreme Court's decision, he refused to answer. He explained he had a duty to support and enforce the rulings of the Court, and that it was enough that everyone understood he would do just that. He did not think it was his duty to question policy, certainly not Supreme Court policy, and made that clear: "I would never give an opinion about my conviction about the Supreme Court decisions because such a statement would have to indicate either approval or disapproval, and I was never going to do it about any of their decisions."

Nor did he want to usurp the legislative territory of Congress. Throughout the 1952 presidential campaign, Eisenhower talked about

---

[8] Alan Shank, "Mayoral Leadership by a Modern Boss-Politician," in *Political Power and the Urban Crisis*, ed. Alan Shank, 2d ed. (Boston: Holbrook Press, 1969), p. 272.

the need to end "executive usurpations of power" and "to restore the Congress to its rightful place in the government."

He wanted to leave politics and policy-making to someone else, and focus on administration. During his campaign he promised to bring in "the best business brains" to help run the government. The federal government, he dreamed, could be run like a big corporation, and he perceived his job as that of the corporation head. All he needed to do was to find the right people and promote sound administration.[9]

The *implications* of this administrative role perception for citizens seeking influence are important. This kind of president is unlikely to be an important ally if one is seeking policy changes, but may be a crucial ally and more receptive if one is seeking a certain administrative response. Then too, access is likely to be easier for those who have something to offer the President on administrative matters.

None of this means that a chief executive can ignore any aspect of the job completely—certainly a president cannot. However, knowing which job the chief executive considers the most important is information relevant to political action, specifically to strategy development.

Something to think about
Does the current President appear to emphasize one aspect of the job more than the others? With what result?

So what can be said to *summarize* the job of chief executive, and what influences them as players?

1. Each will be influenced by a way of seeing the job—as an activist, an initiator of change; as a stabilizer, a harmonizer of interests; or as an executive manager. This helps define the kind of ally or opponent the chief executive is likely to be as well as the possibilities of influence.
2. While there are some formal differences in authority, each chief executive has a legislative and administrative job to do. In addition, each has a political job that influences success at the other

[9] Sydney Hyman classifies presidential roles and offers these illustrations in "What Is the President's True Role?", *New York Times Magazine*, September 7, 1958, p. 17.

two. While personal skills will differ, as will the nature and magnitude of the task to be done, the ability and willingness of the chief executive to persuade and to negotiate will make the difference between a strong executive leader and a weak one. This is a difference that is important to action-oriented citizens, for it helps one calculate whether or not the chief executive will be a strong ally, a strong opponent or too weak to be worth attempting to influence.

How chief executives get their jobs.   Gerald Ford became President under very strange circumstances—some would call them bizarre. Instead of getting the job because he received a majority of the electoral college votes or because of a President's death, he got it through a series of unlikely events.

The story begins with Spiro Agnew, former governor of Maryland and vice president of the United States under Richard Nixon. It seems Mr. Agnew, as governor of Maryland, forgot to tell the Internal Revenue Service that he had been receiving cash payments from consulting engineers doing business with his state. Coincidentally, these firms were offered lucrative contracts. For example, under the Agnew administration, Green Associates, Inc., an engineering company, was awarded approximately 10 contracts, with fees approximately $3 million to $4 million.

Well, people do talk, and several people involved in Agnew's financial network began talking to a federal grand jury. The result? Things got hot for the vice president, and on October 10, 1973, he admitted wrong-doing and entered a plea of *nolo contendere* (no contest) to one charge in a U.S. District Court in Baltimore. When he did so, all other allegations were dropped, and this meant there would be no trial. He also resigned from public office.

Enter Gerald R. Ford. The Twenty-Fifth Amendment to the Constitution required that the post be filled. Under the procedure it specifies, the President submits a nomination to Congress. Once confirmed by a majority of *both houses*, the appointee is in. Ford was in quickly. As someone who had been in the House of Representatives for 25 years and who had served as minority leader, Ford was positively received. He was just what President Nixon needed, someone who would help him mobilize congressional support for his programs (and perhaps for his future political survival), but also someone perceived as "safe and moderate." As one congressional leader put it, "You can count on Jerry Ford not to rock the boat."

Not that vice presidents get many opportunities to rock the boat. Their only formal authority is to preside over the Senate. Any other boat-rocking opportunities must be kindly bestowed by presidents, and they don't often do that.

Neither formal authority nor headlines seem to be necessary for vice presidents in recent years. They have a habit of becoming presidents anyway, and realization of this gives them an unusually important resource.

Well, the same thing happened to Gerald Ford, the vice president. Without much of a struggle, without spending a dime on campaigning, he became President of the United States. The occasion? Richard M. Nixon's resignation on August 9, 1974. The reason? To avoid almost inevitable impeachment and probably conviction.

Fortunately, this isn't the ordinary way of becoming President of the United States. However, the formal process is not necessarily less complicated. It begins by winning the nomination of one's party at its national convention. That support must come in the form of a majority of delegate votes. The next step involves the crucial win, acquiring a *majority* of the nation's *electoral votes*. Each state has as many electoral votes as there are people in its congressional delegation. When combined, this constitutes the *electoral college*. So the largest states with the greatest number of electoral votes understandably receive the greatest attention from candidates.

Among the problems associated with this way of electing presidents (and vice presidents) is this: *All* electoral votes in a given state go to the candidate who wins a plurality—even if only a plurality of one. *Plurality* simply means the greatest number of votes. This winner-take-all approach tends to disenfranchise a substantial minority of the electorate. It may also contribute to the election of a candidate who received a majority of the electoral votes but not the highest popular vote. Remember, a majority is 50 percent plus one vote. This rule certainly worked to the advantage of Benjamin Harrison in the 1888 election. Grover Cleveland received the greatest number of popular votes, but Harrison won the election anyway. He had a 67-vote majority in the electoral college. Strange system, isn't it? Furthermore, this isn't the only problem associated with the way we elect presidents. If no candidate receives a majority of the electoral vote, the House of Representatives decides the election. However, the size of a state's delegation in the House does not give it an advantage. In this case, each state has one vote. The power of small states is enhanced. Under this system the candidate from the majority congres-

"I'd Feel Better Without That Guy Sitting In The Back Of The Cockpit"

From *Herblock's State of the Union* (Simon & Schuster, 1972)

sional party may not win. For example, if the House were Democratic, representatives from conservative Democratic states could join with those from Republican states to elect a Republican. The Senate chooses the vice president in the same manner, and that person will have to serve as President if the House is unable to reach a majority decision by Inauguration Day. The founders must have really struggled to develop such a complicated system.

For other chief executives there are much simpler ways of winning. At the state and local levels they are elected by receiving a majority of the popular votes or a simple plurality. Where only a plurality is required, the likelihood that a nonmoderate will win is enhanced. Where no candidate receives a majority and election laws require one, runoffs are held. These tend to produce moderate candidates.

Something to think about
Why do elections requiring a majority vote tend to produce moderate winners?

What do chief executive elections have to do with political action? Are they really a vehicle through which citizens can influence policies? To a limited extent, yes. However, the chief executive is just one of many public officials involved in the policy process, and this role is subject to the checks and balances of other institutions. The previous discussion of resources, however, suggests that the chief executive is usually a key ally, particularly if he or she is able and willing to use political skills.

Still, sometimes voters can't even decipher the issue positions of candidates. How then can an election possibly offer a policy choice? One way is by having candidates *clearly define* the issues. This happened in the 1968 Democratic primary. Voters perceived a difference between the major contenders for the nomination on the issue of the war in Vietnam.[10] In the 1968 general election, however, voters perceived no differences between the two major candidates on that issue. Why? The explanation is *not* that the voters lost interest in the issue or were less sensitive to the candidates' positions. The explanation is that either there was no significant difference between Nixon and

[10] Benjamin I. Page and Richard A. Brady, "Policy Voting and the Electoral Process," *American Political Science Review*, September 1972, pp. 979–995.

Humphrey on the war issue or they didn't clarify it. At least the differences were not revealed in their major campaign addresses. Because we have a two-party system and no one candidate can afford to antagonize a large block of voters, issue differences become blurred in general elections.

There is a second way in which the policy orientations of candidates for chief executive become important. That is through *retroactive judgment* by voters. Voters tend to look at what candidates have done rather than what they say they will do—not generally, but about specific issues. This happens, in part, because elections are perceived as a means of protecting vital interests. That is, while voters do not make policy choices in an election (most cannot describe the policy positions of candidates), they are sensitive to particular issues and what party has done what. For example, labor is generally sensitive to the way Democratic candidates have behaved with regard to workers in this country. Civil rights forces observe how candidates from each party have responded to that issue. These "issue publics" are knowledgeable and work to defend their specific interests. More important, once they are elected, government officials *act in anticipation* of certain consequences if they do not continue to respond to an issue in the way their supporters would like. So in a sense, elections set policy boundaries by preventing actions that infringe on perceived vital interests.[11]

Well, what can interest groups do to influence even indirectly the way candidates for chief executive will behave once they are elected?

1. They can try to get candidates to clearly and frequently clarify their positions on certain issues, for we now know voters aren't completely oblivious to issue orientations if they are made clear.
2. Interest-group leaders can make sure their members know about a candidate's issue position and previous record on the issue.
3. They can communicate frequently with the chief executive, once elected. He or she should be reminded that the group is watching executive actions closely.

So chief executives get elected in several different ways. Once in office, however, they need to quickly get on with the job. This requires a number of supporting executive players.

[11] Gerald M. Pomper, "Controls and Influence in American Elections," *American Behavioral Scientist*, November–December 1969, pp. 215–230.

Who are they, what precisely do they do, and how do they get their jobs? Who among them could have helped Mrs. Lillie Gravely?

The Executive Office

Bob Haldeman was on the phone: "I'll do my best, Mr. Secretary, but it doesn't look good. The President plans to be tied up all week on Vietnam. If you could possibly put it in writing and get it over here, I'll make sure he sees it first thing in the morning." A sigh was heard on the other end of the line, but no verbal complaint. No loyal cabinet officer could object to the President spending so much of his time on Vietnam then. "Okay, whatever you say, Bob. But I was hoping to talk to him in person about this. We need a final decision fairly soon." "I'll convey your wishes on that point, Mr. Secretary. . . ." [12]

This telephone conversation was between Robert Haldeman, the White House chief of staff in the Nixon administration, and a member of the Nixon Cabinet. It conveys the fact that even a Cabinet member does not always have either direct or easy access to the President. It also conveys that key members of the White House staff can isolate a President by controlling communication.

What is the *White House staff* and how does it fit into the executive office? The executive office of the President is organizationally closest to the President. In addition to the White House Office, it consists of bureaus, other offices, and councils. Created by executive order in 1939, the executive office exists solely for presidential needs. It is designed to help the President collect information and plan programs.

The White House Office consists of personal assistants to the President. Nixon's staff was pyramidal, with Haldeman at the apex; President Ford's was more horizontal. Several people on Ford's staff could walk into the Oval Office at any time—although they didn't do it without good reason.

Governors and mayors aren't quite as fortunate as presidents. Their immediate personal staff is far more limited. In a number of states it merely consists of an executive secretary and some stenographers and clerks. Many mayors are lucky to have even a secretary. However, where there is an executive office of any size, personal staff perform similar functions.

[12] Dan Rather and Gary Paul Gates, *The Palace Guard* (New York: Harper and Row, Publishers, 1974), p. 162.

Why does a chief executive who has a Cabinet even need a personal staff? A personal executive staff member has at least two advantages over a Cabinet staff member. First, personal staff members need not be selected for political reasons—to please particular interests. Second, they need not be selected for any particular expertise. Instead, a chief executive is free to appoint people who agree with him or her philosophically, who are consistently loyal, and who may have general skills that can be used in a variety of ways. The problem with this highly personal staff is that in seeking to serve, they may isolate and overly protect the chief executive and abuse their "special" positions. President Nixon experienced each of these problems.

Executive offices consist of more than just personal staff, however. They usually include a budget office and special advisers. The *budget office* is particularly important, for except in some city and county governments, virtually all chief executives are responsible for assessing administrative costs and making budget recommendations—and they have a great deal of money to spend. In some cities budgets are as high as $1 billion, in large states as high as $15 billion, and nationally, about $370 billion. So it's not surprising that a special budget office is necessary. At the national level, that office includes about 700 staff members and employees, but their responsibility is broader, as implied by their name—Office of Management and Budget. The director must oversee the execution and management of all programs.

Just as a teenager in a family tries to influence budget decisions ("Can't you pay for the car insurance if I buy the car?"), so do various interest groups. Because a budget is a statement about relative values and spending priorities, influencing that statement is an activist's dream. Furthermore, it is better to do this before the budget reaches the legislature, because most legislative bodies don't alter requests in major ways.

Helping to define that budget, however, usually can't be done directly. Ordinarily it must be done by influencing the recommendations and appraisals made by department and agency heads that are to be sent to the budget director. If that doesn't work, the chief executive and legislators have the final word, so tactics will have to be used to persuade them.

Something to think about

What tactics are used in families to influence budget decisions? Can similar tactics be used to influence governmental budget decisions?

Figure 5
Executive office of the president.

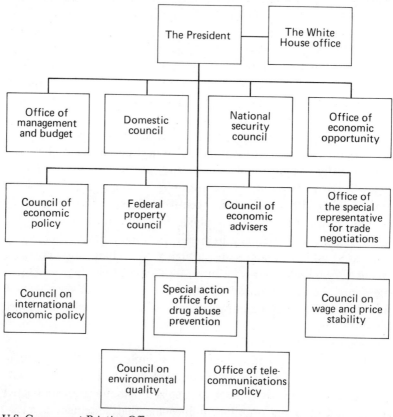

U.S. Government Printing Office.

What factors in a family help to define the shape of the final budget?
Would any of these factors apply to governmental budgets?

In addition to a budget director, executive offices include special
advisers. These are people with particular expertise who help the chief
executive make policy recommendations. Among the major advisers
on the national level are the Council of Economic Advisers, the National Security Council, the Domestic Council, and the Energy Policy
Office, but these are only a few, as Fig. 5 reveals.

Along with the director of the budget, the special advisers within
executive offices frustrate most activists. Because they are more
politically isolated than executive staff or Cabinet members, and be-

cause much of their decision-making is shrouded in secrecy, access and influence appear to be impossible. The specific source of the frustration is the knowledge that these are the experts closest to the chief executive and that as a group they have considerable influence over executive proposals.

Something to think about

Should these executive players just be written off as immune to influence? Are there any direct or indirect approaches that might work?

Cabinet Secretaries

Mario Obledo grew up on welfare in the 1930s Depression. He is a Mexican-American, one of a dozen children in a fatherless family. He is also a former Harvard Law School faculty member and currently a member of Governor Jerry Brown's cabinet in California.

His job couldn't be more relevant to his own life. For example, he oversees the State Department of Corrections. Three of his brothers served time in prison. He also oversees the department that administers welfare payments. As a child in San Antonio, Texas, he experienced squalor, poverty, and the hopelessness that goes along with being poor. Finally, he is responsible for health programs in the state. One of his brothers died of tuberculosis in a public sanitorium, and another died of infant diarrhea in a public hospital. Secretary Obledo admits, "These experiences do not make me an expert," but they do contribute to caring and a commitment to working hard and with dedication.

This is an unusual background for a cabinet secretary—or for any high governmental official—but it contributes to a particular way of seeing the job and a unique approach to it. For example, Obledo doesn't wait for people with problems to come and see him, he goes to them. As he puts it, "I won't be made a prisoner up in Sacramento. I won't lose touch." He knows what can happen. "People call you by your title, make you feel important. . . . They pay you big money. You buy better clothes, eat better food. You get tied up in the office all day with civil servants telling you what you want to hear. Then before you know it, all you see are numbers and names, names and numbers, and you lose the feeling for what's behind it all—the broken lives, the despair, the misery."

It would be easy for Mario Obledo to fall victim to this fate. He is not just another member of a California cabinet, he's an important one. The departments under his supervision spend around $7 billion of an estimated $11 billion executive budget.

Still, he takes the time. Visiting the employment services office in one city, he listened to a middle-aged woman who complained that she was penniless because of a "conflict" over whether she was entitled to unemployment benefits. He listened to Frank Mullany, a 43-year-old unemployed father of four children, who told Obledo, "They (welfare officers) seem to be playing Russian roulette with my life. I find myself asking questions like, 'would my family be better if I just split,' unthinkable questions I never would have thought of asking before." As he visits patients in public hospitals and inmates in prisons, Mario Obledo will hear other stories from desperate people—stories he understands.[13]

Needless to say, fulfilling both the administrative and the political functions while remaining loyal to the chief executive requires a balancing act by cabinet members. Mario Obledo is trying hard. Others, like Martin Durkin, have found it an impossible combination. Durkin was appointed Secretary of Labor by President Eisenhower, but proved such an embarrassment to that administration that he lasted less than eight months. An active Democrat and head of the AFL Plumbers' Union, he was expected to perform in a pro-business Republican administration. President Eisenhower had told Durkin that "he would be expected to represent labor's viewpoint in the government but—he would no longer owe personal allegiance to labor, only to the nation." Durkin simply couldn't cope with the built-in job conflict.[14]

What makes those who are able to maintain this balance more approachable than the executive office staff and advisers? Politically, the cabinet member needs to listen to particular interests to build and maintain support. If, for example, the secretary of agriculture failed to understand the demands of farmers, and inaccurately communicated them to the chief executive, the administration's farm policy might be misconceived, and in the end the farm vote might be jeopardized. In addition, a secretary of agriculture who did not listen to and gain the support of farmers would be losing an important re-

[13] This account of Obledo's activities is primarily that of Mel Ziegler, "He's Been Where They Are Now," *San Francisco Chronicle*, April 29, 1975. © 1975 Chronicle Publishing Co. Reprinted by permission.
[14] Dwight D. Eisenhower, *Mandate for Change* (Garden City, N.Y.: Doubleday & Company, 1963), p. 91.

source in ensuing legislative battles. The secretary needs interest groups to help in defending the chief executive's programs. Clearly, cabinet members are open to a wide variety of influence and are approachable because they have a political job to do.

Their administrative function also makes them approachable. Since it is in their interest to see that policies are implemented efficiently and with sensitivity, they are open to administrative recommendations. A conflict that results from an ill-conceived executive rule is not in the interests of either a secretary or the administration. The public hearing, which is widely used in some departments, is a way to avoid such conflicts.

Independent Agencies

Have you ever heard of the Veterans Administration or the Federal Communications Commission? Both are independent agencies, but they are independent in different ways. The Veterans Administration is known as an *independent executive agency*. It is one of approximately 45 such agencies at the national level. They are called independent because they are not under a Cabinet department. They aren't, however, independent of the President, who appoints the director of each, or independent of Congress, who oversees what they do and pays their bills.[15] The major distinction between these agencies and Cabinet departments is the scope of their activities. Their function is usually more narrowly defined; many, in fact, are called *single-purpose agencies*.

The Federal Communications Commission is a different kind of independent agency. It and six other agencies on the national level are responsible for regulating certain segments of industry. The segments are apparent from the agency names:

- Civic Aeronautics Board (CAB)
- Federal Communications Commission (FCC)
- Federal Maritime Commission (FMC)
- Federal Power Commission (FPC)
- Federal Trade Commission (FTC)
- Interstate Commerce Commission (ICC)
- Securities and Exchange Commission (SEC)

---

[15] Other major independent agencies at the national level include the Civil Service Commission, Atomic Energy Commission, National Aeronautics and Space Administration, United States Information Agency, and General Services Administration.

The powers of these commissions are vast. Without their approval, no railroad, airline, interstate trucker, pipeline, or barge may introduce a new service—or, for that matter, discontinue an old one or set a rate. In addition, no radio or television station may operate, and no gas producer may market fuel or figure its price in interstate commerce. No interstate public utility may build a power plant, and no sizable firm may market a new security or even safely plan a merger.

Similar regulatory agencies with broad intrastate authority exist on the state level. However, they are more likely to govern business activities associated with the sale of alcohol, banking, real estate, insurance, public utilities, and savings and loans institutions.

What makes these commissions independent, and how are they different from other independent agencies? The *ostensible* reasons for their independence are their members' terms of office and their bipartisan nature. Instead of having terms that coincide with that of the President (or other chief executive), commissioners serve for fixed terms of different lengths. They cannot be removed at the whim of the chief executive. FDR discovered this when he tried to fire FTC Commissioner William E. Humphrey. The U.S. Supreme Court rejected his reason: "Your mind and mine do not go along together." The judges ruled that commissioners can only be fired for causes specified by law.[16] The fact that commissions must reflect a party balance also tends to contribute to their independence. A chief executive cannot appoint only members of one party and, in fact, may never be able to appoint a member from his or her own party. So unlike other independent agencies, regulatory agencies are in theory independent not only of departments but of the chief executive and any one party as well.

Now let's get down to reality. In fact, *these agencies are not independent.* They are strongly influenced by the industry they should be regulating or overseeing, by the chief executive, and by the legislative branch.

On the national level the interdependence of industry and regulators has been quite apparent. Unusual forms of FCC influence became so glaring during 1958 and 1959 that the federal court finally intervened. The court reminded the FCC of an unprecedented number of cases involving improper outside influences, including decisions

[16] George Bookman, "Regulation by Elephant, Rabbit, and Lark," *Fortune*, June 1961, pp. 136–139+.

on TV channels in Boston, Miami, and Springfield, Illinois. Part of the problem stemmed from close personal relations between the commissioners and the regulated. Former FCC Chairman John Doerfer, for example, admitted accepting a free vacation aboard the yacht of a broadcast executive. Doerfer argued there was nothing wrong with the excursion because the yacht did not get far from the dock. This led the *Baltimore Sun* to invent "Doerfers Law": "The extent to which a public official can be influenced improperly aboard a yacht varies inversely with the shallowness of the water." [17]

The influence of industry persists. A 1975 report by the General Accounting Office revealed that 42 of the U.S. Geological Survey's top 223 officials owned stock in oil or mineral exploration firms, and 5 of these officials were former oil company employees who were receiving retirement income from the firms. This becomes relevant and interesting information when one realizes that the U.S. Geological Survey's responsibilities include supervision of companies operating oil and gas leases on federal lands, establishment of the maximum rates of production for offshore drilling, and operation of the Earth Resources Observation Program, which uses satellites and remote sensor data to detect the whereabouts of natural resources on the planet.

The influence of legislative bodies is both personal and legal. The fact that these agencies were created by legislatures in the first place and continue to have their authority defined by them means that the legal influence is real. Of course it doesn't help an agency to be out of favor with the legislature, for there is always that budgetary control.

Apart from the legal dimension, the personal and political aspects suggest a means of access for citizens. Many members of Congress, for example, feel they must badger commissioners on behalf of constituents. The late Sen. Everett Dirksen (R., Ill.), Senate minority leader, was particularly good at this. Dirksen explained, "Meeting a commissioner at a cocktail party, you say, 'Hi Joe.' You know him by his first name." Then, when someone asked Dirksen to help out with a particular problem pending before a commission, he would know someone to contact. He explained it this way: "I think that is part of my job with two and a half million people on the payroll, and agencies all over the lot, where the average citizen becomes thoroughly bewildered." [18]

[17] *Ibid.*
[18] *Ibid.*

The chief executive's influence over independent regulatory agencies also has two dimensions—the legal and the political. Legally, the chief executive appoints some members and approves budget requests. While the formal authority seems very limited, it may not be. President Nixon, for example, was pleasantly surprised to discover that many commissioners with fixed terms of office resigned. Of 38 positions on six major regulatory bodies (FAB, FCC, FPC, ICC, SEC, and CAB), President Nixon, after four years in office, had filled 28 of them. He named the chairmen of all six.[19] This allowed him to exercise far more control. He chose people who agreed with him philosophically whether they were from his party or not.

The political dimension of this influence is defined by the person who occupies the office. A chief executive who is popular and has strong legislative support has a good chance of having commission rules and judgments conform to his or her policy perspectives. After all, how long can commissioners withstand open opposition from the executive office and the legislature? Executive influence usually takes the form of a request by the chief executive for a particular commission study. While the request isn't binding, it's not likely to be ignored.

So while regulatory agencies have some independence, they are also dependent on certain groups in obvious ways. To the extent that they are tied to the industry they should be regulating, it is crucial that the public's interests be represented by legislators and chief executives. The history of regulatory decisions doesn't indicate that that is occurring.

Let's see where we are. The major executive players have been identified. They are a very diverse lot, with completely different functions, and they are selected in dissimilar ways. However, their selection can be influenced, as can the way they do their job. They need more than formal authority to be effective, and this fact makes citizens key players in executive games.

What Influences Executive Moves

The previous discussion has suggested general conditions under which certain groups will be influential. However, because it is crucial for citizens playing executive games to know what influences the moves of executive players, a more systematic overview might help.

[19] John Herberg, "Nixon's Imprint Is Deep at Regulatory Agencies," *New York Times*, May 6, 1973, p. 1.

The previous discussion suggests that there are *two categories of executive players* to be considered—the political and the nonpolitical. The first category includes those members of the executive branch who are *elected* to public office and those who are *appointed*. The second category includes public administrators, people who acquire their positions by virtue of training and specialization. Civil service examinations are usually the vehicle of employment for those in this category.

Those in the second category are *permanent employees*, not usually removed when a new party gains control of the executive branch. We haven't talked much about these people so far, but they are important. Those who occupy middle- and upper-level jobs in the bureaucracy have substantial discretion in their activities.[20] Of course, some of these permanent employees also have a political dimension to their job, but it's important to make this distinction because it helps explain who will move how, under what conditions.

The Way Players See Their Job

Our look at John Reading and Richard Daley conveyed the importance of the way the executive sees the job. Even "political" leaders may see their jobs as nonpolitical, but when they do, they are unlikely to be strong players. Usually becoming a political player implies understanding that strong leadership requires cultivating anyone or any group who will help you get things done.

The nonpolitical players also need interest-group support, but the middle- and upper-level players see their job *primarily* as professional —the player is a scientist, a technician, or a manager. That means they are primarily motivated by the norms of their profession. When there are bureaucratic rules or recommendations to be made that are highly specialized, this professional influence is particularly dominant. When, for example, scientists in the Public Health Service had to make a policy decision with respect to the smoking of cigarettes, professional data were crucial, and health bureaucrats felt obligated to bring that professional perspective strongly to bear on the decision. This means, of course, that these players will be particularly sympathetic to interest groups equipped to use highly technical information.

One word of caution, however. When executive players see themselves primarily as professionals, they may resist influence from any-

[20] Ira Sharkansky emphasizes the importance of this distinction in "State Administrators in the Political Process," in *Politics in the American States*, eds. Herbert Jacobs and Kenneth Vines (Boston: Little, Brown and Company, 1965), p. 239.

one who does not belong to the "club." For example, various studies of urban school systems have revealed that the education bureaucracy has become virtually self-contained, sealed by its special training and knowledge. Educational issues are treated as though they were wholly dependent on expert judgments that school professionals alone are competent to make. Differences in judgment are challenged as being inexpert or naive. Quite naturally, many citizens are intimidated by this attitude and those who hold it.[21] Those who are not, like a variety of civil rights groups, can effectively put pressure on elected school boards, who in turn have power over professionals. Remember, however, that school boards and other elected officers can also be intimidated by professionals. Be prepared.

Clearly, not all nonpolitical bureaucrats are influenced by professional norms. Those Mrs. Gravely encountered probably saw themselves as primarily rule followers. Most lower-level bureaucrats do. To move these players, either a new rule, a redefined rule, or an okay from the boss to reinterpret the rule would be required.

Something to think about
Which approach would be the most effective? How could Lillie Gravely do it?

Political Pressures

Interest groups.   Let's go back to the middle- and upper-level bureaucratic employee. For both political and nonpolitical executive players, "politics" influences moves. When the agency, department, or commission needs the support of particular *interest groups* to get financial support for a program from the legislative branch, the groups' point of view carries weight. Of course, this may lead to problems. An agency may rely so strongly on the political support of an outside group that the agency gets trapped. The group begins to exercise a certain veto power over programs it doesn't like. This is nice for the group, but perhaps detrimental to a broader public interest.

This has occurred in many regulatory agencies. Commissioners get trapped not only by their political needs but by their technical

---

[21] Marilyn Gittel, "Urban School Politics: Professionalism vs. Reform," *Journal of Social Issues,* Summer 1970, pp. 69–84.

needs as well. For example, regulatory decisions on rate regulation are frequently made on the basis of industry figures and forecasts. Most state departments of insurance, in fact, have far too few staff members even to review adequately the figures provided by the large and expert staffs of the underwriters' associations. The same is true for product testing: regulators depend heavily on the results of industry tests. The result? Particular groups with specialized information have access not enjoyed by others. Public-interest advocates are trying to correct this imbalance, but more about that later.

Political parties also influence the moves of some executive players. They may do it in direct ways when the player (such as a chief executive or cabinet member) needs partisan support in the legislative branch to get the votes for certain policies. The party also influences other players in less obvious and less direct ways. It influences, for example, the substance of some regulatory decisions. This was quite apparent in a study of voting behavior on the Federal Communications Commission. When decisions had a broad philosophical dimension (e.g., to what degree should commissioners regulate the content of radio and television programs), partisan voting was quite apparent. This isn't to say that the party put pressure on the commissioners to vote in a particular way, but rather that the partisan affiliation of a commissioner consistently influenced votes on this kind of issue. So who gets appointed to commissions and the partisan balance may well be important in predicting certain moves.[22]

Public opinion.   There was just no way Gerald Ford could continue supporting the South Vietnamese government. *Public opinion* was quite clear on the subject. He knew it and Congress knew it. Ordinarily, however, the influence of public opinion is not quite that clear, and ordinarily it depends on other factors: whether the President's party holds a significant plurality in Congress, whether the President has received a strong election mandate, the sudden emergence of a crisis, and so on.

Interestingly, other executive players are also influenced by public opinion, and that influence extends to administrative as well as policy areas. For example, as agencies try to get legislative approval for their programs, they hope they can depend on their favorable public image. To assure this, many executives spend time on public relations

[22] Bradley C. Canon, "Voting Behavior on the FCC," *Midwest Journal of Political Science,* November 1969, pp. 587–612.

activities. Through public speaking and issuing favorable news releases and reports they attempt to build up the image of their department in order to help them get what they want. Law enforcement agencies and military services have been particularly adept at this.

Sensitivity to public opinion is also involved when middle-level administrative moves are considered. To a certain degree every administrative act is evaluated on the basis of its public impact.

> Each employee hired, each one demoted, transferred, or discharged, every efficiency rating, every assignment of responsibility, each change in administrative structure, each conversation, each letter, has to be thought about in terms of possible public agitation, investigation, or judgment. Because of this scrutiny, [real or imagined] every governmental executive lives and moves in the pressure of public dynamite. Every action he may take is influenced by this condition—whether before or after the explosion.[23]

This sensitivity, which of course varies from agency to agency, is one of the things that makes government administration different from private administration. Therefore, if the agency has a great deal of public exposure, educational campaigns to build opinion could have some effect.

Other Institutions

While political sensitivity is important to understanding the behavior of executive players, so is sensitivity to the way other institutions must by law behave. In very formal ways, both *legislatures* and *courts* can influence executive moves. President Nixon discovered judicial power when the U.S. Supreme Court forced him to turn over to the House Judiciary Committee various Watergate-related tapes and documents. "Executive privilege," they ruled, was not applicable in this case. The House had a right to investigate charges with a view toward possible impeachment.

Various departments in Nixon's administration were also forced to vary their moves because of judicial action. For example, even when ordered by the President, departments did not have unlimited authority to withhold funds appropriated by Congress. Much of the $1.8 billion impounded by the Nixon administration was ordered

[23] Paul Appleby, "Government Is Different," in *The Administration of Public Policy*, ed. Michael D. Reagan (Glenview, Ill.: Scott, Foresman and Company, 1969), p. 3.

released in more than 20 separate court actions. Congress, state and local governments, and special interest groups went to court to challenge those impoundment actions.[24]

Other administrators at all levels are also subject to judicial influence. Roughly 20 percent of the Supreme Court's written opinions concern administrative matters,[25] and many other administrative decisions are successfully challenged in lower courts—but not enough, according to Martin Shapiro.

> The overwhelming typical action of courts exercising review is to refuse to substitute their own decisions for those of the agency, and . . . only in a handful of the thousands of agency decisions made each year is there even an effort by the adversely effected party to get a second decision from the courts.[26]

In spite of this record and in spite of the many important administrative decisions that are isolated from public view,[27] this is a method of influence that sometimes works in far-reaching ways. Civil rights forces in the 1950s discovered this as the courts became the only institution that would order desegregation.

We are already aware of the many ways in which legislatures influence the moves of executive players. Their authority to fund programs, to oversee (however badly) the operations of the executive branch, to confirm appointments made by chief executives, and to override vetoes is vast indeed. Federal executives, including President Ford, experienced a sharp blow when the veto of the amendment to the 1966 Freedom of Information Act was overridden. No longer would bureaucrats be able to stall when the media, Congress, or the public wanted information. No longer would Defense and State Department members be able to arbitrarily withhold foreign policy and national defense information. The amendment allows a petitioner to ask that a federal judge privately review classified information to determine if it should be made public.

The degree to which legislative influence in states is important was revealed in a 1967 study of department heads in various states. The

---

[24] Harry B. Ellis, "Nixon 'Impounds' $11.8 Billion but Few in Congress Protest," *Christian Science Monitor,* April 11, 1974.

[25] Martin Shapiro, *The Supreme Court and Administrative Agencies* (New York: The Free Press, 1968), p. 13.

[26] *Ibid.,* p. 95.

[27] The 1976 sunshine legislation has forced about 50 federal regulatory agencies to open their decision-making process to public scrutiny.

Table 10–1
Attitudes of American state executives on political relationships

	Percentages* (N = 933)
"Who exercises greater control over your agency's affairs?"	
Governor	32
Each about the same	22
Legislature	44
Other and n.a.	2
	100
"Who has the greater tendency to reduce budget requests?"	
Governor	25
Legislature	60
Other and n.a.	15
	100
"Who is more sympathetic to the goals of your agency?"	
Governor	55
Each about the same	14
Legislature	20
Other and n.a.	11
	100
"What type of control do you prefer?"	
Governor	42
Independent commission	28
Legislature	24
Other and n.a.	5
	100

* Tabled percentages may not add to 100 because of rounding.
Source: Deil S. Wright, "Executive Leadership in State Administration," *Midwest Journal of Political Science*, XI February 1967, p. 4.

legislature was perceived to have the greatest internal control over administrative activity, as shown in Table 10–1.[28]

The implications of this perception for citizens seeking to influence executive moves are obvious. If bureaucrats can't be influenced directly, going to individual legislators and legislative bodies is the next step.

[28] From Hugh LeBlanc and D. Trudeau Allensworth, *The Politics of States and Urban Communities* (New York: Harper and Row, Publishers, 1971), p. 112.

Executive superiors.   "You can always go to the boss!" This works in both private and public bureaucracies. The lines of authority or chain of command serve as general guides to who is going to have influence over whom. While civil service bureaucrats can't easily be fired for failing to be sensitive to orders, their advancement can be blocked and their lives made generally miserable.

Top-level bureaucrats are a special case. One would think that the chief executive, as the super boss, would always have the greatest influence. As we know, however, that depends on several things. When the chief executive controls a large block of legislators and/or has strong public support, agency heads will usually knuckle under, but if the chief executive lacks that political clout, the agency will attempt to use its own political base (interest-group and legislative support) to act as independently as it can. J. Edgar Hoover, as director of the FBI, was a master at this, regardless of the political strength of his various bosses. Rarely were his decisions reversed by any president. However, he was an exception. Executive superiors usually have more control.

There is, it appears, a special sensitivity to the wishes of the "appointer." In a 50-state survey, department heads *who were appointed* as opposed to elected or promoted through civil service procedures felt they were controlled by the governor and were generally sympathetic to that control.[29] So an indirect way of reaching appointed bureaucrats is to exert pressure on the appointer.

To summarize what one needs to know about executive arenas in order to be politically effective, these points seem important:

1. If a citizen is trying to get a program implemented in a different way or get regulations altered, the executive arena is involved. In essence, this is a likely strategic choice, although there are other institutional possibilities.
2. Players in this arena usually have clearly defined jobs, operate according to formal and informal rules, and are related to other executive players *somewhat* hierarchically. That doesn't mean, as we now know, that various players will not have considerable independence or that power is always associated with formal lines of authority. In a word, activists must escape from organizational charts to know what is happening in this arena.

[29] Deil S. Wright, "Executive Leadership in State Administration," *Midwest Journal of Political Science*, February 1967, pp. 1–26.

3. The moves of executive players are influenced by a variety of factors, but certain factors are more important for political players and others are more important for permanent employees. While the way an individual player sees the job will account for some variations, generally political players can be the focus of both direct and indirect forms of political pressure, while permanent employees may only respond to indirect forms of pressure.

The joy is, although Mrs. Lillie Gravely didn't realize it, that executive players can be budged. They are so different and there are so many of them that initially it may be confusing, but it is quite possible. Knowing who the key players are, their power, and their vulnerability to various types of influence is, of course, only the initial preparation for playing executive games. The rules must also be understood—and that's the next focus.

Key Words

Bureaucracy
Senatorial courtesy
Electoral votes
Plurality
Majority
Retroactive judgment

Suggested Activities

1. Determine the administrative and legislative authority of your mayor, county administrative officer, and governor.
2. Develop a third-party strategy that would allow the candidate of that party to benefit from the electoral college.
3. Attempt to get chief executive candidates to clarify their policy position on a particularly controversial issue.
4. Identify the independent agencies that exist in your state. Do any of the top-level personnel have a close affiliation with the industries they are supposed to regulate? Is there any apparent connection between these people and the appointer?
5. Survey state or local newspapers to determine the public relations activities of particular departments or agencies. Were these activities related to any pending pieces of legislation?

11
Rules of the Executive Game

Can you imagine trying to fight a revolution against a huge, righteous marshmallow? Even if you had enough troops not to be suffocated by it, the best you can hope for is to eat it. And, as you know, you become what you eat. And that is the point. For a revolution to be meaningful it must take into account the nature of organizational life.[1]

This is a bureaucrat speaking. His name is Matthew Dumont. In 1970 he was assistant commissioner for drug rehabilitation in the Massachusetts Department of Mental Health. Do you know what he's talking about? He's talking about the difficulty of playing the executive game. More specifically, he's concerned about the difficulty of changing bureaucratic organizations so that they can be more responsive to people.

The difficulty, he feels, has to do with rules. The rules of bureaucratic life become so important to some executive players that the real purpose of the game is forgotten. Instead the game becomes how to use formal and informal rules to maintain and enhance power.

[1] Matthew P. Dumont, "Down the Bureaucracy," *Transaction*, October 1970, p. 24.

Rules as Determinants of Power

Well, rules do distribute power. Examining those that apply to legislative games made that quite clear. It was also clear that citizens trying to influence institutional players need to know just how that distribution occurs.

The previous discussion of executive arenas identified several rules that executive players use as resources to enhance their power. Among those identified were the chief executive's rights of veto, appointment, and budgetary authority; the commissioner's established term of office and independence from departments; and the middle-level bureaucrat's required expertise and tenure. These, of course, are formal resources—among the many given executive players through constitutional, statutory, or judicial authority. When combined with informal rules and resources, these can make executive players formidable allies or opponents.

Just how that happens can be understood by looking at rules in three ways: how rules distribute power *within* a bureaucracy, how they distribute power *between* different bureaucracies at the same level of government, and how they distribute power *between* bureaucracies at *different levels* of government.

The Distribution of Power within Bureaucracies

Generally, *within bureaucracies* rules distribute power hierarchically. The general is given far more authority than the private. This means, of course, that the major decisions that get made in a bureaucracy are made by those at the top. Subordinates are expected to obey.

We know, of course, that the formal chain of command can be broken when middle-echelon officials have important informal resources of their own—interest-group and legislative support as well as technical skills. However, even in the face of these obstacles, some semblance of hierarchical power remains.

The trick for activists is to discover *who has final authority over what* in a given bureaucracy. Obviously, there are administrators other than the chief executive or cabinet secretary who have "the last word," but usually the further down in the chain of command one looks, the more limited is the authority. Forest rangers, for example, have final authority in very few matters; most of their decisions have to go to regional or national headquarters for review before they become final.[2] Governmental organization charts, civil service manu-

[2] James W. Davis, Jr., deals with different types of bureaucratic authority in *National Executive Branch* (New York: The Free Press, 1970), p. 91.

als, and statutes give only part of the answer. Still, they are a place to begin. Hopefully, they will keep the activist from using sophisticated persuasive tactics on the wrong person.

Let's say the "right" person has been discovered. Be prepared for some realities of bureaucratic life—the realities that concerned Matthew Dumont when he referred to the "huge, righteous marshmallow." They are influenced by rules.

Reality number one.   The person with the authority to act may not have the knowledge to make the right decision. Subordinates who do have the knowledge, who do see the dimensions of a decision clearly, ultimately may be frustrated because of their lack of authority. It is very risky for these subordinates, in aiding an interest group, to circumvent the authority of an immediate superior and go to someone else who has greater authority coupled with some knowledge. *Follow the chain of command* is a bureaucratic rule. In order to get what it wants, the group will probably have to circumvent that chain of authority on its own, perhaps with the help of the media and/or a legislator.

Reality number two.   Some bureaucrats may only be concerned with "putting in their time," not with doing their job. Matthew Dumont thought this was so common that he called it an informal rule of bureaucratic life—*maintain your tenure.* If it is an informal rule, it distributes rewards to the inactive employee.

This is how one follows the rule, according to Dumont. First, the bureaucrat must appear occupied. This means walking briskly at all times, or looking down at your desk rather than up into the distance when thinking. It means always having papers in your hand and responding to the question, "how are things going?" by saying "very hectic" rather than "terrific" or "lousy." It may also mean usually saying no to any request from a subordinate or citizen. Mildred Perlman who retired in 1975 as director of classification for New York City's Civil Service Commission told the *New York Times*: "You start by saying no to requests. Then if you have to go to yes, okay. But if you start with yes, you can't go to no." [3]

Also, the bureaucrat must seem inconspicuous. That means the bureaucrat must express himself or herself quietly and without affect. The opposite of that would involve "deviant" forms of behavior like looking people directly in the eye for a moment too long, walking

[3] "How It Really Works," *Newsweek* (Dec. 15, 1975), p. 46.

around on a weekday without a tie, refusing to write memos, laughing too loud or too long at a conference, and so on.

Maybe Matthew Dumont is exaggerating a bit when he describes his fellow bureaucrats' tendency to follow this rule.[4] However, if maintaining one's tenure is an important rule of bureaucratic life, activists need to know that a person with authority may not want to make the decision they are urging. If this is the case, understanding the other factors that influence bureaucratic behavior as well as the tactical possibilities is crucial.

Still another informal rule, related to the individual tenure rule, that Dumont identified apparently preserves the status quo but may actually be useful to activists. It is, *keep the boss from being embarrassed.* This means that the civil servant who runs interference effectively, who can anticipate and prevent impertinent, urgent, or obvious demands from the boss's boss, from the press, from the public, or from the legislature will be treasured and rewarded. Many CIA employees testifying before the Senate Intelligence Committee in 1975 were experts at protecting their superiors. Rarely was it ever clear just who had ordered what activities to be investigated. To the extent it is observed, the rule may prevent the public's business from being done. The bureaucrat's primary function in the hierarchy becomes preserving a superior's tenure rather than fulfilling assigned responsibilities. Still, this rule may be useful to citizens. A bureaucrat may be responsive if the alternative is embarrassment to the boss.

Within bureaucracies, then, rules distribute authority hierarchically, but that distribution provides no guarantees. It neither guarantees that the person with authority has adequate knowledge to act nor assures that the person will be willing to act. If Matthew Dumont's assessment is correct and those informal rules are pervasive, then getting bureaucrats to budge will require every ounce of skill.

The Distribution of Power between Bureaucracies at the Same Level of Government

Rules also distribute power *between bureaucratic organizations.* Again, these rules are both formal and informal.

---

[4] An apparent contradiction to Dumont's observations is a study of middle-level bureaucrats. It revealed that compared with private bureaucrats, public personnel are more energetic (achievement-oriented). They have a greater desire to accomplish something as an end in itself. See James F. Guyot, "Government Bureaucrats Are Different," *Public Administration Review,* December 1962, pp. 195–202.

Formally, when legislatures establish new programs or strengthen ongoing ones and ask that they be administered by an existing agency, this formal grant of authority may enhance that agency's power relative to another agency. Ordinarily, bureaucratic organizations attempt to expand their informal resources so that when a legislative opportunity to increase that authority presents itself, they are in a position to fight. When President Nixon attempted to eliminate the Office of Economic Opportunity, which had been the key administrative unit in President Johnson's War on Poverty, the battle was on. The OEO mobilized every interest group and legislative friend it could find to assure its survival. However, the mobilization wasn't enough. The battle ended in 1975 when the OEO was abolished. The department that gained most from the dismantling was Health, Education and Welfare. This increase in HEW's formal authority came about partly because HEW shared a constituency with OEO. Interest groups, mayors, governors, and poverty workers believed that if OEO was doomed, HEW would be the department most willing and able to provide a sympathetic home for various programs (Head Start, Follow Through, Comprehensive Health Service, and the Native Americans Programs).

Increasing its jurisdiction is not always the way for an agency to increase its power, however. This is particularly true if the jurisdiction is going to involve future political risks. In their study of New York City, Sayre and Kaufman describe just such a situation, where agencies actually:

> ... compete to avoid program assignments that are especially difficult and controversial. The commissioner of hospitals and the commissioner of correction have both tried to prevent lodging responsibility for treatment of narcotics addicts in their departments, and the Department of Health has been restive under burdens of building inspection the commissioner and the Board of Health would generally prefer to have placed entirely on the Department of Buildings.[5]

So formal grants of authority, money appropriated, and personnel added will distribute power to agencies unequally, but none of this will help if these resources cause the agency to lose its friends.

That's why informal rules are just as important as the formal ones in distributing power to different bureaucratic organizations. To the

---

[5] Wallace S. Sayre and Herbert Kaufman, *Governing New York City* (New York: Russell Sage Foundation, 1960), p. 262.

extent that an agency follows the rule that it must *maintain a stable visible constituency*, advantages flow. To the extent that it follows another rule, *promulgate the myth (or reality) of professionalism*, advantages will also flow. Both can increase the leverage of the agency relative to others within the executive arena, and also in the legislative arena as well.

These informal rules have two implications for citizen action. Those who are considered part of the stable and visible constituency should have some clout. Being "serviced" by the agency, however, does not automatically put you in that position. The constituents of welfare departments tend to be not welfare recipients but social workers. The constituents of educational programs are generally not students but educators. The constituents of health programs are not the consumers but the providers of health care, the professionals.[6] For a strategy to work, certain groups may first have to develop tactics that will help them become part of that constituency.

Something to think about
What tactics would work, given what we know about what influences bureaucrats? Can you think of any groups presently attempting to become part of a department's ongoing constituency?

The other implication for citizens seeking to influence bureaucrats has to do with "professionalism." Groups shouldn't be intimidated by it; they should use it to their advantage. Environmentalists, for example, "out-professionaled" bureaucrats as expert after expert testified before congressional committees considering whether or not to authorize a supersonic transport plane. Civil rights groups refused to be left out of local policy-making that involved the future of minority children, and they frequently mobilized enough community support to cut through the aura of professionalism.

The broader implication of these rules is that they count in assessing the relative power of agencies. To the degree that a bureaucratic organization uses them, it can be a powerful ally or opponent in legislative games and a friend or stumbling block in executive ones.

---

[6] Matthew Dumont develops this point. "Down the Bureaucracy," p. 13.

The Distribution of Power between Bureaucracies at Different Levels

Finally, rules distribute power *between bureaucrats at different levels* of government.

One would think that the crucial rule involved, the Tenth Amendment to the U.S. Constitution, would have cleared up any and all confusion. Remember what it says? All powers, unless specifically mentioned elsewhere in the Constitution, are reserved to the states or the people.

This didn't help the confusion because even the founders weren't clear about how power should be distributed between the state and national governments. This has required Supreme Court action at various times. One of the earliest and most far-reaching cases was *McCulloch* v. *Maryland* (1819). In the process of settling a dispute, the court had to take a look at Article 1, Section 8 of the Constitution. Most of that section describes something called *enumerated powers*. Those are the powers expressly delegated to Congress. Then, as if to negate the Tenth Amendment (which had not yet been inserted), the authors of the Constitution dealt the states a blow. At the end of Section 8, Congress was granted the power to make all laws that shall be *necessary and proper* for carrying out all the earlier enumerated powers.

When the Court told the State of Maryland that it couldn't tax a branch of a national bank in that state, people started to get the picture. They slowly understood that while the U.S. Constitution doesn't actually grant Congress the authority to do many things, that "necessary and proper" clause implies that Congress can also do other things. These *implied powers*, according to the Court, gave Congress the right to establish a bank in the first place. Furthermore, the State of Maryland couldn't tax a legitimate unit of the national government. People also began to understand, as a result of this case, that states have very little to say about the operation of the national government. What had emerged was a principle of *national supremacy* that, in effect, denied the states any right to interfere in the constitutional operations of the national government.

These early rules suggest that formal rules tend to be to the advantage of the national government. Later rules and practices indicate the same thing. All these rules fundamentally influence what happens in which executive arena.

Some people call what emerged "feudalistic federalism," as opposed to "cooperative federalism." Instead of state and local governments' sharing *responsibility* (if not the money) for programs that improve the quality of people's lives, professional bureaucrats at the *federal* level have called most of the shots.[7]

The argument goes this way. In addition to the Constitution and some judicial decisions, specific actions by Congress have also distributed advantages to the federal government. Congress authorizes a great many programs that somehow have to reach the people. Congress can do this because it has the money. As of 1971, Washington collected 59 percent of all tax revenues in the United States. This is primarily because the federal government tends to monopolize the single greatest source of revenue—the income tax. State and local governments, on the other hand, tend to rely more on sales and property taxes for most of their revenue. These are more limited resources because what citizens pay is not necessarily related to their ability to pay.

So Congress has the ability to authorize programs that ultimately cost a great deal of money. However, although Washington has the money, bureaucrats in states and cities must implement the programs so that they reach people.

This is where the feudalistic relationship comes in. It has traditionally been associated with *federal grants-in-aid*. These are funds that Congress makes available to the state and local governments to spend according to certain standards and under certain conditions. However, the receiving government is required to match these funds according to a prearranged formula. Essentially, what grants-in-aid have done, apart from helping states and local communities cope with increasing financial problems, is distribute power to permanent bureaucratic employees instead of chief executives, and to the federal level of government instead of state and local levels.

Harold Seidman says that generally under twentieth century federalism these professionals gained so much power that their departments were referred to as "vertical functional autocracies." Programs approved and money provided by Congress would go from federal bureaucrats who performed a general function (e.g., administering health programs) to those on the state and local levels who performed

---

[7] This and the subsequent discussion is essentially the point of view of Harold Seidman in *Politics, Position, and Power* (New York: Oxford University Press, 1970).

a similar function. Former Governor of North Carolina Terry Sanford described these vertical functional autocracies in this way:

> The lines of authority, the concerns and interests, the flow of money, and the direction of programs run straight down like a number of pickets stuck into the ground. There is, as in a picket fence, a connecting cross slat, but that does little to support anything. In this metaphor it stands for governments. It holds the pickets in line, it does not bring them together. The picket-like programs are not connected at the bottom.[8]

Apart from the broader power effects of this kind of federalism, the immediate effects have been to encourage the fragmentation of executive authority and to promote the isolation of bureaucratic departments.

If chief executives on state and local levels had fully shared in the administration of these programs, perhaps there would have been less isolation and less fragmented authority, but they didn't. Generally they were not given the resources under federal law. For example, governors could rarely select the heads of agencies administering federal programs.[9] They couldn't compete because they didn't have the budget.

It took a while, but governors and mayors finally looked at what was happening to their power. The chief executives at each level decided to organize to change the rules and restore some of their resources. More recent federal laws have reflected their success. For example, in 1968 a federal law (the Intergovernmental Cooperation Act) allowed state agencies to administer programs. No longer must new agencies be established to administer federal benefits. This law also did more, perhaps in an attempt to bring the fence stakes closer together by strengthening political units. It provided that (1) governors and state legislatures should be *informed* of federal grants to state agencies; (2) federal aid, as far as possible, should be *consistent* with and further the objectives of state, regional, and local comprehensive planning; and (3) loans and grants should be made to *units of general local government* rather than to special-purpose units.[10] It was a start.

[8] Terry Sanford, *Storm over the States* (New York: McGraw-Hill Book Company, 1967), p. 80.
[9] A 1969 report issued by the National Advisory Commission on Intergovernmental Relations illustrates this point. It is summarized in Seidman, *Politics, Position, and Power*, p. 142.
[10] *Ibid.*, p. 160.

Something to think about

In addition to chief executives, who gain some power under this legislation, who else might gain or lose?

The major victory for chief executives (and perhaps loss for federal permanent employees) came in 1972 with congressional approval of general *revenue-sharing*. This is a system in which the federal government automatically and regularly turns over a certain amount (or percentage) of tax money to other units of government. The decision, in this case, was to distribute $30.1 billion to state and local governments over five years. Precisely how much each unit receives is based on population, per capita income, and the receiving government's tax effort, but two-thirds of the money goes to local governments (cities, towns, and counties) and one-third to state governments.

Needless to say, governors and mayors were ecstatic in 1972. This was something they had been working toward for years. However, their continuing ecstasy depended on the federal government's not pulling the rug out from under past financing. State and local executives urged the continuation of federal grants-in-aid, as bad as they were. Accepting dependence in one federal aid program along with independence in another seemed okay as long as the two added up to increases in money and power. Even though the two approaches were not equally funded (in 1974 revenue-sharing provided $6.1 billion to state and local governments, while grants-in-aid accounted for $42.1 billion), it was a place to start.

So how do these new rules alter the distribution of power between executive branches at different levels? If spending is used as an indicator, federal bureaucrats still prevail. That usually means that state and local bureaucrats who administer the programs will be more responsive to their counterparts in Washington than to local political leaders. Although the 1968 rules gave chief executives in the state somewhat more influence, the balance under grants-in-aid favors the national level.

Something to think about

What strategy should be used to influence how this money gets administered?

Apart from local and state executives, who derive political benefit, who else benefits from revenue-sharing? Is the power of citizens enhanced? According to President Nixon, in a message to Congress (February 4, 1971), it would be:

> Giving states and localities the power to spend certain federal tax monies will increase the influence of each citizen on how those monies are used. It will make government more responsive to taxpayer pressures. It will enhance accountability.

It *might* someday, but that doesn't seem to be happening now, in the first few years of revenue sharing. A six-state study conducted by the League of Women Voters Education Fund, The Center for Community Change, and the Center for National Policy Review concluded that citizens were frequently not participating in revenue-sharing decisions. Of the respondents, 55 percent said there was no participation; 20 percent said there had been participation; 17 percent said they didn't know; and 8 percent gave other responses.[11]

Well, maybe citizens don't *need* to participate. Perhaps local and state chief executives are sensitive enough to the needs of their constituents to be able to be responsive without citizen input. Or perhaps they are politically sensitive enough to be responsive to the needs of the citizens *who play the game*. The conclusions of a 1974 General Accounting Office survey prompt speculation. The GAO revealed that of the money passed along to state and local governments, only three-tenths of 1 percent has been spent directly on the handicapped, and 1 percent on children. Another study revealed that only two-tenths of 1 percent has benefited the elderly.[12] In all, about 3 percent goes for social services for the poor and aged. Most of the money is spent on three things: public education, public safety, and public transportation. Maybe these are the areas of greatest public need, or maybe these are areas with vocal constituencies.[13]

All this suggests that with revenue sharing, mayors, supervisors, and governors will have more power, and *potentially* citizens will as

[11] League of Women Voters Education Fund, *General Revenue Sharing and the States*, Washington D.C.: League of Women Voters of the United States, 1975, p. 17. Conclusions were based on 300 in-depth interviews with elected officials, department heads, media representatives, and the leaders of community organizations, demographic information studies, reports, newspaper clippings, and budget documents.
[12] See "Revenue Sharing," *New Republic*, June 22, 1974, pp. 7–8.
[13] Spending figures in *Public Interest Alert*, July 1974, p. 176.

well. However, as long as *political* leaders are making the spending decisions, they will be especially sensitive to those who play the political game. As we know, the least advantaged are least likely to play.

Clearly, rules do distribute power, and rule changes tend to distribute it in different ways. Whether one is looking at the distribution within bureaucracies or between them, one must be aware of the formal and informal rules operating and of the political and non-political influences that prevail. They are all very relevant to executive games. Also relevant are the rules associated with access.

Rules of Access to the Executive Game

It's like any game, really. The rules can get you in, they tell you how advantages and disadvantages are distributed, and they help you predict the behavior of other players, but they offer no guarantees. For citizens, at best, executive access rules offer an opportunity to *influence* the outcome of the game; they rarely, by themselves, give one *power*. They are designed that way, to make any disruption of the prevailing distribution of power difficult.

The Points of Access and Informal Rules

Let's begin with understanding how most executive agencies play the game. That is, what are the *stages* of executive policy-making at which citizens *may* have some access? There are essentially five: (1) Rules are initiated, (2) there is a preliminary drafting, (3) the public participates, (4) there is a final drafting, and (5) the rules are reviewed.[14] While only the third stage mentions citizen access, there are opportunities at other stages as well. With each opportunity there are rules, either formal or informal.

In February 1976, an important and highly controversial executive decision was made. The decision maker was William T. Coleman, Jr., federal Secretary of Transportation. The decision? To allow the British-French supersonic transport, called the Concorde, to land in the United States for a trial period. A few years earlier, relying on testimony from scientists and environmentalists, Congress rejected the idea of assisting in the development of a U.S. supersonic transport

---

[14] This sequential look at the process of policy-making in executive agencies is based on a study by William W. Boyer, "Policy-making by Government Agencies," *Midwest Journal of Political Science*, August 1960, pp. 267–288.

plane. The environmental and health risks would be too great, they had concluded.

But the Concorde decision was made, and its ultimate acceptance had not only to do with its thoroughness and limited nature but with the role citizens had been allowed to play in the process. They were a crucial part of this executive game.

Rules can be initiated by almost anyone—bureaucrats, legislators, citizens. *This rule request was initiated* by the Concorde developers. The Atlantic run was crucial if they were to recoup their $3 billion development costs. While ordinarily new aircraft are almost routinely allowed to engage in commercial service, the persisting opposition to supersonic transports required the request to be dealt with at the highest executive levels.[15] President Ford's political advisers urged him to allow Secretary Coleman to make the decision on his own. Not a pleasant task.

The preliminary drafting of a regulation may be carried out by any person within or outside an administrative agency. Students at many colleges and universities, for example, have drafted rule changes relative to grading procedures, school calendars, their systematic participation in collegewide decisions, etc. It seems likely that Department of Transportation staff, in consultation with the Federal Aviation Administration, was primarily responsible for the preliminary drafting of the Concorde regulation. And because the decision might have foreign policy implications, Secretary of State Henry Kissinger was also consulted.

After preliminary drafting, *broader participation* is usually encouraged or mandated by law. Included at this stage are *conferences* with groups whose interests are involved, meetings with *permanent advisory committees*, and/or *public hearings*.

To maximize impact, citizens should follow some *informal rules* at this stage. Know the specific *authority* granted by the legislature; know the *personnel* in the agency who are likely to have the greatest influence in making the decision; know the *guidelines* governing the particular forum for citizen participation—whether it is a conference, committee, or hearing; know the *agenda*; and know the *other likely participants* and their probable contribution.

---

[15] Who in the executive branch has the authority to make what kinds of decisions is indicated in the *U.S. Government Organization Manual*. Congress grants the authority.

Punch

"I said 'we're going deaf', so I suppose that's the balance
of nature at work!"

But remember, being consulted or allowed to participate at this stage is in the agency's interest just as much as it is in the interest of an outside group. Secretary Coleman, knowing he would feel the heat from environmentalists, had to get the support from as many other interest groups as possible. For him, department hearings were crucial. Ultimately, they not only brought him some needed support but they also clarified the implications of several decision options. Most important, they added legitimacy to the final decision.

Following the public hearings and conferences on preliminary proposals, Secretary Coleman hybernated. He was personally responsible for the *final drafting*. One Department of Transportation insider described the process in this way: "Closeted with the record from the hearings and a multitude of official studies on the Concorde, Coleman worked nights and weekends on his decision—writing and rewriting, asking experts to draft language, then 'adding, deleting, making slight changes so that he was totally confident of each nuance.' " [16]

While the final drafting of the Concorde decision was carried out with the greatest secrecy, frequently citizens may even participate at this stage, particularly if they have needed expertise.

The final stage of the executive policy-making process is *review*. Just because a decision has been made doesn't mean it can't be modified or reversed. This occurs after it has been evaluated for its workability and fairness. The Concorde decision is to be reviewed after 16 months of flights. However, in this instance, critics think a review will be futile. Sen. J. Glenn Beall, Jr. (R., Md.) put it this way: "Once we approve the flights, it will just be a matter of time before we will be asked to accept even more flights from more countries". [17] Perhaps, but the importance of the evaluation will probably again assure the participation of a variety of groups. As this occurs, some *informal rules* should be observed. Carefully *collect evidence* of how the rule has been implemented and evidence of its effects.[18] *Draft a rule modification* that is likely to generate support. *Build support* both within the relevant agency and among outside groups (media, legislators, other interest groups, other agencies).

So very generally, these are the informal rules and the points of

[16] "The Concorde Furor," *Newsweek* (Feb. 16, 1976), p. 16.
[17] *Ibid.*, p. 19.
[18] Federal agency regulations are first published in a daily bulletin called *The Federal Register*; later they become part of the *Code of Federal Regulations* (CFR).

access. Clearly, executive policy-making is a continuing process. Citizen input is possible and often encouraged at every stage. Just how well citizens use the opportunities and the rules determines whether they become merely legitimizers of what bureaucrats have already made up their mind to do or whether in fact they are influential.

Conditions of Access and Formal Rules

Now let's get down to specifics. How do formal rules promote citizen access to executive games? We already know about some of the informal access rules.

Probably the most important federal executive rule for citizens is called the *Administrative Procedure Act* (1946). This is what it does.

1. It establishes the essential requirements for administrative proceedings, such as rule-making and adjudication.
2. It requires agencies to furnish the public with information unless they are exempted under the Act or by another statute.[19]
3. It spells out the duties of hearing examiners.
4. It describes the requirements for administrative hearings when they are required by law and sets limits on administrative powers.
5. It establishes legal standards for judicial review of administrative action.[20]

This law and comparable ones at the state level need to be examined in detail before citizens attempt to influence executive agencies. It clearly distributes certain advantages to citizens but also protects the prerogatives of agencies. The following illustration of federal executive policy making demonstrates both. It suggests some of the problems associated with a major access rule.

The Case of the Federal Land Agencies

The federal government owns about 200 million acres of forest land. Control of this land is primarily in the hands of three agencies: the Forest Service, which is in the Department of Agriculture; the National Park Service, in the Department of the Interior; and the Bureau of Land Management, also in Interior. These not always cooperative agencies divide responsibility for the land. The Forest Service has the greatest responsibility; it administers all public lands

---

[19] The Freedom of Information Act referred to in earlier chapters is actually an amendment to this 1964 legislation.
[20] James R. Michael, ed., *Working on the System* (New York: Basic Books, 1974), p. 65.

reserved as national forests. The National Park Service takes care of areas of special scenic or historic significance. The Bureau of Land Management controls large stretches of public lands, much of it treeless but also including choice timberland on the West Coast and other forests in Alaska.

After carefully analyzing the authority granted to these agencies, a conservation-minded law professor by the name of Charles A. Reich concluded that these agencies have been given broad grants of authority by Congress without any accompanying standards or policies to guide them. He also concluded that while particular interest groups may be able to influence these agencies, the public as a whole has little clout.[21]

To develop his first point, Reich calls attention to the authority delegated to the Forest Service. "It is so sweeping and so vague as to represent a turnover of virtually all responsibility." For example, a statute passed in 1960 reads,

> ... The Secretary of Agriculture is authorized and directed to develop and administer the receivable surface resources of the national forests for multiple use and sustained yield of the several products and services obtained therefrom. In the administration of the national forests due consideration shall be given to the relative values of the various resources in particular areas. ...

The language of this law leaves a great deal of discretion to the agency. The term "multiple use," for example, means that forests cannot be used exclusively for one purpose, but beyond that, who decides how the claims of competing interests are to be satisfied? Or, to offer another example, "the relative values of the various resources" are to be given "due consideration," but what are those values and what actions would add up to "due consideration"?

What all this suggests, according to Reich, is that Congress is abandoning its responsibility to represent the people. Instead, the top-level bureaucrats in the Forest Service, none of whom have been elected by or are easily controlled by the public, are able to decide such *major* questions as whether or not the American people need the forests more for resources or for recreation or for wilderness or for dams and public power. Ultimately, decisions to cut trees, build dams, put up hotels, or leave the woods undeveloped would not legally be in conflict with any congressional mandate.

[21] Charles A. Reich develops this point in "Bureaucracy and the Forests" in *The Administration of Public Policies*, ed. Michael D. Reagan (Glenview, Ill.: Scott Foresman, 1969) pp. 284–295.

Even this broad grant of authority would not be a serious problem if agency decisions were made in the open, if they were made after deliberation and debate, if the public had a chance to participate, and if there were checks or reviews of what was decided. Let's see how closely forest agency decisions parallel this model.

With only a few exceptions, the decisions of forest agencies are made wholly within each agency, without notice to or participation by the public. (The 1976 Sunshine Law should change this, however.) In the Forest Service, for example, specific decisions usually follow an upward route from local Forest Service officers who make proposals, through review at a regional level, to final approval in Washington. If the decision requires funds, it will also be reviewed by budget officials in the Department of Agriculture, by the Office of Management and Budget, and, ultimately, by Congress as part of the appropriation procedure.

Does this mean that no one but authorized bureaucrats gets a say? Not quite. Local rangers informally get opinions from civic organizations at the local level; the Service appoints national and regional advisory councils with which it consults from time to time; and on every level there are informal contacts with representatives of interest groups, public officials, and people who write in.

It sounds good, doesn't it—the informal rules of the agency do indeed seem to guarantee access. However, there is a problem, according to Reich. In none of the three forest agencies do the overall procedures provide an opportunity for the *general public* to participate. The close contact maintained with some outside people and groups is not equivalent to public participation. In fact, there are virtually *no formal public rights*.[22] These agencies give no general notice of pending decisions and provide no procedure by which the public can initiate proposals. This is because of a loophole in the Administrative Procedure Act. Somewhere in the legislation it says that the rule-making provisions do not apply to "any matter relating ... to public property." Also, the act says that where an action is clearly *rule-making*, an agency is not required to observe the act if it finds, for good cause, "that notice and public procedure are impracticable, unnecessary, or contrary to the public interest." The result is

[22] Since Charles Reich made these observations about citizen access to decision-making in federal land agencies, opportunities have increased. In addition to the 1976 Sunshine Law, the 1969 National Environmental Policy Act allows private citizens to take legal action to prevent federally funded projects from being implemented if they threaten an area's biological balance.

that particular groups are selected informally for contact, advice, and support, but the broader public point of view is not heard either informally or formally.

The access exceptions, however, are worth noting. If a proposed action would interfere with the contractual rights or other legally protected interests of a particular individual, the individual may ask for a reconsideration of the decision. There are formal procedures in this situation. However, this still confers no rights on the general public. A second exception is somewhat better in this respect. If an announced decision produces a loud enough clamor, an advisory hearing is held. In the Forest Service, these hearings are public and informal. The presiding officer is appointed by the regional forester. After the hearing, the presiding officer prepares a report containing a summary of the issues and the testimony. This is submitted to the Chief of the Service to assist in making a decision.

Something to think about

What should citizens do to maximize this access opportunity? What tactics would increase citizen influence and even power?

Informal hearings have advantages but, at the same time, disadvantages for citizens. The first reason for this is that there is *no procedure to provide detached judgment*. In the Forest Service, a proposal to establish or change a wilderness area is initiated by local Forest Service officials. These same officials are responsible for appointing the hearing officer who presides. The hearing officer reports the testimony to the chief, who, along with subordinates, was responsible for the original recommendation. The result is that one person (the Forest Service chief, in this case) acts as both an advocate and a judge. While this person may not consciously be biased or unfair, it is likely that his or her mind is already made up. This is not unusual human behavior.

A second disadvantage citizens experience in informal hearings is that there is no guarantee that anyone will listen to them. This may relate to the fact that there *is no formal rule requiring the agency head to explain why* a particular decision was made. Such a rule might compel more careful consideration of the various arguments advanced in the hearing. It also would give a reviewing officer some basis for determining whether a decision was well made.

354   Rules of the Executive Game

The third disadvantage suffered by citizens relates to the review procedure. In the Forest Service there is *no formal way for the public to participate in the review* of a decision. If they are dissatisfied, the public has no formal right to object to a decision and argue (at least in writing) before the chief of the Forest Service or the secretary of agriculture. So what ensures that the final decision was indeed made after genuine deliberation?

Well, citizens can always ask the courts to review the decision. Or can they? The Administrative Procedure Act says that judicial review is barred on any agency action that is "by law committed to agency discretion." We already know that Congress has given the three forest agencies broad discretion, placing many of its actions outside the authority of the courts. Thus, the courts may not be a vital resource for citizens seeking changes in some agency decisions.

What are the implications of all this? Reich puts it this way:

> Because the Forest Service, the Park Service, and the Bureau of Land Management, each of which represents a high standard of dedicated professional service, operate so largely without congressional direction, executive supervision, or public participation, the people lack real control over the management of their own land. Loss of control does not necessarily mean bad management; the management may be the finest possible. But the choices are not necessarily those of the people, and it is the core of the democratic faith that in the end only the people know their own best interests.

What all this means is the following: There are many points of access to executive games, but *who* has access and *how significant* it is often is left to the discretion of the agency involved. While specific statutes can compel citizen access, those laws granting broad authority to agencies rarely do that. In some cases, the Administrative Procedure Act will compensate and the 1976 Sunshine Law helps. They require citizen participation of various kinds. However, even then there is no guarantee if the particular administrative action falls within one of the two exempted rule-making areas.[23] Nor need it apply when an action is required for "interpretative rules, general statements of policy, or rules of agency organization, procedure, or practice," or when the agency for good cause finds "that notice and public

---

[23] These are (1) military and foreign affairs functions and (2) functions of agency management, personnel, contracts, loans, grants, benefits, or public property [5 U.S.C. § 553(a)].

procedure thereon are impracticable, unnecessary, or contrary to public interest" [5 U.S.C. § 533(b) (Supp. V)].[24]

Ultimately this major federal rule guaranteeing citizen access ends up assuring us that bureaucrats will have greater formal resources. Similar state rules tend to do the same. For citizens to use formal resources, however limited, they will have to approach the agency from a position of strength. That means getting themselves together and using the appropriate tactics. It can be done, as the next chapter reveals.

Key Words

Enumerated powers
Implied powers
National supremacy
Grants-in-aid
Revenue-sharing

Suggested Activities

1. Discover the degree to which citizens in your city participate in revenue-sharing decisions. What groups predominate in this process? How does the money get distributed?
2. Acquaint yourself with your state's laws giving citizens access to the executive decision-making process. What law most closely resembles the federal Administrative Procedure Act? To whom does it distribute advantages and disadvantages? Does your state have a Sunshine Law?
3. Attend a state or federal public hearing held in your city. Determine whether it was formal or informal and the kinds of groups that participated. While it may take some time, try to discover the result of the hearing.
4. Investigate the 1974–1975 public hearings on the Yosemite National Park master plan. How did they resemble or differ from the model of federal land decision-making described by Charles A. Reich?

24 Reich, "Bureaucracy and the Forests," p. 292.

12
Getting Through to Executives

How can you convince a student aid officer that you are eligible for a loan? What techniques will allow you to convince the governor to sign that day care bill? How do you get the public utilities commission to authorize lower rates?

Each answer requires knowing about the particular executive arena involved; the key players and their resources, both formal and informal; and the rules giving citizens access and those that distribute power. The previous two chapters provided some general information relevant to those answers. It is now necessary to understand specific access techniques.

Some of the ways of getting through to executives are not unusual. They can include any of the techniques of persuasion described in Chapters 5 and 6. The object is to influence people with authority, and executive players are just that.

Unlike legislative players, executive players at each level of government have vastly different resources and ultimately different power. Then too, executive arenas, even at the same level of government, are quite different. All this suggests that the approach chosen and tactics decided upon must be right for the specific decision maker and specific arena. It is not as simple as starting from the least costly tactic and working your way toward those requiring greater and greater resources.

With that warning, let's look at some of the approaches available and their accompanying tactics. They may be direct or indirect, electoral or pressure, normal or extraordinary. Let's begin with the direct and normal.

Direct Techniques

Communicating directly with public officials in the executive branch, we know, is the least costly form of influence. That communication can come in the form of one-to-one conversations, perhaps as an activist assists in drafting a regulation or convinces a "boss" to reinterpret a rule; in group conferences and advisory committees, as groups react to a proposed rule change; and in public hearings, as citizens try to initiate a change or respond to the way in which certain policies are being implemented. These techniques were introduced in the last chapter. They are really forms of lobbying. Whether they are engaged in by professional interest-group lobbyists or active citizens doesn't matter. They are tactics that often work.

Formal Complaint

One way of communicating directly that doesn't sound very serious, let alone effective, is writing one letter to an executive player who has the authority to make a decision. If the one letter skillfully uses a rule to convey its point, bureaucrats, acting in a quasi-judicial capacity, can effect a minor change. They may be compelled to.

Nicholas Johnson, former member of the Federal Communications Commission (FCC), says that to use this tactic effectively, individuals and groups should observe "the law of effective reform."

For him, this involves three things: asserting the factual basis for the grievance and the specific parties involved, specifying the legal principle that indicates relief is due (constitutional provision, statute regulation, or court or agency decision), and indicating the precise remedy sought (a new regulation, license revocation, an order to change practices, or a fine). Rather dramatically Johnson says, "When this principle is not understood, which is most of the time, the most legitimate public protests from thousands of citizens fall like drops of rain upon lonely and uncharted seas. But by understanding and using the right strategy the meekest among us can roll back the ocean." [1]

What Nicholas Johnson means by this statement is illustrated by two stories. In both cases, citizens were trying to curb or eliminate cigarette advertising in broadcasting. The situation prompting action was this: The health hazards of cigarette smoking were clear. The Surgeon General's report left little doubt about the dangers. Yet, despite this ominous report, and despite the warnings printed on cigarette packages, cigarette consumption increased.

Cigarette advertising on television was also increasing. This concerned some people. They were worried particularly about more and more teenagers picking up the habit that television told them was the road to sexual prowess and a fun-packed adult world. A Federal Trade Commission report emphasized this concern and deplored the impact of cigarette commercials. Citizens wrote hundreds of thousands of letters to everybody they could think of—members of Congress, the networks, advertisers, the FTC, and the FCC. Most people got replies; some did not. More important, nothing was done to resolve the problem.

Johnson believes these letters failed because they ignored the law of effective reform. "Vague feelings rather than facts were presented. The letters were not specific about who had done something wrong. They did not refer to any legal principle that had been violated. And, finally, they did not seek a precise remedy. Indeed, many such letters begin, 'Can't the FCC do something about . . . ?'. The answer is that it can't—or at least that it won't—until you tell it just what you want it to do." [2]

John Banzhaf, a New York lawyer in his twenties, wrote a different kind of letter. He called it a "fairness complaint." The offender named was a CBS-owned flagship station in New York City, WCBS. He complained that the station ran great quantities of cigarette commercials, then he referred to a legal principle, the "fairness doctrine." That part of the Communications Act essentially says that a broadcaster has an obligation to treat "controversial issues of public importance" fairly and to present all sides of such issues during the course of programming. John Banzhaf asked the FCC to enforce the regulation by ordering the station complained of to present the other point of view—the antismoking point of view.

---

[1] Nicholas Johnson, *How to Talk Back to Your Television Set* (Boston: Little, Brown and Company, 1967), p. 188.
[2] *Ibid.*, p. 189.

To the dismay of tobacco companies and broadcasters across the country, Mr. Banzhaf got through. Some $50 to $100 million worth of *free* antismoking commercials were soon being presented over radio and television. This rather simple letter containing a clear statement of the problem, rule, and goal produced a result that federal officials and hundreds of thousands of concerned citizens had been unable to bring about: Temporarily, at least, cigarette consumption in the nation declined for one of the first times in history.[3]

The point of this story, Nicholas Johnson reminds us, is not that one person can make a difference (although one person can and did), or even that a given rule is the magic solution to complaints. The point is that for each citizen grievance, whether formal or informal, there is a course of action suggested by this law of effective reform. In certain executive games it can bring the quickest and most thorough results in the most efficient and cheapest way.

Resignation

Getting what you want in executive games is not always that easy. Perhaps there is one crucial executive player who cannot be moved. Even after you have used a variety of normal lobbying tactics, he or she is still unresponsive. One alternative, although a difficult one to pull off, is removing the bureaucrat from office—at least from the office that bestows the particular authority. Sometimes, however, it becomes necessary.

Donald E. Johnson was an Iowa farm supply dealer. He was also a former national commander of the American Legion. In 1969 President Johnson appointed him Administrator of Veterans' Affairs.

Since he was one of their own, the American Legion supported the appointment and were generally satisfied with the way the Veterans Administration (VA) was operating. In 1974, however, the Vietnam veterans were not. Unlike the World War II veterans, who benefited from a GI Bill that covered all education costs at 89 percent of the schools in the country, the Vietnam veterans received (in 1974) a flat $220 per month, or $1,980 for the school year, to cover all expenses. Although they realized that Johnson was not responsible for establishing GI benefits, Vietnam veterans did think he should promote their point of view before Congress and the President. They tried to convince him of this.

Johnson disagreed; he said the Vietnam veterans had misunder-

[3] *Ibid.*, p. 190.

stood the purpose of the GI Bill. It was "to be an assistance to help in readjustment. It was never meant to be a full ride to go to school. If the Congress, representing the people, wants to change the philosophy behind the GI Bill, then they should ask for increased benefits on that basis." [4]

However, Johnson was being attacked for more than his failure to promote the Vietnam veterans' point of view. His administrative skills were being seriously questioned as well. GI Bill checks, vets charged, were consistently sent late, a disaster for those without other income. VA hospitals, according to some, were outdated and geared to provide custodial care to chronically ill older men, not to handle the drug problems, emotional disorders, and physical rehabilitation needs of the Vietnam veteran. Finally, it was argued, veterans were offered little assistance in finding jobs despite President Nixon's pledge that "the men who fought on the battle lines should not come back to job lines." In 1971 Congress had authorized the immediate hiring of 67 federal employment specialists to help young veterans get jobs, but by 1974 less than half those slots had been filled by the VA.[5]

For Johnson the direct heat started at a Nixon press conference. A Texas newsperson took the Nixon administration to task for the alleged inefficiencies of the VA, and particularly its chief. "He's not giving you the correct information," news reporter Sarah McClendon told the President. That was the cue. Media coverage of the statement prompted the less traditional veterans' organizations to act. One group after another contacted members of Congress. Their message was clear—Johnson must go. Soon, the veterans' supporters on Capitol Hill joined in. Their message was directed to the executive branch, which was in no position to resist. The Watergate crisis plus the unresolved charge by Sen. Alan Cranston (D., Calif.) that VA officials had pressured their underlings into making cash contributions to Nixon's 1972 re-election campaign made it uniquely vulnerable. That vulnerability plus the systematic pressure resulted in Johnson's resignation.

The resignation, of course, provided no guarantees for the future. The only hope was that the new chief would be sensitive to an additional constituency—the *Vietnam* veterans. If nothing more, that constituency had demonstrated clearly that they had some independ-

---

[4] "A Square Deal for Veterans? VA Chief Defends His Record," *Newsweek*, April 11, 1974, pp. 37–40.
[5] "Why the Vets Are Up in Arms," *Newsweek*, May 6, 1974, pp. 28–29.

ent clout. That fact couldn't be easily overlooked. Timing their actions to take advantage of executive department turmoil, in a limited way the Vietnam veterans won.

Indirect Techniques

The approach the Vietnam veterans used was a serious step, not a strategy selected carelessly. Such a step seriously damages an individual's reputation and may not in the end produce the desired result— a change in policy. The story that follows involved an equally serious strategy, and one even more costly in terms of resources. While the approach of the veterans primarily involved direct pressure on the executive branch, the recall approach to be described involved indirect pressure—going to citizen decision-makers in order to get executive action.

Recall

Brenda Brown is a housewife, around 30 years old, and in her words, "a political novice." Yet she and a number of other citizens in the tiny suburban community of Corte Madera, California, successfully organized a *recall* election in the winter of 1973. Removed from office were the mayor and two other members of the five-person town council.[6]

For Brenda, the story began when she agreed to be a member of the town's General Plan Study Committee. This was one of many committees in towns and cities throughout the state that were making recommendations on changes in master plans. It was a perfect opportunity for citizen action. However, Brenda and a number of other people who served on the committee or its subcommittees soon discovered that while *they* were taking the responsibility seriously, the mayor and his fellow council members were not. Each recommendation, arrived at after much time and study, was either rejected outright or "filed away."

Others in the town had experienced similar frustration. When petitions were circulated earlier and presented to the mayor and council, they were disregarded—"These issues are too complicated to be resolved by citizens." So the issues—the town's increasing population density and a proposed shopping center on nearby marshlands

---

[6] In this form of government, the mayor is elected by and is part of the town council.

—were dealt with without serious consideration of the citizens' point of view.

What could be done? These active citizens had really tried all the persuasive methods they knew about. However, someone knew about another, the recall. It was legal in their state. Of course, recall was a serious political move; it couldn't be accepted without realizing the implications. Feelings could be hurt, reputations might be damaged, and the town could become divided. Not necessarily, they concluded. If the issues were carefully explained, and if the tone of the campaign remained impersonal, it might be *good* for the town politically.

The number of people consulted about the possibility grew. A meeting of 20 led to a meeting of 60, which led to other meetings. These were mixed groups—not conservative, not liberal, just people angry about being ignored. Some citizens were concerned about environmental issues, others about economic and social ones, but they all had had enough. The decision was made. The mayor and the two other council members who appeared least responsive would be given a formal notice of intent to recall. Fortunately, there were a few lawyers in the group who made sure the state's recall guidelines were observed.

The first task of the campaign was to educate the other residents about the issues. There were four separate mailings before and after formal recall petitions were circulated. Part of the educational problem had nothing to do with the issues. Instead it concerned the method used. People were nervous about "recalling" public officials. It seemed radical or undemocratic. After various assurances, the message appeared to get through: This was a legal way of removing public officials through elections and perfectly "respectable" political activity. The more important issue, the failure of local public officials to be responsive to citizens, also got through.

Brenda, the coordinator of the recall campaign, believed residents were persuaded in very personal ways. While the mailed literature and newspaper articles helped, support grew mostly because a person's friend or neighbor was supporting the recall. Recognizing a name among those that were listed in pro-recall newspaper ads or a name that was on the petition being circulated helped Corte Maderans to develop confidence in the cause.

This was clear on the day of the election. The poll watchers, relying on information provided by canvassing, made sure that pro-recall residents voted. The turnout was large. The organizers' efforts paid off. The mayor and other two councilmen were turned out of office—all because they wouldn't listen to the people they were suppose to be representing.

In some respects, recalling a public official is a negative act.[7] It doesn't produce any positive policy. It provides no guarantees that the newly elected won't perform in the same way. Realizing this, the recall committee prepared for a second election to be held three months later. They would run their *own* candidates, people committed to citizen input. Again they were successful. Corte Madera had essentially a new town council and a new mayor.

Two years later the proposed shopping center that concerned many Corte Maderans had still not been built, serious efforts were underway to limit population density in certain parts of the town, and most important, citizens had become an integral part of the policy-making process. So out of that initial negative action, a recall, came a town government to which many people felt connected. The players were open to citizen influence.

In the case of the recall campaign, voters had the formal authority to influence executive actions. A more common approach to executive influence, one existing in all states, is using another institution to get the executive to budge. Going through legislatures or courts can be effective indirect techniques of influence. Those institutions, we know, have formal resources that may compel the executive branch to move a particular way.

Establishing a New Agency

One of the ways in which *legislatures* control the moves of executives is by altering their resources. This may involve changing the rules under which a particular department operates, disapproving a departmental budget request, or failing to approve the chief executive's nominee to direct the department. Still other ways in which legislatures can influence executive moves are by eliminating an agency, combining it with another, or establishing a new one that will affect the authority of related others.

These legislative actions may be the result of interest group pressure. Groups use one or more of these indirect approaches when direct pressure on executive players fails. This failure often occurs when a department, agency, or commission does not perceive a group as part of its ongoing constituency. With those groups that are thus

---

[7] Impeachment is a more serious step, frequently requiring at least a misdemeanor indictment.

perceived, the agency develops a mutual dependence that allows each side to get what it wants at least some of the time. That dependence can be established by interest groups in a variety of ways. One way is by being instrumental in the establishment of the agency.

Something to think about
What other actions can help groups become part of the ongoing constituency of an agency?

This has been the hope of consumer groups in this country. After attempting, without much success, to become part of the ongoing constituency of a variety of state and federal agencies, they have been trying a new approach. They want a federal agency of their own, one that would advocate the consumer point of view consistently.

The problem that led to this attempt has been documented by studies and personal accounts. First, the number of agencies that have some responsibility for consumer affairs is so large that consumer organizations can't keep track of their activities or focus organization efforts. For example, a 1969 *Congressional Quarterly* study found that at least 39 different agencies had responsibility for administering aspects of hundreds of federal laws. Often responsibility for a single law was split among several agencies. The Truth in Lending Act, part of the 1958 Consumer Credit Protection Act, to name one, is enforced by nine departments and agencies. Three different agencies enforce the Fair Packaging and Labeling Act of 1966.[8]

A second aspect of the problem, in addition to the diffusion of consumer efforts that comes from the involvement of so many agencies, is the lack of response from those agencies that are responsible. According to consumer advocate Ralph Nader, consumers are at a major disadvantage relative to industry. "Unlike corporations which have the money and power to control or influence federal agencies, individual consumers have none of these assets." A November 1974 decision by the Civil Aeronautics Board (CAB) illustrates this. That decision gave airlines permission to raise domestic air fares by 4 percent. In establishing that figure, Nader charged, the agency violated its own regulations by secretly bargaining with the airlines in their

---

[8] "Who Should Protect the Consumer: The White House; Justice Department; or an Independent Consumer Agency?", *Congressional Quarterly* (1970 Chronology), pp. 676–677.

*"Frankly, I keep forgetting what I'm with—the F.T.C.,
the F.P.C., the S.E.C., the F.C.C., or the F.A.A."*

Drawing by Dana Fradon; © 1974 The New Yorker Magazine, Inc.

bids for increases. "These hundreds of millions of dollars in costs to consumers were approved with no independent advocates of the consumer point of view as to whether a smaller increase, no increase, or even a decrease in fares to stimulate air travel was justified by economic conditions prevailing at that time." [9]

A 1974 study of the Federal Energy Administration makes the same point. Since the FEA adopted, at Common Cause's urging, a regulation requiring top policy makers to keep logs of their meetings, the public has, for the first time, a very precise picture of industry access. After analyzing these logs, Common Cause concluded that during a six-month period at the FEA (1974), 91 percent of Administrator Frank Zarb's meetings with outside groups had been with representatives of the energy industry. Over the same six-month period, the FEA's top 10 officials held 458 meetings with nongovernmental representatives. Only 6 percent of these were nonbusiness groups such as consumer and environmental organizations, state conservation agencies, educators working on consumer projects, and so on.

While it is natural and proper for FEA officials to meet frequently with the industry they regulate, the logging requirement reveals how rarely they meet with anyone but the industry concerned.[10]

So this is the problem, according to consumers. The strategy, they knew, would be difficult to implement, but the congressional battle was launched in 1970.

The players were easily identified. The opposition was led by the U.S. Chamber of Commerce. In fact, the Chamber labeled preventing the establishment of an independent agency "a top-priority issue." Their strategy was to deflect consumers' charges that they were "the enemy" by supporting a different approach to consumer protection. They argued that consumer functions should be transferred to the White House adviser's office.[11] In essence, they wanted a statutory office of consumer affairs in the White House, whose head would be authorized to appear as a witness—not a party—in proceedings of other agencies. In addition, the Chamber argued, the Federal Trade Commission should be revitalized to defend consumers more effectively.[12] The National Association of Manufacturers (NAM) was

[9] "Hearings: Nader vs. Industry," *Congressional Quarterly*, March 1, 1975, p. 443.
[10] "Executive Agencies in CC Spotlight," *In Common: The Common Cause Report from Washington*, April–May 1975, p. 3.
[11] This was an office created in 1964 by executive action. The office chief is called the special assistant for consumer affairs.
[12] "Who Should Protect the Consumer," pp. 676–677.

less in the mood for compromise. They objected to any and all consumer agency legislation. So why did the proponents (the Consumer Federation of America, Ralph Nader's Congress Watch, and the Consumer Committee of the AFL-CIO) reject this compromise? Their view was that a White House office, even a statutory one, would just be more of the same. Consumer interests would again be pitted against the interests of business and other special interests, for the nature of the White House is to accommodate diverse views as it formulates and coordinates policy. The proponents wanted something quite different, a *partisan* advocate to represent the buyers of goods and services without taking into consideration the positions of those other groups. The agency, they believed, should be free to oppose *any* policy it felt was detrimental to consumers.

The philosophical conflict was clear. However, between 1970 and 1975 the preservation of the status quo meant a victory for the opposition. In 1970, for example, a consumer protection agency bill was passed in the Senate but was killed by the House Rules Committee. In 1971, the House approved a new, rather weak, version, but the Senate leadership in 1972 was forced to shelve their stronger measure. They could not, even after three attempts, shut off the filibuster against the bill. The last attempt failed by three votes. The 1974 battle was more of the same. The House passed a strong version of the bill, after rejecting an administration-backed substitute that would have curbed sharply the new agency's powers. The Senate, however, again could not overcome the filibuster, even after four tries. On the last cloture attempt, the proponents were two votes short. It was only in 1975 that the climate seemed right. Not only was the filibuster easily broken, but the bill establishing an Agency for Consumer Advocacy passed overwhelmingly. This was not the case in the House, however. While the bill passed 208 to 199, the vote was not enough to override a probable veto by President Ford. The President's opposition was related to his unwillingness to add to the size of the federal bureaucracy.

So that, in summary, is the history. Establishing a new executive agency that will assure access is not always easy, particularly when that access might disrupt the present distribution of power. However, even tactics associated with failure can be instructional. They provide some interesting clues as to why the status quo has prevailed for so long.

A major reason for the continuing failure of the bill was the power the filibuster gave to a few senators. Each attempt, except the last, to invoke cloture demonstrated substantial support for the consumer agency, but it wasn't enough. The tactics used to break the filibuster were countered with comparable tactics from the other side. Only, the crucial rule was on the opponent's side; their task was easier. Essentially both sides focused on the senators believed to be *uncommitted* on a cloture attempt. In the 1974 battle, they numbered about 16. While the Chamber of Commerce used a computerized mailing system to generate letters (and personal visits) from its national membership, the Consumer Federation relied on a Wide Area Telephone Service (WATS) long-distance line to mobilize their membership at the local level. Simultaneously each side was *directly* lobbying the undecided.[13]

Weapons used in these persuasive efforts included, for the proponents, the various studies indicating the inadequate representation of consumer interests, and for the opponents, a public-opinion poll. The poll, conducted by Opinion Research Corporation of Princeton, New Jersey, found that only 10 percent of those questioned favored "setting up an additional consumer protection agency over all the others." The overwhelming number of respondents (75 percent) wanted to make the agencies we now have more effective. Realizing the potential impact of this survey, the opponents timed and staged its release carefully.

The poll's impact was probably reduced, however, by the immediate reaction from consumer groups. They countered that the questions on the poll were distorted to produce a negative response and to exploit public ignorance about the proposed agency. More directly, the Consumer Federation of America asked for and received an agreement by the Senate Government Operations Permanent Investigations Subcommittee to investigate whether such commissioned polls violated the law against deceptive trade policies. They pointed out that few people realized that the poll had been commissioned by the Business Roundtable, a lobby group of executives of large corporations.[14] So much for the dramatic effect of polls!

Another reason for the preservation of the status quo was that until 1975, the White House had been persuaded to stay out of the fight, or at least to cloud its opposition. For example, in 1974, while Virginia H. Knauer, presidential special assistant for consumer affairs,

---

[13] "Consumer Protection: Mismatch of Lobbyists," *Congressional Quarterly*, July 20, 1974, p. 1873.
[14] *Ibid.*

urged support for a strong bill, Office of Management and Budget Director Roy L. Ash appeared to favor torpedoing the measure. In fact, Ralph Nader uncovered a secret White House memo to Ash from top presidential lobbyist William E. Timmons. The memo urged Ash to signal a probable veto from the administration.[15] Carol Tucker Foreman, executive director of the Consumer Federation of America, viewed the White House's stance as the most important reason for the bill's continuing defeat. If it had not been for "the ominous silence of the White House regarding the agency," those few more votes needed to achieve cloture between 1972 and 1974 would have been there.

To counter the effects of the cloture rule and the Presidents' (both Nixon and Ford) disinclination to support a strong bill, the proponents knew they would have to agree to some substantial compromises. One of the most important, which dismayed business groups, was a concession to labor. The only way the pro-agency people could get the necessary support from the AFL-CIO was to bar the proposed agency from intervening in labor-management disputes or agreements such as those handled by the National Labor Relations Board or the Federal Mediation and Conciliation Service. They agreed to this provision in spite of the position of many consumer advocates that unions, on their own and in collusion with employers, frequently disregard the public interest, pushing up prices or limiting competition.

However, not all the concessions were to labor. A 1974 compromise amendment specified that the new agency would be prevented from seeking information directly from businesses. Instead, it would have to channel its questionnaires through the regular agencies. This was to prevent the harassment that business feared. In addition, the Senate-passed version of 1975 was designed to increase support from the broadcast media. The agency would be prevented from participating in FCC decisions regarding broadcast license renewals. Finally, to discourage a presidential veto, backers of the bill did something else. They included a wholesale reshuffling of the present federal consumer bureaucracy—a move designed to save taxpayers $10 million a year. This action came in the form of a last-minute amendment to the bill.

All this was done just to create an executive agency that would

---

[15] "House Approves Compromise Consumer Protection Bill," *Congressional Quarterly*, April 6, 1974, p. 898.

clearly represent the interests of consumers. It has been a long battle. The techniques have included preparing and circulating studies supporting the need for such an agency; lobbying directly and indirectly the undecided senators, particularly those who could break the persisting filibuster; countering immediately the opposition's public-opinion poll; and finally, giving up (it's called compromising) those issues preventing them from winning. Yet as of the summer of 1976 the techniques had not worked. They don't always, even when they are well planned and coordinated. A major opposing player had a resource difficult to match—the veto.

Something to think about
Strategically, what should proponents do next?

Taking Judicial Action
The *courts* are the other institution that can influence executive moves. They can declare an executive appointment illegal, force the release of impounded money, declare an executive decision in violation of the law, and force the law to be applied when it isn't. These actions also are frequently the result of citizen action. The courts only act in response to a suit. Both individuals and groups, if they follow the rules of litigation, can initiate these.

However, judicial actions require special resources. Money to hire a lawyer who understands executive games and endless patience are only two. In addition, for ordinary citizens, there is a special liability:

> The courts have been so reluctant to second-guess agency decisions that an entire, course-length body of law has sprung up to describe the "standing" and "ripeness" required to sustain a complainant's petition for review. When regulatory decisions are overruled at the judicial level, it is almost always at the behest of an aggrieved company or trade group. They alone have the legal resources, the detailed knowledge of agency decisions, and the common interest necessary to launch a costly and extended litigation.[16]

In spite of the disadvantages of this approach, sometimes it is the only remaining choice. This was the situation in Philadelphia in 1969.

---

[16] Richard C. Leone, "Public Interest Advocacy and the Regulatory Process," *The Annals of the American Academy of Political and Social Science*, March 1972, p. 49.

A citizens' advisory committee believed their rights had been violated, and they decided to sue. The defendants were the city and the federal department of Housing and Urban Development (HUD).

The reason for the suit was the failure of the mayor of Philadelphia and HUD to properly implement the Demonstration Cities and Metropolitan Act, more commonly referred to as the Model Cities Program. The legislation had been designed to improve the quality of poor neighborhoods through *decentralized* planning. That is, instead of federal bureaucrats and legislators designing and implementing programs, control was to be local. Public officials, the residents of poverty areas, and representatives of private service agencies were to join together to deal with community problems *they* defined as important. The federal government would pay the bills.

However, the legislation didn't say that power should be equally dispersed among these players. On the contrary, while "widespread participation" of citizens was to be encouraged, local public officials were to have the authority to approve or disapprove the projects to be forwarded to HUD. This authority was the result of intense lobbying by mayors who were still angry about their tenuous control over the community action programs that had been established by the earlier Economic Opportunity Act.

Some citizens in Model Cities Programs didn't like the fact that they had so little power. In Philadelphia, for example, a broad-based coalition of active community organizations that called itself the Area Wide Council (AWC) attempted to share that power. Specifically, the members of the AWC acted on the assumption that they had a partnership with City Hall. Programs, they believed, would be jointly planned and administered. For a while, City Hall cooperated, perhaps because the AWC was so highly organized, cohesive, and determined.

Then things got out of hand—or at least, city officials and the incoming Nixon administration thought so. The new HUD leadership was receiving too many reports of trouble from "overzealous" citizen groups threatening the position of city governments. That broad statement about "widespread participation" would have to be clarified. In April of 1969, HUD issued a more precise rule about citizen participation. Thereafter, citizen participation in all Model Cities Programs was to be limited to *advisory roles*. Control would remain in the hands of city officials. The implications of this rule clarification were that if such community coalitions as Philadelphia's Area Wide Council didn't like the city's point of view, funds for programs would no longer be filtered through them, and their authority to represent poverty-area residents would be withdrawn.

The Philadelphia Area Wide Council didn't like the terms, nor did they like being bypassed on decisions. They decided to challenge the interpretation of the rule. In June 1969 they took the city and HUD to court. This was their explanation:

> We want to tell you right off that the AWC is no longer recognized by the power structure as being in the Model Cities business. HUD and the city foreclosed on us in May 1969 because they got up-tight about the degree of power we managed to achieve over the program.
>
> If only we knew two years ago what we now know about city and federal politics, it might have been a different story. But we were political novices, and they [the establishment] were experts in political chicanery. We were trying to change things, and they were trying to keep us boxed in. It's so much harder to bring about change than it is to sit there and resist it. They had the upper hand, particularly the money and the sophisticated methods for maximum feasible manipulation.
>
> As long as we were able to centralize the community's demands for change, the city feared us, and we were able to achieve stunning victories. When they finally managed to splinter us, we lost the only real power we had—people power. . . .[17]

The splintering of the AWC didn't matter as much in the judicial arena. The game here is very different. While money and time are important, the law is the crucial resource. The law specified, according to the plaintiffs, that citizen participation was an important requirement of the legislation establishing the Model Cities Program. They presented evidence that HUD and the city of Philadelphia had violated this requirement when they changed the local program without the participation of the citizens of the target area.

Two and a half years later, after two defeats at the federal district court level, the Third Circuit Court of Appeals delivered its opinion. The court upheld the claim of the AWC and called for its reinstate-

---

[17] This is a statement by the North City Area Wide Council of Philadelphia as told to Sherry R. Arnstein, "Maximum Feasible Manipulation," *Public Administration Review*, Special Issue, September 1972, p. 378. Philadelphia city officials responded to this assessment and criticism by emphasizing their difference in viewpoint. The city saw the role of citizens as one of influence, while the AWC saw it as one of power. Ultimately, the officials' belief that the program was being badly administered by the AWC prompted the City Hall–appointed manager to assert his control. See "The View from City Hall," *Public Administration Review*, Special Issue, September 1972, pp. 393–394.

ment as the citizen participation organization for the Philadelphia Model Cities Program. It was a hollow victory. By this time the AWC was only a skeleton organization, existing entirely to pursue its claim in court. Ultimately time had been on the side of the defendants. Their loss was a win for HUD and the city.

Something to think about
Did this court action produce *any* direct gain for the plaintiffs or indirect gain for other citizens?

In the situation just described, it was clear that the plaintiffs had a gripe. They felt they had been "injured" in some way. Usually, unless the court believes a person or group has sustained a direct personal injury, that person or group will not be granted *standing* to sue. There is a way around this rule, however. By using *taxpayer suits* citizens can force executive players to make different moves. As a taxpayer, the citizen can sue, in effect, even if he or she was only indirectly injured.

Wait a minute. What does one sue about? All kinds of governmental actions are subject to challenge. The most common include challenges to the increasing state and local government exercises of the *right of eminent domain*, a right that allows private property to be condemned for public use; challenges to the various methods of *bond financing*; and challenges to the particular way in which *contracts for public projects* have been awarded.[18]

If a person isn't a taxpayer, is this technique precluded? The general rule is that where tax payments exceed a *de minimus* level, any taxpayer may bring a taxpayer's suit. "Where the expense . . . is too trifling to constitute an injury to a taxpayer, such expenditure does not offer a basis for an equitable proceeding." (*Ryan* v. *City of Chicago*, 1938) In most states the de minimus requirement would probably be interpreted to allow payers of various forms of excise and income taxes to bring taxpayer suits. In fact, very few judges are even concerned with the question of who is a taxpayer.[19]

If taxpayer suits can be brought by those who pay very few taxes and if the objective may have little to do with a tax increase, what is

[18] "Taxpayers' Suits: A Survey and a Summary," *Yale Law Journal*, April 1960, pp. 907–908.
[19] *Ibid.*, p. 905.

the purpose of this kind of suit? Actually, it is to enable a large body of the citizenry to challenge a governmental action that would otherwise go unchallenged in the courts because of the personal injury requirement. It also has an interesting positive side effect. It extends the concept of judicial review by allowing numerical minorities ineffective at the ballot box or disadvantaged in traditional pressure politics to invalidate statutes or ordinances on constitutional grounds and to force bureaucrats to do their job differently.

All this sounds fine, but what about the cost? A successful taxpayer-plaintiff can usually recover costs, such as filing fees and service fees. However, the plaintiff may not recover what is probably the greatest expense, attorney's fees. Citizens with very few financial resources may have to rely on a federally funded legal services lawyer to use this technique. However, in a handful of states (Arizona, Ohio, and South Dakota), the law allows a successful taxpayer of whatever means to recover reasonable attorney's fees from the municipal or state government.[20]

As important as the taxpayer suit may appear to be as a way to influence executive games, it cannot be used everywhere. While most states (34) and almost every municipality can become defendants, the *federal government cannot*, unless the issue is *clearly* a constitutional one. In 1923, Miss Frothingham made this discovery. She had alleged that a federal grant-in-aid program aimed at reducing maternal and infant mortality was unconstitutional and that expenditures under the program would, by increasing her burden of future federal taxes, constitute a taking of property without due process of law. In Massachusetts (*Frothingham* v. *Mellon*) the court dismissed the contention on the grounds that the taxpayer's interest was so remote that her suit presented no justifiable case or controversy within the meaning of Article III of the Constitution.[21] So, for federal executive games, as Miss Frothingham discovered, the taxpayer suit is not easy to use, but in state and local ones, clearly, it is important.

Recall, resignation, executive reorganization, formal complaints, and court actions—all these ways of getting through to executive players are *normal*. They are consistent with people's expectations about how one should play executive games, in spite of the fact that they go beyond the more common forms of persuasion. However, the executive branch is not exempt from *extraordinary* techniques of in-

20 *Ibid.*, p. 914.
21 *Ibid.*, p. 916.

fluence. Sometimes these indirect techniques are used by the least likely citizen players.

Protesting Rules

It was a beautiful weekend in the San Francisco Bay Area, the kind of weekend that might make you want to drive to the wine country or to the Mendocino Coast, but no one was driving anywhere that weekend. Between September 21 and September 24, 1973, 90 percent of all gasoline stations in northern California were shut down. In addition, during that weekend and the next, there were shutdowns in other parts of the country. In Seattle, Tacoma, and Olympia, Washington, 65 to 70 percent of the gasoline stations were closed. In Houston, 60 percent were shut down. Stations in St. Louis and northern Indiana also participated.

Now gasoline dealers are hardly rebel types. They usually go quietly about their business of pumping gas and offering customer services. What prompted this action? What prompted one of the most effective shutdowns this country has seen in recent years?

It was an executive decision. President Nixon's Cost of Living Council (CLC) had announced its Phase IV guidelines. (The guidelines were designed to deal with the country's inflation.) Among its decisions was one that prevented gasoline dealers from raising the price of gasoline to customers. Simultaneously, however, the Cost of Living Council did not prevent the oil companies from raising the prices they charged dealers. This was the dealers' gripe.

At first, no one dared to voice the idea of a shutdown. That would be too radical. Rather, petitions were circulated, members of Congress were visited, and telegrams were sent to the President. Judicial and legislative actions were also taken. The National Congress of Petroleum Retailers appealed the CLC decision in court, and remedial legislation was introduced in Congress. They were playing the traditional game, using only normal tactics.

Nothing happened, or at least nothing that satisfied the dealers' sense of fair play. The situation was growing more serious. Other tactics were considered. Interest in a limited work stoppage was growing. Could they pull it off?

Dealers recognized they had at least two things going for them: sympathetic media coverage and, not unrelated, sympathetic customers. Their cause was perceived as just. The time seemed right for action.

To play this game successfully, however, they had to follow some rules. A formal one, the Sherman Antitrust Act, precludes agreements between two or more persons to, among other things, restrain trade. Thus, any decision about a shutdown would have to be purely individual. Still, the pressure was on. As one dealer put it the night before the stoppage, "If I go past an open station in the morning, I will be very disappointed." A second rule was informal: Maintain the support of the public and press. Station operators spent the weekend before explaining their position to any customer willing to listen. Members of the press were kept informed by an association representative whose job was to help them "feel" the dealers' position. The supportive coverage would follow.

Something to think about
What kind of media coverage would this be? Why would it be effective?

It worked. Two decisions followed. The first was to allow a 1 to 2 cent increase in pump prices. That wasn't enough, according to the dealers, and the pressure continued. Finally, after a 3½-month battle, dealers got essentially what they wanted. Effective at noon on October 15, 1973, the CLC announced that dealers could adjust their ceiling price to reflect increased wholesale prices.[22]

Let's take a look at the elements of the victory. What allowed the dealers to win? First, they had an issue that was understandable and had the potential to generate widespread support. Second, the tactic was used throughout the country. Although its effectiveness varied, the stoppage got the attention of the media, citizens, and public officials in different geographic areas. More than a few members of Congress were feeling the heat, and a President with a nationwide mandate couldn't easily be indifferent. Third, there was no active opposition to the dealers' demands. While the CLC members were identified as opponents, they didn't conduct any kind of educational campaign to explain their decision, and they were not independent. The President, responding to widespread legislative and citizen pressure, could and did get them to budge. They had no independent source of power; there were no groups available to rally to their support.

[22] The dynamics of this strategy were revealed in a 1973 interview with Robert Moore, executive secretary of the California Petroleum Retailers Association.

Under what conditions might dealers have failed? If the shutdown had lasted longer and/or had been 100 percent effective, citizen support might have weakened. Sustained inconvenience and in some cases actual physical or economic hardship could have produced this result. A presidential sales job might also have resulted in failure. If President Nixon had been willing to use all his resources to build support for the CLC decision, the dealers' position would have suffered. However, none of these things occurred. As a result, players who were inexperienced in protest politics but frustrated, organized, and committed to their position won an important executive game.

Whether direct or indirect, what most of these ways of getting through to executives have in common is that they are never used as a first course of action. Instead, they are used by citizens unable to influence executive games through more usual strategies and tactics. They are used by citizens who have given up on less costly forms of persuasion. Still, don't be misled. Such tactics as lobbying, letter-writing, publicity, and testifying at hearings all work under certain conditions, and the lessons learned by examining their application to legislative games can be appropriately applied to executive ones. Yes, executive players can be moved, Mrs. Gravely.

Key Words

Recall
Taxpayers' suit

Suggested Activities

1. Design a strategy for influencing a top-level appointed bureaucrat that would *not* involve the threat or reality of job loss.
2. Determine which interest groups are part of the ongoing constituency of each Cabinet department at the federal level. Does the connection *help* explain the relative power of departments?
3. If you believed you were eligible for food stamps but were unable to get them, what could you do to get yourself declared eligible?

VI
Judicial Games

13
About Judicial Games

An Introduction to the Arena

Charles Baker, a black man in his forties, has worked half his life for the Campbell Soup Company in Chicago. He is still a relatively low-paid factory worker; by any realistic standards, he and his family are poor.

Nevertheless, Baker was able to save a little money, and, a few years ago, he welcomed the opportunity offered by a realtor selling small row houses on Chicago's West Side. Baker was told he needed only to make a down payment of a few hundred dollars and sign a contract for additional monthly payments to the realtor. He could rent out half of the house to help make these payments. After several years, the realtor promised, Baker would qualify to get a mortgage loan and could begin buying title to the home.

Only later did Baker find out that he had been tricked, along with hundreds of his black neighbors in the crowded West Side section of Lawndale. Dishonest real estate operators had doubled the prices of the small houses on the contracts the families signed and then charged exorbitant interest on top of that. Most Lawndale families wound up owing four times the real value of their homes, and eventually they were told they had little chance of ever qualifying for the mortgage loans necessary actually to purchase title.

The experience was not altogether new for the families of Lawndale. They had been cheated before in the ghetto—by slum landlords in the rundown tenements from which they had come, credit clothing and appliance merchants who gouged them on installment payments for inferior goods, insurance companies that charged everyone in that part of the city higher rates, and countless others. The low-income blacks had come to expect such treatment and had learned to live with it.

But this time they were offered unexpected hope of redress. Young Jesuit novices working at a Lawndale parish persuaded Baker and his neighbors to fight back in court, where all Americans are promised justice. Together, they formed the Contract Buyers League and sued the realtors and their financial backers for fraud and racial discrimination. For months, the court suit dragged on while Lawndale residents continued to make their monthly payments.

Finally, Baker and other Contract Buyers League leaders decided to refuse to pay any more, in an attempt to force the realtors to renegotiate their contracts immediately. But, as soon as the payments stopped, the realtors simply went to court to evict for nonpayment the scores of families who were withholding their monthly installments. Baker and his neighbors then returned to court to ask the judge to prevent their eviction on the grounds that the realtors had no right to charge them so much in the first place and that they had sold the houses under false pretenses. The Lawndale residents wanted the judge to sanction their holdout so that the realtors would be forced to bargain. Their day in court, however, turned out to be shattering.

"I had the privilege to see how the courts operate, and it's terrible," Baker said after his experience inside the towering new glass and steel courthouse in Chicago. "If you're behind on your note and want to explain, forget it. They only want your name, address, and to ask, 'Are you behind on your payments?' "

Baker and others asked for an opportunity to explain to a jury why they thought the realtors were acting illegally. But the judge ruled in every case that the law was clearly on the realtors' side and that nothing was left for a jury to decide. The Lawndale families must pay up or lose their homes, he ordered.

"The judge operated by the law," Baker said later. "And the law evicts poor people from their homes." [1]

This story of Charles Baker and the Contract Buyers League begins to tell us something about judicial games. Specifically, it suggests their purpose and ingredients.

Judicial games settle conflicts between two or more people. Some-

[1] Leonard Downie, Jr., *Justice Denied* (New York: Penguin Books, 1971), pp. 72–74. © 1971 Praeger Publishers, Inc. Reprinted by permission.

times the conflicts are between private parties such as the Contract Buyers League and the Realtors. At other times they are between individuals and a government agency. Then too, they may be between two government agencies. Always, for a dispute to be settled in court, someone must have been harmed in some way and be able to show it, and there must be some form of relevant law to help settle the dispute.

What about that relevant law? The first time the Contract Buyers League tried to sue the Realtors, their case was accepted in court. There is a body of law dealing with fraud and racial discrimination. However, the second time they went to court, to ask the judge to prevent their eviction, they discovered they had no case. The judge ruled that there was no law protecting tenants evicted for their particular reasons.

The Types and Functions of Law

The law operating in this country is of several types. *Civil law* consists of statutes generally regulating conduct between private persons. It is the result of legislative activity on the national, state, or local level. Those activities that are the subject of civil law include such things as contracts, domestic relations, business relations, estates, and labor practices. The government may also be involved in civil actions. The federal Equal Employment Opportunity Commission, for example, may sue a private company for failing to comply with federal antidiscrimination laws, or a citizen may sue the department of Health, Education and Welfare for failing to distribute certain congressionally authorized benefits.

If the subject of a conflict is how the government is organized, the extent of governmental powers, or the character of individual rights, *constitutional law* is used to resolve it. That law is expressed in either the U.S. Constitution or state constitutions. If there is a conflict between the U.S. Constitution and a statute, the U.S. Constitution prevails. It is the supreme law of the land.

Common law is a third type. It is judge-made law. It develops as decisions are reapplied to similar situations and is the basis of legal reasoning in most states. While many statutes grow out of common-law decisions, if there should be a conflict, the statute prevails.

One particular kind of *statutory* law is *criminal law*. It defines crimes and provides punishments for violations. In their jurisdictions, both national and state governments have a body of criminal law, but most of the laws exist at the state level. Major categories include homicide, burglary, larceny, fraud, rape, and assault. Unlike civil law, the government is *always* a party to criminal action. A public prosecutor files all criminal charges.

The law, regardless of type, gets developed because societies develop a set of "shoulds." Two of the shoulds operating in the case brought by the Contract Buyers League were (1) people should represent their claims truthfully (to fail to do so may result in a conviction for fraud), and (2) in public matters, people should treat all races equally (to fail to do so may result in a finding of discrimination).

Something to think about
What were the shoulds operating for the Realtors?

These shoulds, of course, are based on what a society values: the protection of property, freedom of religion, individual liberty, equality, and so on. However, not all values are given equal weight in law. A particularly preferred one, as Charles Baker discovered, is the protection of private property. Law professor Jerome E. Carlin says that the law has historically "been oriented toward the protection of property" and the protection of those who hold property and economic power. Subsequently, it "benefits and protects sellers over buyers, lenders over borrowers, and landlords over tenants." For example, a tenant's obligation to pay rent has always been independent of any contractual obligation of a landlord to provide decent housing. A creditor need only prove the existence of a debt, not its legitimacy, to collect it. A seller does not have to prove that a product or service is what the buyer expected—or even that it has any worth at all—to exercise the right to payment. It is the tenant, the debtor, or the buyer who must prove that he or she has been wronged and who must bear the burden and cost of proof.[2]

To go back to the relationship between shoulds and law, shoulds are really society's *norms*. Law is simply a way of formalizing them. Without them, there would be no judicial games, for there would be no standards by which to resolve disputes.

Laws, however, also serve other functions. They help, for example,

[2] *Ibid.*, pp. 76–77.

to maintain some sort of social order: they allow each person to generally predict the behavior of others. How would it be if you were to drive down a street and not know what to expect from other drivers? Then too, laws perpetuate established ethical standards: "Make divorce legally difficult, because divorce is wrong." In this case the function of law is to promote a particular quality and view of life.

Not all communities or states, of course, share the same norms. So one state will allow gambling and prostitution, while another state will not. One state will call smoking marijuana a felony, while another state classifies it as a misdemeanor. This is possible because we have 51 different sets of formal norms (laws) operating in this country—50 state sets and 1 federal set. This requires 51 different court systems. It suggests the variety of judicial games to be played.

Special Words to Understand

If one decides to play, if all other remedies have been exhausted, then there are some words that must be understood. They describe generally what goes on in a game and who the players are.

The *plaintiff* is the individual or group who first institutes the game by filing certain papers with a court clerk. In criminal cases, the *prosecutor* for the jurisdiction (county, state, or nation) is the plaintiff. The papers that pass between the parties in a dispute constitute the *pleadings*. Included in the pleadings is the *complaint*, which sets forth the facts upon which the cause of action is based. In it the plaintiff and defendant are identified. The *defendant* is the individual against whom the complaint is directed. The strategy and tactics of the case are decided by the *counsel* for each side—the attorney who represents each client's point of view. The *case*, of course, is the legal dispute itself. The *trial* is the initial consideration of the case by a tribunal. Held in a courtroom, the trial involves examining specific events associated with the case. These are the *facts* of the situation. In this country, trials must be public and, when criminal, started without unreasonable delay. In addition, they are to be presided over by an impartial *judge*. The judge maintains order in the court; he or she sometimes decides the case and at other times instructs the jury. The *jury* is an impartial body that sits in judgment of charges brought. It considers the facts, the law, and sometimes the punishment. Juries may be waived by the accused, in which case the judge will decide the *verdict*. A favorable verdict is what players want to win in judicial games. It ends the dispute in question, unless the losing side *appeals* the decision to a higher court.

Something to think about
How can some of these words be applied to the Contract Buyers
League case?

Another word used to describe judicial games in this country takes
more explanation. They are always *adversary* proceedings. That is,
they are proceedings during which each opposing player presents one
side of the case and does everything possible to refute the opposition's
position. This is very different from other institutional games, for it
produces *only one winner*. Of course, outside the official arena, compromise can occur. In criminal cases negotiation and bargaining take
place before the trial begins. The prosecutor and the attorney for the
defendant are directly involved. In civil cases, this can continue during the trial, but outside of court. In this case the attorneys for each
side discuss terms.

If the game *in court* produces only one winner, will justice be
served? What gets left out? Under this adversary system a challenge
to a zoning law brought by neighbors who are resisting a public housing project cannot easily be resolved by a compromise. The judge or
jury cannot consider or decide on alternative land uses. They can't
suggest, for example, that another piece of land be used for the public housing project and the disputed land be used for a shopping center. In an adversary system of justice this is against the rules of the
game.[3]

In addition to precluding compromise, this adversary system of
justice may not reveal all the relevant facts. "Lazy, incompetent, uninterested, or corrupt lawyers may not unearth all the needed evidence. Highly competent lawyers may conceal some valuable facts.
Elements of surprise, 'coached witnesses,' or simply the expenditure of
money may affect the quality and completeness of factual evidence." [4]
Of course, the judge may independently participate in questioning
witnesses or request an attorney to find more facts, and the jury must
assess the credibility of witnesses, but generally, both types of players are more passive recipients of the facts.[5]

---

[3] Herbert Jacob discusses this limitation in *Justice in America*, 2d ed. (Boston:
Little, Brown and Company, 1972), p. 15.
[4] Jay A. Sigler, *An Introduction to the Legal System* (Homewood, Ill.: The Dorsey Press, 1968), p. 122.
[5] *Ibid.*

Something to think about

How might the adversary nature of judicial games influence a person's decision to use the judicial arena?

Winning

All these special words help to describe the judicial game. They are part of the natural vocabulary of players. Ultimately, of course, as with any game, the key thing to understand is how to win, how to get a favorable verdict. That understanding comes with knowing what influences the moves of key players, the rules of access and power, and the possible strategies and tactics. Before examining the ingredients of a win, one should realize that judicial wins are quite different from those in other political games.

One difference has to do with the score. Usually the decision applies only to the case considered. It is unlikely to create any precedent or establish any new norms. In fact, the judge will probably not even write an opinion explaining the decision. So, if that kind of win is satisfactory, then the judicial game is suitable.

Gradually, however, individual cases can produce victories that have a broader scope. As social conditions and the political culture change, judges begin to interpret the law in different ways. Without even perceiving it, judges may gradually establish new norms and, ultimately, new law. This in fact has happened in the areas of criminal justice, divorce, personal injury litigation, and labor disputes.

Sometimes, though not often, a judge may produce dramatic changes through just one decision. A judge can quite consciously interpret statutes or the Constitution in a new way. In these instances the judge is explicitly making *policies*. The published opinions accompanying the decisions reveal the intent. Ordinarily, however, this occurs only in courts of appeal.

Players cannot go to court assuming that the judge will create a new policy. Not only is the decision more likely to be narrow in scope, but the judge may not even accept the case. The justices of the U.S. Supreme Court, for example, wanted nothing to do with making policy about the war in Vietnam. In 1970, when they had an opportunity, they refused to rule on its constitutionality. This is consistent with their general disinclination to get involved in foreign affairs.

Another difference in judicial games is that the outcome is frequently more ambiguous than that of legislative or executive games.

This is especially true when judges create new policy. The reason has to do with judicial decision-making. Courts make policies only in response to the particular case being considered. While judges may intend their decision to apply to many similar situations, that intention is usually not clear until after other cases have been decided and the new doctrine has been extended to them. This is what is occurring in the area of obscenity. Beginning in 1957 with *Roth* v. *United States*, the Supreme Court, while apparently making policy, has with each subsequent case qualified the meaning of obscenity. As of 1975 the intention of the court was still not clear.[6]

Of course, legislative and executive policy is not always clear either, but for a different reason. Neither a legislature nor an executive makes policy on the basis of a single situation or an undefined precedent.

So if judicial wins are usually narrow in scope and if, especially when broad, they are frequently ambiguous, why bother? Individuals and groups "bother" when there is no other choice—when the dispute cannot be suitably settled through other games or when other institutional players refuse to deal with the question. This arena is particularly important for those without a numerical majority and/or without the resources to successfully engage in other forms of pressure and electoral politics. Over the years racial and religious minorities, prisoners, juveniles, and the mentally ill have won judicial games while they could not win other ones. Despite the costs, the limited results, and the patience required, judicial games are an alternative. Now let's take a look at where they occur.

Different Judicial Arenas

Tony Greg, 25, was convicted of killing two men who gave him a ride when he was hitchhiking in Florida. He dumped their bodies in a ditch near Atlanta and stole their car and money. Charles W. Proffitt earned his living as a warehouse worker. He was convicted of breaking into an apartment in Tampa, Florida, where a couple was sleeping. He stabbed the husband to death and beat his wife before fleeing. Jerry L. Jurek was a seventh-grade school dropout. He was convicted of raping a ten-year-old girl in Cuero, Texas, then strangling her and

---

[6] For all the various qualifications to the meaning of obscenity, see Harry Kalven, Jr., "The Right to Publish," in *The Rights of Americans*, ed. Norman Dorsen (New York: Random House, 1970), pp. 253–266.

throwing her into the Guadalupe River. James Woodson and Luby Waxton of Dunn, North Carolina, held up a convenience food store. In the process they shot to death a store attendant and wounded a customer. Tony Roberts, at the age of 26, was convicted of the robbery slaying of a gas station attendant in Lake Charles, Louisiana.[7]

Apart from their convictions in state courts, what each of these men had in common is having been sentenced to death. However, only three of the six were likely to die. The reason concerns the fact that state legislatures define crimes and punishments differently, compelling state courts to treat criminal defendants in different ways. For example, the state legislatures of North Carolina, Louisiana, and 21 other states said death was mandatory for certain crimes. James Woodson, Luby Waxton, and Tony Roberts had to die because they were convicted of those mandated crimes. But the state legislatures of 14 other states including Florida, Texas, and Georgia allowed judges and juries some discretion. They provided guidelines or legal standards. So even though a defendant might be convicted of a capital crime, judges and juries could examine his or her background and consider any special circumstances before sentencing to death. This occurred in the trials of Troy Gregg, Charles Proffitt, and Jerry Jurek. The judges and juries found no special circumstances that warranted their waiving the death penalty.

So if each of the six men was sentenced to die, why is it likely that only three will receive that punishment? The answer has to do with a U.S. Supreme Court decision announced in July, 1976. Clarifying a 1972 decision in which they declared capital punishment unconstitutional because of the arbitrary way in which states were imposing it, in 1976 the judges said the death penalty *is* constitutional. As long as states do not mandate it for certain crimes and as long as they provide guidelines so that the decision of judges and juries is not arbitrary, states are not violating the Eighth Amendment ban on cruel and unusual punishment. Speaking for the 7–2 majority, Justice Stewart put it this way: Mandatory sentences are a kind of cruel and unusual punishment because they treat "all persons convicted of a designated offense not as uniquely individual human beings, but as members of a faceless, undifferentiated mass."

The struggle to clarify the constitutionality of the death penalty reminds us of the *federalism* principle. Power to make laws is divided

---

[7] "Death Penalty Upheld by the Supreme Court," *San Francisco Chronicle* (July 3, 1976), p. 10.

between state and national governments, and power to interpret those laws resides in a *dual court system*. The result? Fifty-one legislatures and 51 judicial structures. The apparent confusion is real. While generally consistent with the U.S. Constitution, each state has its own laws, its own definitions of crime and punishment, and its own procedures.

But out of that confusion comes a resource. A dual court system creates a choice of arenas for the plaintiff as well as defendants. When possible, it may be an advantage to obtain a transfer from a state to a federal court. It certainly has been an advantage to southern black citizens. Knowing they could litigate to protect their civil rights in either state or federal court, they chose the more receptive arena—federal court.

While they share power, the death penalty decisions illustrate that not all the court systems are equal. The national court system, specifically the U.S. Supreme Court, has the final word. Through the powers of *judicial review* and statutory interpretation, the U.S. Supreme Court is the final arbiter of disputes, if they choose to be. This means, specifically, that the 50 state courts, their legislatures, governors, and constitutions are all inferior to the Constitution of the United States. So too are Congress and the President. While not a part of the July 1976 decision, the federal law mandating the death penalty for murder during the course of an air hijacking could also be declared unconstitutional.

Of course, the system isn't perfect, even though the U.S. Supreme Court has the final say. When lower court judges disagree with Supreme Court rulings, they may simply not comply. They may continue to use their own standards of judgment. For example, in *Betts v. Brady* in 1942 (overruled in 1963 by *Gideon v. Wainwright*), the U.S. Supreme Court ruled that defendants in capital cases were entitled to state-appointed counsel if special circumstances were present making it impossible for defendants to represent themselves adequately. Special circumstances included youth, mental incompetence, or inexperience. However, lower courts rarely found that special circumstances existed, thus freeing the states from the necessity of providing counsel. In Pennsylvania in 1961, the state supreme court even ruled that an 18-year-old boy with an IQ of 59 (the equivalent of a mental age of nine) did not need legal aid (*Simon v. Maroney*, 1961).[8]

[8] James P. Levine and Theodore L. Becker discuss this and other inadequacies of the "trickle-down" theory of justice in "Toward and Beyond a Theory of Supreme Court Impact," *American Behavioral Scientist*. March/April 1970, pp. 561–584.

Well, how do they get away with it if the decisions of the U.S. Supreme Court are supreme? How can lower courts ignore and evade such high-level policies? Levine and Becker suggest several ways:

> First, lower courts have the authority to make crucial findings of fact which can only be partially controlled by appellate courts. Second, since the fact constellations of any one case are not exact replicas of those of other cases, lower courts can often distinguish away alleged precedents ordained on high. Third, the verbiage of Supreme Court language can be manipulated with favorable sentences elevated to the states of a "holding" which is binding and unfavorable words discussed as "mere dicta." Fourth, state courts can often insulate themselves from Supreme Court review by grounding their decisions in state law. Thus, judges who want to be obstructive have adequate tools.[9]

Fortunately, most lower court judges are not intent on being obstructionists.

State Court Systems

Now let's get down to the basics: what are the arenas available, and how do they vary? All 50 states have *three general levels* of courts. Each is involved in a different phase of the legal process. There are *courts of general jurisdiction* that accept broad categories of trial cases, there are *special courts* that focus on particular subjects, and there are *appellate courts* that review cases already heard.

Cases are *first* heard in courts of general jurisdiction or special jurisdiction. Those of general jurisdiction have the broadest scope of authority in holding trials. Depending on their location, they have different names. They may be called courts of common pleas, superior courts, district courts, or circuit courts. Criminal cases that might involve a long prison term and civil suits that involve more than $1,000 are first heard here. Minor criminal matters and suits involving small amounts of money are heard in courts of special jurisdiction. Among them are traffic courts, juvenile courts, probate courts, and so on. In this category the *small claims court* is particularly important. Its simple procedure allows citizens to represent themselves when their claims are less than $500 (or some other figure the state may establish).

While relatively few cases are appealed to higher courts, every litigant has the *right to at least one appeal*. Many states have intermediate appellate courts, and all states have supreme courts. Appeals

[9] *Ibid.*, p. 562.

courts are not trial courts in the commonly accepted sense. They do not retry a case; they only look at the record of the lower court and review the law. If a retrial appears necessary, they send the case back to lower court. The "they," in this case, is not a jury. Appeals cases are decided by three or more judges.

The kinds of cases that are appealed are not necessarily the most important ones or the ones where the loser is convinced he or she has not had a fair hearing. The decision to appeal depends on the financial resources of the litigants as well as their ability to endure the pressures and uncertainties of the possible years of waiting until the final decision is rendered. In *some states* that time may be shortened by bypassing the intermediate appeals level. Unlike at the federal level, cases may go directly from trial courts to state supreme courts.[10]

Just as this country's dual court system provides greater access opportunities, so does the presence of different kinds of courts within each state. The existence of various courts operating under different rules, in different political climates, with judges with different attitudes and policy preferences can assist the political activist. Certain courts may be used or avoided as part of a general strategy designed to achieve one's own goals and confuse or defeat opposing interests.[11]

The National Court System

Article III of the U.S. Constitution suggests the types of cases that are heard in the national court system: "all cases, in law and equity, arising under this Constitution, the laws of the United States, and treaties made . . . under their authority." So, access to this arena depends on whether a dispute involves the federal Constitution, statutes, or treaties. Access is also possible when one party to a suit is the United States government, a state government, or a foreign emissary, or if citizens of different states are parties in a suit.[12]

Sometimes citizens have an access choice. For example, in suits involving a contract claim between citizens of different states, the

---

10 For these and other differences in state court structures, see Henry R. Glick and Kenneth N. Vines, *State Court Systems* (Englewood Cliffs, N.J.: Prentice-Hall, 1973).

11 *Ibid.*, p. 32.

12 Access to Article I federal courts, called *legislative courts*, is based on different rules. Created by Congress to administer particular national statutes, they include the Territorial Courts of Guam, Virgin Islands, and the Panama Canal Zones; the Court of Military Appeals; and Tax Courts.

parties can choose to sue in either federal or a state court, unless the monetary value of the controversy is under $10,000, in which case access is limited to state courts.[13] More about access later.

The national judicial structure is similar to the state structures, although fortunately less complicated. The first level consists of *U.S. district courts*. This is the trial court level, where judges hear criminal matters involving the violation of a federal law, such as transporting narcotics across state borders. This is also where civil matters are first decided, such as an antitrust charge filed by the federal government against a large company.

There are 89 of these courts, and most of them have jurisdiction over a large area. This requires judges to travel to the more important cities to hear cases. Many districts have several judges, each operating a branch of the court. The southern district of New York is particularly busy; it requires 24 judges to get the job done.

The first appeals level gets cases not only from U.S. district courts but from various federal agencies. The 97 judges who preside are distributed among 11 separate *courts of appeal*. Unlike at the trial level, usually three judges will hear one case.

The *U.S. Supreme Court* is the final appeals court for both the national system and state systems. It may also be a trial court if a party to the suit fulfills the access criteria previously mentioned. Most of its business, however, comes from the federal courts of appeal. These can be bypassed only by statute or in cases "of such imperative public importance as to require immediate settlement." If a "substantial federal question" is involved, appeals may also come from state supreme courts.

With appeals coming from all these other arenas, how do the nine Supreme Court judges get the job done? By limiting access, usually. Of the more than 3,000 cases they are requested to hear each year, they dismiss nearly 90 percent as unworthy of review. Most consist of pleas from persons in penal institutions, seeking review of their convictions.

So these are the arenas and their general jurisdiction. Both the *appeal process* within each system and the existence of a *dual system* offer citizens choices. The implications of each choice should become clear as we look at the players involved, the distribution of power, and specific access rules. First let's look at the players.

[13] Sigler, *Introduction to the Legal System*, p. 73.

The Players of the Game

The Police

Lawrence Washington has a habit of getting drunk. He doesn't get violent, and he doesn't own a car so he isn't a dangerous driver, but he does get publicly drunk. When he does, he ends up in jail. The fact that he is black and poor and lives in a "bad section" of the city contributes to that destination. When Tom Adams gets drunk, which he does just about as often, the neighborhood cop sends him home. Oh sure, sometimes he has to post collateral or pay a fine, but he isn't shuffled through drunk court and sent off to a dirty cell. Tom is white and well dressed and lives in one of the city's "better neighborhoods."

The reason Lawrence Washington is likely to end up in jail and Tom Adams at home safely "sleeping it off" has to do with *police discretion* in making arrests. The police are the gatekeepers in judicial games involving crimes. For that reason, they are key players. So what do we know about them, how they get their jobs, and the discretion they use in making arrests?

In most cities, the police department is the largest agency under the direct control of City Hall. They are part of the *executive* branch of government. Who controls their activities depends on whether or not the mayor has the power to appoint the police chief, whether there is a special police commission that serves as a buffer between the mayor and the police, the degree to which the police are under civil service regulations, and the extent to which police officers are unionized.[14] When police chiefs are under the supervision of city managers and are appointed from civil service promotion lists, they tend to be less subject to political influence than when they are appointed by an elected official (the mayor or a police commissioner). How they get their job has two implications. If they are removed from the direct authority of an elected official, the department may be better able to deal with serious crime. Police officers may spend less time on crimes with political mileage. However, if they are removed from this direct authority, citizen influence is more difficult.

While police chiefs get their jobs in a variety of different ways, members of the force get the job on the basis of a competitive examination. Once on the job, the police officer has a great deal of independence. No supervisor can observe what patrol officers do between

14 Herbert Jacob, *Urban Justice* (Englewood Cliffs, N.J.: Prentice-Hall, 1973), p. 25.

radio calls or when responding to a call. Of course, they fill out a report of their activities, but the information is rarely checked.

Police discretion in making arrests is the result of this lack of supervision, ambiguities in the law, and the situations police officers encounter. No one is there to tell them how a situation should be handled. The police officer must decide whether or not to arrest the apparently dangerous driver, the husband threatening his wife, or the protesters in front of the foreign embassy. The law isn't much help. There are so many activities defined as crimes that police officers must make choices: Do they raid the local bordello or maintain surveillance on the local drug dealer?

Since the police control the process by which criminal laws are applied, since they are the crucial gatekeepers to criminal courts, how do they choose whom to pursue and arrest? What influences their moves? Certainly their own norms and prejudices are important, but as Herbert Jacob says there are other important influencing factors:[15]

1. The characteristics of the crime. In serious crimes and public crimes, police discretion is reduced. Murderers must be pursued, and a fight in a local bar must be stopped. Petty theft, illegal poker games, and, surprisingly, rape get less attention.
2. The relationship between the alleged criminal and the victim. When the parties in a dispute know each other or are related, police use greater discretion. "Extenuating" circumstances will often keep the police from arresting the pimp doing battle with one of his "girls" or the husband and wife ready to attack each other. Crimes involving strangers are more likely to be pursued.
3. The relationship between the police and one or more parties in the dispute. Objectivity is difficult. A complaint made by someone who is polite and deferential is treated more seriously than one made by someone who is antagonistic. A complaint made by a white-collar worker is likely to get more attention than one made by a blue-collar worker. The nature and intensity of the complaint also influence the way the police officer will respond. If the police officer does act the attitude of the alleged wrong-doer is also likely to be important. Being nice, calm, and deferential may mean release.
4. The policies of the police department. Some departments are most concerned with the *maintenance of order*. In these cities arrests are made only when an incident threatens to become un-

[15] *Ibid.*, pp. 27–29.

controllable. Violations not threatening to public order are likely to be dismissed. Other departments emphasize strictly *upholding the law*. The police officer is instructed to enforce the law even when the public order is not disturbed. Still other departments are most concerned with *service*. Here police officers are concerned with maintaining good public relations. They do this by responding quickly to calls from citizens and by handling complaints informally, with discretion.

Which approach to use and the policies to follow are often decided by the controlling players: commissioners, the mayor, or a city council. Those policies can be influenced. Citizens may want their police department to focus on violent crimes rather than crimes without victims. Or they may want the department to provide more services to neighborhoods rather than to downtown business and tourists. Whatever approach to law enforcement is preferred, demands need to be communicated and promoted.

Sometimes the courts impose policies, as the U.S. Supreme Court did in a variety of cases in the 1960s. Even locally, judicial decisions influence police behavior and discretion. In the spring of 1975, for example, several California judges told police departments that "Johns"—prostitutes' clients—must be arrested and detained as well as the prostitutes themselves. As a result of a suit brought by the American Civil Liberties Union, Alameda County Superior Court Judge Spurgeon Avakian wrote that for officers merely to cite male customers while arresting and holding female prostitutes constituted a violation of the women's constitutional rights of free speech, due process of law, and security against unreasonable search and seizure. In this case, Judge Avakian was limiting police discretion.

Lawyers

In the adversary system of justice, a lawyer is regarded as both an officer of the court and a representative of a client. Just as the police are the principal gatekeepers regulating the flow of criminal cases, lawyers are the chief regulators of the flow of civil cases. Certainly, their job is crucial in criminal cases, but civil law gets most of their attention.

Rarely do poor people become lawyers. The cost of college and then law school makes it a middle-class profession. Think about it. As of 1975, the average annual cost of a college education was $1,600 in public institutions and $3,500 in private institutions. It's therefore not very surprising that fewer than 10 percent of all 20- to 24-year-olds had a college degree in 1970. Then there is law school. That requires three more years of tuition payment and room and board with little scholarship assistance. Many law schools also discourage students from engaging in part-time work. So who is likely to be able to pay the expenses? [16]

Law school education is consistent with who the students are. Middle-class, usually upper-middle-class, interests are the primary focus. For example, courses on contracts and property typically form the core of the first-year program.[17]

Law school education is also consistent with whom lawyers generally serve. About 15 percent of the nation's lawyers work for the government. The majority of these have jobs that have little to do with trial courts or the legal problems of the average citizen. More than three-fourths of the other 85 percent, who are in private practice, primarily work for business interests, in real estate, or handling the estates and trusts of the wealthy. Thus, only about one lawyer in five works in trial courts and handles the legal business of the ordinary American.[18]

This is particularly hard on the middle class. While the poor have free access to federally funded legal services lawyers, legal aid society lawyers, and public defenders, middle-class citizens who need lawyers face a host of problems. First, they don't know which lawyers are good. Whether their problem is buying a house, drafting a will, obtaining a divorce, or settling a disputed charge account, they go to whomever they happen to know or hear about. Even more don't go at all. They can't afford a lawyer. Those whose cases involve contingency fees—the lawyer gets one-fourth to one-third of whatever he or she wins in a personal injury or malpractice case—have no problem, but what about the others? [19]

Some rely on the many do-it-yourself legal books available. Most of those who really need a lawyer, however, bear the cost. The judicial game is usually too complicated for novices. The forms to be filed, deadlines to be met, motions that can be made, negotiations, preparations for trial, and conduct are all matters that require some expertise. This special knowledge that lawyers possess gives them an almost complete monopoly over access to the courts.

[16] Jacob, *Urban Justice*, p. 38.
[17] Downie, *Justice Denied*, p. 166.
[18] *Ibid.*, p. 166.
[19] Jacob, *Urban Justice*, p. 44.

Apart from technical expertise, there are two legal skills that are particularly important to lawyers in judicial games. Like the legislator or chief executive, a lawyer working for a pretrial settlement needs *skills in negotiation*. Most are working for this. In noncriminal cases, the plaintiff wants to get money quickly, rather than waiting years for a final judgment. The defendant wants to pare down the size of the plaintiff's claim and achieve a financially certain conclusion of the dispute. Both want to be free of the psychological strain, the costs of a trial, and the loss of time involved. Criminal defendants want a pretrial settlement for many of the same reasons. Most (85 percent) plea-bargain, even if they are innocent. They will plead guilty to a lesser offense rather than run the risk of a conviction in a trial for a greater offense and rather than spend the time and pay the cost of court.

If a trial does occur, the lawyer's negotiating skill is no longer the important one. In addition to knowledge of the law and procedures, the lawyer needs the *skills of cross-examination and verbal disputation*. The lawyer has to emphasize, while questioning witnesses, the facts that will help a client and discredit the testimony that will not. Unfortunately, few Americans seeking legal assistance know in advance whether or not a particular lawyer possesses these skills. They take their chances and generally have no choice.

Public Defenders

Particularly without choice are poor defendants in criminal actions. They receive either court-appointed counsel or a public defender— and they wouldn't receive either if it weren't for the Sixth Amendment to the U.S. Constitution, the due process clause of the Fourteenth Amendment, and the U.S. Supreme Court ruling in *Gideon* v. *Wainwright* (1963) that indigent defendants must be furnished counsel. In 1970, Congress authorized the appointment of federal public defenders by federal courts of appeals or, as an alternative, the establishment of community defender organizations financed by federal grants.

Ideally, the public defender system is supposed to be an improvement over court-appointed counsel. Assigned counsel, the argument goes, vary not only in ability but in willingness to devote attention to the defendant's interests.

So how does reality stack up against this ideal? Although they recognize that the public defender system is an improvement, some critics say it offers "assembly-line justice." While a private defense counsel handles a client's case from beginning to end, in many large cities different assistant public defenders handle different stages of the trial. An assistant may be quite knowledgeable and skilled in dealing with one particular stage, but there is little opportunity to build a trusting relationship with the defendant.

Second, some critics believe that public defenders sometimes forget whose side they are on. In one study of a big-city public defender's office on the West Coast, David Sudnow observed public defenders becoming part of the "core personnel" in the courthouse. Many public defenders came to think of themselves as part of the government team rather than as adversaries for client interests. For example, they freely expressed their belief that most of their clients were guilty. They tried in their initial interviews with new defendants to force them to admit their guilt and, later, to agree to plead guilty in front of a judge. They had only words of scorn for those who appeared guilty but refused to "cop a plea." One public defender put it this way:

> What the hell are we supposed to do with them? If they can't listen to good reason and take a bargain, then it's their tough luck. If they go to prison, well, they're the ones who are losing the trials, not us.[20]

A third kind of criticism focuses on the vigor with which public defenders pursue the job. In the same study, David Sudnow observed public defenders merely going through the motions of a trial to avoid being considered negligent. The prosecutor could count on the public defender not to test the validity of traditional courthouse procedures or challenge the integrity of the prosecutor's case. The public defender would never contend, for example, that police witnesses might be lying.[21]

In spite of all this criticism, there are defenders of the system. An American Bar Foundation study found that the vast majority of judges and prosecutors believe public defenders to be much more capable than the courthouse regulars and more experienced in criminal law than court-appointed attorneys. Their problems, according to this study, are due to their being overworked, underpaid, and insufficiently supported by staff.[22]

[20] Downie, *Justice Denied*, p. 179.
[21] *Ibid.*, p. 180.
[22] Lee Silverstein, *Defense of the Poor in Criminal Cases in American State Courts*, 3 vols. (Chicago: American Bar Foundation, 1965), vol. 2, p. 178.

Prosecutors

Opposing public defenders in criminal cases are the prosecutors. They exist at the county, state, and national levels. At the county level the prosecutor is usually elected for a two- or four-year term. Depending on the state, the prosecutor may be called the county solicitor, commonwealth attorney, or district attorney. At the state and national levels, the prosecutor is called the attorney general. The attorney general is ordinarily elected at the state level and appointed by the President at the national level. Whatever they are called and however they are chosen, prosecutors have the authority to investigate and enforce the criminal law. In court, when representing the government, they must assume the burden of proof. That means a prosecutor must prove the defendant's guilt beyond a reasonable doubt.

In terms of decision-making *discretion*, prosecutors, like police, have enormous power to determine who will be criminally tried. A prosecutor who believes that no crime has been committed or that the available evidence is too weak to prove guilt in court is obligated to refuse to prosecute. *Grand juries* may be theoretically responsible for making this decision, but they consist of ordinary citizens who look to the prosecutor for advice. The prosecutor presents evidence to them, gives an evaluation of the likelihood of a successful prosecution, and generally controls their activities and information.[23] So this device to protect citizens from the arbitrary power of government is often used as the government sees fit. The case following illustrates the point.

In New York in 1969, 21 members of the Black Panther Party were indicted on 12 counts of plotting to bomb police stations and midtown department stores; of actually bombing police stations and a school building in Queens; and of attempting to murder police officers. Subsequent to the indictments, the police acted. In a series of predawn raids on April 2, 1969, 150 New York City detectives fanned out over the city to arrest 12 members of the Black Panther Party. Two more indicted Panthers were arrested the next day; two were already in a New Jersey jail on other charges. Five were not apprehended. Of those arrested, 13 stood trial together; the trial began on February 2, 1970. After eight months in the courtroom, 12 jurors arrived at their verdict in less than half an hour. All the defendants were acquitted on all charges (30 in all). The case had probably cost the taxpayers about $2 million.

---

[23] In some states a grand jury proceeding may be avoided. A person may be held over for trial as a result of a preliminary hearing before a judge.

What had gone wrong? Shocked at the verdict, New York County District Attorney Frank Hogan blamed the grand jury. In a *New York Post* interview after the trial, he said that grand jury members had presented such a wide-ranging and unsupportable indictment that they must be held responsible. However, could they be, when the prosecutors really called the shots? For example, the district attorney brought the case to the grand jury's attention. He gathered evidence and wrote the indictment's language. The grand jury had no investigators of its own. It was highly dependent on the information and judgment of the prosecutor. Gerald Lefcourt, one of the attorneys for the defense, was more severe in his judgment of the prosecutor's role in the grand jury proceedings.

> There was gross unfairness in the grand jury process. It was totally unrepresentative in its composition. There was tremendous pressure on them, keeping them late at night, inflaming them, telling them they had to prevent bombings the next day, which was absurd in the context of the evidence. There was no one there to put it into context.[24]

Apart from discretion in the indictment process, what other discretion and control does the prosecutor have? The prosecutor is the one who decides whether or not to negotiate with a defendant—a guilty plea for a lesser offense. Since the prosecutor ordinarily has more information about the case than the defense counsel, he or she is in a good position to deal. The result is a good public record for the prosecutor, since the cases actually prosecuted are ones that the prosecutor thinks can be won.

How prosecutors get their job influences how they pursue it. The majority of elected prosecutors are chosen on the basis of their political skill rather than their legal qualifications. Ordinarily their immediate background involved the practice of civil law and working in party politics. Because they are generally elected and frequently go on to higher elective offices, they may give their attention to those cases that will make their public record a glowing one. That means prosecuting the cases that they not only believe they can win but that will attract public attention, cases like the New York Panther one. Then too, guilty pleas out of court add to that record.

It's not the kind of job where a lawyer remains. Tenure rarely extends beyond two four-year terms. Then if they do not go on to

24 This case is described in detail by Stephen C. Chaberski, "Inside the New York Panther Trial," *Civil Liberties Review*, Fall 1973, pp. 111–155.

Tilt

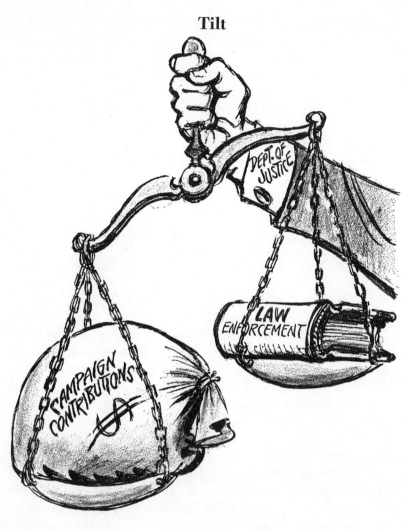

From *Herblock's State of the Union* (Simon & Schuster, 1972)

higher office, they go back to private practice, but a private practice that will be far more lucrative. Working for "the people" pays off.

Juries

Apart from being a defendant or plaintiff, the most important role a citizen can play in judicial games is that of a jury member. In fact, of all the institutional games, this is one where the citizen is no longer an indirect player, influencing the lives of others. The citizen is the key decision maker.

The right to a trial by jury was part of the English system of law. It was one of the many judicial procedures of theirs we borrowed. It applies to both criminal cases (Sixth Amendment) and civil cases (Seventh Amendment). Its purpose was and is to limit the arbitrary power of government, particularly the power to use the courts against one's political opponents.

There are two kinds of juries used in this country. The *grand jury,* already mentioned, issues formal criminal accusations (indictments) after investigating charges. It consists of persons selected by various means and numbers from 5 to 23, depending on the state. Apart from its unique function, there are two things that further distinguish it from trial juries: its proceedings are secret, and most of the due process rights guaranteed to those testifying before a trial jury are not guaranteed to citizens called before a grand jury. The assumption is that since the grand jury's powers are far more limited, those rights are not crucial. Not everyone agrees.[25]

Trial (petit) juries are the ones that actually issue verdicts in both criminal and civil cases. They do, that is, if they get the chance. While studies indicate that most citizens would want a jury trial, in both criminal and civil cases, the number actually using them is declining. Most defendants waive this right in favor of judge trials.

When juries are used, their size varies. In some states 6 members decide minor crimes and 12, major ones. In others, 12 are required in all criminal cases and fewer in civil cases.

Just as the size varies, so does the jury selection procedure. Remember, we're dealing with 51 judicial systems. *Initial selection* is more or less random, but there are minimum qualifications. Generally, one must be a citizen of a certain age, a registered voter, and a resident of the judicial district in which the jury is to be impaneled. *Final*

---

[25] In addition to issuing criminal indictments, grand juries perform a civil function. They investigate and report on the activities of public institutions.

selection is more precise. It is the job of the attorneys for the defense and for the plaintiff. Each prospective juror is questioned in order to eliminate any who may be unfit to serve for one reason or another, or who may have prejudices for or against the defendant, or who may be acquainted with any of the parties involved.

This process sometimes takes weeks. In December 1970 Black Panthers Bobby Seale and Ericka Huggins were put on trial in New Haven. They were accused of murdering a fellow Panther member. To get the final jury lawyers questioned 1,035 prospective jurors over a four-month period. After the trial ended in a hung jury, the judge dismissed the charges because he thought it would be impossible to select another jury.[26]

The kinds of juries found in trial courts reflect the selection process, particularly the way in which initial selections are made. First, if one must be a registered voter in order to serve, the young, the poor, and the nonwhite are likely to be underrepresented. They are the least likely to be registered voters. Vastly overrepresented on juries are professionals, managers, and proprietors. In a Baltimore study, for example, professionals, managers, and proprietors constituted only 18.7 percent of the population but contributed 40.2 percent of the jurors in a federal court. Working-class people, on the other hand, constituted 41.4 percent of the population but only 13.4 percent of the jurors.[27]

Second, if one must lose wages, only the economically secure or the compensated will serve. The law does not require employers to compensate employees serving on juries, and the government hardly lightens the financial burden. The 1966 President's Commission on Law Enforcement and the Administration of Justice discovered that jurors in most jurisdictions are paid between $10 and $20 per day, and less in some. Fortunately, some union contracts now provide for compensation during jury service, and some employers do continue to pay their workers even when this is not part of a union contract. More frequently, however, jurors are not compensated and therefore must ask to be excused from jury duty because of the financial hardship.

If serving on a jury would be an undue hardship, most courts are lenient about excusing those initially contacted. There are, in addi-

26 "Seale Jury Seated after 4 Months of Questioning 1,035," *New York Times*, March 12, 1971, p. 43. Also described in Jacob, *Justice in America*, p. 125.
27 Edwin S. Mills, "Statistical Study of Occupations of Jurors in a U.S. District Court," *Maryland Law Review*, Spring 1962, pp. 205–214.

tion, categories of people who are automatically excused from serving. For example, those occupational groups whose services seem vital to the community may not have to serve. This frequently includes teachers, doctors, nurses, police officers, firefighters, and so on. Until a recent U.S. Supreme Court ruling, a state (Louisiana) could even bar women.

So defendants are often not tried by a jury of their peers. As long as certain categories of people are not systematically excluded, the selection is perfectly legal.

Something to think about
What are some of the implications of the composition of American juries?

How juries make up their mind—that is, what influences their moves—is a subject that hasn't been thoroughly investigated. However, the few studies that have been done suggest the following: *Verdicts are often arrived at quickly.* For example, after interviewing jurors in 213 different criminal cases, a University of Chicago team reported the following:

1. Almost all juries took a vote as soon as they retired to their chambers. In 30 percent of the cases it took only one vote to reach a unanimous decision.[28]
2. The initial majority view usually prevails. In the same Chicago study, where more than one vote was required, the first-ballot majority prevailed 90 percent of the time. This was true regardless of who sat on the jury—rich or poor, men or women. The voting minority can rarely convince their colleagues to switch over.
3. Personal characteristics also influence deliberations. Various observations of simulated juries reveal that men talk more than women, and that the better-educated participate more frequently than the less well-educated. Ethnic background is also a factor. One study found that jurors of German and British background were more likely to favor conviction than those of Negro or Slavic descent.

[28] D. W. Broeder, "University of Chicago Jury Project," *Nebraska Law Review* 38 (1959): 744–760. This and the subsequent studies discussed are reported in Jacob, *Justice in America*, pp. 127–129.

4. Informal factors prevail over formal consideration of the case. The testimony heard in one simulated trial, as well as the judge's instructions, were given far less attention than decision-making procedures, opinions about the trial, and personal reminiscences.

One result is, at least according to the Chicago Jury Project, that jurors' values and their notion of fairness take precedence over the law. For instance, in personal injury cases they take into account whether the defendant is insured or wealthy. When jurors know the defendant is insured, awards tend to be higher than when they don't possess this knowledge; and awards are arrived at not by any formal calculation of what the reimbursement for damages should actually be but by jurors negotiating among themselves.

What tentative inferences can be drawn from this information? Should the jury system be abandoned because verdicts appear to be arrived at quickly, minority views get overwhelmed, personal characteristics influence perceptions, and personal values take precedence over the law?

When defendants waive their right to a jury trial and choose a judge as the principal decision maker, there is little difference in decisions. In criminal cases, judges and juries appear to agree about 75 percent of the time,[29] and in personal injury cases resulting from automobile accidents, agreement, at least in the Chicago study, was 83 percent.

Where there are differences in jury and judge decisions, some patterns are clear. In the Chicago study judges were more likely to convict those accused of crimes than were jurors. This was particularly true in statutory rape cases and first offense drunk-driving cases. However, judge and jury agreed in every narcotics case. In civil cases, the type of defendant made a difference. Juries decided in favor of the plaintiff more frequently than judges when the defendant was the government, a large corporation, or a railroad. The wealth of the defendant worked against it.

Given the special training of judges and their inclination to examine the facts against the law, it is remarkable that this study revealed so few differences in verdicts. Judges may well be influenced by some of the same personal factors that influence jurors.

Why bother about what influences the moves of jurors? Citizens can't lobby them or help select them as they do other public officials.

---

[29] See Harry Kalven, Jr., and Hans Zeisel, *The American Jury* (Boston: Little, Brown and Company, 1966) pp. 63–64.

While that is true, the representatives of citizens in court, lawyers, can and do. They are becoming more sophisticated about *jury selection* and *jury education*. Relying more frequently on psychological and sociological research, they are asking different kinds of questions as they attempt to get a sympathetic jury, and they are taking advantage of the educational opportunities available in the courtroom.

In the 1975 trial of Joan Little psychologists served as consultants. They were part of a 35-member staff specializing in various aspects of the trial. Their job was particularly important. Joan Little, a young black woman, was accused of stabbing to death Clarence Alligood, her jailer. Joan's position was that the stabbing was done in self-defense against rape. She fled the jail in fear for her life. The trial was held in Raleigh, North Carolina. The psychologists' job was twofold. First, they had to demonstrate, through polling, that Joan Little couldn't get a fair trial in Beaufort County, where the crime was committed. They did this, and their study indeed indicated bias. As a result, the defense won a *change of venue*. Once in Raleigh, their job focused on jury selection. Using the psychological devices developed for such trials as those of Angela Davis and the Wounded Knee Indians, the pollsters sampled the population of Raleigh and surrounding Wake County. They probed attitudes toward blacks, women, the poor, and law officers to help construct the model of a "friendly" jury. To see whether prospective jurors fitted the profile, the defense attorney quizzed them: Do you feel blacks are often victims of racial prejudice? Have you ever eaten lunch with a black person? Is the word of a law officer more important than anyone else's? On the basis of these questions, and whatever questions the prosecutor chose to ask, the jury of 12 was selected.

Lawyers handling political cases—those where the client's political outlook may affect the outcome—rely strongly on courtroom educational opportunities to mold the friendly jury. Trial lawyer Allan Brotsky, in fact, always advises a jury trial because of these opportunities. Speaking about a case involving a conscientious objector, he explains his preference for juries this way:

> First of all, a judge is unlikely to give the draftee the benefit of the doubt that twelve jurors will if they can. Secondly, I think the courtroom can be an educational forum. In trying a case to twelve jurors, you're educating them on matters that are vital to them, but on which they may never have been educated before—namely, the attitude of those young people toward the draft, their reasons for their opposition to the [Vietnam] War, and their hatred of war. You have a captive audience that has to sit there and listen

to you. And, believe me, after every draft case that I've tried, at least one or two jurors have come up and thanked me and said, "We really had no idea how deeply the young people felt about this until we sat through this case."

Now you might ask, "well what the hell does that have to do with defending your client? After all, you don't have an independent duty to educate people."

Of course we don't. But we have learned that only if jurors are educated during the case about the political issues on the War and the political opposition of the defendant to the War will they really be able to give him deliberation that is free of the narrowmindedness, know-nothingism and prejudice that is present when they haven't had this kind of education.[30]

So, knowing about the behavior of juries, the way they are likely to move in certain judicial games, is *relevant information*. It helps lawyers plan both judicial strategies and tactics. Specifically, if a jury is involved, it suggests questions to ask in jury selection and messages to communicate during the course of the trial. As long as both sides have access to this information and the opportunity to use similar courtroom tactics, justice can prevail.

Judges

Finally, judges need to be examined. Who are they, how do they get to be players, and what influences their moves? After all, they are usually the most important decision makers. Even when they don't actually decide who wins what, judges guide the juries, shaping the issues to be decided and explaining how the law applies to them. They rule on what witnesses and lawyers can and cannot say. They sentence criminal defendants. They put pressure on opposing lawyers to settle out of court. Most important, they set the tone of the game —rushed or deliberate, serious or farcical, fair or prejudicial. The judge's behavior in the courtroom is not easily challenged.[31]

Let's take a look at how judges are selected. There are presently five different selection systems in use by the states. Each is political. They include:

1. *Gubernatorial appointment.* The power of selection is exercised directly by the governor, using patronage, professional, or other considerations.

[30] Ann Fagen Ginger, "Trial of a Conscientious Objector," in *The Relevant Lawyers* (New York: Simon and Schuster, 1972), pp. 103–104.
[31] Leonard Downie, Jr., makes these and other points about the power of judges, *Justice Denied*, p. 186.

2. *Legislative election.* The choice is made by vote of the legislature on the basis of gubernatorial influence, patronage, or other factors.
3. *Nonpartisan election.* Judges are chosen in elections that formally exclude political parties from participation. Informal influences from political leaders or bar organizations may influence the election results.
4. *Partisan election.* Judges are chosen through elections in which political parties participate. Party primaries are normally part of the election procedure.
5. *Missouri Plan.* This is the most complex selection system; it has three essential parts. First, slates of candidates are chosen by a nominating commission appointed by the governor. The governor then selects a judge from the list of names submitted by the commission. Finally, voters review the appointment by means of a referendum in which the judge runs unopposed on his or her record.

As the above plans suggest, most state judges are popularly elected. About half of these must run in partisan elections, the other half in nonpartisan. In 17 states the governor plays the crucial selection role, either through independent appointments (7 states) or through cooperative appointments (10 states), called the Missouri Plan. In only 5 states does the legislature get to decide.[32]

So what are the implications, professional and other, of these state selection procedures? First, there is no evidence that the plan that is supposed to produce the most professional judges does so. The supposed greater objectivity and legal expertise of judges operating under the Missouri Plan doesn't exist. They do not have notably better legal educations than judges chosen under other plans, although they do have somewhat greater previous judicial experience.

Second, as one would expect, the influence of certain groups varies according to the selection procedures. The organized bar has most influence in cities where the "merit" or Missouri Plan is used. The nominating commissions that exist under this plan always include representatives of the legal profession, and their knowledge of judicial affairs gives them more influence than lay members.

The bar has far less influence over judicial selection where judges are elected or appointed. Rarely do these legal associations have enough clout to veto a nominee. Their published recommendations

---

[32] See Harold W. Chase, "Johnson Administration Judicial Appointments 1963–66," *Minnesota Law Review,* 1967–1968, p. 40.

simply fail to reach many voters or convince chief executives. The groups that do have influence in judicial elections and appointments are party activists, other elected officials, and campaign contributors. A study of the recruitment of Chicago judges revealed, for example, that half the judicial candidates in one election were recruited by party leaders. In addition, nearly all these candidates consulted with party leaders. Of course not only does Chicago have partisan elections, but it has a powerful party organization. It becomes the gatekeeper to the bench.[33]

All this suggests two possible means of citizen influence—through the bar or through politicians. While the latter is more likely, the bar also presents an opportunity. It is not homogeneous. Different factions compete to produce nominees of a particular ideological persuasion, and interest groups concerned with the system of justice could promote certain candidates within one faction. More possible, however, is citizen influence with those who make the appointments and with those (e.g., the party) who promote certain candidates for election. Amazingly, few people play this aspect of the judicial game, even when it is so important.

The same two points for influence exist in the *federal selection system*. The political players on whom groups focus attention are the President, the attorney general, and U.S. senators. The professional players are the members of the ABA's Standing Committee on the Federal Judiciary.

This is how the process works. The Department of Justice, under the U.S. attorney general, recommends judicial appointments to the President. Other members of the White House staff may supply additional names. Some of these come from the ABA's report on proposed nominations.

The President's choice is sent to the Senate for confirmation. The Senate Judiciary Committee is responsible for screening all nominations. They too will solicit the advice of the ABA. Senate confirmation of lower federal court judges is usually assured if the President has followed the informal rule of "senatorial courtesy." This involves getting the approval of those senators from the state(s) involved who are from the President's own party. While Supreme Court nominations are rarely rejected, the rejection or obstruction rate for lower court judges is about 20 percent.

[33] For these and other consequences of selection systems, see Jacob, *Urban Justice*, pp. 72–79.

The politics of this process are interesting. A President will often consult with party leaders, state and national, before making a nomination. Trying to get their support and the support of the relevant senators involves considerable negotiation. The President will often stall, delay, and haggle in order to bargain for a particular candidate. Apart from the advantages gained from patronage, the President is still responsible for the quality of the nominees. President Nixon's prestige was certainly not enhanced by either the quality or the rejection of two Supreme Court nominations.

The politicking is not just at the federal level. It also occurs in states, where a lawyer may try to pave the way for an appointment. In a speech before the Chicago Bar Association Joseph Samuel Perry described how he got to be a federal judge:

> Since we are talking confidentially I will be perfectly frank with you folks in admitting that I tried to obtain this appointment seven years ago and learned that it requires [the support of] not one but two senators. At that time I was out of politics and they did not need me. Therefore, I decided that this time if I wanted that appointment I had better get back into politics—which I did. When I learned, as I soon did, that everyone shoots at the top man—that he is everyone's target—I went to each of the senators and said "Listen here, if you are going to back me, for heaven's sake don't make me number one. Be sure to back me and get me on the list but don't make me number one."
>
> As it turned out that proved to be pretty good strategy because everybody else was shot off and no use lying about it, I helped to shoot them off. The result of it was I landed on top. I have the job now and I am going to stick.[34]

In all likelihood Joseph Samuel Perry did stick. Long-term judicial tenure is a fact of life. In the federal courts, appointed judges remain until they resign. In state courts, appointed judges are usually reappointed without question and elected judges re-elected without challenge. That is why influencing initial judicial appointments is serious business.

Of course judges can be removed, although it is difficult. *Impeachment* is a remedy in cases of serious misconduct; 43 states and the federal government provide for removal from office through impeachment procedures. The procedures, however, are not often used. On

[34] Joseph Samuel Perry, "How I Got to Be a Federal Judge," in *Courts, Judges, and Politics*, ed. Walter F. Murphy and C. Herman Pritchett (New York: Random House, 1961), pp. 93–96.

the federal level, of the eight judicial impeachment efforts, only four have been successful.[35]

There are also easier ways of removing judges. In a few states the legislature may ask the governor to remove a judge. In others, a joint resolution of the legislature will do it. A few states allow the recall of judges. Each of these procedures is possible without a trial.

Then there are removal procedures that keep the matter within the legal profession. The ABA, for example, supports the use in several states of a *special court*. In this instance a specified person (the chief justice, the governor, the attorney general, a lawyer, or a citizen) will file a formal complaint. The complaint is considered in a public proceeding. Also receiving professional approval is the use of *commissions*, a practice in some states. Charges of judicial misconduct are investigated and decided by a special panel of judges, lawyers, and lay persons. Out of public view their deliberations may result in a private request to resign or a formal request to the state supreme court for disciplinary action. With both approaches judges may be removed from office for physical or emotional disability as well as for judicial misconduct.[36]

However, regardless of the procedure, removal doesn't occur often. Every judge will have an opportunity to make a significant impact on the distribution of justice within the jurisdiction. Citizens have an opportunity to evaluate that impact and to observe any decision-making patterns. It is important to be able to predict how a particular judge is likely to play the game. Under certain conditions, *how is he or she likely to move?* Probably the best way of predicting judicial moves is to look for decision-making patterns.

Those considering appeals to the U.S. Supreme Court, for example, are diligent pattern spotters. For them strategic information included these data about the 1974–1975 term: The power of the four justices former President Nixon nominated to the Supreme Court remained strong.[37] Led by Chief Justice Warren E. Burger, their generally conservative viewpoint prevailed, and they were frequently backed by two more moderate members of the court (Byron R. White and Potter Stewart). The result was decisions that generally

[35] Sigler, *Introduction to the Legal System*, p. 102.
[36] *Ibid.*, pp. 103–104.
[37] The Nixon appointees were Warren E. Burger, Harry A. Blackmun, Lewis F. Powell, Jr., and William H. Rehnquist. In the 1974–1975 term they voted together 69 percent of the time; in the 1973–1974 term they voted together 75 percent of the time.

favored a strict interpretation of the Constitution, curbed enforcement of the antitrust laws, enforced criminal sanctions vigorously, and cut back on federal court jurisdiction. The Burger bloc was most consistent in the area of criminal law, which constituted nearly one-quarter of the 1974–1975 docket. The four justices formed the nucleus of a majority, voting together 88 percent of the time. One more pattern was evident, an inclination to reverse lower court decisions. The justices rejected as legally unsound the reasoning of the lower court (state or federal) in two out of three disputes it heard.[38]

Something to think about
How might lawyers considering Supreme Court appeals use this information? What other information would be useful?

Judicial decision-making involves *three interdependent factors*— institutional, external, and personal. The first refers to the rules of the game; the second, to the political climate in which the judge resides; and the third, to the way in which the judge sees the job and the law. Together they influence moves, moves that are generally consistent.

Let's begin with the institutional factors. The most important rule of the courts as an institution is *precedent*. It is fundamental to judicial reasoning. This is how it works. A judge sees some similarity between the present case and previous cases. If the similarity is great enough, the judge will use the rule of law that emerged from the previous cases and apply it to the current case. The rule is, a judge should observe precedent. It is part of the doctrine of *stare decisis*, which generally means "to stand by the decisions and not disturb settled points."

The trick is determining similarities and differences. That is the judge's job. The judge has some flexibility if there is no clear statute involved. For example, a judge may find irrelevant the existence or absence of facts that prior judges thought important and that influenced their decisions. A judge may consider other facts to be of fundamental importance. This influences whether the judge will use

---

[38] This and other information about the 1974–1975 term was compiled by the *New York Times*. See Warren Weaver, "4 Nixon Justices Dominate Decisions," *New York Times*, July 3, 1975, p. 19.

a particular precedent or not, the degree to which a precedent will be stretched to fit, and so on.

If this process sounds somewhat vague, it is because it is. As new situations arise, and as people's wants change, the ambiguities of precedents permit new ideas and new rules to emerge.[39] The U.S. Supreme Court has recognized this need for flexibility. They have said that whether stare decisis "shall be followed or departed from is a question entirely within the discretion of the court, which is called upon to consider a question."

However, this way of reasoning is not departed from lightly by judges. It's too important a decision-making tool. It gives stability to the entire process. For example, lower court judges know that when decisions are appealed, the application of the appropriate precedent will be one of the aspects of the case examined. Lawyers are also able to predict that a particular precedent is likely to play an important role in the ultimate decision. So each key actor knows the rules and is able to generally rely on their being observed. Of course, this way of reasoning also allows judges to make decisions more easily. When they rely on previous decisions, they do not have to treat the legal aspects of each case as new situations. This, then, is a crucial institutional norm that usually supersedes personal ones.[40]

Because of its application to judicial games played in *every* arena, stare decisis is the most important institutional factor. There are others, however, that need to at least be identified. They include other decision-making rules, customs, and procedures. In some states, for example, appellate judges supervise the entire state court system in addition to reviewing cases. This is bound to affect judicial behavior. Also, where judges decide cases as a group (at the appeals level), the need to achieve a majority point of view will influence moves. Finally, the way a judge gets and keeps the job must come into play. Those trial judges who need to run for re-election may need the continuing support of political parties and interest groups. These and other institutional factors vary from state to state but cannot be dismissed as unimportant in understanding how judges make up their minds.

What about the *personal* factors? To what extent do they mitigate the importance of the institutional ones? One personal fac-

[39] Edward H. Levi elaborates on these points in "An Introduction to Legal Reasoning," in *Courts, Judges, and Politics*, ed. Murphy and Pritchett, pp. 371–376.
[40] This was the conclusion of Theodore L. Becker in *Political Behavioralism and Modern Jurisprudence* (Chicago: Rand McNally & Company, 1964), p. 128.

tor is the way each judge views the job. That view, of course, is the result of various influences. One is the general political culture, most relevantly an abstract belief in equality before the law and the value of impartial justice. A second is law school culture, which conveys a more explicit respect for law and legal procedure along with a set of ideas about the qualities and expected behavior of a "good" judge. Finally, there is the court culture itself, which communicates the various traditions and practices that are a part of that arena.

Obviously those cultural factors don't produce judges who are all alike. Judges do end up with differing views of the job, and that will influence their moves. One way of dichotomizing how judges see their job is as *traditionalist* and *activist*. The traditionalist believes that judges should be strictly bound by precedent, while the activist believes that judges should exercise their own value preferences or those they perceive to be in the best interests of the society. While most judges are not entirely at one or the other pole, the pole to which they are closest is important. Former Supreme Court Justice Benjamin Cordozo explained his approach to decision-making in this way:

> My analysis of the judicial process comes then to this, and little more: logic, and history, and custom, and utility, and the accepted standards of right conduct, are the forces which singly or in combination shape the progress of the law. Which of these forces shall dominate in any case must depend largely upon the comparative importance or value of the social interests that will be thereby promoted or impaired.[41]

Several studies have attempted to analyze precisely how judges see their job. The results of interviews with state supreme court judges in four states (Delaware, Maryland, New York, and Virginia) revealed that most tend toward the traditionalist view. Specifically, over half the judges interviewed strongly believed they should restrict themselves almost exclusively to interpreting the law rather than making law. Very few were believers in judicial activism or positivism. They were not adverse to creating new law when they were convinced that circumstances warranted it. Generally, however, they believed that that should be up to legislators and only secondarily up to judges. One-third of the judges interviewed, however, refused to commit

[41] Benjamin N. Cordozo, *The Nature of the Judicial Process* (New Haven, Conn.: Yale University Press, 1921). This and other excerpts are from *Courts, Judges, and Politics*, ed. Murphy and Pritchett, p. 29.

themselves fully to either approach. They felt it depended on the particular case before them.[42]

How a particular judge sees the job is ultimately going to depend not only on the socialization that occurs in law schools and among judicial peers, but also on personal values, attitudes, and beliefs. For example, the previously mentioned study of state supreme court judges also revealed that how they saw their job was related to their political outlook. Those who labeled themselves politically conservative uniformly adopted the law-interpreter position. Political moderates were strongly attracted to the eclectic position. More political liberals adopted the lawmaker (activist) orientation than did either moderates or conservatives. One-half of the liberals, however, took the eclectic position.[43]

The implications of the study for understanding judicial moves are twofold. First, state supreme court judges, and perhaps others, feel relatively free to approach their decisions from their own norms. The pressure to conform to one view of the job does not appear strong. Second, one cannot describe judicial decision-making simply in terms of attachment to legal precedent. Almost one-half of those interviewed perceived a sound degree of innovation and sponsorship of legal change to be either a necessary or a proper part of their job. Some even admitted the necessity of legislation through the courts.[44]

Something to think about

Why is this information important, and how can citizens interested in playing the judicial game determine how a particular judge sees the job?

A particular factor that has received a great deal of attention is party affiliation. The question asked has been, does a judge's affiliation with one party or another reflect or produce certain attitudes that in turn influence certain moves? At least one political scientist who interviewed appellate judges in 48 states concluded that there was a

---

[42] John T. Wold, "Political Orientation, Social Backgrounds, and Role Perceptions of State Supreme Court Judges," *Western Political Quarterly*, June 1974, pp. 239–248. The study by Glick and Vines also revealed the tendency to favor the more traditional approach, law interpreting, *State Court Systems*, p. 61.

[43] Wold, "Political Orientations," pp. 246–247.

[44] *Ibid.*, p. 247.

clear connection.[45] However, others have found that the political climate of the *state* is the important external factor. If that climate is highly partisan, if the party plays an important role in the election or appointment of judges, then the party affiliation of judges does allow one to predict decision-making.[46]

Something to think about
How is one likely to know whether party affiliation is important to judges in a given state?

So after all this, what do we know about judicial games? First, there are various types of law operating, but all reflect the values and norms of a given society. Second, to play the judicial game one needs to know not only this law, but the different characteristics of the appropriate arenas in which it is interpreted. For most citizens and their legal representatives, the characteristics of their own state's judicial system are most important and, depending on the nature of the case, the federal system is important as well, but understanding the subtleties of all 51 legal systems is too overwhelming and not at all necessary. Third, wherever the game is played, a special vocabulary is used. Citizens who want to follow or play judicial games will have to become familiar with that language. They must also become familiar with the different kinds of wins—those that are narrow in scope, with little impact beyond the case at hand, and those that represent fundamental policy changes. Finally, each player in the game has a different degree of power. Police officers, prosecutors, and judges, for example, have an unusually great amount of discretion to play the game as they want, but how each plays will depend on the rules, how each gets and sees the job, and the political climate in which they are operating. The job for citizens and their lawyers is to look for the decision-making patterns. These must be considered as strategies and tactics are developed.

---

[45] Stuart Nagel, "Political Party Affiliation and Judges' Decisions," *American Political Science Review*, December 1961, pp. 843–850.
[46] Sidney Ulmer, "The Political Party Variable in the Michigan Supreme Court," *Journal of Public Law* 11 (1962): 352–362, and David W. Ademany, "The Party Variable in Judges' Voting: Conceptual Notes and a Case Study," *American Political Science Review*, March 1969, pp. 57–73.

This overview of judicial games provides the background needed to begin. However, as with other institutional games, citizens need to know the specific rules that give them some leverage and rules that give them access. On to that.

Key Words

Civil law
Constitutional law
Common law
Statutory law
Criminal law
Plaintiff
Prosecutor
Pleadings
Complaint
Defendant
Counsel
Case
Trial
Facts
Judge
Jury
Verdict
Appeals
Adversary proceedings
Judicial review
Precedent
Stare decisis

Suggested Activities

1. Visit a trial. Apply as many of the "key words" as are relevant.
2. Determine the arrest and prosecution priorities of your local police department and prosecutor's office.

14
Rules of the Judicial Game

Now that we have examined all the players involved, the various arenas and kinds of law, and the special words and moves, the complexity of judicial games should be apparent. What is not apparent thus far is that each player has rules that give an advantage and that allow him or her to play. For citizen players the most important rules to know about are those that become *their* resources in judicial games. These will be the focus of this chapter.

Rules as Determinants of Power

Due Process of Law
In 1961 Clarence Earl Gideon was 51 years old. He had just been convicted of robbing the Bay Harbor poolroom in Panama City, Florida. This wasn't his first conviction. He had frequently been in and out of prisons and he had that look: a wrinkled, prematurely aged face; a voice and hands that trembled; a frail body; and white hair. However, despite his frequent visits to prison, Clarence Gideon was not a professional criminal or a man of violence. He just had a hard time settling down to work, and so he made his way by gambling

419

and occasional thefts. Most who knew him called him a perfectly harmless human being, just one tossed aside by life.[1]

This "perfectly harmless man," however, treated this conviction differently. Not only did he say he was innocent of the charges, but he said that his conviction was unconstitutional. Writing in pencil, using carefully formed printing like a school child's, on lined paper probably provided by the Florida prison, he wrote to the U.S. Supreme Court.[2] The issue, Gideon explained, was due process. To deprive a poor person of the right to counsel, as Florida had, was to deprive that person of due process of law.

This was, of course, his last chance to appeal. The Florida Supreme Court had previously denied his *writ of habeus corpus*, an order freeing him on the ground that he was illegally held.

Gideon's persistence paid off. In 1964 the U.S. Supreme Court ruled in his favor. They agreed that by being denied the right to counsel Clarence Gideon was indeed denied due process of law. Delivering the opinion for the Court, Mr. Justice Black made these comments:

> In our adversary system of criminal justice, any person hauled into court, who is too poor to hire a lawyer, cannot be assured a fair trial unless counsel is provided for him. This seems to us to be an obvious truth. Governments, both state and federal, quite properly spend vast sums of money to establish machinery to try defendants accused of crime. Lawyers to prosecute are everywhere deemed essential to protect the public's interest in an orderly society. Similarly, there are few defendants charged with crime, few indeed, who fail to hire the best lawyers they can to prepare and present their defenses. That government hires lawyers to prosecute and defendants who have the money to hire lawyers to defend are the strongest indications of the widespread belief that lawyers in criminal courts are necessities, not luxuries. The right of one charged with crime to counsel may not be deemed fundamental and essential to fair trials in some countries, but it is in ours. From the very beginning, our state and national constitutions and laws have laid great emphasis on *procedural and substantive safeguards designed to assure fair trials* before impartial tribunals in which every defendant stands equal before the law. This noble idea cannot be realized if the poor man charged with crime has to face his accusers without a lawyer to assist him. (*Gideon v. Wainwright*, 372 *U.S. 335.*)

---

[1] Anthony Lewis, *Gideon's Trumpet* (New York: Random House, 1964), pp. 5–6.
[2] *Ibid.*, p. 4.

Justice Black was talking about procedural and substantive justice, better known as *due process of law*. Overruling the immediate relevant precedent (*Betts* v. *Brady*, 1942), the Court restated an earlier opinion. In *Grosjean* v. *American Press Co.* (1936), "We concluded that certain fundamental rights safeguarded by the first eight amendments against federal action, were also safeguarded against state action by the due process clause of the Fourteenth Amendment, and among them the fundamental right of the accused to the aid of counsel in a criminal prosecution."

So Gideon, denied this right by the State of Florida, regained it through his rights under the due process clause of the Fourteenth Amendment of the U.S. Constitution—rights states sometimes forgot to take seriously.

The reason for focusing on due process of law is that it is the most fundamental rule for citizens in *both criminal and civil cases*. It is our crucial resource in judicial games. Briefly stated, "nor shall any State deprive any person of life, liberty, or property, without due process of law...." [3]

Well, what does it mean specifically, apart from guaranteeing defendants the right to counsel in criminal cases? Take a look at the first eight amendments to the U.S. Constitution. What *procedures* of justice must the government follow? These amendments include protection against unreasonable searches and seizures; the right to a grand jury hearing in criminal cases; protection against double jeopardy and self-incrimination; the right to a speedy and public trial by an impartial jury, to be informed of accusations, to be confronted with witnesses, and to obtain witnesses on one's own behalf; and protection against excessive bail, excessive fines, and cruel and unusual punishment. Clearly, the Bill of Rights is a citizen's dream. The procedural provisions are all summarized in the simple words *due process*.

So far we've been talking about *procedural due process*. There is another kind, referred to as *substantive due process*. In this case, the particular law itself is involved. It too must be fair and reasonable and not arbitrary. A city cannot pass an ordinance, for example, that compels companies to shorten work days by two hours yet pay the same salaries. This would be not only an arbitrary use of law but a denial of the property rights of employers.

[3] The same language appears in the Fifth Amendment and protects citizens in federal cases.

Well, assuming someone is denied due process of law and proves it in court, what can the court do about it? If substantive due process has been denied, the court will strike down the particular legislative or executive acts involved. If procedural justice has been denied, an appellate court might simply release the accused or order a retrial under different procedures. This is what happened to Clarence Gideon. He was retried in the original Florida court, only this time with a court-appointed attorney. New evidence was found, and Gideon was declared not guilty.

This also happened to a Louisiana man accused of bank robbery, kidnapping, and murder. While awaiting trial in 1961, the accused man admitted in a conversation with the sheriff that he had committed the crimes. A local television station televised the conversation from the man's jail cell. Three of the twelve jurors in the original trial admitted having seen the televised confession before the trial. His conviction was set aside by the Supreme Court, and he was retried in another city. The verdict—guilty.[4]

Denial of due process can be expensive business, and the courts can order the guilty to pay. This is what the U.S. Justice Department and Washington, D.C., police discovered. They were the defendants in a very unusual case. In May 1971, the last great wave of organized protest occurred in Washington, D.C. The war in Vietnam was the issue. Thousands of protestors swarmed through Georgetown and across the Virginia bridges to disrupt rush-hour traffic. City police, joined by Marines and soldiers, swept them up by the thousands, ignoring formal arrest procedures, eventually fencing those detained inside a stockade on the Redskins football team's practice field. Later in the week, hundreds of other demonstrators marched on the Capitol for a last rally. Police this time arrested 1,200 of them and carted them by bus to a makeshift detention center in the Washington Coliseum.

To civil libertarians, these mass arrests without any procedural safeguards were appalling. To President Nixon and Attorney General John Mitchell, they were praiseworthy. To a Washington jury hearing the case 3½ years later, they were obviously outside the requirements of due process of law. The jury awarded $12 million in damages to the petitioners arrested at the Capitol—or roughly $10,000 apiece. In addition to being one of the largest nonbusiness civil awards, it is

---

[4] John Paul Hanna, *The Complete Layman's Guide to the Law* (Englewood Cliffs, N.J.: Prentice-Hall, 1974), pp. 441–442.

thought to be the first case in U.S. history in which damages were awarded directly for violation of rights granted by the U.S. Constitution.[5]

Rights of the arrested and accused.   Well, what are one's *rights when arrested and accused* of a crime? Knowing them is an obvious resource for citizens who find themselves in this predicament. A description of a few of the more important ones will help.[6]

First, those arrested and accused have the *privilege against self-incrimination*. It's all there in the Fifth Amendment: no one shall be compelled in any criminal case to be a witness against himself. What's wrong with asking someone if he or she did it or didn't do it? There are two reasons. First, if police are given permission to ask, they may be inclined to use unusual techniques to get the answer. Second, someone who is arrested is presumed innocent—the burden of proof is upon the state. So in light of that presumption, the state must respect the integrity and dignity of the individual.

The U.S. Supreme Court has been saying this for a long time. In 1936 (*Brown* v. *Mississippi*), for example, the courts definitely came out against coerced confessions. In this case, Mississippi police had tortured the defendants in order to extort a confession. The court overturned the conviction, using the Fifth Amendment. They continued to slap the hands of police in 1940. In a Florida case (*Chambers* v. *Florida*) the man arrested was not presented with a warrant, was denied contact with friends and with his attorney, and was subjected to long periods of questioning by different squads of police officers. The Court threw out the conviction. Other similar cases followed, and the direction of the Court's decisions was clear. Then came Escobedo.

Danny Escobedo was imprisoned in 1960 after he allegedly confessed to plotting the murder of his sister's husband in Chicago. In 1964, the U.S. Supreme Court overturned his conviction on the grounds that police had not advised him of his right to remain silent and had prevented him from seeing his lawyer.

The case (*Escobedo* v. *Illinois*) is particularly important for several reasons. It reaffirmed the privilege against self-incrimination. If a lawyer is present during questioning, a person's rights are more

---

[5] "Paying for Mayday," *Newsweek*, January 27, 1975, p. 46.
[6] For details, see the American Civil Liberties Union booklet on the rights of the accused, available from most ACLU offices.

likely to be guaranteed. Also, under the Fourteenth Amendment, it extended the Sixth Amendment right to counsel to the states. Remember, the Court had done this a year earlier in the *Gideon* case. Speaking for the majority, Justice Goldberg had this to say:

> We hold ... that where, as here, the investigation is no longer a general inquiry into an unsolved crime but has begun to focus on a particular suspect, the suspect has been taken into police custody, the police carry out a process of interrogations that lends itself to eliciting incriminating statements, the suspect has requested and been denied an opportunity to consult with his lawyer, and the police have not effectively warned him of his absolute constitutional right to remain silent, the accused has been denied "the Assistance of Counsel" in violation of the Sixth Amendment to the Constitution as "made obligatory upon the States by the Fourteenth Amendment," *Gideon* v. *Wainwright*, and that no statement elicited by the police during the interrogation may be used against him at a criminal trial.

Two years later (1966) the Supreme Court finally got down to specifics on the subject of self-incrimination. In *Miranda* v. *Arizona* the judges extended the Fifth Amendment guarantee against self-incrimination to the states, making them aware of their obligation, but the Court, in addition, specified the *rules* to follow. They didn't want any more confusion.

> To summarize, we hold that when an individual is taken into custody or otherwise deprived of his freedom by the authorities in any significant way and is subjected to questioning, the privilege against self-incrimination is jeopardized. Procedural safeguards must be employed to protect the privilege, and unless other fully effective means are adopted to notify the person of his right of silence and to assure that the exercise of the right will be scrupulously honored, the following measures are required. He must be warned prior to any questioning that he has the right to remain silent, that anything he says can be used against him in a court of law, that he has the right to the presence of any attorney, and that if he cannot afford an attorney one will be appointed for him prior to any questioning if he so desires. Opportunity to exercise the rights must be afforded to him throughout the interrogation. After such warnings have been given, and such opportunity afforded him, the individual may knowingly and intelligently waive these rights and agree to answer questions or make a statement. But unless and until such warnings and waiver are demonstrated by the prosecution at trial, no evidence obtained as a result of interrogation can be used against him.[7]

7 Jonathan D. Casper, *The Politics of Civil Liberties* (New York: Harper & Row, Publishers, 1972), p. 262.

Law enforcement agencies hadn't liked the way the courts had been moving. They felt the courts were favoring the rights of the accused over the rights to law and order of society at large. The *Miranda* decision was considered the worst yet. Police claimed it would undermine the entire enforcement effort. The result? According to two studies, police did a poor job of enforcing it,[8] even though the case could be thrown out during the trial or on appeal, and even though, according to still another study, confessions are not as crucial to convictions as one might expect. Clearly, when the attitudes of those responsible for implementing the law are adverse to it, the process is very, very slow.

In addition to the protection against self-incrimination and the right to counsel, those accused of crimes are guaranteed *protection against excessive bail*. At least, this is what the Eighth Amendment to the U.S. Constitution says. In practice, in federal court under Rule 46 and in most state courts, bail is granted in noncapital cases. The only significant Supreme Court decision dealing with bail occurred in *Stock* v. *Boyle*, 1951. In this case the Court emphasized that the only constitutionally permissible function of bail was ensuring that a defendant would appear at trial. Any bail set at a "higher figure than an amount reasonably calculated to fulfill this purpose is 'excessive' under the Eighth Amendment."

This sounds fair, if somewhat vague, but the vagueness has contributed to some problems. Instead of being set to assure a defendant's appearance in court, bail is almost always related to the seriousness of the offense involved. For example, in New York City, persons charged with robbery and burglary must meet higher bail than those charged with sex offenses or forgery.[9]

There are more problems with this supposed citizen resource than the incorrect function it serves. Let's look at the process involved. Most arrests are made without a warrant. Since they usually occur at night, the police generally hold a suspect until morning. At that time the suspect is brought before a magistrate (a judge of a minor criminal court). Here the suspect is informed of charges, reminded of rights, and informed of the bail necessary for release. Sometimes, however, the bail isn't set until the following day, at another hearing. The fact that bail is set within one or two days means that the judge knows almost nothing about the defendant—only the offense charged.

[8] *Ibid.*, pp. 263–266.
[9] Herbert Jacob, *Justice in America*, 2d ed. (Boston: Little, Brown and Company, 1972), pp. 167–168.

It is only in small cities and rural areas where the workload is not too great that a judge has time to deliberate over bail decisions.[10]

The implications of this process are many—mostly negative. The story of Julio Roldan is particularly illustrative.

Nearly 300 cases were being processed in Part 1-A on October 14, 1970, when Julio Roldan, thirty-four years old—a high-strung Puerto Rican poet, seller of handicrafts, and new member of the Young Lords, the radical Puerto Rican political party in New York—was brought before the judge on a charge of arson growing out of a Young Lords street protest the night before. The protest was over poor garbage collection. In vain, Roldan had complained to the arresting policemen that he and a friend were only trying to stamp out garbage set on fire on the sidewalk by someone else.

After waiting in jail overnight, and in the courthouse lockup from 7:30 a.m., Roldan came before the judge for his brief arraignment at 2:30 p.m. The prosecutor had already processed thirty new cases during the hour following the lunch break. He had not seen the papers on Roldan before 2:30, when, glancing at the information placed before him—including the fact that Roldan was a Young Lord, an identification that frequently draws a hostile reaction from law enforcement agents in New York—he recommended that $2,500 bail bond be set. Roldan's lawyer was in court, but he had not been given an opportunity to interview his client in the lockup during the long wait before arraignment. He protested and asked that Roldan be freed without bond or at least have the opportunity to confer with him first. Roldan himself, obviously upset, cried out, "There is no justice in this court. There is no one here to represent us. This is only happening because I am Puerto Rican."

The Judge, pointing out that he was swamped with business, granted a delay, and the lawyer, who did volunteer work for the Young Lords but had not met Roldan previously, began to argue that his client's emotional condition suggested he should be sent to a hospital for observation. Before the lawyer could argue further, as a transcript of the proceedings later showed, the judge cut him off in midsentence and set bail at $1,500. There was no more time to waste on this case, the judge told the lawyer. "We are working under adverse conditions . . . I can't create the Utopia here."

Roldan did not have the bail money or the premium payment ·of more than $100 that was required to obtain a bail bond in that large an amount. He was sent next door to the towering Tombs jail and there put in an 8-by-8-by-6 foot all-steel cell. During the next two days, Julio Roldan apparently grew increasingly irrational. On

[10] Herbert Jacob, *Urban Justice* (Englewood Cliffs, N.J.: Prentice-Hall, 1973), p. 68.

the third morning of his confinement, guards coming by to count prisoners at 8:30 a.m. found him dead, hanging by his belt from a steel bar in the rear of his cell.

"Ordinarily, in view of his outbursts in court, he would have been assigned to an observation cell used to keep potential suicides under surveillance," according to a detailed report from the city's corrections department made later to Mayor John V. Lindsay. "However, word of his outbursts did not reach jail officials, so he was treated as a routine case." [11]

Julio Roldan's story is, fortunately, not the usual one for those denied bail. However, the usual story, because of its frequency, should be examined.

Bail means money. It is a monetary guarantee that the accused will appear in court. If the accused has sufficient funds to put up the stipulated bail, he or she is freed. In some states, the defendant must pay 10 percent of the required bail to the court. If the defendant appears in court, 90 percent of what is paid is returned. The remainder is kept to administer the bail system. In most states, however, bail is provided by sellers of bail bonds, who require 10 percent payment. These are people engaging in private business, so the fee is nonrefundable. If the seller of bail bonds does not consider the defendant a good risk, he or she may refuse to sell a bond. The defendant then remains in jail.[12]

The poor, like Julio Roldan, are well represented in jail. They usually don't have property or savings, or friends and relations who will lend them the amount of money required. In Philadelphia, recent studies reveal, one-quarter of those charged with felonies in state courts and one-half of those charged in federal courts could not make bail.[13]

Something to think about
What are the implications of being in jail? What are the costs, other than confinement?

Jail because of nonbail is serious business. It is not unusual to be confined for 30 days while awaiting trial, and for serious charges the

[11] Leonard Downie, Jr., *Justice Denied* (Baltimore, Md.: Praeger Publishers, Penguin Books, 1971), pp. 42–43. © 1971 by Praeger Publishers, Inc. Reprinted by permission.
[12] Jacob, *Justice in America*, p. 97.
[13] *Ibid.*, p. 169.

time could run from three to six months. In 1970, according to the Law Enforcement Assistance Administration, there were 160,000 prisoners in local and county jails throughout the United States. Of those, 35 percent were awaiting trial and another 17 percent had not yet been arraigned—and people in jail, whether convicted or awaiting trial, are treated in the same way. Yet we say our system of justice believes a person is innocent until proved guilty.

In addition to the obvious costs of confinement because one has been denied bail, there is another. Studies done in both New York and Philadelphia reveal that those who were unable to post bail and remained in jail were much more likely to be found guilty and to receive severe punishment than those who had been free.[14] There is an alternative, fortunately. The federal government has had since 1966, and many cities now have, something called the *own recognizance* system (OR). Where it exists, people with no previous criminal record and firm roots in the community are freed simply on the promise they will appear in court. In such cities as New York and San Francisco the results are encouraging. The percentage of those failing to come to court is far lower than under bail systems. While the poor still have a harder time meeting OR requirements, the system is a substantial improvement.

With all the problems implicit in bail, how can the Eighth Amendment be considered a citizen resource? It *is* for the nonpoor and for those with access to OR systems, and to the extent that this country becomes more serious about the inequities pervading our criminal justice system, it will become a resource for others.

Another of the due process guarantees discussed earlier is the *right to an impartial jury,* provided for in the Sixth and Seventh Amendments of the U.S. Constitution and extended to states through the Fourteenth. This rule can distribute power to citizens if they choose to use it. It is a resource that is applicable to *both criminal and civil* proceedings.

We know how jurors get chosen, a little about how they make their moves, and something about the problems associated with jury selection. However, since having a jury is a potential resource, as lawyer Allan Brotsky seems to suggest in the previous chapter, the rules spelling out the dimensions of the right should be identified.

The U.S. Constitution, of course, establishes the basic right, and several Supreme Court decisions have clarified how it should be ap-

[14] *Ibid.,* p. 170.

plied. One involved the case of *Duncan* v. *Louisiana* (1968). Gary Duncan was convicted of simple battery in the District Court of Louisiana. Under Louisiana law simple battery is a misdemeanor, punishable by a maximum of two years' imprisonment and a $300 fine. Duncan wanted a trial by jury, but the Louisiana Constitution granted jury trials only in cases in which capital punishment or imprisonment at hard labor could be imposed. So Gary Duncan was denied a jury. He was convicted by a judge and sentenced to serve 60 days in the parish prison. He also had to pay a fine of $150. Obviously unhappy, he appealed to the state supreme court. They denied the appeal; the state constitution was clear on the subject.

The U.S. Supreme Court accepted the appeal, however. Its final decision in favor of Gary Duncan was important for two reasons. First, it established the fact that by virtue of the Fourteenth Amendment, the Sixth Amendment guarantee of an impartial jury applies in state courts. Thus, Louisiana had to offer Gary Duncan that choice. Second, it clarified the categories of crimes for which people must be given the right. According to Justice White, who delivered the opinion:

> It is doubtless true that there is a category of petty crimes or offenses which is not subject to the Sixth Amendment jury trial provision and should not be subject to the Fourteenth Amendment jury trial requirement here applied to the states. Crimes carrying possible penalties up to six months do not require a jury trial if they otherwise qualify as petty offenses. But the penalty authorized for a particular crime is of major relevance in determining whether it is serious or not and may in itself, if severe enough, subject the trial to the mandate of the Sixth Amendment.

This six months imprisonment definition of a serious crime was further emphasized in 1970 (*Baldwin* v. *New York*). If a defendant faces the possibility of six months or more imprisonment, states must grant that defendant the right to a jury.

The founders eased the definition problem in the Seventh Amendment. "In suits at common law (civil suits), where the value in controversy shall exceed twenty dollars, the right of trial by jury shall be preserved."

Does this mean the reverse right is also preserved? Can a person who does not want a jury independently waive that right? Not according to a 1965 Supreme Court decision (*Singer* v. *United States*). Singer, charged with mail fraud, didn't want a jury trial, but he didn't know about Rule 23(a) of the Federal Rules of Criminal Procedure:

Cases required to be tried by jury shall be so tried unless the defendant waives a jury trial in writing with the approval of the court and consent of the government.

No, Mr. Singer, the Court said, "The ability to waive a constitutional right does not ordinarily carry with it the right to insist upon the opposite of that right. . . ." In this case, while the trial court consented, the prosecutor (the government) refused.

One other aspect of this citizen resource needs clarification. How many jurors assures fairness? Under common law, a jury consisted of 12 people. However, in *Williams* v. *Florida* (1970), the U.S. Supreme Court expressed the view that this was really an arbitrary figure. "The relevant inquiry, as we see it, must be the function which the particular feature performs and its relation to the purposes of the jury trial. Measured by this standard, the twelve-person requirement cannot be regarded as an indispensable component of the Sixth Amendment." So Duncan, who was on trial for robbery in the state of Florida, had to be satisfied with the six-person jury provided by Florida law in all but capital cases. A jury with fewer than 12 persons is also quite common in other states, particularly in civil cases.

Something to think about
What would be the advantages and disadvantages of having a 12-person jury rather than a jury of 6 or 8?

In summary, juries can be a citizen resource in judicial games when a serious crime is involved or when a civil dispute involves more than a certain amount of money (the amount varies). The right cannot always be waived. When juries are used, they may consist of fewer than 12 people. Whether or not a jury indeed would be a resource in court probably depends on the case, but this is a major strategic decision best made in consultation with one's attorney.

Something to think about
What would influence a person's decision about whether or not to have a jury trial?

Equal Protection of the Law

Fredrico Gonçalvez is the father of eight children. He and his family spend each year following harvests. Wherever they end up there are few comforts. They sleep where they can, sometimes in the open. If they happen to find a dwelling they can afford, it is probably a cheap skid row hotel or shack. Heating is unlikely, and mattresses are often flattened pasteboard boxes. Every member of the family who can works 10, 11, or even 12 hours a day, often in temperatures of over 100°F. They eat where and when they can.

Fredrico's 18-year-old son, Juan, was arrested recently. He was accused of stealing a car. Confused, frightened, and angry, Fredrico visited him in jail. His son said that he was innocent. What kind of justice could Juan Gonçalvez expect?

Statistically, people such as Juan are in bad shape when it comes to criminal justice. According to the President's Advisory Council on Civil Disorders (1968 Kerner Commission), from arrest to sentencing the poor are denied equal justice.

A look at the inequities in sentencing suggests what Juan is up against. A 1969 report by the administrative office of the United States courts revealed that those with assigned counsel rather than private counsel are sentenced more than twice as severely. There is no doubt that Juan is not able to afford private counsel. In addition, if Juan demands a trial to prove his innocence rather than plea-bargaining with the prosecutor, if found guilty he is likely to be given a far harsher sentence. Specifically, according to the same 1969 report, those who were convicted after trial were sentenced more than twice as severely as those who pleaded guilty ahead of time. Then too, the type of crime makes a difference. Car theft is not one of the favored crimes. Federal Judge Marvin E. Frankel has this to say about the status of crimes:

> There's a traditional difference in sentences for different types of crimes, and it tends to discriminate against the uneducated, unloved, social reject. The guy who steals packages from the back of the truck is going to get four years. And the guy who steals $45,000 is going to get three months.[15]

Good luck, Juan.

[15] Leslie Oelsner, "The Uneven Hand of Justice," *San Francisco Examiner and Chronicle*, "This World," October 29, 1972.

Viewing the problem historically, there has been some progress.[16] We have been moving steadily toward various forms of equal protection. The Revolutionary and post-Revolutionary period produced gains for religious minorities. During this time taxes for religious support were eliminated, as were restrictions on public worship. The Jacksonian period gradually removed religious tests for public office and removed property qualifications for voters and for candidates for public office. The Civil War era produced a subtle shift toward racial equality. At least, slavery was abolished. With the passage of the Sherman Antitrust Act in 1890 there was an attempt to equalize the competitive battle in economic spheres. Labor's bargaining position relative to business was enhanced. From early twentieth century to the present there have been very gradual gains for nonwhite citizens and for women. Today, ostensibly, citizens of all races and religions and both sexes are guaranteed *equal protection of the law* in education, housing, employment, politics, and criminal justice—in fact, in every area in which the government has the right to make laws. The equal protection clause of the Fourteenth Amendment is the major rule involved.[17]

These guarantees, however, are difficult to apply. They offer very little hope to Juan Gonçalvez. When the power of the majority is perceived to be threatened, acceptance of the rules comes slowly. So, each right has had to be established through legislative, executive, and judicial battles, and subsequent battles, often more heated, have been necessary in order to have them applied.

Yet, if citizens are up to it and have other resources, the right to equal protection of the law is undeniable. It is a major source of leverage in judicial games. Always, in deciding who wins, judges and juries will focus on these two questions: (1) Was the specific law involved administered impartially? (2) Did the legislature, in adopting a law providing for differential treatment of different segments of the public, set up a *reasonable classification* of the objects or persons treated, in view of the overall purposes of the law? The second question means that people and things may be treated differently if the classification is *reasonable*. Landlords and tenants can be treated differently, but white and black citizens cannot.

In the late 1960s a third question was used to determine whether

16 This overview of the growth in equal protection is from M. Glenn Abernathy, *Civil Liberties under the Constitution*, 2d ed. (New York: Dodd, Mead & Company, 1922), pp. 453–454.
17 Excluded from equal protection of the law, generally, are private actions.

or not citizens have been denied equal protection. Does the law impinge on fundamental rights? If it does, unless the state demonstrates a compelling reason, the law is unconstitutional.

Applying the standard adopted in the 1960s, the Supreme Court has declared a variety of laws to be inconsistent with the Fourteenth Amendment. These have included laws making persons who have resided in a state for less than a year ineligible to vote and/or to receive public assistance, laws making it a crime for a doctor to prescribe a contraceptive device to an unmarried person but not to a married one, and for anyone other than a doctor or pharmacist to give a contraceptive device to any person; laws imposing such high fees on candidates in primaries that it becomes difficult for those without funds or financial backing to run; and laws making it difficult for minor parties to obtain places on the ballot.[18]

While most of the Court's attention over the years has been given to denial of equal protection on the basis of religion, race, and national origin, cases involving sex discrimination are increasingly being decided. Again, the same kinds of questions are used as guides.

Sometimes rules other than the Fourteenth Amendment are involved. For example, Title VII of the Civil Rights Act of 1964 says that it shall be an unlawful employment practice for an employer "to fail or refuse to hire or to discharge any individual, or otherwise to discriminate against any individual with respect to his compensation, terms, conditions, or privileges of employment, because of such individual's ... sex. ..." Employment agencies and labor unions are also barred from making classifications or otherwise discriminating on the basis of sex. The only exception is "in those instances where ... sex ... is a bona fide occupational qualification reasonably necessary to the normal operation of that particular business or enterprise." [19]

So that is a specific resource for women seeking employment or presently employed. The Equal Employment Opportunity Commission (EEOC), created by the act, is supposed to help enforce it. In 1972 Congress gave the EEOC the authority to go to court on behalf of claimants. Here are some results. In June 1974, in a case against the Corning Glass Company, the Supreme Court ruled for the first time that employers must pay men and women equal wages for what is essentially equal work. The decision cost Corning $1 million in

[18] These and other recent equal-protection cases are identified in J. W. Peltason, *Understanding the Constitution*, 6th ed. (Hinsdale, Ill.: The Dryden Press, 1973), pp. 159–160.
[19] Abernathy, *Civil Liberties*, p. 462.

"You Can't Have A Balanced Court If They _ALL_ Believe In Civil Rights"

From _Herblock's State of the Union_ (Simon & Schuster, 1972)

back pay at one plant for women who had been receiving a lower base rate for daytime work than men who did similar jobs at night. In another major 1974 case the Bank of America reached an out-of-court settlement of a suit filed on behalf of its women employees. The settlement brought them $10 million in higher salaries, set up a $3.75 million trust fund for education and "self-development" programs, and was to increase the overall proportion of women officers to 40 percent by 1978. These decisions followed other similar rulings or settlements with AT&T, Standard Oil of California, and almost the entire steel industry.[20]

In recent years students also have been increasingly receiving equal protection of the law. While these are not precisely Fourteenth Amendment cases, the results are the same. Take the right of free speech. We know that has been an adult right for some time, but students have generally been excluded. In 1969, however, the case of *Tinker v. Des Moines Independent Community School District* came before the Supreme Court. Iowa students who had worn black armbands to protest the war in Vietnam were appealing a decision against them. Although the students had done no more than engage in peaceful protest, they had been ordered by school authorities to remove their armbands. The Supreme Court found that the students' First Amendment right had been violated. No action of the students, they explained, had created any material and substantial interference with appropriate requirements of school discipline. Unfortunately, they made no mention of the "clear and present danger test" used to evaluate adult free speech cases.[21]

The Tinker case was consistent with the landmark case on student censorship, *Dickey v. Alabama Board of Education* (1967). Gary Dickey was the editor of a college student newspaper. He refused to obey a rule that prohibited criticism of the Alabama legislature in the paper. Instead of not printing the article, he printed it with the word "censored" across the page. His expulsion was followed by a federal court action for reinstatement. Dickey prevailed. He had, the court concluded, a First Amendment right to criticize state officials. The school's prohibition could not be justified.[22]

Finally, and this in no way exhausts the subject of student rights, students have a right to academic due process. That is, they have a

---

[20] "The Job-Bias Juggernaut," *Newsweek*, June 17, 1974, p. 75.
[21] Roy Lucas, "The Rights of Students," in Norman Dorsen, *The Rights of Americans*, ed. Norman Dorsen (New York: Random House, 1970), p. 576.
[22] *Ibid.*, p. 577.

right to a full and impartial hearing prior to suspension from school (*Goss* v. *Lopez*, 1975). So whatever the issue—free speech, free press, due process—those under the age of 18 are gradually being guaranteed equal justice. The legal handicap of being classified a "student" is being removed.

All these due process and equal-protection rules and many more distribute power to citizens in judicial games. Clearly, they also distribute power to citizens in other arenas. As people are guaranteed due process of law and equal protection of the law, their opportunities generally are enhanced. That can't help but influence the political culture. One's respect for the law and those administering it is bound to grow if one receives the benefits of fairness and equity. Still, we have a way to go.

Rules Relevant to Access

In addition to distributing resources in judicial games, rules dictate *access opportunities.* They spell out what is and isn't a legitimate case, who has standing in court, and how interest groups may participate.

A Legitimate Case

Judges won't allow just any conflict to be settled in court. Attempting to preserve the separation of powers and their own legitimate domain, they use four rules to determine whether or not a case is legitimate. First, it must be *an actual case,* not a trumped-up suit. An attempt to sue a company, for example, in order to damage its public image would be in violation of this rule. Second, the person bringing the suit must have *a direct interest* at stake and have *standing* to sue. Someone who has not been injured in some way, according to this rule, would be unlikely to be a plaintiff. Third, the case must be *ripe for adjudication,* other remedies having been exhausted. A civil service employee who charges discrimination, for example, would not have access to the courts until the internal administrative procedures for dealing with the charge had been exhausted. Fourth, the *court must have jurisdiction* over the subject. The Supreme Court probably refused to rule on the constitutionality of the war in Vietnam because of the "political" nature of the question. This was the territory of Congress and the President.

While these basic access rules may limit someone's opportunity to play the judicial game, they also prevent the courts from being overwhelmed. They mean that those who do gain access have a better chance of getting a fair hearing.

The second access rule is particularly important. Because it is also complex, it warrants some further attention. Just how is standing determined? The general way of determining standing is by asking whether or not the litigant has a *sufficient personal interest* in getting the relief sought or is a *sufficiently appropriate representative* of other interested persons to warrant giving this relief, if the litigant can establish the illegality alleged. The long-term controversy surrounding standing is directed to the question, what sort of interest is "sufficient" for the plaintiff to be regarded as a proper party to bring action? [23]

Since 1968, the U.S. Supreme Court has interpreted "sufficient interest" very liberally. For example, in that year they gave taxpayers standing to sue in federal court when a constitutional question is involved (*Flast* v. *Cohen*). Previously they had ruled that being a taxpayer was not a sufficient interest to justify suing the federal government (see *Frothingham* v. *Mellon*, 1923). Two 1970 rulings by the U.S. Supreme Court produced a flexible two-part standing test (*Association of Data Processing Service Organizations* v. *Camp* and *Barlow* v. *Collins*). Justice Douglas said these questions should be asked in order to determine standing:

> The first question is whether the plaintiff alleges that the challenged action has caused him injury in fact, economic or otherwise. The second question is whether the interest sought to be protected by the complainant is arguable within the zone of interests to be protected or regulated by the statute or constitutional guarantee in question.

This two-part test for standing is considered liberal for two reasons. The court has great discretion to define whether or not an injury has occurred. It need not involve economic loss or physical injury, as it once did. Second, the court has great discretion to determine what interests are to be protected by the law. Judges, particularly those who consider themselves activists, may define those interests in terms of social needs.

The 1972 case of *Sierra Club* v. *Morton* indicates just how far the

[23] These and subsequent points about standing are from K. E. Scott, "Standing in the Supreme Court—A Functional Analysis," *Harvard Law Review*, February 1973, pp. 645–692.

Court is now willing to go. The plaintiff was the Sierra Club, a well-known environmental organization. They were suing to prevent the secretaries of the interior and agriculture from issuing certain permits necessary to the development of a large-scale ski and resort project in the Mineral King Valley in California. Standing was denied the Sierra Club for failure to make a sufficient allegation of injury to the interests of itself or members. The Sierra Club was claiming to represent the interests of the general public, but to challenge governmental action groups must demonstrate an interest that goes beyond the interest of society generally.

This was only a technical defeat for the Sierra Club. Once it alleged it was representing the interests of its members rather than the public, it could be granted standing. Its members—environmentalists, hikers, campers, etc.—would be, the club could argue, uniquely injured. Using this approach, the Sierra Club successfully gained access.

So standing can be gained by individuals and groups who demonstrate an interest that is unique—that can be separated from the interest of the general public. It need not be economic; even environmental injury counts. However, plaintiffs must demonstrate that the interest to be protected is within the "zone of interests" protected by a statute or the Constitution.

Group Access

The Sierra Club case, in addition to illustrating the liberalizing of standing, suggests that groups can play judicial games effectively as long as they fulfill the general access criteria. The fact that a group of individuals is involved rather than one person who has sustained an injury doesn't seem to matter. This was clearly the position of the U.S. Supreme Court in *NAACP* v. *Button* (1963). Prior to that time various states had prevented groups from going to court. However, for some citizens, particularly minorities, the courts represented the only practical avenue for redress of grievances. Given the successes minority groups have experienced in courts, this was an important opinion.

Well, how do groups play and what are the special access rules? We know from the Sierra Club case and the NAACP decision that groups may actually be plaintiffs. In addition, they may finance an individual's case and/or provide lawyers if it will help promote their cause. However, rules also give groups access in another way, through *amicus curiae* briefs.

Amicus curiae means "friend of the court." Originally it referred to a bystander who, without having an interest in the case, from personal knowledge made suggestions on a point of law or of fact for the information of the presiding judge. Now it is more likely to refer to a group (governmental or private) that has an interest in the outcome but is not a direct party in the suit.

There are several ways in which amicus briefs may help one side or the other to win. First, when there is evidence of weakness in the legal talent of one side, an amicus brief may compensate. The relevant law, perhaps, will be more clearly indicated, new information revealed, or the facts more adequately stated. Second, an amicus brief can be used to introduce subtle variations of the basic argument, variations that a direct party may not want to use. Arguments that might anger the justices, doctrines that have not yet been found legally acceptable, and emotional presentations that have little legal standing can all appear in amicus briefs. This is the opportunity to take legal chances, and they might work. Finally, an amicus brief can help just by serving as an endorsement. If it is filed by a prestigious organization, it is another resource.

So what are the rules on the subject? Under the rules of the U.S. Supreme Court, amicus curiae briefs may be filed *with the consent* of *both* parties, or by permission of the Court if consent is denied. State courts also normally require consent.

This consent rule, however, was not taken seriously by the U.S. Supreme Court until 1949. Rarely was permission to file refused. Then the court began to feel overwhelmed, particularly after the "Hollywood Ten" case produced 40 briefs on behalf of the defendants. The case involved Hollywood personalities who refused to testify before the House Un-American Activities Committee. The rule was tightened and expanded. In addition to gaining consent, amici would have to file briefs "within a reasonable time" prior to the decision and would have to file the request to appear as a friend separate from the document in which they presented their point of view about the case. No longer did the justices want to be rushed or to have to wade through entire arguments before deciding whether or not such a brief should be given their attention.

Their toughness became evident after 1949. Whereas the Supreme Court at one time rarely denied permission to file, the justices in the five terms after 1949 denied permission in 39 instances.[24] Simultane-

[24] Samuel Krislov, "The Amicus Curiae Brief: From Friendship to Advocacy," *Yale Law Review*, April 1963, pp. 694–721.

ously, the U.S. government, as a party to about half the cases before the Court, refused consent in nearly every case. Speaking for the government in 1957, the Solicitor General attempted to make the consent standard clear. The Department of Justice, he said, frowns upon the filing of briefs by amici with merely an academic interest at one extreme, or by those who wish merely to engage in propaganda. When the government is a party to a suit, consent is given "where the applicant has a concrete, substantial interest in the decision of the case, and the proposed brief would assist the court by presenting relevant arguments or materials which would not otherwise be submitted." There it is, the guide to access through amicus curiae briefs.

Clearly these rules suggest that the Court neither wants to be overwhelmed with briefs nor wants to eliminate them. In addition, because they ask the parties to the dispute to consent to the filing, the justices are emphasizing the importance of groups being not just a friend to the Court but a friend to the litigants as well.

This second consideration is important to litigants, for it assures them that their "friends" won't be working at cross purposes. The strategic and tactical role of each can be planned and coordinated. This is crucial, for the amicus brief is in many ways the judicial counterpart of lobbying and testifying at hearings in the legislative and executive arenas. In each case the approach must be part of an overall plan.

Class action suits.   One additional rule relevant to group access is the *class action suit*. Remember the previous discussion of the Washington, D.C., protesters who were illegally detained and arrested, who won $12 million in damages? Their victory was far broader and more significant because the 1,200 arrested brought the suit together, although only 8 were actually tried.

On the federal level, class actions are permitted by the Rules of Civil Procedure. They apply to those persons who have a *common* legal right where the group is "so numerous as to make it impractical to bring them all before the court." States too allow class action suits, although certain procedural rules or court decisions as a practical matter forbid them in a few locations.

Not just everyone with a common legal right can legitimately be called a "class." In federal court class action suits can be filed only if a single defendant claims damages of more than $10,000 or if the case is being brought under specific statutes that allow group suits. The

Clayton Act, the Securities and Exchange Act, the Civil Rights Act, and the Truth in Lending Act, for instance, all provide for class actions. In addition, in 1974 the U.S. Supreme Court said that all members of a class are to be notified if they are to be included in a suit. While this rule sounds reasonable, it presents a problem. For example, one class action suit pending in 1974 charged 11 oil companies with limiting oil supplies and boosting prices. The class of plaintiffs was everyone in the United States who used gasoline, heating oil, natural gas or anything else made from oil; the damages sought were $270 billion. This 1974 decision (*Eisen* v. *Carlisle & Jacquelin*) made cases such as this impossible. Instead, the number of plaintiffs would have to be reduced to those who could be found with reasonable effort. The effect? According to Peter Schuck of Consumers Union, "there will now be injustices without remedies. The more widespread the violation of the law, the more difficult it will be to give notice and bring a suit." [25]

The other side of the argument is that this rule change bestows certain rights on former unnotified plaintiffs. In class action suits everyone included in the class is legally bound by the ultimate outcome of the case. Without the notice required by the 1974 decision, a "co-plaintiff" would not be afforded the opportunity to either withdraw from the suit or possibly even pursue an independent course of action.[26]

On balance, although they have been more restricted since 1974, class action suits remain an important means of group access. Instead of a single plaintiff paying a lawyer between $40 and $100 per hour to handle a case, citizens with a common injury can join together and share the cost. Also, whether there are 10 or 1,000 of them, they will share in the victory. There are also two other possible advantages over a single-litigant suit. The principle (e.g., companies should not rip off consumers) tends not to get lost. There is far less chance that the plaintiffs will compromise with the defendant, for that can't happen in class action suits without the permission of the court. Second, standing is less likely to be lost. For example, in a desegregation suit brought by parents of teen-age children, by the time the appeal process is nearly completed the children may well have graduated and therefore no longer be defined as "injured." In a class action suit,

---

[25] "A Curb on Class Action," *Newsweek*, June 10, 1974, p. 48+.
[26] *Ibid.*

when one plaintiff loses standing another can be substituted, and the original litigation may proceed without interruption.[27]

So, a welfare recipient who feels he is not receiving legally guaranteed benefits, an automobile purchaser who believes the car she purchased was defective, or members of a minority group who feel their rights were violated by an employer all have access. The economics of going to court make the class action procedure an important one.

Clearly rules are resources in judicial games, as they are in all games, and they frequently distribute power to citizen players. In this chapter we've seen them bestow advantages as they guarantee through law certain rights. Among these are the rights of the arrested and accused; the protection against unequal treatment of the law; and the opportunities to gain standing in court, to have the assistance of interest groups, and to join with others to take legal action. Of course, many more advantages exist, and they sometimes compensate for one's liabilities—those that would preclude winning in other arenas. Think about it: would Clarence Gideon have been able to play a legislative game successfully?

The next chapter illustrates more clearly how these rules are applied in actual court cases. What should become apparent is how rules help to define the techniques used to win judicial games. On to that discussion.

Key Words

Due process of law
Self-incrimination
Bail
Equal protection of the law
Standing
Amicus curiae
Class action

Suggested Activities

1. Investigate your city's bail system. What criteria are used to decide whether or not to release someone accused of a crime? If an OR program exists, what criteria are used to determine eligibility?

---

[27] Walter F. Murphy and C. Herman Pritchett, eds., *Courts, Judges, and Politics* (New York: Random House, 1965), p. 277.

2. Interview a local American Civil Liberties Union lawyer. Determine the conditions under which the local ACLU will file an amicus curiae brief or help finance a case.
3. Survey recent local newspapers. Identify cases that were class actions. Determine what gave the "class" standing.

15
Techniques of Winning Judicial Games

What a nightmare! There are different arenas, each with its own rules and means of access; they all have professional players, for the most part; their moves are influenced by innumerable factors. Perhaps just this *one* kind of political game could be left to the professionals. What can ordinary citizens do?

Ordinary citizens, we've seen, can play important parts in this game as jurors, witnesses, and contributors to legal expenses. However, most lawyers would say, when it comes right down to one's own case, civil or criminal, "Step aside, leave it up to us, it is just too complicated for you to directly participate in the planning. The strategies and techniques are much too subtle for the lay person to comprehend." Perhaps—but there is another point of view of which citizens should be aware.

Paul Harris has a criminal law firm in San Francisco. He is particularly experienced at handling draft cases, both as a lawyer and as a former law clerk to a federal district court judge. Currently he is trying to approach law in a nonelitist way, that is, to allow more people to participate in trial decisions. This is what he has to say about leaving it up to professionals and the implications of the traditional lawyer-client relationship.

I really believe that a lawyer plays the role that a priest does, to a large extent: he's put on a pedestal. Lawyers understand the mysteries of the law; they carry out the rituals; they understand its dogma, and they interpret it to the laymen, who find it very difficult to understand. It's not just lawyers; I think it's true to some degree of doctors and all professionals.

Not every lawyer plays this role with his clients, but it's typical of the legal profession, including the radical lawyers. We are taught in law school, and I have friends who tell me they were taught in medical school, that it's wrong somehow to let the client or patient in on everything, for his own good and for efficiency's sake. My law school course in trial practice was taught by a practicing trial attorney, a younger guy, who should not be insensitive to these things. He said, "You do not tell your tactics to your client, because then he's going to have all these stupid theories that just mess things up. You have to run the case." I hear the same thing from radical lawyers. This is store-owner psychology: "I'm in business here, you come into my store; if you don't like my wares, you go next door. If you're a big enough buyer, then we'll talk longer."

One result is that the lawyer is treating people like shit. I was medically disabled and on welfare for a couple of years, and most of the doctors I had to deal with treated me the way most lawyers treat their clients. They would not explain things to me, they ran me through, did not take time to listen to what I said, and as a result several doctors did things that other doctors had tried and that hadn't worked. Some doctors in the same situation did spend time to talk and listen to me. Listening is very important. When you interview clients, a good percentage of what they say is irrelevant, but if you listen long enough you will find out things that do not come to light any other way.

I have a friend on welfare, a very intelligent girl. Her mother had some kind of court proceeding coming up and did not understand it. She was going to the OEO legal service office. The daughter wanted to find out what procedure was going on, and I kept urging her to call the lawyer, but she didn't do it. Finally, she said, "If I call the lawyer it will be the same as when I call the welfare worker or any agency. Either the lawyer will tell me that he can't give out that information or he'll just rap on some things that I don't understand and then hang up." Many poor people have that feeling.

The second result of this behavior is political. When a person goes to a doctor or a lawyer usually he's in trouble; therefore he's dependent on them. Psychologically, when a person feels his own dependence, he either reacts with hostility or just sort of shrivels up, which is more common. When the lawyer rattles off the law and doesn't really explain things to the client and take time with his feelings, he's reinforcing the client's dependence on him. If the lawyer works in a poverty neighborhood, his clients are people who have been traditionally, historically dependent on other people. Their big problem is that they feel they have no power, they don't know how to use power, they are afraid, and they have no concept of their own resources. If, instead of developing his clients' political effectiveness, a lawyer reinforces their subservience and dependence, I think that is a really serious problem.

The lesson of the Student Nonviolent Coordinating Committee in the South was just that. White SNCC organizers would come down in the summer, they'd run the paper, they'd do all the activities themselves—because, of course, white college kids could do it better than poor black people—and at the end of the summer they'd leave, and the people didn't know what to do anymore because they hadn't done it themselves.[1]

Regardless of how much say a lawyer is willing to let clients have, and most will allow very little, just knowing the available tactical choices will at least let people be intellectually active in court. They are less likely to feel intimidated and isolated. However, for those who share Paul Harris's view, the fact that there are a few nonelitist lawyers around indicates that there is a professional choice.

The purpose of this chapter is to promote participation in judicial games—intellectual and/or actual—by introducing some of the techniques used and necessary strategy considerations. To do this, we will analyze three different kinds of cases. The first involves an attempt by a group of citizens to get a federal housing law enforced, the second involves an attempt to actually get public policy changed, specifically to change the way public schools are financed, and the third involves an attempt to get 13 men declared innocent of several criminal charges.

Unfortunately, the amateur's role in each of these cases was limited. Only in the criminal case were nonprofessionals actively involved. In the housing case, the plaintiff organization was systematically kept informed of all moves and sometimes consulted. In the public-education case professionals had their own way completely —it was their case from the beginning.

Regardless of the role played by nonprofessionals in these three cases, and regardless of the fact that these cases are clearly unusual, each illustrates possible strategies and tactics. Many of these may be applied to more traditional criminal and civil judicial games. So don't be intimidated by their importance! Just notice how the rules and the

---

[1] Ann Fagan Ginger, *The Relevant Lawyers* (New York: Simon and Schuster, 1972), pp. 325–327. Copyright © 1972 by Ann Fagan Ginger. Reprinted by permission of Simon & Schuster, Inc.

law, the predispositions and skill of judicial players, and the facts of the case all come together to influence the win.

Getting the Law Enforced: Some Techniques

Yerba Buena means "good grass." It also refers to a federal urban renewal program in San Francisco—except the program doesn't exist. It doesn't exist despite a cost since 1949 of more than $10 billion and the destruction of 300,000 more housing units than have been replaced, most of them the houses of minority people and the poor. Judicial battles have been responsible.[2]

The interests of each side can be described in this way. Those who want to bring "progress" to San Francisco want Yerba Buena because it will bring more business, more jobs, more conventions, a larger tax base, slum clearance, and a revival of the downtown area. The "progress" group understandably includes the city's larger corporations, City Hall, hotel owners and others in the convention and tourist industry, building and construction trade unions, and the newspapers and other media. What they have been supporting is a proposed 87-acre, half-billion-dollar complex of convention and sports facilities, office buildings, and parking garages. Representing this side is the San Francisco Redevelopment Agency (SFRA).

Those opposed to Yerba Buena see it as the ultimate example of the horrors of redevelopment: The conscious destruction of an entire community and an attempt to remove its population from the city altogether to make room for bigger business. They claim that this project and others undertaken by the city of San Francisco have systematically destroyed the homes, jobs, and neighborhoods of thousands upon thousands of working-class and poor people, especially racial minorities and the elderly. Representing this side is an organization that calls itself Tenants and Owners in Opposition to Redevelopment (TOOR).

Strategically, TOOR selected the judicial arena as the way to prevent Yerba Buena, as conceived, from happening. Specifically, the litigation had three purposes. The most important was to assist the people living in the designated renewal area to assert their *statutory right* to decent, safe, and sanitary relocation housing at rents they could afford. In this sense, the goal was *law enforcement*, not law

---

[2] This description of the legal battle over Yerba Buena is from a case study by Chester Hartman, *Yerba Buena* (San Francisco: Glide Urban Center Publications, 1974).

reform. Clearly, the law was on TOOR's side. Redevelopment agencies, under federal statute, must demonstrate to the U.S. Department of Housing and Urban Development (HUD), as a prior condition for receiving federal funds, that adequate housing meeting federal statutory standards exists for the people who will be uprooted by the project, or that it will be provided.

The second purpose of the litigation was to stop the practice of redevelopment agencies across the country of circumventing the law. They had the habit, according to the opponents, of juggling statistics in order to obtain required HUD approvals.

The third purpose was to document and expose to the public, to Congress, and to state legislative bodies the destructive effects of urban renewal when replacement housing requirements are evaded, as they were in San Francisco.

Seeking an Injunction

The strategy developed to accomplish these purposes was a lawsuit that would produce an *injunction*. This is a command from a court forbidding named defendants to perform certain specified acts. Its purpose is not to punish or secure damages, but to prevent a future injury of some kind or the continuation of a present injury. In this particular situation, half a dozen named individuals plus TOOR filed a complaint in federal district court against both HUD and the SFRA. They contended that the Redevelopment Agency had not located decent, safe, and sanitary housing for displacees as required by the 1949 Housing Act. They asked for immediate injunctive relief.

Now why did the TOOR legal staff choose this strategy? The most important reason was that they felt they couldn't win any other way. They had tried. The Department of Housing and Urban Development (HUD) could have forced the Redevelopment Agency to make its relocation plan comply with the law, but they didn't. In fact, HUD wouldn't even grant a hearing on the matter when, in 1968, a group of tenants filed a petition for one. Their reason for the denial was that little actual displacement had yet occurred. However, residents were being displaced, sometimes with very little notice, and the indifference of both HUD and City Hall made them angry and frustrated.

The second reason this strategy was chosen had to do with strategic "information." One year earlier a different neighborhood association had successfully filed suit for a federal injunction against relocation, demolition, and federal funding in an area called the Western

Addition. This was the first time in the 20-year history of urban renewal that a court had actually enjoined an urban renewal project. This earlier case provided TOOR with both tactical guidelines and hope.

The tactical approach appeared simple—just gather enough evidence to indicate that the law was clearly being violated by SFRA. Specifically, it was necessary to show that there were serious flaws in SFRA's relocation plan. Charles Hartman describes the evidence presented:

> Inspection sheets of the building inspectors employed by SFRA showed that many "approved" relocation resources were in poor physical condition, had illegal wiring, an absence of dual means of egress and fire exit signs, access to fire escapes through locked doors, and other serious infractions. Most of this evidence was available to HUD in 1966; it evidently chose to look the other way.
>
> TOOR shored up its evidence by commissioning the nationally known Bureau of Social Science Research to conduct a vacancy survey of those hotels the Redevelopment Agency was using for relocation purposes. After eliminating vacant units renting for over $100 per month and those for which the Agency inspection sheets showed gross physical deficiencies, the survey team counted slightly over 200 vacancies citywide. This survey exposed the extraordinarily small number of standard low-rent units in San Francisco at a time when "turnover theory" predicted just the opposite. TOOR also submitted official crime statistics from the San Francisco Police Department to show the high incidence of crimes against persons in the areas into which most YBC [Yerba Buena Center] displacees were being relocated—Sixth Street and the Tenderloin. These data were particularly important, since older persons and alcoholics are especially vulnerable to muggings and street crime. Impersonal statistics were accompanied by some 60 affidavits from present and former residents of the YBC area describing personal experiences as displacees and their fears of being displaced. This factual demonstration of the housing crisis faced by YBC displacees contrasted dramatically with the official relocation plan HUD had earlier approved.[3]

Relying on a Temporary Restraining Order

Whether or not all this fancy detective work would pay off was to be determined in three hearings before a federal district judge. At the end of the first day, the judge had heard enough to issue a *temporary restraining order* halting involuntary relocation and demolition inside

[3] *Ibid.*, pp. 125–126.

the YBC area pending an opportunity to rule on the motion for an injunction. Prior to the third hearing the judge dictated an additional order prohibiting all relocation activities except in instances where residents *signed a statement* before a notary attesting to the voluntariness of the action. SFRA's dedication to removing YBC area residents, even after the second court order, was apparent when one resident was visited in the hospital by two relocation workers and a notary. The relocation workers had already placed the woman's possessions in storage for "safekeeping" while she was hospitalized, making her forcible relocation an accomplished fact.

Federal Judge Weigel preferred not to have the suit settled in court. He wanted both sides to come to some sort of compromise, but SFRA's blatant violation of one agreement meant out-of-court compromise at this time was impossible. The result was the most sweeping injunction against an urban renewal project ever issued. It halted all demolition and relocation and established July 1, 1970, as the date for cutting off federal funds if the YBC relocation plan was not satisfactorily revised.

Settling on a Consent Decree

Even this drastic action was not enough to get SFRA and TOOR to come to an out-of-court settlement. Instead, Judge Weigel drafted a *consent decree* establishing precisely the obligations of SFRA and the housing rights of the residents of the YBC area. Only by accepting its provisions could SFRA get the judge to lift the injunction. They did and he did.

Again, however, this was only a temporary victory for TOOR. One year later TOOR produced evidence that SFRA still had made no significant progress in providing adequate replacement housing for residents. Their acceptance of the consent decree had, among other things, obligated them to produce within three years (by November 1973) 1,500 to 1,800 new or rehabilitated units of low-rent housing. To deal with this administrative malaise TOOR again went to court and asked for a second injunction. However, all this injunction business was apparently causing HUD some embarrassment. Remember, they were the agency providing and controlling the federal money. The result of this embarrassment was another review by HUD of SFRA's plans. This time they reported to the court that the plans were entirely inadequate. The result? Instead of a second court injunction, HUD assumed responsibility. They imposed what amounted to a continuing administrative injunction until they were satisfied. In

September 1972 HUD officials said they were satisfied, but TOOR still was not. Their request for an injunction continued.

Ultimately, because of the combined pressure of TOOR, HUD, and the federal courts, SFRA realized they would have to comply with the consent decree. The fact that an increase in the local hotel tax would help provide the required housing eased their resistance. In May 1973, a settlement was reached. The lawsuit was dropped in exchange for an absolute commitment by SFRA not only to the 1,500 to 1,800 units of replacement housing but to 400 units of permanent new low-income housing within the YBC project area itself. How reliable the commitment was remains to be seen.

Moves and Countermoves

Now let's take a look at what went on tactically during this long legal game. First, the request for an injunction brought the federal court and Judge Weigel into the game. His granting the first injunction plus his continuing oversight, at TOOR's request, kept the pressure on SFRA. They ultimately agreed to the points in Judge Weigel's consent decree and more.

However, they did it reluctantly. They had thought they could win by stalling and harassing residents of the area, by attempting to influence public opinion, and by attempting to remove and/or circumvent Judge Weigel.

The first of these tactics was designed to remove the reason for the case. With virtually no one moving into the Yerba Buena area, the combination of "voluntary" movements, sickness, and death was reducing the area's population rapidly. The original population had dropped from 4,000 to about 1,300 by late 1970, and to about 700 by late 1972. To SFRA's delight, TOOR found it increasingly difficult to get people to stay in the area. SFRA's position was to maintain that providing housing units for people no longer there was absurd. Therefore, SFRA should be released from its full replacement housing commitment.

In Judge Weigel's court this stalling tactic didn't work. He recognized the ploy for what it was. In his July 1972 ruling he noted:

Defendant Agency urges that there has been a reduction in the number of families and individuals who continue to reside in the Yerba Buena. That is true. But it is immaterial. The commitment was made to comply with the law in the light of an overall shortage of such housing throughout the city of San Francisco. Defendant cannot get rid of its obligation to provide a minimum of

1,500 units of new or rehabilitated low-cost housing by getting rid of some of those who need it.[4]

A second tactic used systematically by SFRA (and also by TOOR) was to mobilize *public opinion*. SFRA did this by continually asserting that the redevelopment project was being held up by malcontents and the publicity-seeking lawyers representing TOOR. For example, in November 1971 there was a fire that caused fatalities in an old hotel within the YBC area. This particular hotel had two years earlier been cited for 18 housing code violations, including the absence of sprinklers in the halls and stairways and illegal cooking in rooms. Immediately after the fire, SFRA issued press releases blaming TOOR for the loss of life because it had initiated litigation that kept the Agency from moving families out of "slum fire traps" —despite the fact that TOOR had urged rehabilitation of that particular hotel.

Another approach used by SFRA to mobilize public opinion was to remind the citizens of San Francisco how much the delay because of litigation was costing the public. The sums ranged from $7,000 a month to keep hotels open for remaining residents (who were protected by court orders), to $7,000 a day for increased interest and administrative costs, to $1 million per month because of construction cost inflation. The role SFRA played in causing the delay was hidden.

TOOR's attempt to mold public opinion was less direct. Each time it went to court, it would make its claim and arguments known, hoping that the public's awareness of public housing and relocation issues would increase. In addition, it was hoped that TOOR's suit would reduce the general credibility of SFRA and the public's confidence in its ability to get things done.

As with most authoritative decision-making, the link between public opinion and judicial decisions is a tenuous one. If indeed public opinion was mobilized one way or the other, it would be difficult to assess how it contributed to Judge Weigel's decisions. More likely the attempt to influence public opinion was an attempt on the part of each side to get the best deal in the inevitable out-of-court settlement.

The third major tactic employed recognized that who the judge is makes a difference. Democratic Mayor Joseph Alioto, a strong supporter of the SFRA and the Yerba Buena project, was shocked when Judge Weigel issued his injunction. When SFRA appealed the

---

[4] *Ibid.*, p. 149.

decision, it brought in the mayor himself as special counsel. This appeared to be an extraordinary and blatant political move, since the city of San Francisco was not a named defendant. Mayor Alioto was serious. In his words, "No federal judge in the country is going to stop the Yerba Buena project. I won't permit it. I've known Stan Weigel for 20 years and he is not about to do it."

Still, Alioto and SFRA were genuinely worried about what Judge Weigel might do. When the judge left for a six-week vacation, the Redevelopment Agency asked for an immediate hearing on its motion to modify the injunction. Judge George Harris, well known in Democratic circles, appeared to be more sympathetic.

TOOR, however, would have none of this tactic of judge-swapping. In addition to arguing that Judge Harris's district court had no jurisdiction over the injunction, since SFRA had already filed its appeal with the circuit court, TOOR raised the issue of the friendship between Judge Harris and the YBC-SFRA backers. To emphasize the point, it published photographs of Harris arm in arm with his "downtown" friends. This move was probably responsible for Judge Harris's stepping aside and calling in a special *master* (an officer appointed to take independent testimony and make a report to the court).

Judge Weigel still had to be contended with. The next tactic was to question his impartiality and his competence—in a word, to intimidate him. The vehicle for this was a motion filed in U.S. District Court in 1972. The Redevelopment Agency asked that Judge Weigel remove himself from the Yerba Buena case on the grounds of bias and prejudice and being "overwrought and extremely emotional" in his rulings. This was a highly unusual move. Court observers could recall no other such accusation filed within the last 15 years. However, for the SFRA, it was a way to eliminate the principal hurdle to the continuation of the project. A major San Francisco newspaper cooperated in the move. A January 6, 1972, *Examiner* editorial read:

> How much longer must the City of San Francisco put up with the dictatorial decisions on community affairs of U.S. District Judge Stanley Weigel? . . .
> Weigel long has been a central figure in the semi-disastrous delays suffered by the $350 million Yerba Buena redevelopment project. This week he imposed costly new restraints.
> What now, how long, oh lord? . . .
> Weigel and the foundation [the San Francisco Neighborhood Legal Assistance Foundation] refuse to give proper recognition to

the Redevelopment Agency's human and efficient program to re-
locate residents displaced by Yerba Buena. . . .
Is there no way to get this crucial issue out of Weigel's court?

Judge Weigel responded to the motion by asking the chief judge
of the Northern District of California to review the case. Judge
Carter rejected SFRA's bias charges, calling them "incredible." He
noted that SFRA had been perfectly willing to go along with Judge
Weigel's decisions when they seemed in their interest (i.e., the 1970
consent decree SFRA voluntarily signed). "Clearly, when they thought
the cards were with them they enjoyed the game," Carter remarked.
SFRA's appeal of Judge Carter's decision was denied, and a subsequent *Examiner* editorial again urging Judge Weigel to disqualify
himself was ignored. He was to remain a key player.

The final settlement between the two sides demonstrated that
only in some respects did SFRA's tactic work. The stalling action by
SFRA, although obvious to all, did create pressures on TOOR to
compromise. The law, TOOR's diligent research and resistance, a
sympathetic and steadfast federal judge, and exceptionally talented
and tenacious attorneys (two were from the federally funded San
Francisco Neighborhood Legal Assistance Foundation and the third
from the Housing Law Center at the University of California at
Berkeley) obviously aided the plaintiffs. In any other kind of political
battle, the resources of SFRA might have been overwhelming. The
support of business, labor, the press, city government, and usually
HUD would have suggested that almost any pro-YBC tactics would
work. The fact that they didn't gets back to the nature of the judicial
game. With its unique rules, it is a game where numerical and financial minorities can win—even if it takes four years or more to
do it.

There is one more thing about TOOR, the plaintiff organization.
It consisted of 60 to 80 persons, mostly tenants who resided in the
area but also a few owners of small businesses and was essentially
run by four paid staff members. It was not a mass-based organization.
Members would gather monthly to share information. From 1969 on
the TOOR lawyers played the key role. The organization wasn't always without conflict. Perhaps because of the inadequate and spo-
radic participation of members, the attorneys didn't always consult
TOOR. They made decisions that a strong community organization
they would not have permitted them to make. Certainly the decision
to drop the lawsuit in exchange for a Redevelopment Agency promise

to build 1,500 to 1,800 housing units caused dissent. TOOR believed the attorneys had given away their only leverage.

However, loss of citizen control is often one of the costs of choosing litigation as a strategy, and the TOOR staff realized that in settling on that strategy they were reducing even further the slim possibility of developing an alternative or complementary mass-based political organization and set of tactics. They were dependent on the advice of their attorneys and had to defer to their perceptions, skill, and priorities. They won, however, in what was probably the only way they could. The question is, was the cost too great?

Something to think about
List the formal (legal) resources and the informal resources used by each side. Which of these are available and usable in more typical civil cases—i.e., those involving contract disputes, bodily injury, or the denial of certain rights? Which would be difficult to use in more traditional cases, and why?

Effecting Social Change: Some Techniques

Most activists would argue that judicial arenas are the last place to try to effect social change. Court decisions, they say, rarely alter people's attitudes and/or behavior in any significant way. The exceptions, however, make the difference. Certainly the civil rights cases of the 1950s and 1960s helped to produce, however slowly, changes in educational, economic, and political opportunities. A probable positive side effect was a change in the racial attitudes of many citizens.[5]

However, using the courts in this way is complicated business. The case of *Serrano* v. *Priest* (1971) illustrates some of the techniques.[6]

John Coons was a struggling young professor of law at Northwestern University. He had just completed a study of discrimination in city spending between various Chicago school districts. He found the gap between school spending in Chicago and spending in the surrounding suburbs to be immense.

[5] Whether or not the results were directly related to the various Supreme Court decisions, a study released in 1975 by the Institute for Social Research (University of Michigan) revealed an increase in contact between races between 1964 and 1974 and an increase in positive attitudes toward other races.
[6] These details of the *Serrano* v. *Priest* legal struggle are from Gerald C. Lubenow, "The Action Lawyers," *Saturday Review*, August 26, 1972, pp. 36–42.

His interest in unequal school financing continued. In 1966 two of his senior law students at Northwestern, Steve Sugarman and Bill Clune, joined in a broader investigation of the problem. This time the investigation was to lead somewhere, to change. The question was, *what strategy?*

"From the very beginning," Coons recalls, "we felt we wanted to have some impact on what was seen as an indefensible system." The legislative arena was unlikely to be responsive. After all, they reasoned, more money for the poorer districts would have to come out of the pockets of the middle-income and rich districts, and there would probably be an unsympathetic majority of taxpayers and voters. The courts seemed a more fruitful avenue for reform.

Choosing the Legal Argument
Once the decision to use the courts was made, a variety of preliminary tactical questions had to be dealt with. First, *what legal argument* would have the greatest chance of producing the desired decision? The issue was clear: the inequity of spending considerably more on educating a child in one district than in another. However, the precise argument, they believed, needed to be simple, enforceable, and not likely to interfere too much with the legislative process. What emerged from their discussion was a decision to ask the court for a negative principle, a statement saying "don't do it this way." More specifically, they would ask the court to rule that the quality of public education may not be a function of wealth. A *UCLA Law Review* article by law professor Harold Harowitz gave them the legal foundation. He laid out a solid case for applying the equal-protection clause of the Fourteenth Amendment to inequalities in educational opportunity, including those created by the way in which schools are financed.

The Harowitz article attracted the attention of a number of people. An energetic attorney by the name of Sid Wolinsky contacted Harowitz, as did Coons. All were interested in initiating a suit, but they had two problems: no money and no client.

Getting the Support of a Sponsoring Organization
The money problem was solved when they were able to interest Derrick Bell, newly appointed director of the Western Center for Law and Poverty. The center had a lot of money, but not much was being done. Bell explained his support in this way, "We had to show we

weren't just preaching change. We had to do something to show the law could be used in a dramatic way to change people's lives. We had to generate some excitement."

Selecting a Defendant

Most cases are initiated by people with a problem who find a lawyer, but many activist lawyers, such as Coons, Wolinsky, Harowitz, and Bell, see a problem and hunt for an appropriate client. The trick is to find the right one—one who has been "injured" in a way that will produce the correct ruling.

John Serrano was the person. He was a psychiatric social worker active in educational affairs in East Los Angeles's sprawling Mexican-American community. He had had to move to a suburb of Los Angeles (Whittier) because his son's principal had warned him to take his children out of the East Los Angeles schools if he cared at all about their education. Serrano agreed to be a part of a class action suit. He helped find 37 other people—10 parents and their 27 children—who also agreed to join as plaintiffs.

With money and clients on hand, the legal team got down to business. They divided responsibility according to their own expertise. "Bill acted as the administrator, quickly but forcefully cajoling the others, monitoring research into educational disparities in California (the state where the suit was to be brought), and drafting the complaint; Harowitz was the theoretician, dominating many of the initial afternoon-long sessions in his cramped office with an exposition of the legal strands to be brought together. Coons was the resident expert on school finance, and his bulky manuscript became a veritable bible for the litigants. Wolinsky was the trial lawyer, vested with ultimate authority on tactical matters, since it was he who would have to take the case to court and argue it before a judge." [7]

Wolinsky and team had two immediate tactical decisions to make. The first was, *who should be sued?* The idea of suing every one of the state's hundreds of school districts was rejected. Even though that might be necessary in order to get a ruling that would apply statewide, the logistical problems appeared to be overwhelming. Instead, three state officials involved with dispensing funds for public education would become the defendants. Heading the list was Ivy Baker Priest, state treasurer. Although he was considered an

[7] *Ibid.*, p. 39.

additional possible plaintiff, Governor Ronald Reagan was excluded because of a desire to make the case as politically noncontroversial as possible.

The next tactical decision was *where* to initiate the suit. Sometimes lawyers and their clients have no choice. If the law in question is clearly within the jurisdiction of the state court system or the federal court system, that determines where the case must be initiated. However, in some kinds of cases there is a choice. Certainly there has been for civil rights lawyers operating in the South, and for them that choice is crucial. The federal courts have obviously been more sympathetic to the rights of black citizens than the state courts. Likewise, southern whites have won more often on race issues in state courts.[8]

So the choice of where to initiate the Serrano case was an important tactical consideration. There are two schools of thought on the subject. Some activist lawyers believe the U.S. Supreme Court is the ultimate battleground where the broadest national rulings can be gained, and that the most direct route is through a U.S. district court. Other activist lawyers believe in shielding an issue from the Supreme Court while they build up a series of favorable lower court decisions and mold a favorable political climate nationally. The Serrano lawyers chose the more conservative approach. After all, the issue was a controversial one; they needed to act with some restraint.

Some information about the California Supreme Court also influenced their choice. The state courts were regarded as more responsive to practical arguments than the federal courts, and if the case ever reached that level, they would have arguments prepared. The case was in fact heard by the California Supreme Court, and tactician Wolinsky explained his approach in this way: "We went to great lengths to convince the court not only that this was the law but that it made great sense economically, politically, and that, administratively, it could be made to work."

A second piece of information directed the *Serrano* lawyers to the California court system. The California Supreme Court was recognized as one of the outstanding appellate courts in the nation, was believed to be particularly receptive to innovation, and was viewed as stubbornly independent. This was the ideal arena for *Serrano*.

[8] See Kenneth N. Vines, "Southern State Supreme Courts and Race Relations," *Western Political Quarterly*, March 1965, pp. 5–18.

Obtaining the Right Judge

With the court issue settled, the next tactical consideration was the *judge*. While theoretically it is not possible to shop for the right judge, in fact trial lawyers make it their business to know the personalities and predispositions of local judges before whom they practice. A defendant in a drunk-driving case would prefer not to have a teetotal judge; a husband in a domestic litigation case doesn't want to get a judge who has a reputation for being tough on husbands and sympathetic toward wives in such cases. Some attorneys are very skillful at maneuvering their trial calendars to avoid a particular judge.[9]

The *Serrano* lawyers wanted a sympathetic judge, and Wolinsky knew precisely the one. Since there were only two judges who handled such proceedings in Los Angeles County, he had a 50 percent chance. State superior court judges are assigned on the basis of complaint number. All odd numbers go to one judge, all even numbers to another. So, all an enterprising attorney has to do is look over the shoulder of the person in front, check the number, and bend down to tie a shoelace if the next number is wrong. This foolproof system can't miss, but it did. When the person sent by the *Serrano* team to file the complaint arrived at the clerk's office (August 23, 1968), there was no one else in line. He had to take the next number on the complaint roster. It was the "wrong" judge. The case was thrown out of court, but appeals followed. During the appeal process the team continued to reshape the case, placing greater emphasis on the inequity of having the quality of public education depend on wealth. In September 1970, the state Court of Appeals also dismissed the case.

However, a supportive climate appeared to be growing. Articles on school financing and the Fourteenth Amendment were appearing in prestigious journals, suits in other parts of the country were being filed, and national publicity followed.

Planning Amicus Curiae Briefs

Finally, Sid Wolinsky got the word. The California Supreme Court would hear the case. This was their chance. The tactics at this point involved amicus curiae briefs. There were several broad arguments

[9] John Paul Hanna, *The Complete Layman's Guide to the Law* (Englewood Cliffs, N.J.: Prentice-Hall, 1974), p. 151.

the legal team wanted the court to consider. The idea was to have these broader arguments made in prestigious amicus briefs. In addition, these briefs would indicate to the court the broad concern over the issue. Now, who should submit them? The problem was to limit the number. Everyone wanted to write one. They simply had to select those with the clearest and broadest interest in the matter. Each of those finally selected focused on a particular argument. The Youth Law Project, an Office of Economic Opportunity program, submitted a brief arguing that the maldistribution of education funds perpetuated the cycle of poverty. The NAACP and the Mexican-American Political Association filed a joint brief in which they raised the question of racial discrimination. Wolinsky also got the San Francisco Board of Education, one of the wealthiest in the state, to submit a brief; they supported the principle of financial equalization.

The tactics and preparation were designed not just to win a case but to win a clear majority. This would then be a clear mandate to the state legislature to change the way the state's public schools were financed. In addition, if they were overwhelmingly successful, the case and approach would be likely to be a model for all the other groups operating around the country with the same goal in mind. It would provide the basis for a national strategy whose culmination would be a similar decision by the U.S. Supreme Court.

John Serrano, the 37 other plaintiffs, and the activist lawyers got their wish. The nearly unanimous decision (6 to 1) read this way: "This funding scheme invidiously discriminates against the poor because it makes the quality of a child's education a function of the wealth of his parents and neighbors. Recognizing, as we must, that the right to an education is a fundamental interest which cannot be conditioned on wealth, we can discern no compelling state purpose necessitating the present method of financing."

The *national* strategy, however, suffered a setback. In *Rodriguez* v. *San Antonio*, the U.S. Supreme Court did not accept the equal-protection argument. Those who argued the case, however, unlike the Serrano team, focused on racial discrimination, which the Court didn't see as connected to the manner of financing.

Timing the Strategy

Perhaps it was the particular argument used that produced an unfavorable response from the U.S. Supreme Court, or perhaps it was a question of *timing*. The proper time to initiate a suit or an appeal is a major tactical consideration. Leaving *Serrano* for a moment, let

"*Do you ever have one of those days when everything seems un-Constitutional?*"

Drawing by Joe Mirachi; © 1974 The New Yorker Magazine, Inc.

us look at how other plaintiffs schedule litigation. The American Jewish Congress has challenged a number of practices in this country that legally favor Christian traditions. It times its challenges carefully. It prefers, for example, to begin its objections to Christian celebrations in public schools well in advance of such holidays as Christmas or Easter rather than during the holiday season. This assures a more favorable climate of opinion.[10] More relevant to the Rodriguez failure may be the attitudes of the members of the Court itself. If rulings on similar cases have been negative, it may be wiser to postpone litigation that would only build unfavorable precedent. Some of the lawyers associated with the Serrano case believed that the timing was wrong for Rodriguez as well as the major argument.

The NAACP has been particularly sensitive to timing and the prevailing attitudes of the judges. For example, for years it tried to get the Supreme Court to declare restrictive covenants on the rental and sale of housing a violation of the Fourteenth Amendment. Several attempts to get a *writ of certiorari* had failed. This writ is a decision by a higher court to review a lower court's decision. In the case of the U.S. Supreme Court, a writ of certiorari requires the approval of four of the nine justices. Suddenly, in 1945, the climate changed. The NAACP learned that Justices Murphy and Rutledge were willing to grant a writ, and tried to provide enough leverage to bring two more judges to their side. Prior to this time, their plans were like those of the Serrano team: Test cases had been initiated in several cities, and conferences were held during which the NAACP lawyers could compare notes to produce a consistent trial record. The idea was to be sure there was agreement on the arguments so that regardless of which case would be reviewed, all would benefit. The planning paid off when the timing was right. Restrictive covenants on housing were declared contrary to the equal-protection clause of the Fourteenth Amendment.[11]

At some point the timing will be right to again challenge inequities in school financing before the U.S. Supreme Court. A different case or a different argument may well be accepted. In the meantime, the *Serrano* case and those won in other states stand as major strategic and tactical victories, and they are likely to stand because of the authority of state constitutions and state laws.

[10] L. Harmon Zeigler and G. Wayne Peak, *Interest Groups in American Society*, 2d ed. (Englewood Cliffs, N.J.: Prentice-Hall, 1972), p. 201.
[11] *Ibid.*, p. 202.

Something to think about
List the formal and informal resources used by the Serrano lawyers.
Which of these would be available and usable in more typical civil
cases? Which would be difficult to apply to more traditional cases
and why?

Getting Declared Innocent: Some Techniques

People go to court for a variety of reasons: to get the law enforced,
as in the Yerba Buena case; to effect policy change, as in the Serrano
case; to resolve personal disputes; and, for some, to be cleared of
criminal charges.

Most of those accused of crimes plead guilty, usually to a lesser
charge, and thus avoid a trial. For those citizens who have been
arrested and indicted and who are willing to endure the costs (emotional as well as financial) of proving their innocence, a criminal
trial is a grueling ordeal.

The New York Panther trial referred to in Chapter 13 was not a
typical criminal trial. It had far too many political implications. Still,
it conveys various techniques used by counsel for the defense to get
clients declared innocent. Some of these techniques are used in civil
trials as well. Whenever they are used, their availability indicates
that getting a favorable decision involves much more than looking
at the facts and looking at the law.

The New York Panther trial, as you remember, involved 13 men
indicted by a grand jury for 30 criminal acts, including plotting to
bomb police stations and midtown department stores, actually bombing police stations and a school building in Queens, attempting to
murder police officers, and possessing weapons and explosives. On
September 8, 1970, 17 months after the arrest and jailing of the
Panthers, the formal trial began. Strategic and tactical planning by
the defense, however, began soon after the arrests.[12]

Selecting the Appropriate Defense
The broad strategy adopted was to stress the prosecution's failure to
prove the case. The defense would be reasonable doubt. Remember,

[12] This description of the Panther trial is from Stephen G. Chaberski, "Inside the
New York Panther Trial," *Civil Liberties Review*, Fall 1973, pp. 111–155. Copyright © 1973 by the Civil Liberties Union, Inc. Reprinted by permission.

the burden of proof beyond a reasonable doubt is on the prosecution. To succeed, the Panther lawyers would have to successfully discredit the government's witnesses and information. Among the witnesses whose information the defense had to discredit were police infiltrators. Tactically, this was done from the outset of the trial and continued throughout. The attack began in the opening remarks by one of the lawyers for the defense, Gerald Lefcourt, a 28-year-old graduate of Brooklyn Law School:

> The infiltrator mind is a mind that needs a plot. It needs subversion like a private detective needs an adulteress or adulterer . . . needs to find organizational guilt rather than individual guilt, as part of this studied attempt to get a plot. . . . The infiltrator mind is very selective in what he hears. It extracts sinister language and excludes the good or the explanation for the acts. The infiltrator mind is the worst kind of fact reporter, unreliable because it has a purpose. . . . Before the Black Panther Party was very old here in New York, the infiltrators and agents were there with these purposes in their minds.

In essence, Gerald Lefcourt was saying, the infiltrator's testimony is not to be trusted because the nature of the job precludes objectivity.

Discrediting the government's case was not the only strategy available. The defense might have decided to conduct the case primarily along political lines. Charles Garry, nationally known for his defense of political clients (Huey Newton, Bobby Seale, and Los Siete de la Raza), believes it is impossible to have a successful nonpolitical defense for a political defendant. He might well have selected this alternative strategy had he been counsel for the defense. Speaking of his defense of Black Panther Huey Newton, Garry reveals how he openly made the political position of his client known:

> Before the trial even started, when I was questioning the prospective jurors in voir dire examination, to decide which ones I wanted to strike from the jury, I went into my client's political views, his opposition to the war in Vietnam, his correlation of the war in Vietnam and the bombing of Hiroshima and the Korean War and all of the other things that were going on, as genocide against people of color. . . . In my opening statement to the jury, I gave the ten point program of the Black Panther Party. I told them that Huey Newton was a militant who believed that revolutionary change was necessary; I explained that revolutionary change meant abrupt change. When Huey took the stand he spent two days talking about his philosophy and the Black Panther Party's

political outlook. Because you don't duck it. It's there. There's no way of hiding it; what you have to do is project it. . . .

You've got to tell the jury, "This is exactly what my client believes. Do you have any prejudgments about it?" Don't let the prosecution sneak it in by innuendo, by saying, "Now, we're not trying the Black Panther Party, here, ladies and gentlemen of the jury, we're not trying the revolution; we're trying this man because he did something wrong: he killed a human being." Don't let him get you in that box. Make it very clear that this man is being tried because of his beliefs.[13]

While the political dimensions of the case were not part of the central strategy, the New York Panthers' lawyers decided not to conceal them. The issues were being raised by the prosecutor. He told the jury that it was not the Black Panthers that were on trial, but the very first page of the indictment identified the alleged criminals as Black Panthers, gave their rank in the party and described the party itself as a paramilitary organization. So the defense had no choice. Relying on Charles Garry's approach and successes, in the voir dire and cross-examination of witnesses the defense described the party. They dealt with its purpose, the social situation against which the party organized itself, the ten-point party program, the "free breakfast" program conducted by the party, and other community services provided. The defense was trying to show that the defendants were concerned with rectifying a broad range of social ills.

Clearly, this initial strategic decision is a difficult one to make. There are a number of defenses in a criminal trial. Here are some possibilities: This act was an *accident*, and thus not a crime. The defendant has a foolproof *alibi*. The accused did not have the mental or physical *capacity* to commit the crime. The violation of the law was an act of good conscience, an act of *civil disobedience*. The act was committed with the *consent* of the victim. The accused was *entrapped*, that is, tricked into committing a crime by the police. The trial constitutes *double jeopardy*; the defendant was previously tried for the same crime. There is a *reasonable doubt* that the accused committed the crime. The act was in *self-defense*. The rights of the accused were violated, thus denying *due process*. Only those of a particular minority group are accused of a certain crime; this is a denial of *equal protection of the law*. Possible defenses go on and on.[14]

[13] Ginger, *The Relevant Lawyers*, pp. 72–73.
[14] John Paul Hanna explains these and others. *Complete Layman's Guide to the Law*, pp. 319–323.

Deciding Whether or Not to Have a Jury

In addition to choosing the major strategic approach, the New York Panthers' lawyers had to decide quickly whether or not to have a jury. It must have been a difficult decision because the information was contradictory. On the one hand, lawyers such as Charles Garry who are experienced in handling political trials urge a jury. Garry says he doesn't have any faith in juries, but he has more faith in juries than in judges. This is particularly true, he says, in controversial cases in which the law is technically against you. In such cases lawyers need to get people to look beyond the law to their own conscience, and judges, he believes, are less likely to do this. Even the courts admit the legitimacy of this approach to jury decision-making. In the case of Dr. Spock, the baby doctor–writer turned politico, the U.S. Court of Appeals for the First Circuit said the jury was supposed to be the "conscience of the community" and was supposed to "look at more than logic," particularly in controversial areas, such as free-speech cases, where "a community standard or conscience was to be applied" by the jury.[15]

In addition to Garry's advice, the social and political climate of Manhattan, where the trial was to be held, indicated the use of a jury. Manhattan is likely to produce more jury members who are professionals of one kind or another, who are black and Puerto Rican, and who consistently vote "liberal" in elections than the rest of the city, state, or country.

Finally, without a jury the defense would have to rely on a prosecution-picked judge. In New York County (contrary to practice elsewhere) a prosecutor not assigned to a specific courtroom can move a case for trial in any court at virtually any time he or she wishes. This enabled the prosecution to select Judge Murtagh, who, it can only be assumed, was sympathetic to the government's case.

The information that argued against having a jury was jury behavior in previous political cases. Juries have been fairly pliable in the hands of vigorous prosecutors, particularly in conspiracy cases. In the 1950s and 1960s especially, jurors readily followed the prosecutor in Communist-conspiracy and loyalty-security cases. They believed the government's contentions of danger to the society. Justice Felix Frankfurter denounced conspiracy law as the "prosecutor's darling" largely because of the ease with which a jury could be convinced of guilt despite meager proof.[16]

---

[15] Ginger, *The Relevant Lawyers*, p. 82.
[16] Chaberski, "Inside the New York Panther Trial," p. 150.

Despite the prosecution-oriented juries in past political cases, they decided to have a jury, and the advice of Garry and others, the likelihood that a judge would be sympathetic to the prosecution, the social and political climate of Manhattan, and perhaps the defense team's confidence in their ability to discredit the government's case before a jury probably all contributed to this decision.

So these were the initial strategic choices. The tactical decisions to follow included how to select a sympathetic jury; how to select, prepare, question, and cross-examine witnesses; and, not unrelated, how to educate the jury. These decisions would provide the techniques to win.

Selecting a Sympathetic Jury

Voir dire means "to say the truth." It refers to the preliminary questioning of a witness or potential juror to see whether that person is qualified to testify or to sit on the jury. An "unqualified" juror may be one who is unfit to serve for one reason or another, or one who is prejudiced for or against the defendant, or one who is acquainted with any of the parties involved in the case. However, potential jurors may be considered unfavorable for other reasons. Where questioning by attorneys is permitted, questions are designed to eliminate the "unfavorable."

On the basis of the information derived, there are two ways of eliminating jurors. One is called the *peremptory challenge*. This is a request by an attorney to have a particular juror excused without the attorney stating reasons. The number of peremptory challenges available to each side is limited. The kind of challenge that is unlimited in number is a *challenge for cause*. An attorney for the defense or prosecution who challenges for cause must state reasons, if they are not obvious to the court. The judge then either will allow the challenge and excuse the juror or will disallow the challenge. If the challenge is disallowed, the attorney may use one of the available peremptory challenges.

In the New York Panther trial the voir dire questions asked by Assistant District Attorney Joseph Phillips were routine. From each prospective juror he elicited essentially the same information: personal history; prior knowledge of the case, or of guns and bombs, and of the law; opinions or bias; attitudes toward violence; and willingness to be fair. In addition, he managed to interject during the course of questioning a condemnation of racism and police brutality. He was preparing the prospective jurors for defense questions. At this point Phillips appeared willing to accept anyone not obviously on the side of the defendants. However, he used his peremptory challenges to eliminate social workers, artists, journalists, and people connected with show business.

The voir dire conducted by the defense was more thorough and paved the way for the main defense strategy. It was the beginning of the jury education process. For example, one juror was asked, "You realize there may come a time when there will be a parade of infiltrators called to testify in this case, and the fact that they are undercover agents of the New York City Police Department, would that influence you in providing the defendants with a fair and impartial treatment of the case?" Other questions asked of several prospective jurors dealt with the juror's political beliefs, the effect of the juror's background on present views, the credibility the juror might accord to police testimony, and any fears about blacks and violence. An attempt was made to get certain jurors to excuse themselves from the case by pleading bias or financial incapacity to sit for the duration of the trial. More than half of those initially selected took this way out. This saved the defense some peremptory challenges.

Particular categories of people received special attention. The defense lawyers believed that some categories of people, especially white "ethnics," were inevitably hostile. Nor were blacks readily accepted. Several working-class or middle-class black men were asked if they knew what the phrase "Uncle Tom" signified.

At the end of the questioning the defense team of six lawyers *plus the defendants* would enter long huddles before deciding whether to accept or reject a prospective juror. (Two of the defendants acting as their own counsel had participated in the questioning.) The jury agreed upon by the defense and prosecution, after the six-week voir dire, included 5 of the 48 blacks questioned and 7 of the 163 whites, including one Puerto Rican. Occupationally, they were quite diverse. They included a building superintendent, a construction foreman, a composer of classical music, a casework supervisor for the Welfare Department, a retired longshoreman, a post office employee, an office worker, two teachers, two book editors, a film editor, and a graduate student. Whether or not the voir dire techniques would produce a win for the defense remained to be seen.

On October 19, 1970, the presentation of evidence began. Every fact that each side wanted to establish had to be backed up by evidence, either physical (e.g., a gun or bomb), documentary (e.g., a letter), or testimony (e.g., a statement by a witness). The defense's strategy, remember, was to discredit the government's case. This meant they had to convince the jury that the prosecution's evidence was so weak and/or inaccurate that the defendants couldn't possibly be guilty beyond a reasonable doubt. Preparing the jury for the presentation of the prosecution's evidence, Charles McKinney, the only black lawyer on the defense team, spoke:

> Proof will show that the D.A. is trying to build a case upon certain alleged truths, half-truths, and distortions, seizing upon the understandable public concern and the hysteria of the moment to draw inferences upon inferences.... Remember, the burden rests upon the prosecution and I urge you to insist that they meet that burden.

Questioning and Cross-examining Witnesses

As each category of prosecution witness appeared, a similar tactic was used. The first group consisted of detectives from the New York City Police Department whose jobs were political surveillance and undercover work. After they told about the arrest and evidence seized, each was cross-examined. The defense tried to show their prejudice and ultimate lack of objectivity. The questions and answers went this way:

Question:
Then, would it be correct to say that you personally despised the Black Panther Party?
Answer:
I despise the tactics, sir.
Question:
And you feel they should be eliminated?
Answer:
Yes sir.
Question:
Do you feel that it's your patriotic duty and obligation to assist in the elimination of the Black Panther Party and its members?
Answer:
It's my duty to common decency, sir.[17]

The next category of witnesses was the police infiltrators. Again the defense attempted to show the imprecision of their statements and their lack of objectivity. However, even before the defense began,

---

[17] Michael Tabor, one of the defendants acting as his own counsel, asked Police Detective Coffey these questions.

the prosecution witnesses appeared weak. Ralph White, one of the infiltrators, was to give crucial testimony supporting the charges. However, this testimony, according to at least one juror, was unconvincing. These were his thoughts at the time:

> White's done, and we're not much better off. Even if you believe the dynamite switch, what have you got? Who exactly did something? White didn't see anyone do anything. He didn't hear anyone say he was going to bomb something. But there are hints and bits and pieces, but, remembering what the cross-examination did to Roberts (another infiltrator who testified), I think it will all seem meaningless. Unless (Prosecutor) Phillips has got something more, which I don't think he does, there's going to be a string of acquittals.

As unconvincing as the testimony might have been, the defense tried to diffuse White's statement about one defendant's possession of dynamite and a plan to use it on a police station. During the successful cross-examination, White admitted that he hadn't seen any Panthers do anything illegal except carry guns. However, weakening the testimony of White and the other infiltrators involved two special techniques. The first was to *emphasize the context* of the testimony. When an infiltrator related a conversation he had overheard or described an incident he had observed, the defense had to be sure the context was described fully. If the participants were all drunk or high on dope, that had to be shown; if the agent missed significant parts of the event, this had to be brought out. The second technique was to *emphasize the unique role of the infiltrator*. The defense counsel had to demonstrate the infiltrator's divided loyalties, the way in which he was used by his superiors, his selective memory, the selective use by his superiors of his reporting, his motivation for assuming a dual identity, and generally, the tensions underlying his position. The idea was to undermine his credibility by pointing to peculiar, perhaps neurotic, lapses in behavior.

When it was the defense's turn to present evidence, their approach was to call only witnesses who could help dispute further the factual testimony by prosecution witnesses. There were eight defense witnesses in all, and at least one juror believed their testimony to be insignificant and unnecessary.

Selecting and Preparing Witnesses

Let's leave the Panther trial briefly and think about the subject of preparing witnesses to testify. How do lawyers do that? Trial attorney Malcolm Burnstein gives this advice:

You have to avoid making the witness sound like he's been coached. He shouldn't give the same answers in exactly the same words on cross-examination that he gives on direct examination. That's one of the key indications that a witness was coached. So, tell your witnesses, "I'm not trying to get you to memorize any particular answers. What I want is that the subject matter of your answers always be the same when I ask you this question, not any particular words in the answer."

To prepare my own witnesses, I start by asking them what happened. Then I sit down with the story and put it into some kind of order that will make a good direct examination. Then I question my witness just as if he were on the witness stand, and we discuss his answers until he sees what I'm getting at with each question. I do that a couple of times. Then I cross-examine him. To do this you have to ask yourself what the hell a competent DA could ask your witness that might trick him up or hurt him or confuse him. You ask him precisely those questions. You fire them at him, and you insist on an answer. Then, after he has answered, you discuss his answers.

Now, I don't tell my witnesses what to wear, but I do tell them, "Whatever you wear, the jury is going to react better to you if you look neat and clean." I don't tell them to cut their hair or shave off their beards and any of that. To some extent it's taking on the life style battle at the same time you're fighting the rest of the issues in the case. But I have found that if the witness at least looks neat and clean, even if he has long hair or whatever, the jury can accept him. I just don't think it's my business to make my witnesses or my clients change their life style. I try to tell them, "Look, the jury is square and middle-class. You would probably impress them more if you were to put on a suit and tie, but if not we can overcome that particular little handicap."

Each time you put a witness on the stand, you should ask enough preliminary questions so that the jury gets some notion of who that witness is. Ask him, "How old are you?" "Where do you live?" "What do you do?" "Have you got a family?" If you want the jury to believe what that witness says, you have to give them some appreciation of him as a person.

One stupid problem comes up all the time, especially with witnesses who have never been involved in a trial before. The prosecutor will ask, "Have you discussed your testimony with anybody before coming to court?"

The witness's first thought is to say, "No."

Then the DA says, "Well, you've discussed it with Mr. Burnstein, haven't you?"

"Well, yes, I guess I have."

"You've discussed it with your wife, haven't you?"

"Well, I guess I have." Pretty soon the witness looks like a fool. So you have to tell your witnesses that the prosecutor may ask that question and that the answer is "Of course I've discussed the case."

Another trick to warn your witnesses about is that the cross-examiner will try to make them mad, because when a witness gets mad he forgets what he was going to say and he's liable to say anything. Even if he doesn't say anything damaging, it makes a bad impression on the jury when a witness blows up. The witness is for one side or the other, but the jurors aren't, so they don't react as hostilely to the DA. You have to warn your witness, "Don't play into the prosecutor's hands. You're a friend of Joe's, right? That's why you want to be a witness. So don't blow up. Keep your cool."

You have to try to assess whether each person is going to be a good witness or a bad witness. If he's going to be a bad witness, but he's got some crucial testimony, keep the direct examination as short as possible and hope for the best on cross-examination. If you think a witness will respond well to questions, then you can have a much longer direct examination to bring out more things.

Frequently you need testimony by experts in a criminal case or in a personal-injury case—chemists or psychiatrists or whatever. I try to get people who can adjust to the judicial format and still be able to tell a story. A lot of guys may be really good shrinks or chemists but they freeze up when they get into court with all the restrictions as to the form of the question, relevancy, scope, and so forth.[18]

The New York Panther lawyers probably didn't have to deal too seriously with preparing witnesses. One reason for this was that they had so few, and another was that the strength of their case rested on their ability to discredit government witnesses.

However, they did have a tactical problem to deal with regarding witnesses: whether or not to have the Panthers testify. What would be gained and what lost? If the primary strategy had been to conduct a political trial—that is, to convey to the jurors that the defendants were being tried not for the alleged deeds but for their political views —then the defense team would probably have decided to have the accused testify. Their testimony would have included extensive questioning to produce information about ghetto rhetoric, black psychology, poverty and deprivation, black culture, and police provocations and surveillance. It would have required careful witness preparation.

However, the strategy was not primarily political, and the essential political dimensions had already been revealed during the extensive

[18] Ginger, *The Relevant Lawyers*, pp. 59–60.

and lengthy cross-examinations. Could they risk antagonizing the jury by extending the trial for two more months?

Two not very substantial pieces of information made them decide against calling the defendants to testify. First, they were beginning to feel "good vibrations" from some of the jury members, and they did not want to jeopardize these. Second, they felt their clients' anger might be too much for the jury. After all, they had been locked up for two years on supposedly trumped-up charges.

The Panthers wanted to testify, and they felt very strongly about it. If they were being railroaded into 100 years in jail, they at least wanted the satisfaction of defending themselves. However, this testimony not only would expose the jury to rough talk for which they might not be prepared, but could allow the prosecution to cross-examine. That cross-examination would probably involve the defendants' prior criminal records and political activity. After an intensive five-day discussion of this tactical point, the defendants and counsel voted against testifying.

Ultimately, through skillful examination and cross-examination, and after effectively sensitizing the jury to their historic role of asserting popular control over governmental authorities, the defense team heard the vote for acquittal. The trial lasted eight months, but the jury needed only three hours to deliberate.

In this case, it wasn't only the planning and techniques used by the defense that produced the win. They had other things going for them: a simmering distrust of government (fed by the war in Vietnam), a case with heavy political and/or racial overtones that may have appealed to the jury's sense of justice, and, above all, extraordinarily weak evidence submitted by the prosecutor. Still, the defense counsel had to know how to build on each of these factors, and they did.

Generating Publicity

Before we leave the subject of techniques to use in criminal trials, we might think about the role of publicity. Should publicity and favorable public opinion be encouraged and planned? Is this necessary to win?

The New York Panther lawyers did not employ publicity techniques. They did operate, however, in a negative publicity climate. In part this was natural. Before a controversial trial, the press is generally a captive of the district attorney and police. An indictment such as that of the Panther 21 is a front-page headline event. After the initial publicity, the police continued to reveal unsympathetic bits of information. They talked about continuing investigations linking the Panthers to other crimes, and the media reported these "leaks." The pressure to get scoops overwhelms even the most conscientious of journalists. The defense just didn't have any scoops to offer. Saying "we didn't do it" is hardly front-page news.

In addition to the problem of journalists reporting what the prosecution and police wanted to release, the style of reporting seemed blatantly unsympathetic to the defense. Those who were attempting to raise money for the Panthers' bail and legal expenses were treated as rowdies and rioters. Also, while disturbances during the pretrial hearings were played up, the media paid little attention to the defendants' complaints about outrageous jail conditions and to the near death several times of the epileptic defendant Lee Berry.

Well, can't the defense play that game, build sympathetic media coverage? Trial lawyer Charles Garry believes it is crucial to build community support for the defense. He thinks public trials should indeed be public. Speaking of the trial of Panther Huey Newton, Garry said:

> The prosecution would have been very happy to try Huey in some star-chamber proceeding, where no one would hear anything about it; he would have been snuffed out in a day. The fact that he got a manslaughter conviction instead of first-degree murder was accomplished by the concern of the community. It's just as simple as that. So don't sell "Power to the People" short.

When asked how the community interest helped Newton, precisely, Garry responded:

> Well, it was a positive public interest to offset the negative interest of Huey Newton's enemies. It created for the first time, a balance —not a full, complete balance, but somewhat of a balance [the jury] heard the community. And those on the jury who had some feelings responded to what we were presenting.[19]

In the Newton trial publicity was coordinated by a "Free Huey" committee. They planned marches, rallies, press releases, speaking engagements, and so on. The trials of Joan Little, Angela Davis, and Daniel Ellsberg involved a great deal of similar activity. These, of course, were highly controversial trials, usually with a political or racial dimension. Perhaps generating public interest did help assure

[19] *Ibid.*, p. 82.

careful rulings and ultimately greater justice. Whether in fact they did, no one knows. The techniques, however, would be difficult if not impossible to employ in most criminal trials. There is little interest in most cases of burglary, battery, robbery, forgery, etc. Building favorable publicity is simply not a strategy available to most people accused of crimes.

The New York Panthers won without it. They won in a negative publicity climate. Whether or not to attempt to generate public support depends on the nature of the particular case, the resources of the defense, and the probable behavior of the media with and without a publicity strategy. If the case for the defense is perceived as strong enough, even in controversial criminal trials publicity will ordinarily not be a concern of the defense counsel.

In summary, many aspects of a criminal trial require special techniques. These aspects include the voir dire, the preparation of witnesses, the examination and cross-examination of witnesses, and generally jury education (assuming that there is a jury). The important strategic decisions are what shall be the defense, whether or not to have a jury, and whether or not to try to generate favorable publicity and public attention.

Something to think about

What types of criminal cases are more typical? What resources did the Panthers' lawyers have that might be applicable to these cases? What were the defendants' liabilities? Are these common to other cases? Identify tactics by which lawyers might compensate for their clients' liabilities.

Yerba Buena, *Serrano*, and the New York Panthers—three judicial games of three different types. Each conveys the importance of strategic and tactical planning if one is to win. Each also illustrates particular techniques that may be used. The fact that these are primarily planned and employed by professionals doesn't lessen the need to know about them. It is easy to stay passive in these games and not get involved precisely because they are so professional. However, as with other political games, inaction has costs. To get excused from jury duty because "it's too much of a hassle," to make yourself unavailable in order not to be called as a witness, to refrain from contributing to the legal defense of a person or cause you believe in, or to accept without question the advice of your lawyer contributes, ultimately, to injustice. That is the fundamental cost.

Key Words

Injunction
Temporary restraining order
Consent decree
Special master
Writ of certiorari
Voir dire
Peremptory challenge
Challenge for cause

Suggested Activities

1. Select a recent trial that was given substantial publicity. Collect as many details about it as possible. Identify and evaluate the strategy and tactics used by each side.
2. Invite a trial lawyer to class. Ask him or her to talk about courtroom strategy and tactics. Have specific questions prepared in advance.

Conclusion

Where does this overview of the game of American politics lead? Hopefully, it leads to more effective political participation. That is the primary pay-off for people who care about a problem, see a political solution, and want to make their participation count.

In Chapter 1, however, another kind of pay-off was suggested—achieving a social order more consistent with democracy as both a moral system and a political system. Let's return to those values as we assess the message of this book.

Democracy as a moral system, remember, has to do with the ends or objectives of a popularly controlled government—the promotion of individualism, liberty, equality, and fraternity. Implicit in looking at democracy in this way is the assumption that people should make judgments about the ends of political action as well as the means. However, each political game described throughout this book involved conflict. The players were promoting different values or, at a minimum, different norms. Were they all promoting the moral aspects of democracy?

Now we are entering dangerous territory. Regardless of the side, each player probably perceived his or her action as entirely consistent with the ethical dimensions of democracy. That is possible because of the apparent conflicts among such values as individualism, liberty, equality, and fraternity. At some point citizens must order these values, and that's why they often seem to be working at cross purposes.

Something to think about
Which of the democratic values predominated for the following groups:

- HOTDOGS
- Pro-gun lobby
- Corte Madera Citizens for Recall
- TOOR

So should we abandon the idea that, somehow, engaging in political action will produce a "better" social system, one more consistent with democratic values? Edgar Litt says no. He says there is a paramount value that should allow us to evaluate any and all political actions. That is the sanctity of human life. This is how he puts it:

> ... the conduct of political action is guided by a basic value norm: a commitment to the sanctity of every human life, physical and personal, not only to its sheer preservation but to its freedom, within limits dictated by the general welfare, to grow and develop according to inner propensities and potentialities.
> ... In this view, existing political institutions, majority rule, and the rule of law are flexible concepts whose utility is judged to the extent they foster basic human rights.[1]

Probably few would disagree with Edgar Litt's point of view, although in application a strange mixture of competing policies would still result. However, does that really matter? Greater and more diverse citizen participation is likely to produce policy decisions of a somewhat different character. After all, public officials will be sensitized to a wider assortment of values and a different ordering of priorities. No one knows whether the "correct" policy would then emerge. At a minimum, the diversity of players with political skills may tend to free public officials to act according to what they perceive to be the public interest, not just the overwhelming private interest.

---

[1] Edgar Litt, *Democracy's Ordeal in America: A Guide to Political Theory and Action* (Hinsdale, Ill.: The Dryden Press, 1973), p. 20.

That action may indeed turn out to reflect a commitment to the sanctity of human life.

However, let's deal with the second aspect of democracy—a political system. Through institutionalized means of participation, citizens are supposed to have some control over the authoritative decisions of government. Did the various attempts to influence public officials in the legislative, executive, and judicial arenas have some value in themselves—apart from the policy results?

Political participation is educational, and regardless of the results, that's a positive side effect. Our old friend Jean Jacques Rousseau, that eighteenth century philosopher, was adamant on the subject. He said an ideal system is one designed to develop responsible, individual social and political action through the participatory process. A citizen will learn to take into account more than immediate private interests in order to gain cooperation from others. In the process, the citizen will learn that public and private interests are linked.

The nice thing about citizen participation, according to Rousseau, is that the education it results in is continuing; it is self-sustaining. The very qualities that are required of individual citizens if the system is to work successfully are those that the process of participation itself develops and fosters. The more individual citizens participate, the better they are able to do so. The human results, then, that accrue through the participatory process are an important justification for a participatory system.[2]

However, Rousseau goes even further. In addition to valuing participation (apart from the objectives) because it is educational, we should value it because it is ultimately integrative—it brings people together. Because of the need to cooperate in order not to be powerless, because people are "excessively dependent on the republic," a feeling of belonging to the community develops. Of course, this is more likely in Rousseau's ideal system, which is essentially one of economic equality and independence, but it is even possible in a system as economically diverse as ours. Even when they were frustrated, target area residents in Model Cities Programs, Corte Madera residents bent on recall, and Yerba Buena residents involved in litigation were brought together. There was an adversary, there was conflict, but there was also some development of community.

[2] Carol Pateman, *Participation and Democratic Theory* (Cambridge: The University Press, 1970), pp. 24–25.

So playing the game of American politics produces no policy guarantees and no guarantees that a particular set of values will be promoted, just the greater probability that policies will reflect more diverse values and altered priorities. Whether these are "right" or "wrong," or whether they are consistent with democracy as a moral system, no one can say. What can be said about political action, apart from its objectives, is that it has some additional intrinsic value. As an educational device it allows people to exercise some control over their lives; as an integrative device it reduces one's sense of powerlessness and isolation; and as a communicative device it may just bring us closer to the ideal—the promotion of the sanctity of human life. This is how democracy as a political system and democracy as a moral system can meet. However, this requires knowing *how to play*.

Hopefully, after 15 chapters, some clues to that process are clear. These are some of the major tasks:

1. Establish a realizable goal. Be prepared to explain that the potential negative side effects are unlikely, and that the goals are consistent with this country's norms.
2. Choose the strategy that will involve the most sympathetic level and branch of government. Of course, not all levels and branches have the authority to act in every policy area. Rely on a pressure rather than an electoral approach, if possible. The latter is more difficult, given the advantages of incumbents.
3. Identify the key institutional, interest-group, party, and media players. Determine who among them holds the key formal decision-making authority and the key informal decision-making power. How strongly do they feel about the issue? How is each likely to move in your game?
4. Identify not only the actual but the potential resources of allies and opponents. How can the potential become actual? Devise ways to control the resources you have.
5. Initially, select tactics that will allow you to increase resources. Then concentrate on tactics that will persuade. This may involve first persuading minor sympathetic players in order to gain access to major ones. If the resources are available, personal forms of persuasion are the most effective.
6. Determine how the rules distribute resources in the institution that is your strategic target. Which of these will be to the advantage of you and your allies? Integrate these rules as you develop

an entire plan. Be sure to follow the rules of access to the institution and the essential tactical rules.

Good luck!

Suggested Activities

1. Individually or in groups, select a problem that you would like to see resolved and that can be dealt with politically.
2. Using the political action steps identified in Chapter 2, plan an entire political strategy. Try to have all three institutional arenas and different levels of government covered by the class members.
3. Exchange written strategy papers with another group or individual. Do an oral critique of the strategy you receive, with the initiating group or person defending it.

State or other jurisdiction	Established by constitutional provision	Basis of referendum (a)	Petition requirement (b)	Referendum provisions are also available to all or some local government units (c)
Alaska	★	Petition of people	10% of votes cast in last general election for Governor and resident in at least ⅔ of election districts	★
Arizona	★	Petition of people Submitted by Legislature	5% of qualified voters	★
Arkansas	★	Petition of people	6% of votes cast in last general election for Governor	★

(a) Three forms of referendum exist: (1) Petition of people—the people may petition for a referendum, usually with the intention of repealing existing legislation; (2) Submitted by Legislature—the Legislature may voluntarily submit laws to the electorate for their approval; and (3) Constitutional requirement—the state constitution may require certain questions to be submitted to the people, often debt authorization.

(b) In each State where referendum may occur, a majority of the popular vote is required to enact a measure. In Massachusetts the measure must also be approved by at least 30 percent of the ballots cast.

(c) In addition to those listed in this column, the following States have a referendum process that is available only to local units of government: Kansas, home rule cities; Minnesota, North Carolina, Pennsylvania, South Carolina, Texas, Virginia, West Virginia, and Wyoming.

(d) Amendments or repeals of initiative statutes by another statute must be submitted to the electorate for approval unless the initiative statute provides to the contrary.

(e) The type of referendum held at the request of the Legislature is not established by a constitutional provision.

(f) Applies only to referendum on legislation classifying property and providing for differential taxation on same.

Source: The Book of States.

Appendix A cont'd.

State or other jurisdiction	Established by constitutional provision	Basis of referendum (a)	Petition requirement (b)	Referendum provisions are also available to all or some local government units (c)
California	★	Petition of people (d) Constitutional requirement	5% of votes cast in last general election for Governor	★
Colorado	★	Petition of people Submitted by Legislature	5% of votes cast in last general election for Secretary of State	★
Florida	★	Constitutional requirement	—	|
Georgia	★ (e)	Submitted by Legislature Constitutional requirement	—	★
Idaho	★	Petition of people	10% of votes cast in last general election for Governor	★
Illinois	★	Submitted by Legislature	—	★ ★
Iowa	★ ★	Constitutional requirement	—	★ ★
Kansas	★ ★	Constitutional requirement	—	|
Kentucky	★	Petition of people (f) Constitutional requirement	5% of votes cast in last general election for Governor	★
Maine	★ (e)	Petition of People Submitted by Legislature Constitutional requirement	10% of votes cast in last general election for Governor	★

State			Method	Requirement	
Maryland	★ (e)		Petition of People / Submitted by Legislature	3% of votes cast in last general election for Governor	★
Massachusetts	★		Petition of people	2% of votes cast in last general election for Governor	★
Michigan	★		Petition of people / Submitted by Legislature / Constitutional requirement	5% of votes cast in last general election for Governor	★
Missouri	★		Petition of people / Submitted by Legislature	5% of legal voters in each of ⅔ of congressional districts	★
Montana	★		Petition of people / Submitted by Legislature	5% of total qualified electors and 5% in at least ⅓ of legislative districts	★
Nebraska	★		Petition of people	5% of votes cast in last general election for Governor	★
Nevada	★		Petition of people	10% of votes in last general election	★
New Hampshire	★	★	Submitted by Legislature	—	—
New Jersey	★	★	Constitutional requirement	—	★
New Mexico	★		Petition of people / Constitutional requirement	10% of votes cast in last general election for Governor	—
New York	★	★	Constitutional requirement	—	—
North Carolina	★	★	Submitted by Legislature / Constitutional requirement	—	—
North Dakota	★		Petition of people	7000 signatures	—

Appendix A cont'd.

State or other jurisdiction	Established by constitutional provision	Basis of referendum (a)	Petition requirement (b)	Referendum provisions are also available to all or some local government units (c)
Ohio	★	Petition of people / Constitutional requirement	6% of electors	★
Oklahoma	★	Petition of people / Submitted by Legislature / Constitutional requirement	5% of votes cast for state office receiving largest number of votes in last general election	★
Oregon	★	Petition of people / Submitted by Legislature	5% of votes cast in last election for Supreme Court justice	★
Rhode Island	★★	Constitutional requirement	—	★★
South Carolina	★★	Submitted by Legislature / Constitutional requirement	—	—
South Dakota	★	Petition of people	5% of votes cast in last general election for Governor	★
Utah	★	Petition of people	10% of votes cast in last general election for Governor	★
Vermont	—	Submitted by Legislature	—	★★
Virginia	★	Submitted by Legislature / Constitutional requirement	—	★★

Washington	★	Petition of people Submitted by Legislature Constitutional requirement	4% of votes cast in last general election for Governor	★
Wisconsin	★ (e)	Submitted by Legislature Constitutional requirement	—	★
Wyoming	★	Petition of people Constitutional requirement	15% of those voting in last general election and resident in at least ⅔ of counties of State	★
Puerto Rico	★	Submitted by Legislature	—	—
Virgin Islands	★	Submitted by Legislature Constitutional requirement	—	★

Appendix B The Book of the States *provisions for recall of state officials*

State or other jurisdiction	Officers to whom applicable	Established by constitutional provision	Petition requirement*	Also available to all or some local government units†
Alaska	All elective officials	X	25% of voters in last general election in district in which election occurred	X
Arizona	All elective officials	X	25% of votes cast in last election for office of official sought to be recalled	X
California	All elective officials	X	State officer: 12% of votes cast in last election for office or official sought to be recalled; county officers: 20%; municipal officers: 25%	X
Colorado	All elective officials	X	25% of votes cast in last election for office of official sought to be recalled	X
Idaho	All elective officials except judicial officers	X	20% of the number of electors registered to vote in the last general election held in the jurisdiction from which the officer was elected	X
Louisiana	All elective officials except judges of courts of record	X	25% of voters voting; 40% of voters in districts of less than 1000 voters	X
Michigan	All elective officials except judges of courts of record	X	25% of voters in last election for Governor in electoral district of officer sought to be recalled	
Nevada	All elective officials	X	25% of voters voting in the jurisdiction electing official sought to be recalled	X

State	Officials subject to recall		Signatures required on petition
North Dakota	All elective officials	X	30% of votes cast in last general election for Governor
Oregon	All elective officials	X	25% of votes cast in last election for Supreme Court Justice
Washington	All elective officials except judges of courts of record	X	25%–35% of qualified electors depending on unit of government
Wisconsin	All elective officials	X	25% of votes cast in last general election for Governor
Guam	Governor	X	Petition for referendum: $\frac{2}{3}$ vote of Legislature or petition of Legislature by 50% of voters voting in last Governor election. Referendum election: "yes" votes must total $\frac{2}{3}$ of votes cast in last Governor election, and majority voting on issue must be "yes"
Virgin Islands	Governor	X	40% of votes cast for Governor in last election

* In each State where a recall election may occur, a majority of the popular vote is required to recall an official.

† In addition to those listed, the following States have a recall process available only to local units of government: Arkansas, Georgia, Hawaii, Illinois, Iowa, Maine, Minnesota, Missouri, Montana, Nebraska, New Jersey, New Mexico, Ohio, Oklahoma, South Carolina, Texas, West Virginia and Wyoming.

Source: The Book of States.

Appendix C   *The Book of the States*
initiative provisions for state legislation

State	Type (a)	Established by constitutional provision	Petition requirement (b)	Initiative provisions are also available to all or some local government units (c)
Alaska	D	X	10% of those voting in the last general election and resident in at least ⅔ of election districts	X
Arizona	D	X	10% of qualified electors	X
Arkansas	D	X	8% of those voting in the last general election for Governor	X
California	D	X	5% of votes cast in the last general election for Governor	X
Colorado	B	X	8% of votes cast in the last general election for Secretary of State	X
Idaho	D	X	10% of votes cast in the last general election for Governor	X
Maine	I	X	10% of votes cast in the last general election for Governor	X
Massachusetts	I	X	3% of votes cast in last general election for Governor	X
Michigan	I	X	8% of votes cast in last general election for Governor	X
Missouri	D	X	5% of voters in each of ⅔ of congressional districts	X
Montana	D	X	5% of qualified electors in each of at least ⅓ of legislative representative districts; total must equal 5% of total qualified electors	X
Nebraska	D	X	7% of votes cast in last general election for Governor	X

Appendix C cont'd.

State	Type (a)	Established by constitutional provision	Petition requirement (b)	Initiative provisions are also available to all or some local government units (c)
Nevada	I	X	10% of voters in last general election	X
North Dakota	D	X	10,000 electors	X
Ohio	B	X	3% of electors	X
Oklahoma	D	X	8% of total vote for state office receiving largest number of votes in last general election	X
Oregon	D	X	8% of votes cast in last election for Supreme Court Justice	X
South Dakota	I	X	5% of votes cast in last general election for Governor	X
Utah	B	X	10% of electors (direct); 5% from majority of counties (indirect) (d)	X
Washington	B	X	8% of votes cast in last general election for Governor	X
Wyoming	D	X	15% of voters in last general election and resident in at least ⅔ of counties in State	X

(a) The initiative may be direct or indirect. The direct type, designated D in this table, places a proposed measure on the ballot for submission to the electorate, without legislative action. The indirect type, designated I, requires the Legislature to act upon an initiated measure within a reasonable period before it is voted upon by the electorate. In some States both types, designated B, are used.

(b) In each State where the initiative may occur, a majority of the popular vote is required to enact a measure. In Massachusetts the measure must also be approved by at least 30 percent of the ballots cast.

(c) In addition to those listed in this column, the following States have an initiative process that is available only to local units of government: Georgia, Kentucky, Louisiana, Minnesota, New Jersey, Pennsylvania, South Carolina, Texas, Vermont, Virginia and West Virginia.

(d) These requirements are established by law.

Source: The Book of States.

The Constitution of the United States

We the People of the United States, in Order to form a more perfect Union, establish Justice, insure domestic Tranquility, provide for the common defence, promote the general Welfare, and secure the Blessings of Liberty to ourselves and our Posterity, do ordain and establish this Constitution for the United States of America.

Article I

Section 1   All legislative Powers herein granted shall be vested in a Congress of the United States, which shall consist of a Senate and House of Representatives.

Section 2   The House of Representatives shall be composed of Members chosen every second Year by the People of the several States, and the Electors in each State shall have the Qualifications requisite for Electors of the most numerous Branch of the State Legislature.

No Person shall be a Representative who shall not have attained to the Age of twenty five Years, and been seven Years a Citizen of the United States, and who shall not, when elected, be an Inhabitant of that State in which he shall be chosen.

Representatives and direct Taxes shall be apportioned among the several States which may be included within this Union, according to their respective Numbers, which shall be determined by adding to the whole Number of free Persons, including those bound to Service for a Term of Years, and excluding Indians not taxed, three fifths of all other Persons. The actual Enumeration shall be made within three Years after the first Meeting of the Congress of the United States, and within every subsequent Term of ten Years, in such Manner as they shall by Law direct. The Number of Representatives shall not exceed one for every thirty Thousand, but each State shall have at Least one Representative; and until such enumeration shall be made, the State of New Hampshire shall be entitled to chuse three, Massachusetts eight, Rhode-Island and Providence Plantations one, Connecticut five, New-York six, New Jersey four, Pennsylvania eight, Delaware one, Maryland six, Virginia ten, North Carolina five, South Carolina five, and Georgia three.

When vacancies happen in the Representation from any State, the Executive Authority thereof shall issue Writs of Election to fill such Vacancies.

The House of Representatives shall chuse their speaker and other Officers; and shall have the sole Power of Impeachment.

Section 3   The Senate of the United States shall be composed of two Senators from each State, chosen by the Legislature thereof, for six Years; and each Senator shall have one Vote.

Immediately after they shall be assembled in Consequence of the first Election, they shall be divided as equally as may be into three Classes. The Seats of the Senators of the first Class shall be vacated at the Expiration of the second Year, of the second Class at the Expiration of the fourth Year, and of the third Class at the Expiration of the sixth Year, so that one third may be chosen every second Year; and if Vacancies happen by Resignation, or otherwise, during the Recess of the Legislature of any State, the Executive thereof may make temporary Appointments until the next Meeting of the Legislature, which shall then fill such Vacancies.

No Person shall be a Senator who shall not have attained to the Age of thirty Years, and been nine Years a Citizen of the United States, and who shall not, when elected, be an Inhabitant of that State for which he shall be chosen.

The Vice President of the United States shall be President of the Senate, but shall have no Vote, unless they be equally divided.

The Senate shall chuse their other Officers, and also a President pro tempore, in the Absence of the Vice President, or when he shall exercise the Office of President of the United States.

The Senate shall have the sole Power to try all Impeachments. When sitting for that Purpose, they shall be on Oath or Affirmation. When the President of the United States is tried, the Chief Justice shall preside: And no Person shall be convicted without the Concurrence of two thirds of the Members present.

Judgment in Cases of Impeachment shall not extend further than to removal from Office, and disqualification to hold and enjoy any Office of honor, Trust or Profit under the United States: but the Party convicted shall nevertheless be liable and subject to Indictment, Trial, Judgment and Punishment, according to law.

Section 4   The Times, Places and Manner of holding Elections for Senators and Representatives, shall be prescribed in each State by the Legislature thereof; but the Congress may at any time by Law make or alter such Regulations, except as to the Places of chusing Senators.

The Congress shall assemble at least once in every Year, and such Meeting shall be on the first Monday in December, unless they shall by Law appoint a different Day.

Section 5   Each House shall be the Judge of the Elections, Returns and Qualifications of its own Members, and a Majority of each shall constitute a Quorum to do Business; but a smaller Number may adjourn from day to day, and may be authorized to compel the Attendance of absent Members, in such Manner, and under such Penalties as each House may provide.

Each House may determine the Rules of its Proceedings, punish its Members for disorderly Behaviour, and, with the Concurrence of two thirds, expel a Member.

Each House shall keep a Journal of its Proceedings, and from time to time publish the same, excepting such Parts as may in their Judgment require Secrecy; and the Yeas and Nays of the Members of either House on any question shall, at the Desire of one fifth of those Present, be entered on the Journal.

Neither House, during the Session of Congress, shall, without the Consent of the other, adjourn for more than three days, nor to any other Place than that in which the two Houses shall be sitting.

Section 6   The Senators and Representatives shall receive a Compensation for their Services, to be ascertained by Law, and paid out of the Treasury of the United States. They shall in all Cases, except Treason, Felony and Breach of the Peace, be privileged from Arrest during their Attendance at the Session of their respective Houses, and in going to and returning from the same; and for any Speech or Debate in either House, they shall not be questioned in any other Place.

No Senator or Representative shall, during the Time for which he was elected, be appointed to any civil Office under the Authority of the United States, which shall have been created, or the Emoluments whereof shall have been encreased during such time; and no Person holding any Office under the United States, shall be a Member of either House during his Continuance in Office.

Section 7   All Bills for raising Revenue shall originate in the House of Representatives; but the Senate may propose or concur with Amendments as on other Bills.

Every Bill which shall have passed the House of Representatives and the Senate, shall, before it become a Law, be presented to the President of the United States; If he approve he shall sign it, but if not he shall return it, with his Objections to that House in which it shall have originated, who shall enter the Objections at large on their Journal, and proceed to reconsider it. If after such Reconsideration two thirds of that House shall agree to pass the Bill, it shall be sent, together with the Objections, to the other House, by which it shall likewise be reconsidered, and if approved by two thirds of that House, it shall become a Law. But in all such Cases the Votes of both Houses shall be determined by Yeas and Nays, and the Names of the Persons voting for and against the Bill shall be entered on the Journal of each House respectively. If any Bill shall not be returned by the President within ten Days (Sundays excepted) after it shall have been presented to him, the Same shall be a Law, in like Manner as if he had signed it, unless the Congress by their Adjournment prevent its Return, in which Case it shall not be a Law.

Every Order, Resolution, or Vote to which the Concurrence of the Senate and House of Representatives may be necessary (except on a question of Adjournment) shall be presented to the President of the United States; and before the Same shall take Effect, shall be approved by him, or being disapproved by him, shall be repassed by two thirds of the Senate and House of Representatives, according to the Rules and Limitations prescribed in the Case of a Bill.

Section 8   The Congress shall have Power To lay and collect Taxes, Duties, Imposts and Excises, to pay the Debts and provide for the common Defence and general Welfare of the United States; but all Duties, Imposts and Excises shall be uniform throughout the United States;

To borrow Money on the Credit of the United States;

To regulate Commerce with foreign Nations, and among the several States, and with the Indian Tribes;

To establish an uniform Rule of Naturalization, and uniform Laws on the subject of Bankruptcies throughout the United States;

To coin Money, regulate the Value thereof, and of foreign Coin, and fix the Standard of Weights and Measures;

To provide for the Punishment of counterfeiting the Securities and current Coin of the United States;

To establish Post Offices and post Roads;

To promote the Progress of Science and useful Arts, by securing for limited Times to Authors and Inventors the exclusive Right to their respective Writings and Discoveries;

To constitute Tribunals inferior to the supreme Court;

To define and punish Piracies and Felonies committed on the high Seas, and Offences against the Law of Nations;

To declare War, grant Letters of Marque and Reprisal, and make Rules concerning Captures on Land and Water;

To raise and support Armies, but no Appropriation of Money to that Use shall be for a longer Term than two Years;

To provide and maintain a Navy;

To make Rules for the Government and Regulation of the land and naval Forces;

To provide for calling forth the Militia to execute the Laws of the Union, suppress Insurrections and repel Invasions;

To provide for organizing, arming, and disciplining, the Militia, and for governing such Part of them as may be employed in the Service of the United States, reserving to the States respectively, the Appointment of the Officers, and the Authority of training the Militia according to the discipline prescribed by Congress;

To exercise exclusive Legislation in all Cases whatsoever, over such District (not exceeding ten Miles square) as may, by Cession of particular States, and the Acceptance of Congress, become the Seat of the Government of the United States, and to exercise like Authority over all Places purchased by the Consent of the Legislature of the State in which the Same shall be for the Erection of Forts, Magazines, Arsenals, dock-Yards, and other needful Buildings;—And

To make all Laws which shall be necessary and proper for carrying into Execution the foregoing Powers, and all other Powers vested by this Constitution in the Government of the United States, or in any Department or Officer thereof.

Section 9   The Migration or Importation of such Persons as any of the States now existing shall think proper to admit, shall not be prohibited by the Congress prior to the Year one thousand eight hundred and eight, but a Tax or duty may be imposed on such Importation, not exceeding ten dollars for each Person.

The Privilege of the Writ of Habeas Corpus shall not be suspended, unless when in Cases of Rebellion or Invasion the public Safety may require it.

No Bill of Attainder or ex post facto Law shall be passed.

No Capitation, or other direct, Tax shall be laid, unless in Proportion to the Census or Enumeration herein before directed to be taken.

No Tax or Duty shall be laid on Articles exported from any State.

No Preference shall be given by any Regulation of Commerce or Revenue to the Ports of one State over those of another: nor shall Vessels bound to, or from, one State, be obliged to enter, clear, or pay Duties in another.

No Money shall be drawn from the Treasury, but in Consequence of Appropriations made by Law; and a regular Statement and Account of the Receipts and Expenditures of all public Money shall be published from time to time.

No Title of Nobility shall be granted by the United States: And no Person holding any Office of Profit or Trust under them, shall, without the Consent of the Congress, accept of any present, Emolument, Office, or Title, of any kind whatever, from any King, Prince, or foreign State.

Section 10   No State shall enter into any Treaty, Alliance, or Confederation; grant Letters of Marque and Reprisal; coin Money, emit Bills of Credit; make any Thing but gold and silver Coin a Tender in Payment of Debts; pass any Bill of Attainder, ex post facto Law, or Law impairing the Obligation of Contracts, or grant any Title of Nobility.

No State shall, without the Consent of the Congress, lay any Imposts or Duties on Imports or Exports, except what may be absolutely necessary for executing its inspection Laws: and the net Produce of all Duties and Imposts, laid by any State on Imports or Exports, shall be for the Use of the Treasury of the United States;

and all such Laws shall be subject to the Revision and Controul of the Congress.

No State shall, without the Consent of Congress, lay any Duty of Tonnage, keep Troops, or Ships of War in time of Peace, enter into any Agreement or Compact with another State, or with a foreign Power, or engage in War, unless actually invaded, or in such imminent Danger as will not admit of delay.

Article II

Section 1   The executive Power shall be vested in a President of the United States of America. He shall hold his Office during the Term of four Years, and, together with the Vice President, chosen for the same term, be elected, as follows

Each State shall appoint, in such Manner as the Legislature thereof may direct, a Number of Electors, equal to the whole Number of Senators and Representatives to which the State may be entitled in the Congress: but no Senator or Representative, or Person holding an Office of Trust or Profit under the United States, shall be appointed an Elector.

The Electors shall meet in their respective States, and vote by Ballot for two Persons, of whom one at least shall not be an Inhabitant of the same State with themselves. And they shall make a List of all the Persons voted for, and of the Number of Votes for each; which List they shall sign and certify, and transmit sealed to the Seat of the Government of the United States, directed to the President of the Senate. The President of the Senate shall, in the Presence of the Senate and House of Representatives, open all the Certificates, and the Votes shall then be counted. The Person having the greatest Number of Votes shall be the President, if such Number be a Majority of the whole Number of Electors appointed; and if there be more than one who have such Majority, and have an equal Number of Votes, then the House of Representatives shall immediately chuse by Ballot one of them for President: and if no Person have a Majority, then from the five highest on the List the said House shall in like Manner chuse the President. But in chusing the President, the Votes shall be taken by States, the Representation from each State having one Vote; A quorum for this Purpose shall consist of a Member or Members from two thirds of the states, and a Majority of all the states shall be necessary to a Choice. In every Case, after the Choice of the President, the Person having the greatest Number of

Votes of the Electors shall be the Vice President. But if there should remain two or more who have equal Votes, the Senate shall chuse from them by Ballot the Vice President.

The Congress may determine the Time of chusing the Electors, and the Day on which they shall give the Votes; which Day shall be the same throughout the United States.

No Person except a natural born Citizen, or a Citizen of the United States, at the time of the Adoption of this Constitution, shall be eligible to the Office of President; neither shall any Person be eligible to that Office who shall not have attained to the Age of thirty five Years, and been fourteen Years a Resident within the United States.

In Case of the Removal of the President from Office, or of his Death, Resignation, or Inability to discharge the Powers and Duties of the said Office, the Same shall devolve on the Vice President, and the Congress may by Law provide for the Case of Removal, Death, Resignation or Inability, both of the President and Vice President, declaring what Officer shall then act as President, and such Officer shall act accordingly, until the Disability be removed, or a President shall be elected.

The President shall, at stated Times, receive for his Services a Compensation, which shall neither be encreased nor diminished during the Period for which he shall have been elected, and he shall not receive within that Period any other Emolument from the United States, or any of them.

Before he enter on the Execution of his Office, he shall take the following Oath or Affirmation:—"I do solemnly swear (or affirm) that I will faithfully execute the Office of President of the United States, and will to the best of my Ability, preserve, protect and defend the Constitution of the United States."

Section 2   The President shall be Commander in Chief of the Army and Navy of the United States, and of the Militia of the several States, when called into the actual Service of the United States; he may require the Opinion, in writing, of the principal Officer in each of the executive Departments, upon any Subject relating to the Duties of their respective Offices, and he shall have Power to grant Reprieves and Pardons for Offences against the United States, except in Cases of Impeachment.

He shall have Power, by and with the Advice and Consent of the Senate, to make Treaties, provided two thirds of the Senators present concur; and he shall nominate, and by and with the Advice and Consent of the Senate, shall appoint Ambassadors, other public Ministers and Consuls, Judges of the supreme Court, and all other Officers of the United States, whose Appointments are not herein otherwise provided for, and which shall be established by Law; but the Congress may by Law vest the Appointment of such inferior Officers, as they think proper, in the President alone, in the Courts of Law, or in the Heads of Departments.

The President shall have Power to fill up all Vacancies that may happen during the Recess of the Senate, by granting Commissions which shall expire at the End of their next Session.

Section 3   He shall from time to time give to the Congress Information of the State of the Union, and recommend to their Consideration such Measures as he shall judge necessary and expedient; he may, on extraordinary Occasions, convene both Houses, or either of them, and in Case of Disagreement between them, with Respect to the Time of Adjournment, he may adjourn them to such Time as he shall think proper; he shall receive Ambassadors and other public Ministers; he shall take Care that the Laws be faithfully executed, and shall Commission all the Officers of the United States.

Section 4   The President, Vice President and all civil Officers of the United States, shall be removed from Office on Impeachment for, and Conviction of, Treason, Bribery, or other High Crimes and Misdemeanors.

Article III

Section 1   The judicial Power of the United States, shall be vested in one supreme Court, and in such inferior Courts as the Congress may from time to time ordain and establish. The Judges, both of the supreme and inferior Courts, shall hold their Offices during good Behaviour, and shall, at stated Times, receive for their Services, a Compensation, which shall not be diminished during their Continuance in Office.

Section 2   The judicial Power shall extend to all Cases, in Law and Equity, arising under this Constitution, the Laws of the United States, and Treaties made, or which shall be made, under their Authority;—to all Cases affecting Ambassadors, other public Ministers and Consuls;—to all Cases of admiralty and maritime Jurisdiction;—to Controversies to which the United States shall be a Party;—to

Controversies between two or more States; between a State and Citizens of another State;—between Citizens of different States;— between Citizens of the same State claiming Lands under Grants of different States, and between a State, or the Citizens thereof, and foreign States, Citizens or Subjects.

In all Cases affecting Ambassadors, other public Ministers and Consuls, and those in which a State shall be Party, the supreme Court shall have original Jurisdiction. In all the other Cases before mentioned, the supreme Court shall have appellate Jurisdiction, both as to Law and Fact, with such Exceptions, and under such Regulations as the Congress shall make.

The Trial of all Crimes, except in Cases of Impeachment, shall be by Jury; and such Trial shall be held in the State where the said Crimes shall have been committed; but when not committed within any State, the Trial shall be at such Place or Places as the Congress may by Law have directed.

Section 3   Treason against the United States, shall consist only in levying War against them, or in adhering to their Enemies, giving them Aid and Comfort. No Person shall be convicted of Treason unless on the Testimony of two Witnesses to the same overt Act, or on Confession in open Court.

The Congress shall have Power to declare the Punishment of Treason, but no Attainder of Treason shall work Corruption of Blood, or Forfeiture except during the Life of the Person attainted.

Article IV

Section 1   Full Faith and Credit shall be given in each State to the public Acts, Records, and judicial Proceedings of every other State. And the Congress may by general Laws prescribe the Manner in which such Acts, Records and Proceedings shall be proved, and the Effect thereof.

Section 2   The Citizens of each State shall be entitled to all Privileges and Immunities of Citizens in the several States.

A Person charged in any State with Treason, Felony, or other Crime, who shall flee from Justice, and be found in another State, shall on Demand of the executive Authority of the State from which he fled, be delivered up, to be removed to the State having Jurisdiction of the Crime.

No Person held to Service or Labour in one State, under the Laws thereof, escaping into another, shall, in Consequence of any Law or Regulation therein, be discharged from such Service or Labour, but shall be delivered up on Claim of the Party to whom such Service or Labour may be due.

Section 3   New States may be admitted by the Congress into this Union; but no new State shall be formed or erected within the Jurisdiction of any other State; nor any State be formed by the Junction of two or more States, or Parts of States, without the Consent of the Legislatures of the States concerned as well as of the Congress.

The Congress shall have Power to dispose of and make all needful Rules and Regulations respecting the Territory or other Property belonging to the United States; and nothing in this Constitution shall be so construed as to Prejudice any Claims of the United States, or of any particular State.

Section 4   The United States shall guarantee to every State in this Union a Republican Form of Government, and shall protect each of them against Invasion; and on Application of the Legislature, or of the Executive (when the Legislature cannot be convened) against domestic Violence.

Article V
The Congress, whenever two thirds of both Houses shall deem it necessary, shall propose Amendments to this Constitution, or, on the Application of the Legislatures of two thirds of the several States, shall call a Convention for proposing Amendments, which, in either Case, shall be valid to all Intents and Purposes, as Part of this Constitution, when ratified by the Legislatures of three fourths of the several States, or by Conventions in three fourths thereof, as the one or the other Mode of Ratification may be proposed by the Congress; Provided that no Amendment which may be made prior to the Year One thousand eight hundred and eight shall in any Manner affect the first and fourth Clauses in the Ninth Section of the first Article; and that no State, without its Consent, shall be deprived of its equal Suffrage in the Senate.

Article VI
All Debts contracted and Engagements entered into, before the Adoption of this Constitution, shall be as valid against the United States under this Constitution, as under the Confederation.

This Constitution, and the Laws of the United States which shall be made in Pursuance thereof; and all Treaties made, or which shall be made, under the Authority of the United States, shall be the supreme Law of the Land; and the Judges in every State shall be bound thereby, any Thing in the Constitution or Laws of any State to the Contrary notwithstanding.

The Senators and Representatives before mentioned, and the Members of the several State Legislatures, and all executive and judicial Officers, both of the United States and of the several States, shall be bound by Oath or Affirmation, to support this Constitution; but no religious Test shall ever be required as a Qualification to any Office or public Trust under the United States.

Article VII
The Ratification of the Conventions of nine States, shall be sufficient for the Establishment of this Constitution between the States so ratifying the Same.

Done in Convention by the Unanimous Consent of the States present the Seventeenth Day of September in the Year of our Lord one thousand seven hundred and eighty seven and of the Independence of the United States of America the twelfth. In witness whereof We have hereunto subscribed our Names.

(The first 10 Amendments were ratified December 15, 1791, and form what is known as the "Bill of Rights.")

Amendment 1
Congress shall make no law respecting an establishment of religion, or prohibiting the free exercise thereof; or abridging the freedom of speech, or of the press; or the right of the people peaceably to assemble, and to petition the Government for a redress of grievances.

Amendment 2
A well regulated Militia, being necessary to the security of a free State, the right of the people to keep and bear Arms, shall not be infringed.

Amendment 3
No Soldier shall, in time of peace be quartered in any house, without the consent of the Owner, nor in time of war, but in a manner to be prescribed by law.

Amendment 4

The right of the people to be secure in their persons, houses, papers, and effects, against unreasonable searches and seizures, shall not be violated, and no Warrants shall issue, but upon probable cause, supported by Oath or affirmation, and particularly describing the place to be searched, and the persons or things to be seized.

Amendment 5

No person shall be held to answer for a capital, or otherwise infamous crime, unless on a presentment or indictment of a Grand Jury, except in cases arising in the land or naval forces, or in the Militia, when in actual service in time of War or public danger; nor shall any person be subject for the same offense to be twice put in jeopardy of life or limb; nor shall be compelled in any criminal case to be a witness against himself, nor be deprived of life, liberty, or property, with due process of law; nor shall private property be taken for public use, without just compensation.

Amendment 6

In all criminal prosecutions, the accused shall enjoy the right to a speedy and public trial, by an impartial jury of the State and district wherein the crime shall have been committed, which district shall have been previously ascertained by law, and to be informed of the nature and cause of the accusation; to be confronted with the witnesses against him; to have compulsory process for obtaining witnesses in his favor, and to have the Assistance of Counsel for his defence.

Amendment 7

In Suits at common law, where the value in controversy shall exceed twenty dollars, the right of trial by jury shall be preserved, and no fact tried by jury, shall be otherwise reexamined in any Court of the United States, than according to the rules of the common law.

Amendment 8

Excessive bail shall not be required, nor excessive fines imposed, nor cruel and unusual punishments inflicted.

Amendment 9

The enumeration in the Constitution, of certain rights, shall not be construed to deny or disparage others retained by the people.

Amendment 10

The powers not delegated to the United States by the Constitution, nor prohibited by it to the States, are reserved to the States respectively, or to the people.

Amendment 11

The Judicial power of the United States shall not be construed to extend to any suit in law or equity, commenced or prosecuted against one of the United States by Citizens of another State, or by Citizens or Subjects of any Foreign State. *(Ratified February 7, 1795)*

Amendment 12

The Electors shall meet in their respective states and vote by ballot for President and Vice-President, one of whom, at least, shall not be an inhabitant of the same state with themselves; they shall name in their ballots the person voted for as President, and in distinct ballots the person voted for as Vice-President, and they shall make distinct lists of all persons voted for as President, and of all persons voted for as Vice-President, and of the number of votes for each, which lists they shall sign and certify, and transmit sealed to the seat of the government of the United States, directed to the President of the Senate;—The President of the Senate shall, in the presence of the Senate and House of Representatives, open all the certificates and the votes shall then be counted;—The person having the greatest number of votes for President, shall be the President, if such number be a majority of the whole number of Electors appointed; and if no person have such majority then from the persons having the highest numbers not exceeding three on the list of those voted for as President, the House of Representatives shall choose immediately, by ballot, the President. But in choosing the President, the votes shall be taken by states, the representation from each state having one vote; a quorum for this purpose shall consist of a member or members from two-thirds of the states, and a majority of all the states shall be necessary to a choice. And if the House of Representatives shall not choose a President whenever the right of choice shall devolve upon them, before the fourth day of March next following, then the Vice-President shall act as President, as in the case of the death or other constitutional disability of the President.—The person having the greatest number of votes as Vice-President, shall be the Vice-President, if such a number be a majority of the whole number of Electors appointed, and if no person have a majority, then from the two highest numbers on the list, the Senate shall choose the Vice-President; a quorum for the purpose shall consist of two-thirds of the whole number of Senators, and a majority of the whole number shall be necessary to a choice. But no person constitutionally ineligible to the office of President shall be eligible to that of Vice-President of the United States. (*Ratified July 27, 1804*)

Amendment 13

Section 1   Neither slavery nor involuntary servitude, except as a punishment for crime whereof the party shall have been duly convicted, shall exist within the United States, or any place subject to their jurisdiction.

Section 2   Congress shall have power to enforce this article by appropriate legislation. (*Ratified December 6, 1865*)

Amendment 14

Section 1   All persons born or naturalized in the United States, and subject to the jurisdiction thereof, are citizens of the United States and of the State wherein they reside. No State shall make or enforce any law which shall abridge the privileges or immunities of citizens of the United States; nor shall any State deprive any person of life, liberty, or property, without due process of law; nor deny to any person within its jurisdiction the equal protection of the laws.

Section 2   Representatives shall be apportioned among the several States according to their respective numbers, counting the whole number of persons in each State, excluding Indians not taxed. But when the right to vote at any election for the choice of electors for President and Vice President of the United States, Representatives in Congress, the Executive and Judicial officers of a State, or the members of the Legislature thereof, is denied to any of the male inhabitants of such State, being twenty-one years of age, and citizens of the United States, or in any way abridged, except for participation in rebellion, or other crime, the basis of representation therein shall be reduced in the proportion which the number of such male citizens shall bear to the whole number of male citizens twenty-one years of age in such State.

Section 3   No person shall be a Senator or Representative in Congress, or elector of President and Vice President, or hold any office, civil or military, under the United States, or under any State, who, having previously taken an oath, as a member of Congress, or as an officer of the United States, or as a member of any State legislature, or as an executive or judicial officer of any State, to support the Constitution of the United States, shall have engaged in insurrection or rebellion against the same, or given aid or comfort to the enemies thereof. But Congress may by a vote of two-thirds of each House remove such disability.

Section 4   The validity of the public debt of the United States, authorized by law, including debts incurred for payment of pensions and bounties for services in suppressing insurrection or rebellion, shall not be questioned. But neither the United States nor any State shall assume or pay any debt or obligation incurred in aid of insurrection or rebellion against the United States, or any claim for the loss or emancipation of any slave; but all such debts, obligations and claims shall be held illegal and void.

Section 5   The Congress shall have power to enforce, by appropriate legislation, the provisions of this article. (*Ratified July 9, 1868*)

Amendment 15

Section 1   The right of citizens of the United States to vote shall not be denied or abridged by the United States or by any State on account of race, color, or previous condition of servitude.

Section 2   The Congress shall have power to enforce this article by appropriate legislation. (*Ratified February 3, 1870*)

Amendment 16

The Congress shall have power to lay and collect taxes on incomes, from whatever source derived, without apportionment among the several States, and without regard to any census or enumeration. (*Ratified February 3, 1913*)

Amendment 17

The Senate of the United States shall be composed of two Senators from each State, elected by the people thereof for six years; and each Senator shall have one vote. The electors in each State shall have the qualifications requisite for electors of the most numerous branch of the State legislatures.

When vacancies happen in the representation of any State in the Senate, the executive authority of such State shall issue writs of election to fill such vacancies: *Provided,* That the legislature of any State may empower the executive thereof to make temporary appointments until the people fill the vacancies by election as the legislature may direct.

This amendment shall not be so construed as to affect the election of term of any Senator chosen before it becomes valid as part of the Constitution. (*Ratified April 8, 1913*)

Amendment 18

Section 1   After one year from the ratification of this article the manufacture, sale, or transportation of intoxicating liquors within, the importation thereof into, or the exportation thereof from the United States and all territory subject to the jurisdiction thereof for beverage purposes is hereby prohibited.

Section 2   The Congress and the several States shall have concurrent power to enforce this article by appropriate legislation.

Section 3   This article shall be inoperative unless it shall have been ratified as an amendment to the Constitution by the legislatures of the several States, as provided in the Constitution, within seven years from the date of the submission hereof to the States by the Congress. (*Ratified January 16, 1919*)

Amendment 19

The right of citizens of the United States to vote shall not be denied or abridged by the United States or by any State on account of sex.

Congress shall have power to enforce this article by appropriate legislation. (*Ratified August 18, 1920*)

Amendment 20

Section 1   The terms of the President and Vice President shall end at noon on the 20th day of January, and the terms of Senators and Representatives at noon on the 3d day of January, of the years in which such terms would have ended if this article had not been ratified; and the terms of their successors shall then begin.

Section 2   The Congress shall assemble at least once in every year, and such meeting shall begin at noon on the 3d day of January, unless they shall by law appoint a different day.

Section 3   If, at the time fixed for the beginning of the term of the President, the President elect shall have died, the Vice President elect shall become President. If a President shall not have been chosen before the time fixed for the beginning of his term, or if the President elect shall have failed to qualify, then the Vice President elect shall act as President until a President shall have qualified; and the Congress may by law provide for the case wherein neither a President elect nor a Vice President elect shall have qualified, declaring who shall then act as President, or the manner in which one who is to act shall be selected, and such person shall act accordingly until a President or Vice President shall have qualified.

Section 4   The Congress may by law provide for the case of the death of any of the persons from whom the House of Representatives may choose a President whenever the right of choice shall have devolved upon them, and for the case of the death of any of the persons from whom the Senate may choose a Vice President whenever the right of choice shall have devolved upon them.

Section 5   Sections 1 and 2 shall take effect on the 15th day of October following the ratification of this article.

Section 6   This article shall be inoperative unless it shall have been ratified as an amendment to the Constitution by the legislatures of three-fourths of the several States within seven years from the date of its submission. (*Ratified January 23, 1933*)

Amendment 21

Section 1   The eighteenth article of amendment to the Constitution of the United States is hereby repealed.

Section 2   The transportation or importation into any State, Territory, or possession of the United States for delivery or use therein of intoxicating liquors, in violation of the laws thereof, is hereby prohibited.

Section 3   This article shall be inoperative unless it shall have been ratified as an amendment to the Constitution by conventions in the several States, as provided in the Constitution, within seven years from the date of the submission hereof to the States by the Congress. (*Ratified December 5, 1933*)

Amendment 22

Section 1   No person shall be elected to the office of the President more than twice, and no person who has held the office of President, or acted as President, for more than two years of a term to which some other person was elected President shall be elected to the office of the President more than once. But this Article shall not apply to any person holding the office of President when this Article was proposed by the Congress, and shall not prevent any person who may be holding the office of President, or acting as President, during the term within which this Article becomes operative from holding the office of President or acting as President during the remainder of such term.

Section 2   This article shall be inoperative unless it shall have been ratified as an amendment to the Constitution by the legislatures of three-fourths of the several States within seven years from the date of its submission to the States by the Congress. (*Ratified February 27, 1951*)

Amendment 23

Section 1   The District constituting the seat of Government of the United States shall appoint in such manner as the Congress may direct:

A number of electors of President and Vice President equal to the whole number of Senators and Representatives in Congress to which the District would be entitled if it were a State, but in no event more than the least populous State; they shall be in addition to those appointed by the States, but they shall be considered, for the purposes of the election of President and Vice President, to be electors appointed by a State; and they shall meet in the District and perform such duties as provided by the twelfth article of amendment.

Section 2   The Congress shall have power to enforce this article by appropriate legislation. (*Ratified March 29, 1961*)

Amendment 24

Section 1   The right of citizens of the United States to vote in any primary or other election for President or Vice President, for electors for President or Vice President, or for Senator or Representative in Congress, shall not be denied or abridged by the United States or any State by reason of failure to pay any poll tax or other tax.

Section 2   The Congress shall have power to enforce this article by appropriate legislation. (*Ratified January 23, 1964*)

Amendment 25

Section 1   In case of the removal of the President from office or of his death or resignation, the Vice President shall become President.

Section 2   Whenever there is a vacancy in the office of the Vice President, the President shall nominate a Vice President who shall take office upon confirmation by a majority vote of both Houses of Congress.

Section 3   Whenever the President transmits to the President pro tempore of the Senate and the Speaker of the House of Representatives his written declaration that he is unable to discharge the powers and duties of his office, and until he transmits to them a written declaration to the contrary, such powers and duties shall be discharged by the Vice President as Acting President.

Section 4   Whenever the Vice President and a majority of either the principal officers of the executive departments or of such other body as Congress may by law provide, transmit to the President pro tempore of the Senate and the Speaker of the House of Representatives their written declaration that the President is unable to discharge the powers and duties of his office, the Vice President shall immediately assume the powers and duties of the office as Acting President.

Thereafter, when the President transmits to the President pro tempore of the Senate and the Speaker of the House of Representatives his written declaration that no inability exists, he shall resume the powers and duties of his office unless the Vice President and a majority of either the principal officers of the executive department or of such other body as Congress may by law provide, transmit within four days to the President pro tempore of the Senate and the Speaker of the House of Representatives their written declaration that the President is unable to discharge the powers and duties of his office. Thereupon Congress shall decide the issue, assembling within forty-eight hours for that purpose if not in session. If the Congress, within twenty-one days after receipt of the latter written declaration, or, if Congress is not in session, within twenty-one days after Congress is required to assemble, determines by two-thirds vote of both Houses that the President is unable to discharge the powers and duties of his office, the Vice President shall continue to discharge the same as Acting President; otherwise, the President shall resume the powers and duties of his office. (*Ratified February 10, 1967*)

Amendment 26

Section 1   The right of citizens, who are eighteen years of age or older, to vote shall not be denied or abridged by the United States or by any state on account of age.

Section 2   The Congress shall have power to enforce this article by appropriate legislation.

Amendment 27

Once ratified by three-quarters of the state legislatures, this amendment will prohibit discrimination based on sex by any law or action of any government—federal, state, or local.

Index